COMMUNICATION AT WORK:
WRITING AND SPEAKING

COMMUNICATION AT WORK: WRITING AND SPEAKING

Roger P. Wilcox
DIRECTOR, COMMUNICATION CONSULTING SERVICES
Flint, Michigan

Houghton Mifflin Company   Boston

Atlanta Dallas Geneva, Illinois Hopewell, New Jersey Palo Alto London

Copyright © 1977 by Houghton Mifflin Company. All rights reserved. No part of this work may be reproduced or transmitted in any form or by any means, electronic or mechanical, including photocopying and recording, or by any information storage or retrieval system, without permission in writing from the publisher.

Printed in the U.S.A.
Library of Congress Catalog Card Number: 76-14651
ISBN: 0-395-24372-6

To
Eva
Jim and Ethie
Kenneth
David

CONTENTS

Preface	xi
PART ONE OVERVIEW	**1**
Chapter 1 The Need for Effective Communication on the Job	**2**
The Need for Effective Communication on the Job	4
The Importance to You of Being an Effective Communicator	6
Problems Encountered in Communicating Effectively	7
Characteristics of Writing and Speaking on the Job	10
Becoming an Effective Communicator	11
Summary	13
Suggested Applications	13
Notes	14
Chapter 2 Writing and Speaking as Communication	**16**
What We Mean by Communication	17
How Communication Falloff Occurs	22
Falloff and Noise	28
How to Reduce Communication Falloff	29
Summary	34
Suggested Applications	35
Notes	36
Chapter 3 Your Reader and Listener	**38**
The Manager: A General Definition	40
The Manager's Psychological Motivations	40
The Manager's Job Orientation	44
The Manager as Communicator	48
The Manager's Style	53
The Manager as a Person of Change	55
Your Other Communication Receivers	56
In Closing	58

Summary	58
Suggested Applications	59
Notes	60

PART TWO BEING CLEAR 63

Chapter 4 Structure 64

What We Mean by Clear Organization	66
Why Clear Organization Is Important	66
An Effective Balance between the General and Specific	68
The Direct vs. Indirect Approach	74
Patterns of Organization	77
Aids in Achieving Clear Organization	82
Use of Headings and Subheadings	87
Summary	88
Suggested Applications	89
Notes	90

Chapter 5 Effective Paragraphing 92

Function of Paragraphing	93
Definition of a Paragraph	93
Guidelines in Formulating the Topic Sentence	94
Guidelines for Developing the Topic Sentence	98
Summary	111
Suggested Applications	111
Notes	116

Chapter 6 Effective Sentences 118

Completeness	120
Coherent Structure	121
Emphasis	134
Appropriate Length	144
Conciseness	148
Variety	151
Word Choice	154
Summary	163
Suggested Applications	164
Notes	174

Chapter 7 Grammar, Punctuation, and Word Usage 176

Abbreviations	177
Agreement	179
Clauses	184
Comparisons	185
Conjunctions	187
Numbers	189
Plurals	192
Possession	194
Prepositions	196

Punctuation	197
Spelling	219
Verb Tense	220
Words—Confused and Misused	222
Revision Exercises	232
Notes	237

Chapter 8   Using Graphic Aids — 238

Basic Considerations	239
Kinds of Ideas Best Presented Graphically	241
Classification of Graphic Aids	241
Tables	241
Figures	248
Check List for Planning Graphic Aids	276
Placement of Graphics	277
Summary	277
Suggested Applications	278
Notes	279

PART THREE   BEING PERSUASIVE — 281

Chapter 9   Persuading Your Reader or Listener — 282

What We Mean by Persuasion	283
The Three Factors of Persuasion: An Overview	284
Adapting to the Receiver's Needs	285
Persuading through Credibility	293
Persuading through Logic	302
Summary	307
Suggested Applications	308
Notes	312

PART FOUR   SPECIFIC APPLICATIONS — 315

Chapter 10   Writing Effective Letters and Memos — 316

Importance of Business Letter Writing	317
Concept vs. Application	318
Creating a Positive Image	318
Parts of a Letter	334
Addressing the Envelope	340
Formats and Mechanics	342
Applications for Employment	347
Memos	361
Summary	366
Suggested Applications	366
Notes	369

Chapter 11   Writing Effective Reports and Proposals — 370

Reports and Proposals in the Business World	372
Real World vs. Verbal World	374

A Classification of Reports and Proposals	383
The Components of a Formal Report or Proposal	386
Sample Reports and Proposals	412
Summary	431
Suggested Applications	431
Notes	438

PART FIVE PRESENTING YOUR IDEAS ORALLY 439

Chapter 12 The Oral Presentation 440

Speaking Compared with Writing	441
Overcoming Speech Fright	443
Delivering the Speech	448
Using Visual Aids	456
Advantages and Limitations in the Use of Selected Visual Aids	458
Making Sure the Main Points Stand Out	465
Handling Questions from the Audience	466
Summary	468
Suggested Applications	469
Notes	473

Index	475

PREFACE

During the winter of 1971 I had the privilege of conducting a series of intensive training programs in report and proposal writing at General Motors divisions in a number of European countries. Since then, I have conducted many similar programs in written and oral communication, both in this country and in Brazil. Represented among the participants has been a wide range of specializations, age levels, management levels, and educational backgrounds. From these experiences has emerged one dominant realization: that men and women, regardless of other differences, are of one mind in attaching great importance to being able to communicate effectively on the job through writing and speaking. This observation on my part is amply supported by evidence from many other sources, some of them cited in Chapter 1, "The Need for Effective Communication on the Job." It would appear that, quite literally, effective communication, like ample illumination, is required if we are to see what we are doing. The absence of either leaves us totally in the dark.

Yet, despite the crucial need to communicate effectively, many of us communicate poorly and few very well. A study published by the United States Office of Education in 1975 revealed that fifteen million Americans are unable to address an envelope well enough to ensure that the postal service can deliver it. *Newsweek* magazine's article, "Why Johnny Can't Write" (December 8, 1975), observes that "The colleges and universities complain that many of the most intelligent freshmen . . . are seriously deficient when it comes to organizing their thoughts on paper. . . . At the University of California at Berkeley, where students come from the top 12.5 percent of high-school graduates, nearly half of last year's freshmen demonstrated writing skills so poor that they were forced to enroll in remedial courses nicknamed 'Bonehead English'. . . . At Temple University in Philadelphia, the proportion of freshmen failing an English placement exam has increased by more than 50 percent since 1968." One result, declared *Newsweek*: "The cries of dismay sound even louder [than among educators] in the halls of commerce, industry, and the professions, where writing is the basis for almost all formal business communication."

The underlying causes of these problems have been analyzed extensively; my purpose here is not to reiterate the obvious. Instead, with *Communication at Work* I wish to make a contribution toward meeting the very great and very real writing needs of most students. More specifically, the text seeks to fulfill the following objectives:

1. To help the student become aware of the importance of communication on the job—not just to the company, but to himself or herself as well.

2. To help the student understand in essence the complex process of communication, how communication falloff occurs, and how to reduce falloff to a minimum.

3. To help the student become aware of the importance of the reader or listener and to provide insights into the personality characteristics of the people he or she will be communicating with.

4. To help the student understand the basic concepts and specific techniques in achieving clarity through basic structure; effective paragraphing; effective sentences, correct grammar, punctuation, and word usage; and graphic aids.

5. To provide the student with a unified theory of persuasion on the job, drawing freely on recent findings in psychology.

6. To acquaint the student with the basic forms of writing on the job and offer specific guidelines for writing each of these.

7. To help the student understand and cope effectively with the problems unique to the oral as opposed to the written presentation.

No text, of course, can by itself achieve objectives such as these. Essential to the process is the capable guidance of the teacher and—even more—the motivation and perseverance of the student. But with these conditions present, it is hoped that this text may provide a useful aid in preparing students to enter their life's work with a solid degree of competence.

Acknowledgments can never do justice to all those to whom an author is indebted. Nevertheless, for their varied contributions, I should like especially to express my appreciation to the following:

Students and program participants—hundreds of them, ranging from college freshmen to upper management levels—whom I've had these past few years. I suspect that I've learned more from them than they have from me.

Former colleagues of mine in the Department of Communication and Organizational Behavior at General Motors Institute; especially John W. Baird, Chairman Tony Hain, C. David Hurt, Gary M. Richetto, Marvin H. Swift, Stewart L. Tubbs, and Robin N. Widgery; also to Rodney L. Boyes, former chairman of the Department of Industrial Management, and Glenn L. Pegram of the same department.

Friends and critics from outside GMI: Erwin P. Bettinghaus, Dean, College of Communication, Arts, and Sciences, Michigan State University; Mary C. Bromage, Professor of Written Communication, University of Michigan; Kareen Hagopian, Supervisor, Technical Editing, Bell Telephone Laboratories, Inc.; Nicholas P. Kyros, Vice-President of Sales and Director of Marketing, Sheraton–O'Hare Motor Hotel, Rosemont, Illinois; Robert P. Mayberry, Associate Director, United Cerebral Palsy Association of Michigan, Inc.; Ernest Mazzatenta, Technical Information Department, General Motors Research Laboratories; Catherine Adams-Wilcox, a law student at Ohio State University; Ruth Barnes, Morehead State College; Harry Crosby, Boston University; Edward Harris, Lorain County Community College; Jack Leahy, University of Washington; and Arthur Wagner, Macomb County Community College.

From the GMI Library, Director William R. Elgood and two of his staff, Betty J. Amboy and Mary H. Martin, who were especially helpful in a variety of ways.

Departmental secretary Dolores M. Lucasse ("Scotty") for her invariably efficient typing of nearly all the manuscript, with occasional assists from Marie Brown, Marilyn Manning, and Mildred Murphy.

Finally, to members of my own family, who offered numerous helpful suggestions, as well as moral support: James and his wife Ethel, both communication professors, one at Bowling Green State University, the other at the University of Toledo; Kenneth, an instructor in German at Ohio State University; David, client service representative with Great Lakes Marketing Associates, Inc. of Toledo; and Eva, my wife, whose tolerance of the enormous demands involved in writing a book I deeply appreciate, even though she has strictly forbidden me ever again to write another—"for another five years, at least."

Roger P. Wilcox

ONE OVERVIEW

THE NEED FOR EFFECTIVE COMMUNICATION ON THE JOB

THE NEED FOR EFFECTIVE COMMUNICATION ON THE JOB
Internal Communication
  Downward Communication Upward Communication
  Horizontal Communication
External Communication
THE IMPORTANCE TO YOU OF BEING AN EFFECTIVE COMMUNICATOR
PROBLEMS ENCOUNTERED IN COMMUNICATING EFFECTIVELY
Problems as Viewed by the Reader or Listener
Problems as Viewed by the Writer or Speaker
CHARACTERISTICS OF WRITING AND SPEAKING ON THE JOB
Characteristics of Business Writing
  Subject Matter Form Style Focus
Characteristics of Business Speaking
BECOMING AN EFFECTIVE COMMUNICATOR

Leaders in business and industry agree that effective communication on the job is important. For instance, several years ago Phillip Bowser, at that time director of research at Buick, summed up the role of communication in his work by stating flatly, "What we do in this department is of no importance at all. The only thing that's important is what we tell others of what we do." Mr. Bowser was expressing essentially what C. F. Kettering, General Motors' pioneer in research, said years ago when he declared, "Success in engineering and research depends as much upon the ability to present ideas convincingly as it does upon the ability to perform calculations and experiments. A presentation made in words which are not understood is a complete loss."

Consultants in management have expressed similar views. Robert R. Aurner, a management consultant, has stated: "The objective record will show that the individual who can write well has a significant 'promotable' edge over the one who cannot."[1] Peter Drucker, another eminent management consultant, in an article in *Fortune,* "How to Be an Employee," said that the ability to communicate effectively heads the list of requirements for success: "As soon as you move one step up from the bottom, your effectiveness depends on your ability to reach others through the spoken or written word. . . . In the very large organizations . . . this ability to express oneself is perhaps the most important of all the skills a man can possess."[2]

The views expressed by these authorities find solid support in numerous surveys over the years. In 1959 the School of Engineering of Purdue University conducted a survey that showed that of all their courses, both technical and nontechnical, English and speech were rated the most valuable.[3] Likewise, a study on managerial and supervisory educational needs of business and industry in Pennsylvania, conducted by Pennsylvania State University, showed effective written communication and effective speaking at the head of a list of needs felt by top management to be most important for their subordinates.[4] And "ability to communicate" received the highest rating in a study reported in the *Harvard Business Review* on "What Helps or Harms Promotability."[5]

Additional evidence comes from a survey conducted in the late sixties at Southern Illinois University by a class in business communication concerning the nature of communication problems as seen by businessmen in the St. Louis area. Among the significant findings were that "all but 9 of the 112 persons interviewed said communications caused trouble for them, and 75 persons (88 percent) ranked communications first or second as a source of trouble."[6] A recent survey of executives of California-based corporations drew the response from a vice president that "One of the greatest weaknesses we see in the college graduates that come to us is the limitation in their ability to communicate both orally and in writing."[7] Finally, here is the advice of an alumnus of the Newark College of Engineering after ten years on the job: "If you do not succeed in mastering Engineering, be certain to obtain a mastery of English. *For in the end it will be the one subject you will need more than any other during your lifetime.*"[8] While some might question the ultimate value assigned by this engineer to the study of English, his general sentiment coincides closely with what we have found to be a broad consensus: ability to communicate on the job is important!

THE NEED FOR EFFECTIVE COMMUNICATION ON THE JOB

Views such as those cited above deserve explanation. *Why* is communication on the job considered so important?

An initial answer is that effective communication is vital in any human encounter, be it at home, school, on a date, at a party, or in business. For communication is the only means we have of asking questions, giving information, offering opinions, getting advice, sharing feelings—in short, satisfying our varying needs as functioning individuals constantly interrelating with others. Deprived of the ability to communicate, nearly everything that makes life worthwhile would be lost.

But this general need to communicate, omnipresent and unceasing, becomes intensified in the complex climate of modern business. Businesses have expanded dramatically in recent decades. A generation or two ago a firm might be limited to one or a half-dozen locations; today it may have branches in dozens of cities, and often in several countries as well. The number of levels of authority from clerk or floorsweeper to the top executive has increased. With new and ever more sophisticated technologies, areas of specialization have proliferated. The pressures of tighter competition, labor demands, consumer groups, and government regulatory agencies have imposed more rigorous demands for communication that is clear, accurate, and persuasive. These demands seem unlikely to diminish. Failure to communicate effectively means failure to survive.

To understand the situation more clearly, let us review the communication activities of a business organization, both internal and external.

Internal Communication

Communication within an organization is usually discussed under the categories of the three directions in which the communication flows: downward, upward, and horizontal.

Downward Communication Downward communication includes instructions, policy statements, and employee information from any level of management to any level or levels below. No organization could function long if its leadership had no way of directing the activities of those responsible for carrying out its policies and operations. Means used by management for communicating downward include newsletters, announcements, handbooks, memos, instructions (both written and oral), and staff meetings. To be effective, these communications must be clear and accurate. Even more important, they must create a willingness to *want* to understand and cooperate.

Upward Communication Upward communication is communication from any level in the organization to one or more higher levels. It was not until the early 1950s that the value of upward as well as downward communication began to be appreciated.[9] Before then, under the traditional concept of authoritarian leadership, the prevailing philosophy was, simply, "I say and you do." Now, with the rise of participative styles of management, not only information from employees but also their ideas are increasingly looked for and welcomed. Both management and employees benefit; management because of the information and ideas acquired, and the employees through the recognition they receive, plus the sense that they are having some say in what goes on.

A common device for implementing upward communication is the employee suggestion system. Doubtless you have noticed items in the paper with headings such as "Atlas Employee Receives Thousand Dollar Award for Suggestion," with perhaps a photo of a company official presenting the award.

Another common form of upward communication, if the employees belong to a union, is the grievance report. For example, a production worker feels that he or she is being told to perform an unreasonable assignment, so he or she files a grievance (a brief form stating who, what, when, where, and so forth) with the union representative, the member of the committee. This calls for the supervisor to write a grievance report, stating as objectively as possible his or her version of the incident. The grievance report then goes to the director of labor relations, who periodically meets with the committee representative to attempt to resolve accumulated disputes. If they are unsuccessful, the case moves to higher levels.

A less publicized but more vital day-by-day channel of upward communication is the report. It may be formal or informal, oral or written, requested by management (typically) or sometimes initiated by the employee. The importance of reports in business is easy to understand when we consider the function of reports in general: to inform someone of a situation or event he or she is not in a position to observe directly. Much of the information we possess we acquire through reports—news reports, sports reports, weather reports, to name a few. This is the only way we can keep informed as to what goes on in the world, simply because we cannot be all places at any given time. So we must depend on others to be our eyes and ears.

In a business organization the situation is the same, for neither can any supervisor or administrator be in all places in the organization at the same time. Yet, a prime function of any administrator is making decisions; this is a good part of what he or she is paid for. In the end, the success of the organization depends on the quality of the decisions the administrator makes. But the quality of these decisions can be no better than the soundness of the information they are based on. As in the world outside, administrators must depend on others to be their eyes and ears. Clear, accurate, objective reporting is part of the lifeblood of a healthy organization. Because of its importance, a major focus of this book, either direct or indirect, is on reporting.

Horizontal Communication   Horizontal communication consists of communication among persons on the same level in the organization for the purpose of better coordinating and broadening their perspective of the activities of the organization outside their immediate area. These persons may belong to the same department, to different departments within the immediate organization, or to different departments in separate divisions of a larger organization. If they belong to the same department, they may work on the same shift or on different shifts. If they are on different shifts, it becomes vitally important that memos written by the supervisor of an earlier shift are correctly interpreted by the counterpart on a later shift.

With the ever-increasing degree of specialization, problems in horizontal communication are greater than might be supposed. Accountants talk one language, salespeople another, and computer technologists another. Worse, each tends to assume that everyone else understands fully the language used. So the communicators may not be understood; often they do not realize they are not understood. They suffer from the illusion that they have communicated successfully when they have not.

External Communication

Downward, upward, and horizontal communication all occur *within* the organization. But business communication does not stop here. A business must purchase new materials or finished products from suppliers. It must sell its own products or services to distributors or to the buying public in general, and having sold must frequently respond to customer complaints. It must comply with a variety of government regulations: federal, state, and local. It probably is affiliated with other businesses in coping with common problems through the Chamber of Commerce, trade associations, or professional societies. All of these activities require still more communication through telephone calls, correspondence, personal meetings, or attendance at conventions.

Estimates vary, but it is certain that a considerable amount of time in business is spent communicating, either within the organization or outside of it.

THE IMPORTANCE TO YOU OF BEING AN EFFECTIVE COMMUNICATOR

Keeping in mind how utterly dependent business is on communication, and realizing the high value placed by business leaders on effective communication, its importance to you as an employee should by now be obvious. Several reasons in particular come to mind.

First is the time factor already mentioned. If writing and talking were activities performed only rarely, you could probably get by with being only a mediocre communicator. In your case, communicating effectively on the job will be a *major* requirement for success, and you will want to do well if you expect to move ahead.

A second reason is to achieve visibility. Whatever technical competencies you possess, often they will remain unnoticed outside your immediate ring of associates except as they reach visibility through memos or letters you write or through reports or proposals you either write or present orally. Otherwise, you will likely be overlooked, and this can hurt, especially if you are overlooked when the time rolls around for promotions and salary increases. On some jobs, such as that of a test engineer, the *only* concrete proof of competence is the report written following completion of a test or investigation.

Finally, there is the matter of personal satisfaction. Few of us actually enjoy doing a poor job; much of the satisfaction in any enterprise is the realization that we have performed well. I recall the glowing pride of a former student who showed me this memo from his supervisor:[10]

> Greg:
> Your latest technical report on "The Cost Estimating Functions" is one of the most comprehensive and well written that I have read. . . . I plan to circulate it to various colleagues, including the managing director. I am sure they will applaud the excellent job you have done.
>
> Jim

Several years ago, Lawrence A. Appley, then president of the American Management Association, wrote an article, "Put It In Writing." He concluded with these words: "Putting it in writing is an art, and the manager who consciously tries to put in writing something that has been created within his own mind is an artist, and receives the gratifications that go with successful art."[11]

Mr. Appley's advice to managers is fully as applicable to beginning employees.

PROBLEMS ENCOUNTERED IN COMMUNICATING EFFECTIVELY

At this point you may be quite willing to concede, "I agree. Effective communication on the job doubtless is important. But what's the problem? I've taken English for years, with grades good enough to get into college. And I've been talking all of my life, and think I can get by in front of an audience."

Problems as Viewed by the Reader or Listener

Some cues on "What's the problem?" are contained in the results of a questionnaire given to top executives at General Motors' Adam Opel Division in Germany in 1970 concerning what they did like and did not like about the memos and reports submitted to them by their subordinates. Here is a list of their responses to selected items revealing practices they were unhappy about:

	Yes	No
1. Are specific problems and objectives of the project clearly stated?	3	10
2. Is introductory information free of irrelevant material?	2	8
3. Are individual sections adequately introduced, logically developed, and appropriately concluded?	0	11
4. Are data in most convenient form and location for the user?	2	10
5. Does concluding information usually fully answer the investigated problem?	1	10
6. Is concluding information effectively organized?	0	10
7. Are subdivisions clearly labeled for easy use and comprehension?	0	9
8. Would it be better for you to receive a one-half page abstract rather than a lengthy report in most situations?	13	0

Additional writing problems as viewed by the reader are found in comments to the same questionnaire when administered to top executives at General Motors Continental Division in Belgium. Here is a sampling:

> In general, prefatory information in reports is rather poor.
>
> Introductory information is frequently too detailed.
>
> Many times the conclusion lacks clear answers to the investigated problems. Often the writer does not differentiate between findings, conclusions and recommendations.
>
> In general, reports do not contain enough illustrations. Often, those that are included are neither located for maximum usefulness, nor properly numbered, titled, labeled or properly keyed to the text.
>
> In general, paragraphs, and sentences lack clarity and are too wordy; and, most often, technical terms are not defined for the remote reader.
>
> Often, people do not know why they are getting reports.

Although the above responses pertain to writing in Europe, my own experience in conducting numerous plant training programs in this country suggests that the same problems abound here as well as abroad.

Nor are communication problems in business limited to writing. Several years ago I attended a national conference of engineers, teachers, and industrial officials interested in industrial education. While there I listened to 28 speakers, nearly two-thirds of whom, in my judgment, did only a fair-to-poor job. Here is a partial list of their faults as I noted them:

Too much abstraction, not enough concrete detail
Too many data, too little interpretation
Failure to define key terms
Lack of adequate preview of what to expect
Failure to sum up adequately the main points to be remembered
Too many screen projections
Lack of coordination between speaker and projectionist
Little rapport with audience
Reading from a manuscript with little or no expressiveness or eye contact[12]

Problems as Viewed by the Writer or Speaker

Participants in writing programs I have conducted in industry have identified on their participant questionnaires a long list of improvements they hoped to achieve in the program. An analysis of their responses discloses that the most frequently mentioned improvements (as indicated by the number following the item) were these:

1. Greater conciseness; avoidance of excess wordiness (43)
2. Clear structure; logical sequence; proper format (36)
3. Clarity; putting ideas in language the reader would understand (34)
4. Spending less time at their writing; being able to complete a writing assignment quickly (15)
5. Vocabulary improvement; being able to use the right terminology (11)
6. Ability to be more persuasive; to "sell" others (10)
7. Improved sentence structure (8)
8. Learning how to be more tactful (6)
9. Being able to edit others' writing more effectively (5)

In speech classes I have conducted over the past three decades, the problem most commonly mentioned by students at the beginning of the course is "overcoming nervousness in front of the audience." Close behind this are usually mentioned such skills as "being clear," "being persuasive," "ability to organize my ideas"—and "knowing what to do with my hands"! The problems of nervousness and what to do with the hands tend to take care of themselves after the speaker has faced an audience a few times—but not necessarily the problems of being clear, persuasive, or well organized.

CHARACTERISTICS OF WRITING AND SPEAKING ON THE JOB

Before concluding, we need to bring into focus what we have been referring to all along: business communication, specifically, business writing and business speaking, the particular concern of this book. What distinguishes it from any other writing or speaking?

Characteristics of Business Writing

Business writing can be defined in terms of four factors: subject matter, form, style, and focus.

Subject Matter The subject matter of writing in business embraces whatever operations or problems the business may be concerned with. Yet even with this limitation, the list seems nearly endless. Research, design, manufacturing, advertising, selling, customer relations, labor relations, training programs, office procedures, accounting, benefit programs, company policy—all these are typical broad categories under which a great multitude of more specialized topics fall. The range of business enterprises is even more inclusive, as a casual glance through the Yellow Pages of any fair-sized telephone directory will reveal.

Form The great bulk of business writing is in the form of memos, reports, proposals (internal communications), and letters (external communications). Since these will be discussed in detail in Part 4, "Specific Applications," we shall not define them explicitly here. Other business writing includes brochures, manuals, handbooks, and technical articles for publication.

Style The style of business writing can be described by such adjectives as factual, objective, impartial, systematic, clear, and concise. These characteristics tend to distinguish it from the kind of writing commonly taught in high school and college composition courses, in which students are encouraged to express themselves creatively in writing essays, short stories, poetry, or term papers based on library research. Models of writing provided for students are typically passages from eminent literary artists, or sometimes outstanding samples of student writing. As a result, style in such courses tends to become almost an end in itself. In contrast, business writing style "calls no attention to itself but does its job in such a straightforward and unassuming way as to be all but invisible, allowing the reader to focus his whole attention on what is being said."[13]

Focus In composition courses such as those just described, the focus is on the message. Put differently, the writer's end product is thought of as the completed manuscript. In business writing, ideally, the focus instead is on the reader, and the end product is the response elicited within the reader—understanding, agreement, favorable attitude, or whatever it may be. The competent business writer, then, tries to adapt to the reader's present understanding and attitude in the most effective way through content, organization, paragraphing, sentence structure, language, format, and tone—whether the reader be one person or many. How the writer accomplishes this will be a major concern of this text.

Characteristics of Business Speaking

All we have said about the subject matter, style, and focus of business writing applies essentially to business speaking as well. The subject matter of business speaking is governed by the immediate business situation; its style is plain, straightforward, and objective; and its focus is—or ought to be—on getting through to the listener. As for form, while the subject matter of memos is often communicated face-to-face and the subject matter of letters by telephone, we do not use the terms "oral memo" or "oral letter." Indeed, the distinctive feature of memos and letters is that they *are* in writing so the wording can be more precise, they can be studied in detail if need be, and they can be filed for future reference. These advantages are so important that a common form found in many business organizations is the "A.V.O."—Avoid Verbal Orders. (In this context, incidentally, the term "verbal" means "oral"; in its broader sense "verbal" means "consisting of words," whether written or oral.)

The subject matter of reports and proposals is also often presented orally, and here we do speak of "oral reports" and "oral proposals"—or, to use a somewhat less precise, more inclusive term, "oral presentations." However, oral presentations differ in some important respects from written presentations, and these differences we shall take up in Chapter 4, "Structure," as well as in the final chapter, "The Oral Presentation."

BECOMING AN EFFECTIVE COMMUNICATOR

Considering the major role played by communication in job success, what are your chances of becoming an effective communicator in writing and speaking?

The answer depends largely on you—your mental capacity, your motivation, and your hard work. If you have the qualities required for success in whatever program you are enrolled in—be it nursing, business administration, social work, engineering, or whatever—you almost certainly possess the qualities for success in communication.

In an article, "Making Technical Writing Easier," L. Clinton Hawes of IBM wrote: "Writing . . . is not as difficult as many people try to make it. Poets and novelists may have to wait for an internal voice, but not technical writers. All writing is at least partly an art, requiring a degree of intellectual and emotional involvement. However, there are techniques which can be used almost routinely to make writing less mysterious and more repeatable."[14]

Keep in mind we are not expecting you to become a professional writer or speaker (though some of you may). Rather, we are expecting you to become a reasonably proficient writer and speaker in your chosen profession. This you can do.

There are, however, a few misconceptions to clear away:

1. "Good writing is a matter of observing the rules of grammar." True, good grammar is an important ingredient in effective writing, because poor grammar can create both confusion and an image of illiteracy. But grammar is a means, never an end in itself. Nearly all of you have already mastered a good portion of the basics. Chapter 7, "Grammar, Punctuation, and Word Usage," will help you with most of the problems you may still have.

2. "A good writer says it right the first time; he or she seldom needs to revise." This is a gross misconception; few writers can achieve their best results the first time around. Missing points need to be added, excess verbiage needs to be pruned, sequence needs to be straightened out, and so on. In business writing, there is this qualification, however: the less formal and important the occasion, the less "perfect" the writing need be as long as it is clear and accurate. But if circumstances warrant, careful writing will repay. To those who protest, "I don't have time," my response is, "Whose time do you want to waste? Yours, or your reader's?" A little extra time used in composing a letter or report can save a great deal of time later to clear up misunderstandings. And effective writing usually means more than one draft.

3. "Engineers can't write." It is true that some engineers—or technicians, or scientists, or accountants, or whatever—may not find writing as easy as performing skills in their own area. Some may not *like* to write. But to argue that "engineers can't write" is a gross overstatement which fails to do justice to the great majority who can and do.[15]

4. "A writer needs a big vocabulary." A writer needs an *accurate* vocabulary appropriate to the subject matter and reader, but not necessarily a big one. I am reminded of a student I once had in freshman English who protested a "C" I had given her on a "friendly letter" assignment. "Mary," I told her, "you never would talk in the style you used in that letter." Her reply was, "Why I thought the purpose in writing was to use as many big words as possible!" "Big words" are the bane of business writing, and authorities like Stuart Chase, Rudolf Flesch, and Robert Gunning have been fighting for years to improve the readability of business and professional writing. Someone has even proposed the "KISS" formula for clear writing: "Keep It Simple, Stupid!"

5. "Speakers are born, not made." Some people do possess a greater flair for facing an audience than others. But the principal barrier to success in

speaking is fear of facing an audience, and any speech teacher can testify that after the first few experiences, speech fright among their students is seldom a problem. After that it is a matter of learning how to sort out, organize, and develop their ideas clearly, interestingly, and persuasively. Good speaking is not a matter of eloquent flights of oratory, but of a clear, straightforward, sincere presentation of ideas in terms the audience can understand.

With such misconceptions as these out of the way, we are ready to proceed. It will be the purpose of this text, with the help of your professor, to provide you with a basic philosophy, some dependable guidelines, some useful techniques, and plenty of experience. The rest, my friend, is up to you.

SUMMARY

1. Business leaders and management consultants feel strongly that ability in writing and speaking is of top importance for success on the job.

2. The reason for the importance to the company of effective communication becomes clear through reviewing the communication activities of a business organization, both internal and external.

3. The importance of employees being effective communicators is due to: (a) the amount of time they will spend communicating, (b) the visibility it provides them, and (c) the personal satisfaction it affords them.

4. Numerous surveys have revealed various problems in effective communication, from the point of view of both management and the employee.

5. Business writing and speaking can be usefully differentiated from other kinds of writing and speaking in terms of (a) subject matter, (b) form, (c) style, and (d) focus.

6. Proficiency in ability to meet writing and speaking requirements on the job lies within the grasp of anyone capable of meeting the other requirements of the job.

7. Common misconceptions concerning writing and speaking include the following: (a) "Good writing is a matter of observing the rules of grammar"; (b) "A good writer says it right the first time; he or she seldom needs to revise"; (c) "Engineers can't write"; (d) "A writer needs a big vocabulary"; and (e) "Speakers are born, not made."

SUGGESTED APPLICATIONS

1. Consult the *Business Periodicals Index* in the library and select two or more articles, as specified by your instructor, on the role of communication in business and industry. Read the articles and write a 400- to

500-word paper in which you summarize briefly the main points and offer your own evaluation. Begin with a brief introductory paragraph, use topic headings (and subheadings if appropriate), and end with a brief summary paragraph.

2. Interview a number of persons in management on the role of communication in their work. These could be department heads, deans, or other administrative personnel in your school, or supervisors or executives in businesses or plants. As an aid, construct a simple interview guide containing such questions as: "What communication activities do you engage in?" "How much of your time do these take?" "What problems do you encounter in downward communication?" "What problems in upward communication?" A few courtesies to keep in mind: ask in advance for an appointment; be sure to be on time; let the person you are interviewing do the talking; avoid arguing (though don't hesitate to draw the person out by asking questions); ask permission if you wish to take notes; do not overstay your time (probably not more than a half hour); and thank the person for his or her time and interest when you leave. Report your experience, either orally to the class or in writing to the teacher, or both as he or she may direct. In addition, you might wish to send a copy of your report to your interviewee, along with a short thank-you letter.

3. Spend a half hour in a place of business (supermarket, department store, restaurant, business office, campus office) observing the communication activities of the people present. These activities could include talking (face-to-face or on the telephone), writing (in longhand or by typewriter), as well as listening and reading. Take notes, then write a report of around 300 words describing the communication you observed. Your report should be clear, accurate, factual, informative. Close with a brief paragraph summing up in general your conclusions based on what you observed.

NOTES

[1] Robert R. Aurner, "Communications Impact: Power Source for Decision Makers," *Journal of Business Communication,* 5:2 (Winter, 1967), pp. 26–29.

[2] Peter F. Drucker, "How to Be an Employee," *Fortune,* May, 1952.

[3] George A. Hawkins, Edward C. Thomas, William K. LeBold, "A Study of the Purdue University Engineering Graduate," *Journal of Engineering Education,* Vol. 49, No. 10 (June, 1959), pp. 930–947.

[4] Samuel S. Dubin, Everett Alderman, and H. Leroy Marlow, "Managerial and Supervisory Education Needs of Business and Industry in Pennsylvania," Department of Planning Studies, Pennsylvania State University, 1967.

[5] Garda W. Bowman, "What Helps or Harms Promotability," *Harvard Business Review,* Vol. 42 (January-February, 1964), pp. 7–26, 184–186.

[6] Homer L. Cox, "Opinions of Selected Business Managers About Some Aspects

of Communication on the Job," *The Journal of Communication,* Vol. 6, No. 1 (Fall, 1968), pp. 3-12.

[7]James C. Bennett, "The Communication Needs of Business Executives," *The Journal of Business Communication,* Vol. 8, No. 3 (Spring, 1971), pp. 5-11.

[8]Herman Estrin, "Engineering Alumni Advice to Freshman on Studying English," *College English,* Vol. 21 (November, 1959).

[9]See, for example, the excellent article by Earl Planty and William Machaver, "Upward Communication: A Project in Executive Development," *Personnel,* Vol. 28, No. 4 (January, 1952), pp. 304-318.

[10]Letter written by James L. Yarbrough. Used with permission of author.

[11]Lawrence A. Appley, "Put It In Writing," *Supervisory Management* (June, 1964), pp. 22-23.

[12]Roger P. Wilcox, *Oral Reporting in Business and Industry* (Englewood Cliffs, N.J.: Prentice-Hall, Inc., 1967), pp. 1-2.

[13]*A Guide for Authors* (Boston: Houghton Mifflin Company, 1974), p. 17.

[14]L. Clinton Hawes, "Making Technical Writing Easier," *Journal of Technical Writing and Communication,* Vol. 1 (April, 1971), pp. 161-172.

[15]See, for example, the editorial, "Engineers Can't Write, Can They?," *Design News,* June 5, 1972.

2 WRITING AND SPEAKING AS COMMUNICATION

WHAT WE MEAN BY COMMUNICATION

Implications of the Definition
    Communication Is a Process
    Communication Depends on Symbols
    Communication Involves Two or More People
    Communication Is Interactive   Communication Is Imperfect

A Communication Model
    Formulation   Expression   Transmission
    Reception   Interpretation   Feedback

HOW COMMUNICATION FALLOFF OCCURS

Problems in Formulating the Message
    Lack of Familiarity with the Subject
    Lack of Familiarity with the Situation
    Lack of Sensitivity to the Reader or Listener
    Presence of Emotional Blocks

Problems in Expressing the Message

Problems in Transmitting the Message

Problems in Receiving the Message

Problems in Interpreting the Message
    Differences Between Sender and Receiver
    The Denotative-Connotative Dimension
    The Content-Relationship Meaning   The Problem of Selectivity

FALLOFF AND NOISE

HOW TO REDUCE COMMUNICATION FALLOFF

Create a Positive Working Relationship

Compose and Present the Message Effectively

Encourage Two-Way Communication

In the book title, and repeatedly throughout Chapter 1, we have used the term "communication." We have emphasized that to be successful in your business career you must communicate effectively. But we have not yet defined the term, and it is necessary now that we do so. For how you conceive of communication will influence the degree of success you achieve at it, and a faulty conception can only invite failure.

If, for instance, you think of communication as "the transmission of information," you are inviting failure.[1] Or, if you believe that the end product of communication is a well-phrased letter or an impressively delivered speech, again you are inviting failure. So it is essential before proceeding further that we clarify what we do mean by this all-important term.

WHAT WE MEAN BY COMMUNICATION

The term "communication" has been used so loosely in recent years that it has come to mean almost anything the user wants it to mean. So we must be more specific. For our purposes we shall define *communication* as "a process of sharing meaning between persons through an exchange of symbols enabling each person to elicit in his or her own mind a meaning similar to that in the mind of the other."[2]

Implications of the Definition

Such a definition requires elaboration. Some of the more important implications are these:[3]

Communication Is a Process Communication is not a product (such as a letter or talk), but a process, and process implies change. "By adopting the process approach," says Almaney, "we can perceive [communication] events as dynamic and on-going systems rather than static and stationary."[4] In the communication process, nothing remains constant. As communicators, our mood, intent, point of view, and mental alertness are constantly changing from day to day, hour to hour, almost from minute to minute. The words we use and the meanings they represent likewise constantly change, depending on the circumstances and the people involved. Finally, the receiver (our reader or listener) is in as constant a state of change as we are, and this has a profound effect on how he or she interprets any message we send.

Communication Depends on Symbols There is no way that we can transmit meaning directly (except possibly through extrasensory perception). Ideas and feelings cannot be transferred like physical objects, such as money or a piece of merchandise can. Only symbols—which stand for the meaning, but are not the meaning themselves—can be transmitted. The symbols may be verbal (that is, words), or nonverbal (such as tone of voice, rate of speaking, gestures, promptness, format, illustrations, and many others). These symbols are the servants that carry the meaning.

Symbols in themselves have no meaning. The only function a symbol can perform is (a) to represent some meaning in the mind of the sender (writer or speaker), and (b) to arouse a meaning in the mind of the receiver (reader or listener). For instance, you might ask a friend, "May I borrow your eraser?" If the friend fails to notice that you are writing in ink, he or she may hand you a pencil eraser. If it happens that this person is a foreigner from, say, Korea, he or she may not yet be familiar with what the word "eraser" stands for, so be uncertain what you want. There is nothing in the word "eraser" itself—or in any other word—that guarantees that it will accurately express what you mean, or will be interpreted by anyone else the way you intended.

Communication Involves Two or More People If we are the communicator, it is only natural for us to think in terms of our own end of the process—writing a letter, for instance, or planning and presenting a talk. When we have finished, it is also natural for us to think of the process as being complete. But this is a gross fallacy; only *half* the process is complete, and the less important half at that! *For in communication it is not what we present that is important, but what our readers or listeners perceive—what they understand, believe, and accept.*[5] Thus, our objective in communicating is not to write a letter or report, or make an oral presentation. Our objective is to help our readers or listeners understand, see for themselves, or whatever we hope their response will be. Our message is not an end, but only a means to an end.

Communication Is Interactive Implicit in our definition is the point that each participant in the process plays the double role of being both sender and receiver. The context which most readily illustrates this is face-to-face communication, where each participant plays both roles simultaneously. A says something to B, using a combination of both verbal and nonverbal symbols, and what A says influences B so that B responds instantly (even no response is a form of response). B may respond nonverbally by such activities as scowling, laughing, shifting weight, or leaning forward. Or B may respond verbally by agreeing, disagreeing, questioning, changing the topic, and so on. Whatever B's responses may be, they in turn influence A. Each, then, continuously interacts with the other.

This same concept, though less obvious, is just as true when we write. The relationship you have with your reader (which is a result of the kind of interaction you have had with him or her in the past) profoundly affects what you write, how you write, and how easily you write. To illustrate, consider how these three variables would be affected by the contrasting nature of the relationship inherent in the two situations following:

1. a "good news" letter to your boyfriend or girlfriend, with whom you are deeply in love

2. a memo requesting a favor from your boss, whom you consider cold, unsympathetic, and critical

Even when we do not know who our reader will be, our writing is still influenced, though in this case by the *absence* of a clear relationship. As one test engineer expressed it, "Eighty-five percent of the time when I write a report I don't know who will read it. And it's pretty hard to write a report if you don't know who your reader will be."

The interactive nature of communication underscores the importance of viewing it as a two-way rather than a one-way process. In a perceptive article entitled "Communication as Participation," Edgar Dale says:

> Effective communication is not a one-way process aimed chiefly to change the receiver. Rather it is a two-way dialogue which changes both sender and receiver. Communication at its best is the *sharing* of ideas and feelings in a mood of mutuality. There is continuing dialogue. In one-way communication, however, the sender assumes that the receiver is a target to be aimed at but with little or no provision for the "target" to shoot back. There is no creative interaction.[6]

The two-way concept is interestingly illustrated in this account written by a student of an experience in a plant where he was employed:

> Whenever time permitted, Waldo and I would have lengthy discussions, usually on religion, and I believe that led to Waldo's decision to introduce me to a group of his friends when we went on break one day.
>
> Nine forty-five each morning Waldo and I would shut off our machines and walk to the cafeteria for our fifteen minute break.
>
> This particular morning Waldo and I sat down near one of Waldo's friends who was reading a pocket size book.
>
> Waldo said, "What are you reading there?"
>
> "A passage from the Scriptures," was his reply. He went on to say, "We were going to discuss the passage, 'And then God made a greater light to light the day and a lesser light to light the night.'"
>
> The discussion progressed with other people joining the group. They decided that the "greater light" was the sun. This conclusion seemed warranted, so I said nothing, but then they decided that the "lesser light to light the night" was composed of the reflection of the sun's light on the moon and stars. I just had to say something.

I pointed out that while the moon does reflect light from the sun, a star is just the same as the sun and gives off its own light. None of them seemed to believe this "fact," a feeling that was hard for me to understand, and then they started to quote the Bible as proof that they were correct. I couldn't understand what I was up against until one of the gentlemen asked me where I got my information.

I told him, "Any science book will tell you exactly what I said about the moon and the stars."

He looked surprised for an instant and then said, "Well, you can believe that instead of the word of the Lord if you want to." He paused for a second, looked at his friends, then said in a semi-mocking tone, "I suppose some scientist has been to one of the stars to see what they're made of."

To this I replied, "Just as much as the Lord descended from heaven to enlighten you." Our break ended at that point. I couldn't help feeling, though, that it was too bad that the gentleman with the Bible was so close-minded. Later, I realized he probably was thinking the same about me.

That one fifteen minute break had taught me a valuable lesson in human communication. I realized that if we become so stubborn as to ignore an opposing view, we no longer have a dialogue, but only a monologue. This is a lesson I shall not soon forget.[7]

Communication Is Imperfect This statement is implied by the last part of the definition, which refers to "symbols enabling each person to elicit in his or her own mind a meaning similar to that in the mind of the other." "Similar to," but not identical—and the reason it is not identical can be summed up by the following pair of statements:

Symbols seldom fully represent our ideas.

Symbols have no inherent meaning; the meaning is in the mind of the person using the symbol.

We shall explore these points more fully when we discuss "communication falloff" later in the chapter. For now it will suffice to point out that by its very nature communication is not a perfect, but an imperfect process.[8]

A Communication Model

Another way of explaining the communication process is by means of a model (a simplified, graphic representation). Figure 2.1 is the model we shall use.[9]

WRITING AND SPEAKING AS COMMUNICATION

From this model we can identify six steps in the communication process:

Formulation A wishes to communicate with B as a means of producing some effect in B's understanding, attitudes, beliefs, or behavior. Deliberating on what message will best achieve this response, A inwardly formulates his message.

Expression A expresses, or "encodes," the message in symbols. As already explained, the symbols may be verbal or nonverbal, and if verbal either written or spoken. Actually, the encoding process begins in A's mind during the formulation stage, but does not become outwardly manifest until the expression stage.

Transmission The symbols (the message) are transmitted to B in person, by mail, and so forth. At another level, as B reads or hears the message, the symbols are transmitted to his or her retina or eardrums by means of light or sound waves.

Reception The light waves or sound waves act as stimuli creating sense impressions that are relayed to B's brain.

Interpretation B interprets the message, or attempts to interpret it, in terms of his or her particular frame of reference.

Feedback B reacts to A's message inwardly, and may formulate a message of his or her own, thus initiating a new communication. If this message reaches A, then feedback has occurred. Even if it does not reach A, but A expects a response, feedback still occurs through lack of response.

Thus, how communication is "a process of sharing meaning . . . through an exchange of symbols" is revealed more explicitly through these six steps of our model.

FIGURE 2.1 A Simple Model of Interpersonal Communication

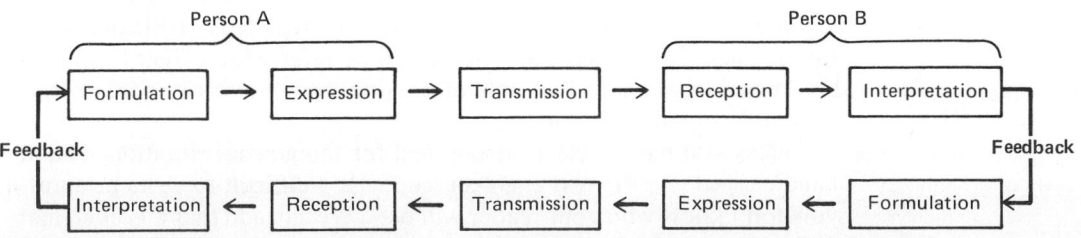

HOW COMMUNICATION FALLOFF OCCURS

As stated above, the meaning as interpreted is never quite the same as the meaning intended. This loss of meaning between sender and receiver is known as *communication falloff*. Why does falloff occur? An analysis of potential problems at each step of our model will provide some helpful insights.

Problems in Formulating the Message

If the content of our message appears faulty, communication falloff occurs as the readers or listeners begin to feel that our grasp of the situation—our facts, our reasoning, our conclusions—is questionable. Moreover, they begin questioning our credibility in general, and this contributes even more to communication falloff. Thus, message formulation, the first step in the communication process, is also the first step at which falloff may commence. A look at possible reasons for faulty content should prove useful in avoiding it. Among the more common are these:

Lack of Familiarity with the Subject If a writer does not know the subject, he or she is in no position to tell anyone else about it. Fortunately, in writing and speaking on the job, this problem is not usually as troublesome as in college assignments in which you may be asked to write a term paper on a topic you know very little about—for example, "An Analysis of the Use of Metaphor in *Moby Dick*." On the job, as a rule, you will be writing from within your own area of expertise. Nevertheless, you may still need to investigate thoroughly, assimilate, select, analyze, synthesize, and organize until the content appears solid and sound to the most critical reader. Otherwise, you risk, at the outset, the possibility of some—perhaps considerable—falloff.

Lack of Familiarity with the Situation Who will the reader be? Your supervisor alone? Your supervisor and the rest of the department? Your supervisor's supervisor as well? What information must be included to adapt to their level of knowledge? What biases do they have you should be aware of? Will this document be used as is, or will your supervisor incorporate it with other similar reports in a report of his or her own intended for higher management? Will it be distributed outside the organization? Will it be pulled from the files to be referred to a year from now? Five years from now? Is it only of passing, routine importance, or "permanent," top-level importance?

Unless you have a clear, strong feel for the general situation, you are handicapped. As the test engineer said, "It's difficult to write a report if you don't know who your reader will be." We can add that it is even more difficult if you do not know the situation in general.

Lack of Sensitivity to the Reader or Listener Having stressed the importance of the receiver in the communication process, we can appreciate why lack of sensitivity to the receiver would be a barrier in formulating (and expressing) a message that "gets through." Yet some writers and speakers are low in such sensitivity. A few years ago Dr. Charles Goshen, a professor both of engineering management and of psychiatry, conducted a series of in-depth interviews with a fairly large number of engineers who had been on the job some 20 to 25 years. Among various personal characteristics he found to be quite common to the group was "their lack of awareness of other people's individualized attitudes and backgrounds . . . [as] demonstrated by a particular type of communication failure." Goshen elaborated on this point as follows:

> Much of their work involved making reports and proposals to others whose own professional activities overlapped with their own to only slight degrees. They themselves very likely would have become deeply immersed for some period in their project and were, consequently, very familiar with it. Their presentations unwittingly assumed a commensurate degree of familiarity on the part of their audience, and they seldom were aware of the necessity for first providing the latter with a body of background information or of first setting a mood conducive to acceptance. Instead, they would tend to plunge immediately into the intricacies of their subject, leaving their audience with no framework on which to build an understanding, thus failing to develop cooperation.[10]

While such lack of awareness would not, of course, hinder formulating a message clear to *themselves,* it would definitely hinder their formulating one clear to their reader or listener. Thus, the falloff could be tremendous.

Presence of Emotional Blocks A final problem we shall suggest is the presence of emotional blocks. Consider, for example, these cases:

> Anderson, a first-line supervisor, sits at his desk fretting over how to start a report requested by his supervisor to explain why efficiency in his department has fallen lower than in any of the other departments. The boss has a quick temper and has frequently criticized Anderson. Anderson, in turn, feels extremely uncomfortable in any of his dealings with the boss. After several futile starts, he tosses the paper in the basket and decides to wait until tomorrow.
>
> Dominguez has recently been promoted to department head. Among her new subordinates are three former colleagues who also aggressively sought the position she won. Their feelings

toward her range from disappointment to cold politeness. She is about to write a memo announcing a new policy change she suspects will be unpopular; she is uncertain of the best approach to use.

Schwartz, a computer technologist fresh from the university, feels that he has been largely ignored during the few months since he arrived. Now he has been invited to address a management group at the plant on certain new applications of computer science. He has seldom faced an audience, and feels unnerved each time he thinks about the prospect. He desperately wants to make the most of this opportunity, but his mind goes blank as he tries to plan what to say.

This list of hypothetical examples could readily be expanded. They are not unusual in illustrating the crippling effect emotional blocks can have in message formulation.

Problems in Expressing the Message

Having determined what ideas to include in your message, you now must decide how best to express them. As we have already emphasized, the only way ideas can be expressed is through symbols, whether verbal, nonverbal, or both. Here is the source of considerably more communication falloff, for *symbols never fully represent what the communicator has in mind*. This is especially true if he or she has not thought through the ideas carefully, or lacks an adequate vocabulary, or is insensitive to very subtle differences in meaning between words, or is using other than his or her native tongue. It is further true if the communicator lacks skill in fashioning words into sentences or sentences into paragraphs, so the main ideas receive too little emphasis or the subordinate ideas too much, or the relationship between ideas is confusing or misleading; likewise if he or she is guilty of wordiness. Superfluous words, rather than clarifying the meaning, tend to blur it. If one is presenting one's ideas orally instead of in writing, feelings of self-consciousness—in addition to all the other problems mentioned above—can severely damage expressiveness. One may mumble, hesitate, forget much of what one planned to say, stare at the ceiling or floor, or drone on through the manuscript (if the speech is written).

In short, since the message that gets recorded on the sheet of paper, or uttered by the lips, imperfectly represents one's ideas, substantial falloff may occur even before the message reaches the reader or listener. In this light we can appreciate the wisdom of the common quip: "I know that you believe you understand what you think I said, but I am not sure you realize that what you heard is not what I meant." Sometimes it appears that the sender doesn't realize either, as shown in this sentence from a motor accident claim received by an insurance office: "One wheel went into the ditch. My foot jumped from brake to accelerator pedal, leaped across the road to the other side and jumped into the trunk of a tree."

Problems in Transmitting the Message

Little falloff normally occurs during this step. If the message is written and never arrives, naturally the falloff is total. If it is delayed, some falloff may result if what was intended as a prompt reply is interpreted—before arrival, anyway—as negligence. If the copy is partially illegible, falloff will occur also.

Speaking probably introduces more possibility of falloff at this stage than does writing. All too often the acoustics are poor, external noises (such as air conditioners, heavy traffic, sirens, someone coughing) intrude, or the speaker talks too rapidly, too indistinctly, or without sufficient volume.

In general, however, the transmission stage—especially in written communication—is not typically a primary source of falloff.

Problems in Receiving the Message

When we recall that reception of written messages refers to the reader's receiving the message into his or her brain through the sense of vision, we realize that little falloff normally occurs in the reception stage either. Usually the reader's sight is clear enough so he or she can read the message, though sometimes in haste he or she may misread it and come to wrong conclusions, temporarily at least.

If the message is spoken, falloff in reception is a little more likely, for if the listener misses a word or phrase because of poor hearing (or for any other reason for that matter), he or she cannot "turn the speech back" and relisten. If he concentrates on trying to decipher what he missed, his attention is no longer on the speaker, so he or she misses still more. Clear audibility on the part of the speaker, and good hearing and attentive listening on the part of the listener are necessary for minimizing falloff in spoken messages at the transmission and reception stages.

Problems in Interpreting the Message

The interpretation stage is where falloff is most likely to occur. The reason is that, just as writers or speakers must depend on symbols to express their meaning, so readers or listeners must depend on symbols to interpret the meaning—and symbols by themselves have no meaning. There is, for instance, nothing in the three letters "c-a-t" inherently related in any way to the four-footed animal we associate with the word. The association is solely in the mind. This illustrates what is the most critical factor in communication falloff: the only meaning symbols possess is in the mind of the person using them—and people are different.

Differences Between Sender and Receiver The extent to which people differ is indicated by the many factors that account for their differences:

age, sex, race, national or cultural background, social status (past and present), intelligence, education, amount of experience, kinds of experience, status in the organization, economic status, marital status and adjustment, temperament, attitude toward the subject, attitude toward the writer, mood at the moment of reading, and so on. Considering that this list is far from complete, and that each factor is highly complex, it is clear that a vast list of factors, both conscious and subconscious, influence how the receiver will interpret the message. Then when we reflect that the particular combination of factors influencing the reader or listener will certainly differ—perhaps drastically—from those influencing the writer or speaker, we can readily see why the amount of falloff may be enormous. However, the more similar in all respects the sender and receiver are to each other, the less the falloff to be expected at the interpretation stage.

In business, as elsewhere, differences between the two may result in quite different interpretations of meaning, as seen in the following examples:

1. The functional relationship between sender and receiver. For example, the word "guarantee" has a very precise meaning to a salesperson, but will probably carry a much vaguer (and more inclusive!) meaning to the customer.

2. Positional relationship. A president might view reduced production as a problem to explain to the stockholders; a newly hired employee would probably view it as a worry about keeping his or her job.

3. Group-membership relationship. A union representative will see a grievance in a different light from that of the supervisor.

4. Differences in heredity and environment. An Ivy League graduate may have little comprehension of a destitute laborer's aspirations—or lack of them.

5. Difference in formal education. The floorsweeper will have virtually no background at all for carrying on a conversation about a project with the computer technologist whose office he or she is sweeping.

6. Past experience. A supervisor offering "good advice" may be entirely sincere, but still be distrusted by a worker who feels he or she was double-crossed by the supervisor six months before.

7. Emotions. A rush typing job given at 4:45 will be regarded quite differently by a harassed office manager and by a secretary with an appointment at 5:15.[11]

The problem of falloff in interpretation is further complicated when we reflect on the various dimensions of meaning. Two of the most important are the denotative-connotative dimension and the content-relationship meaning.

The Denotative-Connotative Dimension The *denotative meaning* is the objective meaning on which people broadly agree. For instance, all of us would agree in a general way on what a cat is. Yet, when we hear the word mentioned we inevitably interpret it in terms of specific cats we have known, which of course will differ from the particular set of specific cats others have known. So even the denotative meaning differs somewhat from one person to another.

The *connotative meaning* is the subjective or emotional meaning aroused in the receiver's mind. Again, to take "cat" for example, mention of this word will arouse feelings of great affection in some people, but of great distaste in others. The term "failed" is another example. When a test engineer writes in a report that a part "failed" after 900,000 cycles (times tested), he or she means simply that it ceased operating at that point; he or she could just as easily have written, "The part operated successfully for 900,000 cycles." But if the report containing the word "failed" happens to be introduced as evidence in a product liability suit, it is almost certain to connote a much more negative meaning to members of the jury than it did to the engineer. Outside the test laboratory the idea of failure generally carries a very negative connotation.

Differences in interpretation tend to be much greater in the connotative than in the denotative aspect of meaning.

The Content-Relationship Meaning Viewed from another perspective, every message carries both a content meaning and a relationship meaning. The content meaning is *subject* oriented; it is impersonal and relates to the subject at hand. The relationship meaning, on the other hand, is *person* oriented, and implies the nature of the relationship between sender and receiver, whether positive or negative, formal or informal, subordinate or coordinate. To illustrate, whether you address a memo to a colleague as "Mr. Jones," "Jones," "Bill," or "You blockhead," the content meaning remains the same, for you are referring to the same person in each case; however, the relationship implied by each salutation is probably quite different. The relationship meaning is always important, but especially so in letters, where *tone* is typically a critical variable. What the writer may intend as purely objective and impersonal may appear to the reader as tactless and offensive. Serious falloff may then result.

Relationship is often more likely to be expressed nonverbally than verbally. Quality of stationery, promptness of reply, tone of voice—all nonverbal symbols—may speak louder than the words themselves.[12]

The Problem of Selectivity Finally, falloff in interpretation is strongly influenced by the problem of selectivity. Since it is humanly impossible to pay attention to or remember *everything* we hear or read, we are selective (subconsciously) in what we listen to, read, or remember. We necessarily attend to and remember what is either most pleasing or most threatening to our interests and needs.

Perhaps you have been asked by your supervisor to gather some extensive information that he or she needs for a report he or she is preparing for his or her superior. Later, you mention that you now have the information, but it will be the first of the week before you have it organized and ready to give to him or her. If it happens that he or she is under sudden pressure to complete the report earlier than expected, the only part of your message your supervisor may hear is that "it will be the first of the week before it is ready"—which means further delay for him or her. The point that you now have the information (which you feel happy about) may scarcely enter his or her consciousness.

Or, your supervisor may show you an evaluation he or she has written of your performance (a standard practice in many companies every six or twelve months). The evaluation may contain one statement that is highly complimentary, several rather neutral, and one highly critical. In all probability, the two statements you pay most attention to will be the one that is complimentary and the one that is critical. The others you may scarcely notice or remember.

Moreover, we tend to perceive messages according to our frame of mind. When you tell your supervisor that the information will be ready the first of the week, he or she is likely to "hear": "will *not* be ready before the first of the week." Furthermore, he or she may think to him- or herself, "Next time I'll ask somebody I can depend on." Likewise, upon reading your supervisor's evaluation, you may be exhilarated the rest of the day because of the one complimentary remark, or in a very blue mood because of the one critical remark—depending on the frame of mind you were in when you read it.

Selective attention, selective perception, selective retention—all influence profoundly how a message is interpreted. Yet neither the sender nor receiver may even be aware of the influence at all.[13]

FALLOFF AND NOISE

We have examined falloff in terms of the steps of our communication model. Another useful way of examining it is through the concept of *noise,* which refers to anything that reduces the fidelity, or accuracy, of the meaning between sender and receiver.

Noise may be classified as *semantic, mechanical,* or *psychological,* and may occur at any stage of the communication process. Semantic noise refers to differing word meanings, and is found in the formulation, expression, and interpretation stages; mechanical noise to interference in transmission or reception; and psychological noise to emotional attitudes in the sender or receiver.

The following table shows typical examples of noise:

	Sending	Receiving
Semantic	use of jargon inability to think of "the right word" faulty sentence structure	lack of adequate background for understanding different denotative meaning different connotation
Mechanical	illegible copy crowded margins indistinct articulation inadequate volume	defective vision faulty hearing inadequate lighting external distractions
Psychological	anxiety about communicating hostility toward reader or listener emotional fatigue	indifference distrust biased attitude

HOW TO REDUCE COMMUNICATION FALLOFF

We have said that by its very nature communication is an imperfect process. Yet, though perfect communication is an unattainable goal, much can be done to reduce the gap between faulty communication and effective communication.

We have pointed out, too, that noise—resulting in falloff—may occur at any point in the process from formulation to interpretation. Nevertheless, the sender can, and should, assume a major share of the responsibility for controlling noise so as to minimize falloff. The receiver likewise should assume a major share of the responsibility. Successful communication, like a successful marriage, requires that each party go more than halfway.

Our advice on how to reduce falloff will involve three approaches: create a positive working relationship between sender and receiver; compose the message effectively; and encourage two-way communication.

Create a Positive Working Relationship

The basic condition for achieving effective communication with a minimum of falloff is a positive working relationship between the persons doing the communicating. This kind of relationship does not necessarily mean agreement. Rather, it means a climate in which agreement may be reached, and disagreement treated with understanding and respect. In short, it means a climate of *trust*.

The importance of trust in successful communication is evident wherever we turn: between friends, associates, husband and wife, parent and child, doctor and client, subordinate and supervisor. Its presence is critical between groups as well: blacks and whites, liberals and conservatives, the poor and the rich, as well as factions in conflict all over the globe. In industry, it is critical between labor and management. Dr. Alan McLean, a psychiatrist, has emphasized how important it is in employee relations "to promote a climate favorable to the growth of understanding."[14] He went on to comment that employees who are resentful and suspicious can and will misinterpret the meaning of downward communication, no matter how clear it might be.

Although the importance of trust is so clearly evident in our relationships with others, it is a curious paradox how often its importance is ignored. The reason for this appears to be rooted in another paradox, which can be expressed by this pair of related principles:

1. We all possess a strong need for esteem—to be well thought of and to be able to think well of ourselves. No one likes one's esteem threatened; everyone wants to be treated with consideration and respect.

2. A consequence of our concern for our own need for esteem is that we tend to be blind to others' need also for esteem.

In other words, the esteem need is one we are keenly sensitive about in ourselves, but often indifferent to in others. Ironically, this is self-defeating, since the less concern we show for others, the less they tend to show toward us.

Precisely how does the breakdown of trust, resulting from threats to esteem, produce communication falloff? The answer is simple. When we feel threatened, we tend to become defensive, and when we become defensive, our concern is no longer with the content meaning of the message, but with protecting our egos. We become angry, we make alibis, we think of comebacks and ways to cut the other down; in short, we react emotionally rather than logically. The communicator's objective of securing understanding, agreement, or cooperation is thus thwarted by the receiver's emotional response. While the content meaning may have provided the reason for the message, the relationship meaning determines *how* the content meaning is interpreted.[15]

Variations can be expected in the degree to which the receiver may react defensively. At least three variables are:

1. Receiver's sense of security. The less sure of oneself one is, the more likely one will become defensive.

2. Threat of message. A message that is severely threatening will tend to elicit defensive reactions more readily than one only mildly threatening.

3. Existing relationship between sender and receiver. A relationship already negative provides a more likely setting for defensive reactions.

Promoting trust—not putting the receiver on the defensive—is important in either writing or speaking, but especially in writing. One reason is that when we write we presumably have time to think through more carefully just how we will express our thoughts and feelings. If our message puts the reader on the defensive, he or she can rightfully assume either that it was deliberate, or that we did not consider him or her important enough to warrant taking the time to be more tactful. Furthermore, since visual and vocal cues, plus opportunity for two-way communication, are sharply reduced in writing as compared with speaking, it is all the more important in writing to be sensitive to the relationship implications. Finally, when our message is written it is "permanent" (until lost or discarded).

Before leaving our discussion on the importance of a positive relationship, we must stress a very important point. The nature of the relationship between any two people is the result of what *both* of them have made it—not just one, or the other, but *both*. Consciously or subconsciously, intentionally or unintentionally, each has contributed in some way.

To be more specific, if bad feelings exist between you and some other person, it may be convenient to say the other is at fault, but you also must share part of the fault as well. By the same token, so also must the other person. This is true whether the person is your roommate, your boyfriend or girlfriend, a parent, a professor, your boss, or whoever. Consider the classic example of the nagging wife and the hen-pecked husband. She says, "I wouldn't have to nag if you'd only act like a man"; he replies, "I could act like a man if you'd only stop nagging." To the outsider it is obvious that each is contributing to the other's behavior. Just as communication is interactive, so is the relationship between the communicators a joint result of their interaction.

To sum up, a critical prerequisite to successful communication is a positive, working relationship; a climate of trust. By itself, trust will not prevent falloff. Without trust, greater falloff is certain to result.[16]

Compose and Present the Message Effectively

Assuming that we have a positive, working relationship with our reader or listener, we must then focus on composing and (if a speech) presenting the message. Composing and presenting the message involve the first two steps of our model: formulation and expression. More specifically, they involve at least the following:

1. Find out as much as possible in advance about the subject, the situation, and the readers or listeners. If your supervisor gives you a writing or speaking "assignment," you should make it a point before leaving his or her office to learn as much as possible relevant to getting a clear feel for the situation—and the supervisor should be willing to help you.

2. Try to become as free as possible of emotional blocks such as those described earlier in the chapter. Overcoming emotional blocks may require more assistance than this text can provide, but it is important to recognize their effect and learn how to cope with them.

3. Work on composing effective sentences and paragraphs (when the message is written), organizing clearly, using language appropriate to the subject and reader, avoiding faults in punctuation and grammar, using graphic aids correctly, and choosing the proper format for memos, letters, and reports or proposals; in short, learn to use whatever techniques will enable you to adapt clearly and persuasively to your reader's understanding and attitudes.

4. Try to be confident and communicative when speaking, using an oral style (as opposed to a written style), planning and using visual aids proficiently, and handling a question period competently.

A review of the table of contents will reveal that offering guidelines in mastering these skills constitutes the major objective of this text.

Encourage Two-Way Communication

It might seem that if one has a favorable relationship with one's readers or listeners, and can use the above techniques in writing or speaking well, one should be a successful communicator. But when we recall our analysis of falloff and noise, we realize that this is not necessarily the case, since much of the falloff occurs later, in the interpretation stage. Never can we fully control how a message may be interpreted, because *we* do not do the interpreting. The receiver does it, and without two-way communication no one would know how closely his or her interpretation approximates our meaning.

In discussing our communication model earlier in the chapter, we limited our discussion to the first five steps. This has amounted to treating communication as if it were a one-way process: sender to receiver. Now we bring in the sixth step, *feedback,* which changes communication from one-way to two-way. For achieving successful communication, this is probably the most important step of all. In fact, it is an extremely critical stage, for whether one thinks of communication as a one-way or two-way process has profound implications on the kind of communication one engages in and the degree of success one achieves.

F. J. Roethlisberger, in a classic article on communication, summarizes the issue in these words:

> In thinking about the many barriers to personal communication, particularly those that are due to differences of background, experience, and motivation, it seems to me extraordinary that any two persons can ever understand each other. Such reflections provoke the question of how communication

is possible when people do not see and assume the same things and share the same values.

On this question there are two schools of thought. One school assumes that communication between A and B, for example, has failed when B does not accept what A has to say as being fact, true, or valid; and that the goal of communication is to get B to agree with A's opinions, ideas, facts, or information.

The position of the other school of thought is quite different. It assumes that communication has failed when B does not feel free to express his feelings to A because B fears they will not be accepted by A. Communication is facilitated when on the part of A or B or both there is a willingness to express and accept differences.[17]

The first school of thought clearly regards communication as one-way—and the implications are devastating. The one-way communicator assumes that meanings are in symbols, not in people, so if the receiver fails to understand or comes up with a different meaning, he or she must be either ignorant, stupid, or too lazy to consult the dictionary. The one-way communicator further assumes that there is only one way to look at anything: his or her way; the other person's way doesn't count. One-way communication is characteristic of the autocratic style of leadership, which thinks of communication as basically downward ("I say and you do"). The one-way approach can hardly avoid sparking reactions of resentment on the part of the receiver, and these in turn destroy the first condition for successful communication: a positive, working relationship.

The two-way communicator, on the other hand, realizes that any message can be interpreted in a variety of ways, so he or she expects that the receiver may give it a different interpretation than was intended. Two-way communication promotes the attitudes of trust and respect so vital to a good relationship, and is characteristic of a democratic style of leadership.

The one-way communicator is a poor listener; he or she may or may not be a good writer or speaker. The two-way communicator is a good listener; probably he or she is a good writer and speaker as well.

How about the applicability of the two-way concept in writing and speaking? It is easy to see how it applies in conversation (though far too many ignore it even here). And it is easy to see how it applies, though less readily, when speaking before an audience—especially through the give-and-take of a good question period afterward; also in the way the speaker adapts to the audience in the speech itself, by showing respect for their attitudes and background and by not talking down to them.

In written communication, the applicability of the two-way approach is less obvious. But it can be applied, and we should seek to use it when possible. Let me suggest some ways:

1. Avoid assuming a dogmatic air that could leave the reader with the feeling that you have the answers and that what he or she thinks doesn't count.

2. Encourage the reader to respond (in person, by telephone, or in writing) with any questions, suggestions, or other reactions he or she may have. If he or she does, show by your manner that rather than being annoyed you are glad to have a response.

3. When you write a letter, report, or proposal—even a memo if important enough—have your supervisor or a knowledgeable colleague review it with you before it goes to the typist. This can easily save time in the long run.

4. Provide the typist with adequate instructions so he or she will realize, for example, whether the typescript is to be a rough or final draft, along with any other special directions on format, deadlines, and so forth. Encourage the typist to raise questions or offer suggestions; if encouraged, he or she may be very helpful.

Two-way communication embraces both a philosophy and a variety of techniques. If utilized, it can yield a high payoff. However, it flourishes best in a favorable environment, and this in turn is basically a function of the management style in the organization. As we have suggested, an authoritarian style is likely to be hostile to two-way communication. Professor Mary C. Bromage, who has done extensive consulting in industry and government, argues persuasively that although executives claim to prize above all others the qualities of clarity, brevity, and directness in the writing they receive, they work in an environment which creates defensiveness and results in writing which is unclear, verbose, and indirect. Her article implies clearly that management sets the tone, and is likely to get the quality of communication it fosters.[18]

With a positive, working relationship between sender and receiver, a message that is composed and presented effectively, and a two-way approach in communicating, communication falloff can be reduced to a point that it is no longer a major problem. But the likelihood of falloff always is present. Effective communicators recognize this, and through means such as those suggested above seek constantly to reduce it to a minimum.

SUMMARY

1. The way one thinks of communication influences the degree of success one achieves as a communicator.

2. Communication may be defined as "a process of sharing meaning between persons through an exchange of symbols enabling each person to elicit in his or her own mind a meaning similar to that in the mind of the

other." Among the more important implications of this definition are that communication (a) is a process, (b) depends on symbols, (c) involves two or more people, (d) is interactive, and (e) is imperfect.

3. Communication may also be defined as involving six steps: formulation, expression, transmission, reception, interpretation, and feedback.

4. Communication falloff is inevitable and may occur at any point in the six steps, but most of it occurs at the steps of formulation, expression, or interpretation.

5. Noise, which refers to anything that reduces the accuracy of the meaning between sender and receiver, is another way of explaining falloff. Noise may be classified as semantic, mechanical, or psychological.

6. Three ways of reducing communication falloff are proposed. Of these, the most basic condition is the presence of a positive, working attitude between sender and receiver. The other two are (a) composing and presenting the message effectively and (b) encouraging two-way communication.

SUGGESTED APPLICATIONS

1. Write a paper of about 500 words in which you (a) describe objectively an incident you were personally part of that involved communication falloff, (b) analyze it in terms of factors discussed in this chapter, and (c) offer some definite suggestions as to how a similar situation could be avoided in the future. Begin with a brief introductory paragraph, end with a brief concluding paragraph, and use topic headings (and subheadings if appropriate).

2. An article in *Nation's Business* some years ago related the account reprinted below of a communication breakdown.[19] Read the account, then write a paper of about 250 words analyzing the breakdown in terms of factors discussed in this chapter. Offer some definite suggestions as to how such an incident could have been avoided:

> A corporation president sent this note to the personnel officer: "I would like to know what procedure we follow in hiring people at our X plant."
>
> This memo set off a historic flap. Subordinate managers, unsure what he had in mind and unwilling to ask, instituted a complete review of the company's personnel policies. More than 300 hours of consultations were held at various levels. Scores of reports were written. Every aspect of the subject was explored.
>
> Finally, after weeks of work, a quarter-inch-thick report was delivered to the president. It gave full details of all the aptitude

and intelligence tests that were used, all the sources of manpower that were tapped, what percentage of applicants were able to make the grade, the cost of the hiring program, and all the reasons anyone could think of to explain why this was a fine system.

The boss took one look at it and almost strangled. "All I wanted to know," he said, "was where I should send a neighbor's young son, who was interested in a summer job. It doesn't matter now—he's gone back to college."

3. Using the communication model provided in this chapter, write a paper of 300-400 words analyzing your own effectiveness as a communicator (written, oral, or both) in terms of difficulties you encounter at the formulation and expression stages. Illustrate your points with examples from your experience, and try to determine what may have been the cause or causes.

4. Describe two persons you have known—one with whom you feel very comfortable, the other with whom you feel ill-at-ease. Show what effect these contrasting situations have on your ability to communicate effectively. Your paper should run around 250-350 words.

NOTES

[1] For further discussion of this point, see Adnan Almaney, "Communication: Is It the Transmission of Information?" *Journal of Technical Writing and Communication,* Vol. 4, Spring, 1974, pp. 107-115.

[2] For this definition I am indebted to two sources especially: Almaney, cited above, and Raymond S. Ross, *Speech Communication,* 2nd ed. (Englewood Cliffs, N.J.: Prentice-Hall, Inc., 1970), p. 6.

[3] For a similar discussion, see Roger P. Wilcox, *Oral Reporting in Business and Industry* (Englewood Cliffs, N.J.: Prentice-Hall, Inc., 1967), pp. 12-16.

[4] Almaney, p. 110.

[5] Wilcox, p. 13.

[6] Edgar Dale, "Communication as Participation," *The News Letter* (Columbus, Ohio: College of Education, Ohio State University), December, 1970, p. 1.

[7] Used with the permission of the author, Mr. William Barrington.

[8] For a more penetrating discussion of this implication, see James R. Wilcox, "The Assessment of Meaning: A Communication Perspective," in *Exploration in Speech Communication,* ed. John J. Makay (Columbus, Ohio: Charles E. Merrill Publishing Company, 1973), pp. 39-62.

[9] R. P. Wilcox, pp. 11-12.

[10] Charles E. Goshen, "Engineering Characterology and Management Careers," *Engineering Education,* April, 1969.

[11] R. P. Wilcox, pp. 15-16, as adapted from Willard V. Merrihue, *Managing by Communication* (New York: McGraw-Hill Book Company, 1960), pp. 18-19.

[12] For an excellent analysis of the content-relationship aspects of meaning, see Paul Watzlawick, Janet Beavin, and Don Jackson, *Pragmatics of Human Communication* (New York: Norton, 1967), especially Chapters 1–5.

[13] An excellent analysis of the selective processes is found in John R. Wenburg and William W. Wilmot, *The Personal Communication Process,* Ch. 7, "Selectivity in Communication," (New York: John Wiley & Sons, Inc., 1973).

[14] Alan McLean, "An Industrial Psychiatrist Looks at Employee Communications," *Personnel Journal,* February, 1955, pp. 340–343.

[15] For a more complete analysis of defensive behavior, see Jack R. Gibb, "Defensive Communication," *Journal of Communication,* Vol. 11, September, 1961, pp. 141–148.

[16] For further reading in this area, consult any of the texts on interpersonal communication now on the market. One recent text especially recommended is Stewart L. Tubbs and Sylvia Moss, *Human Communication: An Interpersonal Perspective* (New York: Random House, 1974), particularly Ch. 12, "Enhancing Interpersonal Relationships." Another excellent source on the subject of trust is the article by T. M. Higham, "Basic Psychological Factors in Communication," *Occupational Psychology,* 31 (January, 1957), pp. 1–10.

[17] Carl R. Rogers and F. J. Roethlisberger, "Barriers and Gateways to Communication," *Harvard Business Review,* 30 (July, 1952), pp. 46–52.

[18] Mary C. Bromage, "Defensive Writing," *California Management Review,* 1970.

[19] Louis Cassels, "Management Is a 3-Part Job," *Nation's Business,* 44 (December 1956), pp. 80–82.

 YOUR READER AND LISTENER

THE MANAGER: A GENERAL DEFINITION

THE MANAGER'S PSYCHOLOGICAL MOTIVATIONS
The Maslow Hierarchy of Human Needs
The Achievement Seekers
The Security and Status Seekers
The Question of Power

THE MANAGER'S JOB ORIENTATION
Pressure from the Job
Consequences of Job Pressure
    More Results-Oriented than Theory-Oriented
    More Task-Oriented than People-Oriented

THE MANAGER AS COMMUNICATOR
The Manager as Writer and Speaker
    The Manager as Writer   The Manager as Speaker
The Manager as Communication Receiver
    The Manager's Dislikes   The Manager's Likes
The Manager as Editor

THE MANAGER'S STYLE
Theory X
Theory Y
Managerial Style of the Older Manager
Managerial Style of the Younger Manager
Exceptions in Style as Related to Age

THE MANAGER AS A PERSON OF CHANGE

YOUR OTHER COMMUNICATION RECEIVERS

Horizontal Communication
Downward Communication
External Communication
IN CLOSING

In Chapter 2 we stressed the importance of the receiver—our reader or listener. "Not what we present . . . is important," we said, "but what our reader or listener . . . understands, believes, and accepts." We quoted the engineer who complained, "It is pretty hard to write a report if you don't know who your reader will be." Further, we showed how essential it is to have a positive kind of relationship with our reader or listener. Therefore, the purpose of this chapter will be to give you a feel for the kind of people you will be writing and speaking to on the job, in order that you can better understand and adapt to them, and establish a positive, workable relationship with them.

For a number of reasons, nearly all of this chapter will focus on upward communication. Nearly all of your writing, as you become a member of an organization, will likely be upward, since the lower end of the ladder is where you will begin. With promotions to higher levels, your upward communication, instead of diminishing, will probably increase. Upward communication, especially at the beginning, usually poses special problems, since you are likely to feel less sure of yourself communicating with the boss than with your peers. Finally, upward communication has more direct effect on your recognition and advancement.

However, at the end of the chapter, some advice will be offered on horizontal and downward communication; also on adapting letters to persons outside the organization.

Before we proceed, some cautions are in order. First, the descriptions given below of your reader and listener are necessarily general. They refer to what *probably* is true, or what *likely* will be the case, but certainly there will be exceptions and varying degrees of applicability. No one person will fit neatly into any of the categories discussed; human nature is much too complex. Thus, it will be your responsibility to decide how best to apply these generalizations to specific cases.

A second caution is that the discussion below is intended to be purely descriptive. There is no intent to pass judgment, favorable or unfavorable, on people in management; only to help you understand them better and the problems they face.

Finally, this chapter will offer little advice on specific techniques for communicating effectively with your reader or listener. That will be a subject for later chapters.

THE MANAGER: A GENERAL DEFINITION

In this chapter the term "manager" will be used to refer to anyone in the organization responsible for performing a management function. At the upper level, the management function consists of deciding broad objectives and policies for the total organization. At the middle level, it consists of implementing those objectives and policies within broad divisions of the organization—such as research, design, purchasing, manufacturing, personnel, marketing, finance, and others. At the lowest levels, the management function is to carry out the day-to-day operations of specific departments.

Although we shall use the general term "manager," those at the upper levels are more commonly called "administrators" or "executives," and those at the lower levels "supervisors." To be still more specific, the titles attached to persons in management are many and varied: foreman, general foreman, superintendent, general superintendent, plant manager, general manager, finance director, personnel director, sales manager, or (in a college) department head, dean, provost, president.

The route by which one enters management usually begins in some technical, or specialized area. Thus, in a college, a chemistry professor may become head of his or her department; later, perhaps, a dean; and eventually he or she might become president. In industry an engineer might begin as a production supervisor and end up as plant manager. A head metallurgist doubtless began as a metallurgist; the comptroller, an accountant; the sales manager, a salesperson, and so on. Thus the manager typically begins as a specialist, gradually becoming more and more a generalist the farther up the ladder he or she moves.

Regardless of level or area of specialization, one characteristic common to all persons in management is this: they must achieve their objectives through others. And the higher they are, the more "others" they must depend on. This is where the need for communication in the organization arises—downward and upward, as well as horizontal. Hence, the reason for textbooks such as this.

THE MANAGER'S PSYCHOLOGICAL MOTIVATIONS

What motivates a person to seek or accept a position in management? What needs is he or she attempting to satisfy? To answer these questions, we must understand motivation in general.

The Maslow Hierarchy of Human Needs

Psychologists have described human needs in various ways, but one of the most useful classifications is found in Maslow's Hierarchy of Human Needs, shown in Figure 3.1.[1]

Starting at the bottom, the physiological needs include the need for air, food, water, sleep—what a person needs simply to survive. Safety, or security, needs result in such activities as putting locks on doors, having bank accounts, buying insurance, maintaining fire and police departments, as well as labor unions placing high priority on the seniority system in the plant. Love or affiliation needs find expression in friendship groups and family relationships. Esteem needs are twofold: to be able to think well of ourselves (have a positive self-concept), and to be well thought of by others. Our need for others' esteem—their approval and recognition—is revealed in many ways: by the neighborhood we live in, the clothes we wear, the cars we drive; by our rank or title on the job, the size and decor of our office (if we have one), and in numerous other ways, often very subtle. Finally, self-actualization refers to the need for personal growth, to become what we have the potential to become, whatever our talent or field may be. This need is also often called the need for self-fulfillment, or the achievement need.

The position of the need on the diagram indicates relative importance or rank (hence the term "hierarchy"). The physiological needs are the most basic, but have motivational effect only when they are *not* being met; otherwise we tend to take them for granted (for example, the act of breathing). As each level of needs is satisfied to at least a reasonable degree, the next level becomes increasingly relevant.

The hierarchy is not as rigid as might at first seem. William V. Haney has proposed several qualifications to the Maslow model that are useful to keep in mind:[2]

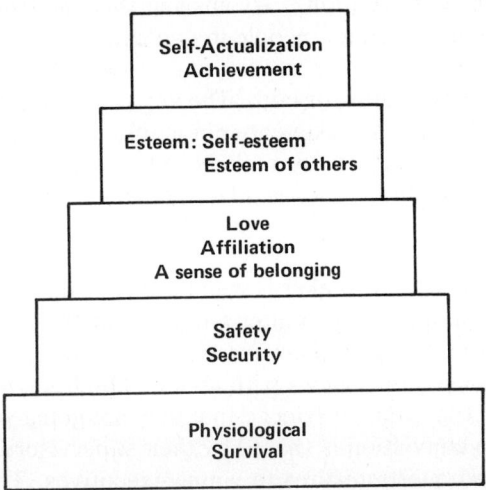

FIGURE 3.1
Maslow's Hierarchy of Human Needs

1. Multiple levels. A person may satisfy more than one need level at a time. For example, a hostess might serve an elegant dinner to a group of close friends and satisfy all five needs the same evening. Your seeking an education probably contributes to satisfying all five needs. One writer, Tim Hostiuk, argues that the achievement need coexists with the other needs at all levels; it simply assumes different forms at different levels. What represents achievement to the laborer struggling for security may be quite different from what represents achievement to the successful executive.[3]

2. Need conflict. When two or more needs conflict, the immediate situation rather than the hierarchy may determine which need gets satisfied first. While writing a final examination (satisfying, perhaps, security, esteem, or achievement needs), one may need desperately to go to the bathroom (physiological need). Yet the need for a good grade may be so great that one defers meeting the physiological need until the exam is finished. A higher order need takes priority, contrary to the general principle of the Maslow concept.

3. Modifying factors. Needs vary from one person to another. With some the affiliation need is much greater than for others. Initiative in fulfilling needs varies greatly also. Some people depend heavily on others for need fulfillment; others show much greater independence. Finally, some persons seem able to discipline themselves more rigidly in suppressing "lower order" needs in their drive to fulfill "higher order" needs. Haney suggests that "This may help to explain people such as Albert Schweitzer, Tom Dooley, and Mohandas Gandhi—men who seemingly lived primarily at the self-fulfillment level."

With this brief review of Maslow's Hierarchy, we can return to our original question: What motivates a man or woman to seek, or accept, a management position? To answer this question, it appears useful to classify management people in two categories: those motivated *primarily* by the need for achievement, and those motivated *primarily* by the need for security, status, or both. The key word here is "primarily." Certainly, the achievement seekers are not indifferent to security and status, nor are the security and status seekers indifferent to achievement. But the primary focus differs, so the classification seems useful to employ.

The Achievement Seekers

The achievement seeker is well described through evidence gathered in a study conducted by Walter Guzzardi in the early 1960s for a series of articles in *Fortune* magazine. Guzzardi engaged in a series of "lengthy and intense" interviews with about a hundred young executives ("young men on the train, convinced that they are going somewhere, and knowing that the conviction is shared by their supervisors"). Then he sent several thousand questionnaires to young executives. The project led eventually to a book, *The Young Executives*.[4]

Listen to Guzzardi's characterization of these men, sometimes in his own words, sometimes quoting directly from them:

> His greatest . . . ego satisfaction, comes when he succeeds in making a change of an important kind in his company's or his industry's business methodology.[5]

> "My basic drive [said one executive] is for excellence—the standard I want to meet." Another young executive embroiders on this theme. "My boss says . . . 'Don't come in tomorrow.' But I *have* to come in. . . . People say, 'Don't bring your briefcase home.' But I *have* to."[6]

> . . . promotions . . . [bring] "more challenge and more responsibility," and toward those goals he drives with real ferocity. As he wins a larger share of them, one need is submerged, a higher need emerges, and the man presses on to gratify that need. . . . The young executive . . . corresponds to Maslow's "self-actualizing person."[7]

> "Before you reach a certain salary level [says a systems engineer], money is the important thing. After that, job satisfaction takes over."[8]

In the questionnaire, Guzzardi asked, "What is the greatest single source of satisfaction to you on your present job?" The top answers were: "The sense of accomplishment I get from it," and "I have some real creative opportunities. . . ." Very low on the list were, "The fact that it pays very well," and "the knowledge that if I perform ably, I am secure."[9]

The achievement seeker in management, then, is strongly driven to achieve. Security he or she already enjoys; status is a by-product.

A person need not occupy a management position to be motivated to achieve. Research scientists, inventors, artists, writers, teachers, and many others may be driven as strongly to achieve, but may have little interest in directing the efforts of other people.

The Security and Status Seekers

Management people in this category are interested in achievement, too, but this is not their *primary* motivation as managers. Rather, they enter management as a means of advancement in the organization. The road to management, as noted earlier, originates typically at the technical level. However, the technical worker is seldom the one who reaps the rewards. These go to the managers because the responsibilities they bear and the decisions they make exert a much greater impact on the organization.

So, as Goshen observes in his article "Engineering Characterology and Management Careers" (cited in Chapter 2), "The experienced engineer frequently finds his career advancement leading him into managerial positions whether he aspires to them or not."[10] The results can be ironic for—to quote further from Goshen—"The character traits that make for a good engineer are not those that make for a happy manager."[11]

Thus these managers struggle with problems—not the least of which are "people problems"—often beyond their area of technical expertise. Unless they can learn to cope, their promotion may prove to be a poor bargain, for them and for the organization as well.

There is another difference between the two types of managers, and this lies in the origin of their drives. With the achievement seeker, the drive to achieve originates within the person. But with the security-status seeker, though the desire for security and status comes from within, the drive to achieve is more likely to originate from without—in the pressures of the organization. Thus, the achievement seeker would appear more likely to be a force acting on the organization; the security-status seeker more likely to be responsive to forces in the organization.

The Question of Power

In the perspective of the Maslow Hierarchy, power would seem to be not so much a need in itself, as a means of satisfying other needs. Nevertheless, it appears to be an important ingredient in managerial success.

A former executive and professor of business administration at Harvard, J. Sterling Livingston, argues that "Since managers are primarily concerned with influencing others, it seems obvious that they should be characterized by a high need for power. . . ."[12] He goes on to declare that "Power seekers can be counted on to strive hard to reach positions where they can exercise authority over large numbers of people. Individual performers who lack this drive are not likely to act in ways that will enable them to advance far up the managerial ladder."[13]

We can expect, then, that those who feel uncomfortable in the use of power will either tend to avoid managerial positions or will find the exercise of power an additional source of anxiety.

Before concluding this section on motivation, we must stress one very important point. Regardless of what differences may distinguish one manager from another, all of them possess, in common with the rest of us, the need for esteem. They need to be well thought of by their "relevant others"; also to be able to think well of themselves. Just as Hostiuck argues that the achievement need exists at all levels of the Maslow Hierarchy, so I would argue that the esteem need does too (except in cases where one's very survival is threatened). Each of us, from floorsweeper to president, likes to be treated as an individual, not an object. This is of profound importance in human communication.

THE MANAGER'S JOB ORIENTATION

Even though managers possess strong esteem needs, the pressures they work under result in their being more concerned with the job than with the esteem needs of others. In his book *The Managerial Mind,* David Ewing writes: "The main commitment of the managerial mind is to the organization. The administrator considers the survival, operating ability, and growth of his department, task force, or enterprise important for their own sake."[14]

Pressure from the Job

This commitment to the organization—regardless of what inner needs may be served, leads to job pressures. A young executive in Guzzardi's survey refers to "all kinds of pressure on me." A production foreman in a manufacturing plant tells his workers, "I don't care about anything else. Just get that production out." The one slogan that, perhaps better than any other, symbolizes the atmosphere the manager works in is "Get the Job Done." Not getting it done affects adversely his or her chances for salary increase or promotion. From the company standpoint, not getting it done affects adversely its very chances for survival.

Consequences of Job Pressure

Understanding the consequences resulting from this kind of job pressure will enable you better to adapt to your reader or listener in communicating up the line. It will also enable you to cope more effectively with difficulties or discouragements you may encounter.

More Results-Oriented than Theory-Oriented Because of the emphasis on getting the job done, the manager tends to be more results-oriented than theory-oriented. The manager's principal criterion in evaluating a new idea is likely to be "Will it work?" In my experience conducting training programs in industry, I have learned to lay heavy emphasis on practical application. If the participants can see down-to-earth value in what I am offering, they will buy it; otherwise, their interest grows thin. In my own mind, my material must be sound theoretically, but in theirs the theory is secondary.

There is probably another reason the manager tends to be more results-oriented: theory is of less interest to managers than results. If they were more interested in theory, they would probably have gone into an area such as teaching or research where theory is of more pressing concern.

More Task-Oriented than People-Oriented Again, at least in part because of the pressure to get the job done, the manager tends to be more interested in the task than in the people performing the task. Guzzardi comments on one of his young executives as follows:

> The view that congenial social relationships, or the maintenance of heavy joviality at office parties, are important ingredients in business success is contradicted by Jones' experience. He rarely sees his superiors after business hours, or for

any purpose except the explicit conduct of business affairs. And he just as rarely socializes with his subordinates. "I remain aloof on a social basis. I don't want to know their personal problems. . . . Somebody started to tell me that my secretary was getting a divorce, but I interrupted right away. I just don't want to know that kind of thing."[15]

While Jones may represent an extreme case, the manager's task orientation tends to push him or her in that direction.

Pleasing others, then, is not a primary concern of the manager. It would be impossible anyway, for what pleases one employee may displease another, especially if the two are in competition with each other. Thus you might submit a worthwhile idea, only to have it rejected because someone else submitted one even more worthwhile, and it would have been impractical to approve both. Or you may request a favor that by itself is perfectly reasonable, yet find it not granted because to do so would create a precedent not feasible to extend to others. Managers who seek to please all their people will succeed in pleasing no one. Eventually, they will be accused of playing favorites.

Another consequence of a manager's task vs. people orientation is that he or she may actively encourage tension within the department. Referring to the manager's problem of controlling people, Ewing says:

> The manager also copes with the dilemmas of direction and control by placing a value on tension. He regards many forms of it as an essential ingredient of creative relationships and aggressive activity. He is interested not only in maintaining various sources of tension but also in preserving enough balance among them so that one does not overpower another.[16]

The use of tension as described by Ewing is intended to be employed constructively. Unfortunately, creating tension may also be employed destructively, to the detriment both of subordinates and the organization, by insecure managers concerned above all with their own survival. A. H. Chapman, a psychiatrist, has written a book called *Put-Offs and Come-Ons,* describing in part "the rotten things people do to each other." One of the stratagems he describes is called "May the Best Man Win." "Its basic theme is that in the endless struggles that go on in business and professional hierarchies, the skillful strategist is careful to hire or advance not the best man but the man who least threatens the strategist's position."[17]

The manager who plays this game is described as engaging in all kinds of manipulation to shackle or get rid of the subordinate who threatens him or her most. The manager, A, may isolate the subordinate, B, from contacts with all others above them in the organization. A may praise B as little and criticize as often as possible. A may assign B impossible tasks or give B impossible deadlines; A may play one B off against another B, or provoke B into making a misstep and then fire B, or abolish B's position so B is left with no place to go but down—or out.

Such maneuvers are not the mark of the competent manager who feels secure. But managers are human like anyone else, and such maneuvers are sometimes used.

Another consequence, a constructive one this time, of the manager's task orientation is a tendency to "prod employees to break old patterns of behavior and to enlarge their horizons."[18] This may take the form (to paraphrase slightly) of "refusing to take seriously the limitations his people may think they have, trying to encourage venturesomeness, since he recognizes that he himself can never know the true potentials of another man."[19] Though such prodding may seem disquieting to the subordinate at the time, it may also open new doors for personal growth, rewarding to the subordinate as well as to the organization.

Finally, the manager's task orientation over people orientation is often accompanied by a tendency to be "emotion-blind." Writing on this point, Livingston says: "Many men who have more than enough abstract intelligence to learn the methods and techniques of management fail because their affinity with other people is almost entirely intellectual."[20]

As if to reinforce this point, Ewing in his closing summary says: ". . . the manager finds it difficult to respond to some of the feelings people have in private life. Worries about love, death, anonymity, youth, insecurity, morals, and so forth are likely to 'go over his head' except as he experiences them himself."[21]

These, of course, are broad generalizations. Exceptions exist. For instance, one general supervisor in accounting I interviewed on the role of communication in his work gave top priority to the importance of knowing the other person, of putting oneself in his place, of "feeling with him." A plant foreman told me that he was always willing to turn a listening ear to personal problems of his men, even though occasionally he felt that some of them took advantage of him. When I asked whether willingness to listen resulted from a belief that a well-adjusted worker is a better producer, he replied, "Well, yes, I suppose, but I could never turn away from a fellow who has a problem anyway."

Another exception is illustrated by one of Guzzardi's young executives expressing his sentiments on the subject of firing a subordinate:

> Firing people is one thing that doesn't get any easier with practice. The closer you are to it, the tougher it is. . . . I know it has to be done, but I really get sick when the time comes. . . . [By] the time it's over I wish I were playing the guitar for a living instead.[22]

To conclude, we have seen that an important consequence of the pressure on the manager to "get the job done" is that he or she tends to be more task-oriented than people-oriented. Thus, such a manager will tend to view communication as a means of helping him or her get the job done better.

THE MANAGER AS COMMUNICATOR

We have already seen in Chapter 1 that virtually all leaders in business organizations readily extol the virtues of communication. What kind of communicator is the typical manager? Let's take a look at him or her from two points of view: as a sender and as a receiver.

The Manager as Writer and Speaker

An observation to be made at the outset is that seldom is skill in writing or speaking the primary base from which one enters a managerial position. Exceptions might be the English professor who becomes head of the department, or a copy editor in a publishing company who moves up to become a supervising editor. As explained earlier, the typical manager begins in some technical area such as engineering or marketing. Competence in writing, and perhaps speaking, are probably considered important, but these are not the distinguishing requirements of the trade or profession. He or she may be a skilled communicator—perhaps highly skilled—and this doubtless aided his or her advancement. Or, this individual may have been promoted in spite of lackluster ability as a communicator.

The Manager as Writer Considering the importance of writing as a management tool, the manager's writing ability was probably a factor in his or her initial promotion. It would be an increasingly important factor the farther he or she advances; lackluster ability would be a definite handicap beyond the first level or two.

There exists, however, a curious inconsistency between the writing managers expect from their subordinates and the writing they address to those above them. This inconsistency is well stated by Professor Mary Bromage, who has done extensive consulting in industry and government:

> 450 management men . . . in one large industrial corporation . . . [were] asked . . . to respond to this question: "What qualities do you consider most desirable in business communications?"
>
> Three qualities outnumber all the rest in answer to that question: *clarity, brevity,* and *directness.* Yet when samples of the writing done by these same respondents are examined, the results are often at variance with the proclaimed preferences.[23]

The explanation of this inconsistency is not difficult to decipher. The job pressure they work under indicates why harried managers want communications that are addressed *to* them to be clear, brief, and direct. At the same time, their esteem needs suggest why in communicating up the line they may resort to obscurity, wordiness, and indirectness. The following passage from a management text of several years ago sheds additional light on this point:

> because of their sensitivity to the boss and their dependence on him, there is a good deal of distortion of the facts in communicating up the line. Along with a great concern for "giving the boss what he wants," there is a constant tendency to "cover up," to keep the boss from knowing about the things that go wrong or the things that do not get done.[24]

As Professor Bromage points out, "writing is a form of human behavior," and we have already stressed how important a role in human behavior is played by the need to be well regarded.

The Manager as Speaker   Less evidence is available to suggest that the manager is an effective speaker. In fact, one experienced executive, referring to managers' platform competency, wrote an article which he entitled "Executives Can't Communicate," followed by the subtitle, "They talk too much, express themselves badly, and miss the point."[25] He describes fellow executives as getting off the track, using illegible visual aids, failing to look their audience in the eye, droning on through page after page, and putting their audience to sleep.

This may exaggerate the situation a bit, but—in my judgment—probably not a great deal. The manager's schooling—as is true with anyone else, for that matter—almost never provides sufficient training in speech. Further, the job of manager almost certainly calls for considerably more writing than speaking. Finally, until a manager has had some experience, he or she probably becomes nervous and ineffective when facing an audience. As a result, the manager who speaks well is the exception.

It seems fair to offer these generalizations about the typical manager as a writer and speaker: they recognize the importance of good communication; they probably write better than they speak, and they expect their subordinates to be more direct and open in communicating with them than they tend to be in communicating with those higher up.

The Manager as Communication Receiver

What about the manager as a recipient of messages from below? A simple way of describing him or her in this role is to list some of his or her likes and dislikes:

The Manager's Dislikes   Among the things managers dislike in the messages they receive are the following:

1. *Personal gripes*. Gripes tend to be person-oriented rather than task-oriented. They often imply a criticism of his or her ability to manage. And

they confront the manager with an additional problem when he or she probably has enough to worry about as it is.

2. *Criticisms*. Criticisms are possibly a shade more acceptable because they are more likely task-oriented; they may bring to light a problem that needs solving. But, like the gripe, a criticism will often be interpreted as reflecting on the manager's ability to manage.

3. *Alibis*. The manager wants results, not excuses. On the other hand, if the reason is really legitimate, he or she will want to know—and *the sooner the better.*

4. *Attempts to blame someone else*. Trying to blame someone else seems to a manager just another alibi, with the additional bad odor of trying to drag him into an interpersonal conflict he would prefer to avoid.

5. *Not being kept informed*. How much information to supply the boss calls for good judgment. Certainly he or she does not want to be bothered with every trifling detail, but if it is information which being ignorant of could get him or her into a troublesome situation, the manager will want to be informed, fully and openly.

6. *Going over a manager's head*. No one likes to look bad to others, least of all to the boss. Going over the supervisor's head is certain to be interpreted by him or her as a maneuver to make him or her look bad, and it will be resented. In impossible situations it may be necessary, but it should be used only as a last resort.

7. *Unsolicited or unwarranted opinion*. This is not to say a manager never wants your opinion. But it should be opinion you are qualified to offer or that has been requested. In Chapter 11 we shall discuss the criteria for qualified opinion.

Each of these dislikes is understandable when we recall the motivations and pressures associated with being a manager.

The Manager's Likes We have already shown that managers prefer the three qualities of clarity, brevity, and directness. More specifically, they like such characteristics as the following, some of which contribute to clarity, brevity, or directness, while others offer additional advantages:

1. *Getting the gist at the outset*. Because of their heavy work load—including sometimes dozens of memos, letters, or reports in a day—most managers prefer to get the gist of the message, clearly and concisely stated, right at the outset. The murder mystery approach is for evening relaxation, not for the daytime rat race.

2. *Being given the facts*. In the introduction he wrote for Guzzardi's *The Young Executives,* Peter Drucker wrote: "They [the young executives] are highly professional in their approach to their job. 'What are the facts?' is their first question. They are much more concerned with 'what is right'

than with 'who is right.' "[26] A supervisor I interviewed several years ago told me that one communication practice that annoys him is the other person's "not having at hand all the facts."

3. *Being given the whole story.* In spite of the tendency to communicate upward only what makes us look good, managers want "the whole story"—at least as much as is relevant. They do not want to discover later that essential information was omitted or distorted, since their having acted on incomplete information may have either wasted their time or made *them* look bad. Failing to give the whole story can be self-defeating in the long run. (From your own vantage point, it is better that the manager learn the bad news from you than from someone else.)

4. *Being told in language they can understand.* Managers are specialists in probably no more than one or two technical areas. The farther up the ladder they move, the more they become generalists; that is, they acquire a general grasp—but seldom a detailed familiarity—of many areas. They will invariably be short on the time or inclination to dig through a mass of technical jargon, nor do they enjoy admitting that they may be confused. Therefore, messages addressed to them should be phrased in terminology they can understand. How to assemble a message combining both the technical and the general for different readers will be a topic for Chapter 11 on reports and proposals.

5. *Whatever will make their job easier.* Managers welcome whatever will make their job easier. Constructive suggestions and new ideas fall in this category—provided they are clearly explained, meet an existing need, and do not involve costs outweighing the gains.

"Completed staff work" also falls in category five. Completed staff work, as defined by one executive, consists of:

> the study of a problem and presentation of a solution by a staff member in such form that all which remains to be done on the part of the department head is to indicate his approval of the completed action.
>
> Completed staff work deliberately increases the burden on each staff member in order to give more freedom to the department or division head and to protect him against hasty conclusions and incomplete solutions. It is your job to advise your department head what he ought to do, not ask him what should be done. Before presenting any solution, you are expected to exhaust all available sources of information; to write, restudy, to coordinate, rewrite; to test all possible solutions for suitability, feasibility, and acceptability. You must consider all alternatives until you evolve the best advice, in terms of action, of which you are capable. Then, and only then, should you ask your department head for suggestions.

Writing a memorandum to your department head does not constitute completed staff work, but writing a memorandum for him to send to someone else does.[27]

The degree to which the concept of "completed staff work" is appropriate will vary with the situation. In some instances it will be desirable to confer with the manager in advance for general guidelines. Never will it be advisable to "box him or her in"—to leave him or her no alternatives. It is a manager's prerogative to have the final say on any decisions or actions for which he or she is responsible.

The Manager as Editor

Sometimes written material you submit to the manager will be signed (or countersigned) by him or her instead of by you because it is addressed to someone up the line, and the manager's signature will lend the message more credibility. Other times written material submitted to the manager will be incorporated with material from others in the department in a report or proposal he or she will assemble under his or her own name. Or, at times, what you write will go out under your name, but the manager will still wish to check it over because the finished product will reflect on the department or company, favorably or unfavorably. In such situations, the manager functions also as editor.

A training program I conducted some time ago for "supervisor-editors" revealed some interesting facets concerning this role. Points of view expressed by these people included the following:

1. They recognized that one of their important functions was to help the writer understand what was wanted and why—especially helping him or her to understand management's perspective.

2. They were annoyed if the writer did a careless job to begin with in the expectation, apparently, that the supervisor would make the necessary corrections (although they recognized that this tendency by the writer may have been encouraged by excessive editing in the past).

3. They were especially critical of such earmarks of poor writing as faulty organization, not being clear, not being specific, generating unanswered questions, insufficient use of graphic aids, and wordiness.

4. They found it difficult to be tactful in editing a really bad report.

5. Sometimes when they felt that changes were desirable they found it difficult to give clear reasons *why* they were desirable.

6. Although they realized that they should avoid rewriting the report, they sometimes found it difficult to resist the temptation.[28]

A point not brought out above is that you should not be surprised if the manager-editor has some pet biases on style. I have known, for instance, of some who insist, "Never start a sentence with 'but' "; "Never use the word 'however' "; "Always use the passive voice, never the active"; or

"Never use a personal pronoun." As boss, he or she is entitled to his or her views, but that does not mean that they necessarily have basis in sound usage or grammar. In such instances you must decide how important it is to comply with the manager's views. Often the issue may not be worth bothering about.

In analyzing the manager as a message receiver and editor, we have seen that he or she probably has some rather definite likes and dislikes. Being aware of these in your own situation can help you adapt more intelligently.

THE MANAGER'S STYLE

Managerial styles are often described as ranging from authoritarian to participative. The authoritarian style is perhaps best identified by the label, Theory X.

Theory X

Theory X, as described by its originator, the late Douglas McGregor of M.I.T., rests on three basic assumptions concerning human behavior: (a) The average person is inherently lazy; (b) because of this he or she must be "coerced, controlled, directed, [and] threatened with punishment," and, furthermore, (c) he or she "prefers to be directed, wishes to avoid responsibility, has relatively little ambition, wants security above all."[29]

The trouble with Theory X is that in post–World War II industrial societies it is outmoded. The reason is found in the final phrase of the last assumption, "wants security above all." As a result of union negotiations and the higher standard of living generally, most workers have enough security so that it is no longer (as we recall from Maslow) a dominant motivator. As Frederick Herzberg, an industrial psychologist, has pointed out, while meeting the lower order needs in the Maslow Hierarchy can keep a worker from being dissatisfied, this does not motivate him or her to do better.[30] Motivation, says Herzberg, results from the opportunity to achieve. Enter Theory Y, the label commonly given to the participative management style.

Theory Y

Theory Y asserts that the average person is not inherently lazy, is more strongly motivated by the opportunity to achieve than by external controls and threats of punishment, and can learn not only to accept but to seek responsibility.[31]

Theory X and Theory Y describe, of course, opposite ends of the spectrum. In actuality, few managers will be found at either extreme; most will fall somewhere between. But there is reason to believe that, at this point in time, older managers (those past middle age) tend more toward Theory X, and younger managers toward Theory Y.

Managerial Style of the Older Manager

Several factors help explain this divergence. One is that the older manager is less removed from the effects of the Great Depression of the thirties, when jobs were scarce, pay was low, and very little of "the good life" could be taken for granted. Consequently, he or she tends to be more security minded than those of a generation later and to see the authoritarian style as supportive of security.

Second, the authoritarian style is the style these managers grew up with. Their parents were, in general, more authoritarian. If they served in the armed forces, they faced authoritarianism all around them. The authoritarian style was the style they most likely encountered on their first job. To them, this style is part of the natural order of life.

Finally, the participative style as a concept in management did not emerge until sometime in the 1960s. Even though the older managers doubtless have heard of it, perhaps even participated in management training programs on it, they tend to be skeptical that it will work. At age 50 it is difficult to change one's life style.

To the extent that the older manager is more authoritarian, what are the implications for you as you enter the organization? One implication is that he or she is more likely to be a "one-way communicator," a type we discussed above in Chapter 2. Communication to this manager is more likely to be a matter of "You listen to me. When I need to hear from you, I'll let you know."

Closely related is the likelihood that this manager will be less open to new ideas. Erwin Bettinghaus in his book on persuasion describes the authoritarian personality as one who "tends toward absolute judgments . . . and [is] not easily swayed by messages that contradict the authorities he trusts, even though the messages might be judged by others to be rational and logical."[32] Goshen found also a tendency among the engineers he interviewed to "use their expertise to prove that something would not work or could not be done rather than being challenged to find new solutions."[33]

Still another implication is that older managers are more likely to feel threatened by the "bright young men or women" or by minorities under them. Dr. Harry Levinson of the Menninger Foundation describes the situation thus:

> Middle age is for many men an acute psychological loss period. . . . In almost any field, younger men bring new skills and techniques which will ultimately displace the old. The older men fear to lose their self-respect if they admit what they have been doing is no longer adequate. To accept the newer ways, for some, is to make that admission. If they do change, they admit the younger men are right. If they fail to change, they run the risk of seeing the younger men move rapidly ahead of them.[34]

Managerial Style of the Younger Manager

We have described the older manager in somewhat extreme terms. By way of contrast, the younger manager (born around the time of World War II or since) is more likely to possess the following characteristics:

1. They are more likely to use a Theory Y style—partially because they are more familiar and comfortable with it, partially because the young employees of today respond less readily to authority than was true a generation ago. Thus, instead of relying on authoritarian measures as a primary tool, they seek to motivate by promoting, through participative techniques, their subordinates' personal growth in directions consistent with organizational goals.

2. They are not as likely to be "organization men." Drucker, commenting on Guzzardi's young executives, found "not one 'organization man' in the lot."[35] These managers find their security in their own competency, rather than within the organization.

3. They are probably better educated—thanks in large measure to the strong impetus given higher education by the GI Bill of Rights following World War II. Ninety percent of Guzzardi's young executives had college degrees, and half of these also had postgraduate degrees.

4. They are more up to date, in part because they are better educated, but in part also because their education is more recent.

5. They are in general more comfortable with the "bright young men or women" coming out of the colleges, viewing them more as a source than a threat. They also are more comfortable with the influx of minority peoples into the organization.

Exceptions in Style as Related to Age

The pattern proposed above—older managers, Theory X; younger managers, Theory Y—cannot be applied rigidly. Some younger managers, because of factors peculiar to their background, will tend to be quite authoritarian. And some older managers will be oriented rather strongly toward a Theory Y style. But these will tend to be those who have risen several levels up in the organization, who are probably better educated, and probably more secure.

THE MANAGER AS A PERSON OF CHANGE

We have described the manager as though he or she were an unvarying individual—each one different, to be sure, but once we have him or her pegged, there he or she is, static, unchanging, predictable.

Such, however, is not the case. In Chapter 2 we pointed out that people are in a constant state of change. We can understand this in ourselves: confident at one time, depressed at another, sometimes turned on, other times burned out. We need to think of the manager in these terms, too.

Mr. Chan, or Ms. Chan, who seemed cordial at eight o'clock, may scarcely notice us when we bump into him or her at ten. He or she may be calm and unhurried on one occasion; agitated and impatient on another. And the supervisor who gave high priority to Notion N six months ago may seem sold on Notion O today.

So we should never make the mistake of supposing we have the supervisor "psyched out," completely, once and for all. Not only will no two ever be quite the same; no one will ever be quite the same twice. But the guidelines offered above should aid you in understanding better and adapting more effectively in the relationship you seek to achieve with your manager and the interchange of communications you engage in with him or her.

YOUR OTHER COMMUNICATION RECEIVERS

This chapter thus far has focused on examining the managerial mind for better communication up the line. In closing, we offer a brief word on your other communication receivers.

Horizontal Communication

The best advice here is to review in Chapter 2 the discussion of communication falloff at the interpretation stage, then recall from Chapter 1 the comment that "problems in horizontal communication are greater than might be supposed. Accountants talk one language, salesmen another, computer technologists another, and so on." If we can remember to express ourselves in terms meaningful to those outside our area of specialization, then keep the channels open to clear up misunderstandings, we should experience little difficulty.

Downward Communication

Let's project ahead a few years and assume that now *you* are in management. What guidelines will be helpful in communicating with those under you?

One advantage is that your downward communication will presumably be with others in your own area, so problems of misunderstanding between different fields are less likely.

Against this advantage, other aspects of the situation—easy to forget as you move up the line—need to be stressed.

First, those below you—especially the newer ones—will possess a more limited perspective of company matters than do you. Often they will not even be aware of certain policies (written or unwritten) that you take for granted. If they are aware, they may not appreciate the reason for those policies. Further, you will tend to perceive trends in the company that they may be oblivious to. They may not recognize the symptoms, or if they do, arrive at quite different interpretations as to what the symptoms mean. Likewise, you will have been around long enough to understand better than they how to get things done, whom to see, whom to bypass, how to deal with Mr. P or Ms. Q. In short, their grasp of the work environment will certainly be different from, probably more limited than yours; more different and limited than you probably will realize.

Second, your subordinates will possess the same basic job needs for security, esteem, and achievement that you do. They will want to feel increasingly secure; will want to be treated as individuals, not objects; will want opportunity for personal growth. How well they feel these needs are met will depend largely on you; again, probably more than you realize.

Third, because of the critical role you play in their need satisfaction, their behavior will tend to be more guarded with you than with their peers. Any misstep they commit will prove more costly, they suspect, if you become aware of it than if only their peers do.

How best then to cope with these differences and needs? The remedy lies in achieving what was stressed in Chapter 2 as the prerequisite for effective communication: a positive, mutually supportive relationship. Since *you* are the boss, you bear the primary responsibility in promoting this relationship. This will mean understanding and being tolerant of their more limited experience—and helping them expand it. It will mean practicing *two*-way—as opposed to one-way—communication; learning to listen, to see others' points of view.

An example comes to mind. A professor I know who does consulting in industry tells of an executive who called him with the complaint, "My people won't communicate with me." My friend obtained permission to attend the next staff meeting as an observer. At this meeting the executive, at one point, said, "As you men know, we're faced with such and such a problem. I'm wondering if any of you have any ideas how we can lick it." One man spoke up, offering his analysis and a solution. In reply, the executive pounded the table and said, "No! Absolutely not. If we were to do this . . ." and so on. "Now," he added, "do any of the rest of you have any ideas?" Silence; complete silence. After the meeting the executive turned to my friend and said, "You see what I mean? These people just won't communicate."

In establishing a positive relationship, Theory Y style of management almost certainly proves more productive, resulting in communication with your subordinates that is freer, franker, and more rewarding.

External Communication

Finally, in the letters you send to persons outside the organization, it will help to recognize that the characteristic that most distinguishes letters from memos, reports, and proposals is *tone*. The reason is that the letter is the only one of the four types employed primarily for external communication, and since there is less opportunity for establishing face to face the positive relationship requisite to effective communication, more care must be taken in the letter to cultivate this relationship. The importance of the positive relationship is underscored when we reflect that every letter is a projection of the organizational image to the outside world, and naturally the organization wishes to project a favorable image. Thus, letters are relatively more person-oriented. The writer shows more concern for the esteem needs of the recipient and is more careful not to put the recipient on the defensive. Tact and diplomacy, while important in all forms of business and personal writing, become particularly important in letter writing.

IN CLOSING

We began this chapter by referring to the importance of a sound working relationship with your reader or listener. The objective of this chapter has been mainly to give you a feel for the motivations, pressures, communication practices and preferences, and managerial style of those up—or down—the line from you. The aim is not to enable you to outwit them, but to work more effectively with them. Each of you depends on the other. Each has his or her own role, essential to the success of the other. The more clearly you perceive this relationship and can function effectively within it, the more promising the odds that you will receive the rewards that can make your job a source of genuine satisfaction to you.

SUMMARY

1. Upward communication tends to be both the most troublesome, yet the most job-rewarding kind of communication in the organization.

2. Whatever his or her title or level, the manager is involved in carrying out, through others, some phase in the policies and operations of the organization.

3. Managers can be thought of as being motivated primarily to satisfy achievement needs or to satisfy security and status needs. In either case, to be effective they must feel comfortable in the use of power to achieve their objectives. And like all others, they have strong esteem needs.

4. The manager's job pressures tend to make him or her more results-oriented than theory-oriented, and more task-oriented than people-oriented.

5. As communicators, managers are typically better writers than speakers. In the communications that they receive, they dislike whatever makes their job more troublesome; they like whatever makes it easier or more productive.

6. Although there are exceptions, the older manager's style tends to be more authoritarian, and the younger manager's style more participative.

7. The manager, like any other person, is constantly in a state of change; he or she is never twice the same.

8. In horizontal communication we need to keep in mind the special problems in communicating from one area of specialization to another; in downward communication, the needs and different perspective of the subordinate; and in external communication, the importance of tone.

SUGGESTED APPLICATIONS

1. This chapter takes a number of definite positions that may seem controversial. These include:
   a. Some managers are motivated primarily by the need to achieve; others by the need for security and status.
   b. Managers tend to be more results-oriented than theory-oriented.
   c. Managers tend to be more task-oriented than people-oriented.
   d. Managers are typically better writers than speakers.
   e. Older managers tend to be more authoritarian than younger managers.
   f. No manager is ever "quite the same twice."
   g. Theory Y almost certainly results in improved communication with subordinates.
   h. The distinctive feature of letters, as opposed to other business communications, is tone.
   i. Since you and your boss are interdependent, the purpose in understanding him or her better should not be to outwit him or her, but to work with him or her more effectively.

Write a paper of around 400–500 words in which you defend, attack, or otherwise evaluate any one of these positions. Build your case around the two or three strongest reasons you can think of, and support each reason with factual evidence, opinion from authoritative sources, or both.

2. Students often refer to "psyching out" the professor. This chapter is intended mainly to help you "psych out" prospective managers in your future. As author, I am interested in how helpful you have found this chapter to be. Therefore, I would welcome a letter from you giving me your candid reactions, along with any suggestions for improving the chapter should it sometime be revised. You may address me as:

>Prof. Roger P. Wilcox
>Communication Consulting Services
>2954 Helber Street
>Flint, MI 48504

I promise to respond to any correspondence received.

3. Select any six of the controversial statements above and conduct a survey to determine to what extent others may agree. Devise a questionnaire in which each statement is followed with five possible answers, such as:

| *Agree Strongly* | *Agree Somewhat* | *Not Sure* | *Disagree Somewhat* | *Disagree Strongly* |

Type the questionnaire, have it duplicated, and have it answered by at least 20 people—ideally half of them employees and half of them supervisors. Write a 300–400 word report of your study in which you explain your methodology (choice of questions, choice of respondents, procedure for having them answer the questions), summarize the results in one or more tables (as explained in Chapter 8), and offer your interpretation as to why the results turned out as they did.

4. Write an analysis (300–400 words) of your own personality in terms of the Maslow Hierarchy. Your paper should show both an understanding of the hierarchy itself, as well as some insight into your own behavior patterns.

5. Follow the instructions in item 4, but write about someone else whom you know well.

NOTES

[1] First published in an article, "A Theory of Human Motivation," by Abraham Maslow in *Psychological Review,* 50 (1943), pp. 370–396, and developed more fully in his book, *Motivation and Personality* (New York: Harper & Brothers, 1954).

[2] William V. Haney, *Communication and Organizational Behavior* (3rd ed.) (Homewood, Ill.: Richard D. Irwin, Inc., 1973), pp. 146–150.

[3] K. Tim Hostiuck, *Contemporary Organizations: An Introductory Approach* (Morristown, N.J.: General Learning Press, 1974), pp. 37–42.

[4] Walter Guzzardi, Jr., *The Young Executives* (New York: The New American Library, 1964).

[5] Guzzardi, p. 9.

[6] Guzzardi, p. 27.

[7] Guzzardi, p. 33.

[8] Guzzardi, p. 38.

[9] Guzzardi, pp. 176–177.

[10] Charles E. Goshen, "Engineering Characterology and Management Careers," *Engineering Education,* April, 1969, p. 498.

[11] Goshen, p. 498.

[12] J. Sterling Livingston, "Myth of the Well-Educated Manager," *Harvard Business Review,* January-February, 1971, p. 86.

[13] Livingston, p. 87.

[14] David W. Ewing, *The Managerial Mind* (New York: The Free Press, 1964), p. 194.

[15] Guzzardi, p. 90.
[16] Ewing, p. 195.
[17] A. H. Chapman, *Put-Offs and Come-Ons,* (New York: G. P. Putnam, 1968), p. 122.
[18] Ewing, p. 195.
[19] Ewing, pp. 195–196.
[20] Livingston, p. 88.
[21] Ewing, p. 199.
[22] Guzzardi, pp. 152–153.
[23] Mary C. Bromage, "Defensive Writing," *California Management Review,* 13, No. 1, 1970.
[24] Burleigh Gardner and David Moore, *Human Relations in Industry* (Homewood, Ill.: Richard Irwin, 1964), p. 96.
[25] Robert E. Levinson, "Executives Can't Communicate," *Dun's Review,* December, 1972, pp. 119–120.
[26] Peter F. Drucker, "Introduction," in Guzzardi, p. xix.
[27] From a memo by Mr. M. A. Furnish. Used with permission of author.
[28] Adapted from Roger P. Wilcox, "The Writing Team: Writer, Supervisor-Editor, Secretary," in *The Proceedings,* 20th International Communications Conference, 1973, pp. 139–140.
[29] Douglas McGregor, *The Human Side of Enterprise* (New York: McGraw-Hill Book Company, Inc., 1960), pp. 33–34.
[30] Frederick Herzberg, *Work and the Nature of Man* (Cleveland: The World Publishing Company, 1966).
[31] McGregor, pp. 47–48.
[32] Erwin P. Bettinghaus, *Persuasive Communication* (New York: Holt, Rinehart, and Winston, Inc., 1968), p. 87.
[33] Goshen, p. 496.
[34] *Think* magazine, published by International Business Machines Corporation. Copyright 1962 by Harry Levinson.
[35] Guzzardi, p. xx.

TWO BEING CLEAR

4 STRUCTURE

WHAT WE MEAN BY CLEAR ORGANIZATION

WHY CLEAR ORGANIZATION IS IMPORTANT
Advantages to the Reader or Listener
Advantages to the Writer or Speaker

AN EFFECTIVE BALANCE BETWEEN THE GENERAL AND SPECIFIC
General Ideas
Specific Ideas
Effects of an Imbalance
    Too General   Too Specific   The Effective Balance
Achieving an Effective Balance

THE DIRECT VS. INDIRECT APPROACH
The Case for the Direct Approach
Exceptions to Using the Direct Approach
    When Your Reader Prefers the Direct Approach
    When You Prefer the Indirect Approach

PATTERNS OF ORGANIZATION
Rationale for a Clear Pattern
Common Patterns of Organization
    Problem-Solution (Need-Plan) Pattern
    Criteria-Application Pattern
    Cause-Effect or Effect-Cause
    Time (Chronological) Pattern
    Space (Geographical) Pattern   Topical Pattern
    Order of Increasing Importance (Indirect Approach)
    Order of Decreasing Importance (Direct Approach)
Patterns within Patterns
The Introduction and Conclusion

AIDS IN ACHIEVING CLEAR ORGANIZATION
Planning the Brief Message
     Memos   Letters
Planning Longer Messages
     What Outlining Can Do for You   Steps in Outlining
     Mechanics of Outlining

USE OF HEADINGS AND SUBHEADINGS

The reader or listener in business, we said in Chapter 3, is typically busy. In the words of Raymond A. Rogers, a senior research chemist, the executive seems "to operate in a sort of routinely continuing, sustained emergency that varies from acute crisis to the normal everyday administrative quandary." He or she faces the "predicament of not ever having enough time to do all things he [she] needs to do."[1] It follows, then, that such a person, "chronically short of time," will appreciate messages clear enough so (in Rogers's words) "he won't have to work so hard or so long to understand what you have to tell him."[2] In this respect, the executive is no different from you as a student. If you have fifty pages of sociology to read before class tomorrow, you pray you won't have to struggle page after page to decipher the author's meaning.

Being clear in writing results from a combination of ingredients: clear structure, clear paragraphs, clear sentences, clear language, clear grammar and punctuation, clear use of graphic aids, clear use of the components of the form of writing involved (letters, reports, and so forth). In speaking, the ingredients are similar: clear structure, clear development, clear language, clear delivery, and clear use of visual aids. The requirements for clear writing will provide the framework for Part 2 of this book, "Being Clear." Problems unique to speaking will be covered in Part 5, "The Oral Presentation."

Structure, then, or organization is where we shall start. The reason is simple. Any message of a single paragraph or longer consists of one or more ideas and their development. Selecting and arranging these ideas must precede their development, and this requires deciding on structure. Without structure, we are not clear on our objective nor how to reach it. We are like a carpenter trying to build without any plan.

WHAT WE MEAN BY CLEAR ORGANIZATION

Clear organization results when the following conditions are present:

1. The purpose of the message is clear.
2. The main and subpoints are clearly identified and stand out from the supporting material.
3. Ideas at all levels are arranged in a clear, rational sequence.
4. The relationship between ideas at all levels is made clear.
5. The main components of the message (whether a memo, letter, report, or proposal) are identified and utilized effectively.

Organization, then, gives structure and direction to what we write or say. It enables us to know what to include and where, as well as what to leave out. It tells our reader or listener what our message is about, which are our main ideas, which the supporting ideas, and how they all fit together.

WHY CLEAR ORGANIZATION IS IMPORTANT

Organizing a report clearly has several important advantages, both from the reader or listener's point of view, and from our own as writer or speaker.

Advantages to the Reader or Listener

The most obvious advantage of clear writing to readers or listeners is that it helps them to grasp the essential message more clearly and quickly. This point finds support in a study made several years ago, "Some Effects of Message Structure on Listener's Comprehension."[3] This study revealed, not surprisingly, that listeners achieved higher comprehension scores when the message was well organized. When the message also included transitions to point up the organization, the scores were still better.

An additional variable in the outcome was the listener. Through a pretest, listeners were placed in three categories: high ability in organizing materials, middle ability, and low ability. The high ability listeners, as expected, did better than the middle or low ability listeners. However, when the message structure was poor, the high ability listeners had lower scores than the low ability listeners did when the structure was good, or even only fair. Poor structure results in poor comprehension.

Several reasons help explain why receivers can comprehend better when the structure is clear. One is that when there is a rational sequence, they are less likely to get lost; they can stay with it better. Another is that a clear structure provides them with an overall frame of reference to which they can relate facts and details; they see a pattern that helps them "put it all together." Finally, they can better sort out the main ideas, as opposed to the supporting ideas; thus, they can more readily see "what it all adds up to."

A second advantage of clear organization to the reader or listener is that of remembering better. This would be expected from the final point above: being able to see what it all adds up to. Consider, for example, a two-page report, containing, let us say, 200 ideas—some less important than others, to be sure, but still 200. Now, trying to remember 200 ideas would pose a major strain on anyone. But if, among those 200, only four are really main ideas, then remembering these becomes a quite manageable task. Without clear organization, the main ideas are not likely to stand out; with clear organization they definitely will.

Our analysis is consistent with research findings, which "suggest that generalizations or major ideas are better comprehended and retained than are details or specifics. . . ."[4] Indeed, main ideas are what the good listener (and, we assume, the good reader as well) looks for. A study conducted at the University of Minnesota comparing one hundred of the poorest listeners revealed that, "Good listeners focus on central ideas. . . . Poor listeners are inclined to listen for the facts. . . ."[5] However, as we saw above, even good listeners are handicapped when the main ideas are buried.

Advantages to the Writer or Speaker

The temptation is great, when we have a paper to write or a talk to give, to rush quickly through the planning stage. Our mood is expressed by the little girl who said, "How do I know what I think till I see what I say?"

There is some truth, indeed, in this view, for as one writes, new ideas do come to mind. But the writing or speaking should *follow* the planning, not replace it. Taking time to plan carefully before starting to write or speak can more than pay off, to us as well as to our receiver. It can do so in at least these three ways: save time, increase confidence, and enhance credibility. Since time saving will be discussed later in this chapter, we shall move on to the other two advantages.

If our message is to be given orally, having a carefully planned structure can pay dividends through increased self-confidence. The speaker who has not taken time to think through his or her speech structure in terms of central idea, main points, supporting points, and the relationship between them can easily get rattled. He or she is like a tour guide with little idea of where to go or how to get there. With a clear plan, a speaker can proceed with much greater confidence, step by step, from beginning to end.

Perhaps the most significant advantage from our own point of view derives from the relationship between organization and credibility (amount of confidence the receiver places in us). Curiously, studies have revealed no significant gain in credibility from clear organization. However, a study some years ago disclosed a sharp, significant loss in credibility from *poor* organization.[6] The relationship seems analogous to what one wears to a funeral. If one arrives well dressed, one attracts little notice, for others expect it. But should one come dressed in sweaty paint clothes, one would attract plenty of notice—all negative!

Further, taking time to organize promotes the relationship between us and the receiver. It says, in effect, "I care enough about you to plan the message so you can follow it easily."

Clearly, taking time to develop a clear structure offers important gains, to our reader or listener, and to us as well. Failing to do so can result in our forfeiting these gains, besides damaging our credibility.

AN EFFECTIVE BALANCE BETWEEN THE GENERAL AND SPECIFIC

Before we get into more detailed matters of structure, there are two basic principles relating to structure that deserve special attention. One of the most useful ways of classifying ideas is on the basis of whether they are general or specific. It will aid us as communicators if we learn to think of them this way and can achieve an effective balance between them.

General Ideas

General ideas are the main ideas, the broad inclusive ideas, of any message. An everyday example would be a newspaper headline: "Stock Market Takes Dip"; "Electronics Firm Plans Expansion." So also would be a title of a book. Such statements as these are extremely general, for they include everything contained within the news story or book they refer to.

Headings within a news story or textbook are also general, but less so, since they apply to only a portion of the whole. Thus within this chapter (whose title is less general than the book title), the heading "Why Clear Organization Is Important" is general, but less general than the chapter title. To proceed a step further, a topic sentence of a paragraph is general, too. Though more limited in scope than the topic heading under which it is located, it is the most inclusive statement within the paragraph. It sums up in one sentence what the paragraph is about.

In a formal report or proposal the following elements fall in the category of general:

Title
Abstract
Table of contents
Introduction
Conclusions
Recommendations
Major headings; major and minor subheadings
Major points; major and minor subpoints
  (often topic sentences of paragraphs)

While it is true that these elements represent varying levels of generality, or inclusiveness, they nonetheless all stand for ideas that essentially are general rather than specific. Incidentally, when headings of various levels are arranged in an outline, the outline can be thought of as an arrangement of general ideas. So can a table of contents, which constitutes a kind of outline.

General ideas possess at least two important characteristics. One is that they constitute the gist, or essence, of the total message. Whether expressed as a title, a heading, a sentence, or even a whole paragraph (as in the case of an abstract), they represent the meaning of the whole message *in general*. This is their unique characteristic that distinguishes them from specific ideas.

A second characteristic (shared by specific ideas) is that, by themselves, they are incomplete. Suppose, for example, you were to find in your mailbox at work a memo, "New Policy on Vacation Time." By itself, such a statement would raise numerous questions: What is the new policy? How will it affect me? When does it take effect? Why is the change being made? The fact that though a general idea may express the gist of the message, it is still incomplete, gives rise to the necessity of the second category: specific ideas.

Specific Ideas

Specific ideas are those that get down to details, the "nitty gritty" of the subject. Whereas in a formal report or proposal the abstract or conclusions convey the gist of the document, the discussion contains the detailed development explaining or supporting the conclusions. The appendix (if there is one) contains details even more specific, such as tables of data.

In like fashion, while the topic sentence of a paragraph expresses the general idea, the accompanying sentences contain the specific development required to make the general idea clear.

Specific details (sometimes called "support materials" or "forms of support") are of various kinds. Chapter 5, "Paragraphing," will illustrate some of the most common: analysis, classification, description, comparison, contrast, examples, statistics, and testimony. Another kind used often in business communication includes graphic aids (in written materials) and visual aids (in oral presentations).

Just as general ideas possess at least two important characteristics, so also do specific ideas. The first is that while the general idea expresses the gist of the message, specific ideas give factual details or instances that illustrate or support the general. For example:

> *General statement:* Sometimes it is useful to define a term by comparing it with a similar term.
>
> *Specific instance:* For instance, an autogiro differs basically from a helicopter in that the autogiro does not have power supplied to it during flight.

General statement: Inflation continues in an upward trend.

Supporting facts: Food prices were up another 3.6% during August, clothing 3.1%, and utilities 2.9%.

The other characteristic, already mentioned, is that specific ideas by themselves—like general ideas—are incomplete. The most limited kind of specific idea is the single fact; for example: "Jones was absent"; "It rained on Thursday"; "The shipment arrived late." By themselves such statements have limited meaning. They leave us asking, "So what?" Not until they are related to a more general idea do they acquire significance.

To represent the notion that a complete message requires both the general and the specific, we could use a circle:

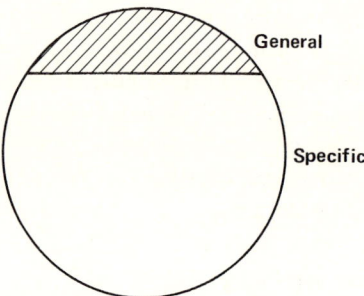

With either the general or specific missing we no longer have a complete circle. Neither do we have a complete message.

Effects of an Imbalance

The notion of classifying ideas as either general or specific is quite simple. Less obvious—and less generally recognized as well—is the importance of achieving an effective balance, or mix, between the two. Let's examine the results when we lean toward either extreme.

Too General A message with too high a ratio of general to specific we think of as being "up in the clouds," "vague," "theoretical," "abstract," "difficult to understand," and so forth. We wish the writer or speaker would "come down to earth," "get down to brass tacks," "give some examples," "offer supporting data."

No doubt you have encountered messages of this kind: textbooks and classroom lectures consisting of all theory and no application; political addresses loaded with generalities but no specifics; sermons heavy with platitudes but lacking in illustrations.

Wendell Johnson, an eminent general semanticist (one who studies the effect of language meanings on human behavior), wrote a well-known book, *People In Quandaries,* in which he referred to "theoretical articles . . . pitched on very high levels of abstraction, and . . . very dry indeed to most people, because they are so lacking in descriptive detail and cannot be understood at all, unless one is already thoroughly familiar with [the subject].''[7] He went on to refer to a colleague doing research in child psychology at a university noted for studies in this field. This colleague checked out a complete year's volume of a scholarly journal, only to find that after forty years the pages were still uncut! The journal had a reputation of containing articles that were virtually unreadable because so highly general.

Such writers and speakers, to draw on a familiar proverb, talk mainly in terms of the forest. They probably wouldn't know a tree if they saw one, nor think it worth their attention. No matter how packed with generalities, the message would still be incomplete. Their messages could be represented like this:

Too Specific By contrast, a message with too high a ratio of specific to general is equally deficient; perhaps even more so. Such a message we label as "lacking interpretation," "lacking depth," "not clear what it all adds up to," and so forth.

While some texts are top heavy in theory, many popular books are too lacking. They offer page after page of how-to-do-it advice or entertaining anecdotes, with only the skimpiest relationship to any set of underlying principles or theory that might give them meaning.

Some people converse (carry on a monologue is more accurate) in the same manner. They spend hours relating trivia over deals they have made, squabbles they have had with their family or neighbors, or operations they have undergone, with no awareness, apparently, of principles of economics, human behavior, or medicine that their anecdotes either illustrate, support, or refute.

An example comes to mind. It concerns a twenty-five-page memo addressed to executives of overseas subsidiaries, intended to offer guidelines governing the release of company information to the public. Two executives (both well educated and fluent in English) from different subsidiaries described their experience with this memo. One read and reread it several times, then wrote his own interpretation, six or seven pages long, to pass on to his staff; but he was not at all sure his interpretation was correct. The other read it once, decided it was not worth the effort of trying to decipher, and threw it in the basket. The fault, both agreed, was that the main ideas—what it all boiled down to—simply failed to stand out.

A similar example consisted of a seventy-five-page technical report, crammed with a mass of disorganized detail. What conclusions there were lay buried near the end, with virtually no relationship shown to the preceding data.

Whereas the theoreticians see the forest instead of the trees, these detail-bound persons can't see the forest for the trees. No matter how many details they pour out, their messages remain incomplete. To return to the circle, their messages are like this:

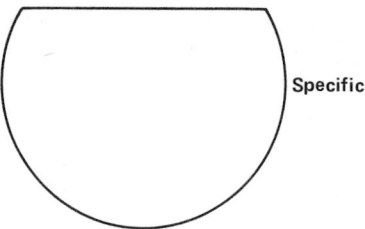

The Effective Balance Neither extreme, then, is complete; neither is effective. The desirability of combining both elements is given special emphasis in Houghton Mifflin's *A Guide for Authors:*

> Suppose a sociologist fills a paragraph with phrases such as "behavioral conformity," "reference groups," and "collective values and norms," without one concrete detail or brief example. The paragraph lies inert and bloodless. Examples add vividness and interest, and they make abstractions easier to grasp and remember. One of the most successful exemplifications in textbook literature occurred in a famous economist's discussion of the choice which every economy has to make between consumer goods and capital goods. He put it in terms of the choice between guns and butter in Nazi Germany. . . . At about the same time another textbook author spoke of "maximizing one's want satisfaction through allocation of one's scarce resources." You can guess which book caught on.
>
> Conversely, a nutshell summary of a generalization, principle, or insight can give instant order to a mass of fact.[8]

In his book, *The Art of Readable Writing,* Rudolf Flesch expresses the same point with the phrase "up-and-down writing"—that is, writing "up" to express the general principle or abstract concept, then writing "down" through use of concrete cases and specific data for clarification.[9]

Viewed this way, good writing should more nearly resemble a series of peaks and valleys:

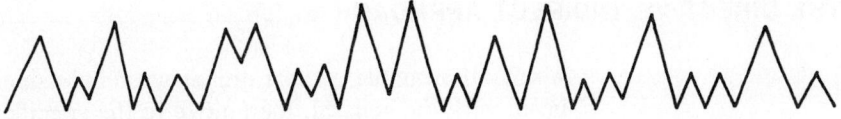

than a straight line:

_____

The rule must be flexible, though, for what constitutes an effective balance will vary. Some messages will consist almost entirely of specific detail with a minimum of summing up or interpretation. For instance, a supervisor's report of a labor grievance (for the information of the director of labor relations in handling the case) will be limited mainly to the who, what, where, when, and how. Little if any opinion is wanted—just the facts; thus, the "why" will be omitted or handled cautiously, for speculations begin creeping in at this point. Another example would be a test report, where the writer—while entirely competent to observe and record data—is not professionally qualified to draw conclusions on what the data signify. Interpreting them will be left for the supervisor.

On the other hand, an announcement of a change in company policy may be highly general, with specifics to follow later, perhaps in a detailed brochure, a question period, or both.

Most business messages fall somewhere between these two extremes. A rough guide might be 10-20 percent general, 80-90 percent specific.

Achieving an Effective Balance

Before we move on, a few suggestions may be useful on how to achieve an effective balance between general and specific.

The first, and most important, step is a mental one: comprehend thoroughly the concept of general/specific, become committed to its value, then learn to *think* general and specific, theory and application, abstract and concrete. As you observe events in your daily environment, look for the principles that will help explain them. Conversely, as you encounter new theory in your reading or classroom lectures, make an effort to apply them in everyday life. Inability to perceive the specific meaning of the general, or the general meaning of the specific drastically limits one's effectiveness in communicating.

The other suggestions concern technique. Learn how to use outlines to get "the big picture." Learn how to use the components of written messages—especially reports and proposals. Learn how to use topic sentences and developmental detail in writing paragraphs. Learn even how to write sentences that contain the right blend of general and specific. All these techniques will be covered in this and succeeding chapters. They are important.

THE DIRECT VS. INDIRECT APPROACH

A second principle of clear organization in business writing is normally to begin with the general, then move to the specific; in other words, to use the direct approach. Using the *direct approach* (called by some the "deductive approach") means coming directly to the point, then proceeding to clarify or support it. You would be using the direct approach if you were to send a letter home beginning, "Please send me $50. I need the money because . . ."

The *indirect approach* ("inductive") consists of presenting the reasons or explanation first, building up to the main point at the end. You would be using the indirect approach if in your letter home you were to describe all the expenses you've been having, then end with, "As you can see, I'm broke. Could you send me $50?"

A common fallacy in writing a report is organizing it in the same sequence as the investigation: procedures, data, then finally conclusions and recommendations. This is specific to general; indirect; the "murder mystery" approach referred to in Chapter 3; or, as one American manager expressed it after reading some German reports organized in this way, "starting with Adam and Eve."[10]

The Case for the Direct Approach

To the writer, going from specific to general may seem like a logical sequence; by the same token it is a *writer*-centered approach. As already mentioned in Chapter 3, the reader normally wants to get at the gist of the report or proposal at once, without having to hunt for it. This preference was clearly revealed in a survey conducted by J. W. Souther years ago in a large industrial corporation:

> managers who were interviewed said they read the summary or abstracts of a report and the sections entitled Introduction, Background, Conclusions, and Recommendations. Very few read the body or appendix.[11]

These findings concern managers. In a second survey, Souther sought to determine what engineers and scientists (not in management) at the research laboratory of a large company looked for in reports from colleagues. The findings were virtually identical. At the top of the list stood conclusions and recommendations; at the bottom, results and detailed data. Souther speculates on the reasons thus:

> When engineers and technical people *write* reports they assume that their associates, at least, want all the details, [even] if management does not. But when they *read* such reports, this is precisely the material they pay least attention to.[12]

This raises a question. If main ideas are all the reader is interested in, why include detail at all? There are several reasons. One is to provide support and explanation. Souther found that when managers did read further, "it frequently was because they were skeptical of the conclusions drawn. Or else they were especially interested in the subject, deeply involved in the problem, or felt that the urgency of the problem demanded full reading."[13]

Another reason for including detail, particularly if the report is of an investigation, is to enable others to replicate the study. Without knowing the procedures, or being able to compare results, meaningful replication would be impossible. As a practical example, suppose a chemist is asked to test a new paint on the market. His or her company has used, on the basis of tests made at the time, a competing brand for the past five years. Now the company wants to know whether the new brand, slightly lower in price, will perform as well. In order to make a valid comparison, the chemist would need to know what procedures were used in the earlier test, and with what results. If these details are included in the report, fine; if not, he or she is out of luck.

There is, however, an exception to be noted. In test laboratories a standard procedure may be devised for all tests of a given category, and this procedure then written and placed on file. When this is the case, there is no need to repeat the description of procedure in each test report. All that is needed is to refer to, or "reference," the appropriate document on file; this can then be consulted, if desired, by the reader. But aside from this exception, the detailed data and explanations should be included in the report so they are on record for anyone to consult if he or she wishes, whatever the reasons.

Exceptions to Using the Direct Approach

There are times, however, when the indirect, specific-to-general approach may be preferable. Such exceptions fall in two categories: (1) when your reader prefers the indirect approach, and (2) when you prefer it.

When Your Reader Prefers the Indirect Approach In spite of the case for the direct approach, your most probable reader for the next year or more will usually prefer the indirect. This reader is your teacher—not necessarily of this course, but of your courses in general.

The reason for a teacher's preference is not difficult to see when you consider how his or her role differs from that of the manager in an organization. To the manager, memos and reports are a means of helping get the job done. The more quickly he or she can sort out, review, and evaluate the utility of this information the better. But to the teacher, reports and term papers are a means of providing you experience in conducting research, analyzing data, arriving at conclusions, and expressing your ideas. Consequently, a teacher is not so much interested in the information per se (he or she probably is quite familiar with it already), as in evaluating your grasp of the material and step-by-step reasoning from beginning to end. Thus, the indirect approach is more consistent with the role of teacher and critic.

In business also you occasionally may encounter the reader who prefers the indirect approach. Such a reader is probably a "detail person" who prefers to study the specifics for him- or herself before considering the conclusions. This assumes, of course, a strong enough interest on the reader's part, because of the importance of the subject, to want to become absorbed in the detail. (It may also imply that your reader does not yet place sufficient confidence in you to accept your conclusions without checking them closely for him- or herself.)

When You Prefer the Indirect Approach One situation in which *you* may prefer using the indirect approach is when your report or proposal presents concepts new to your reader, and you want him or her to understand not only the conclusions or recommendations, but also the rationale. In short, you wish to "educate" him or her. For example, you may propose a totally new method of employee evaluation. It is not enough, you feel, that your supervisor understand the method; in order to implement it, he or she must understand the concepts behind it. To increase the likelihood of his or her reading the discussion as well as the recommendations, you place your recommendations at the end.

A similar case is one in which your proposal is likely to trigger a negative response. The proposal you offer may entail a high cost, or run counter to traditional policy or the biases of your boss. Or it may resemble an idea he or she rejected six months before. You are certain that if your boss encounters the proposal before understanding the reasons, he or she will close his or her mind and read no further. So you want to "lead" him or her through the steps arriving at the controversial recommendations, hoping that as your boss sees for him- or herself the reasons supporting the proposal, he or she will be less likely to say no.

In either of the above cases, your strategy would include the following:

1. In the abstract (if there is one) and introduction, identify the problem and stress its importance, then state that this paper will present and evaluate one or more possible solutions.

2. Begin the discussion with whatever analysis and data may seem necessary to convince the reader of the nature of the problem and the consequences if it is not solved.

3. Continue the discussion by presenting the criteria any solution should meet.

4. Present one or more alternative solutions, showing convincingly how their disadvantages would outweigh their advantages.

5. Conclude with presenting your proposed solution, showing convincingly how its advantages would outweigh its disadvantages.

Obviously, this strategy cannot be guaranteed to work. But the odds are greater than if you get a "thumbs down" at the outset.

There is one other case in which you will not only wish to use an indirect approach; it is customary that you do. This is the case of the oral presentation. Here the situation is quite different. When you submit your material in writing, your readers can spend as much time or as little with it as they wish. But when you give an oral presentation, your listeners consider it important enough to reserve a given amount of time in their schedule. They do not expect to listen two minutes, then walk out; they expect to remain to the end. Thus, not only do you have the opportunity to use the indirect approach; you gain if you do. You gain by being able to present your analysis and rationale first, after which your conclusions and recommendations will make more sense. Also you gain by being able to keep your listeners in suspense, thus more attentive until the end.

Your strategy in the oral presentation would be similar to the strategy outlined above.

PATTERNS OF ORGANIZATION

At the beginning of the chapter we cited several advantages of clear organization. One was that it provides the receiver with a clear frame of reference, or pattern, to which he or she can relate the specifics of the message.

Rationale for a Clear Pattern

The advantage of our building from a sound pattern and making the pattern obvious is twofold. We relieve the readers or listeners of the burden of having to supply the pattern themselves, and we more nearly ensure that the pattern they perceive will be the one we intend.

If we have no sound pattern, or fail to make one obvious, they will seek to impose one themselves so the message will "make sense." If the effort to do this is too great, they will give up and turn their thoughts elsewhere.

Neither alternative is desirable. If our readers or listeners try to decide on the pattern themselves (in terms of their own set of experiences) it will likely differ from the one intended by the communicator. A result will be communication falloff. Moreover, having to decide on the pattern for themselves will reduce the amount of attention they can give to the ideas themselves, thus resulting in still more falloff. If they give up (possibly because there was no sound pattern to begin with), then of course the message does not get through at all. Whichever the alternative, both the message and the communicator's credibility are bound to suffer.

Common Patterns of Organization

To become more specific, let us examine some of the more common patterns used in writing and speaking. We shall examine them in terms of their uses, advantages, and limitations.

Problem-Solution (Need-Plan) Pattern A problem may be defined as any unsatisfactory condition; any deviation from the normal or what is desired; any difficulty in need of correcting. In short, it is anything that someone would like changed because it bothers one. Examples in business and industry could include material shortages, machine breakdown, poor morale, incompetent supervision, communication breakdown, loss of a contract, or declining profits.

A solution is "anything that remedies the need or eliminates the difficulty without resulting in other difficulties still greater."[14] The solution may consist of an improved technique, new equipment, modified routine, a training program, a revised business form, eliminating a position, dropping or adding a product line, and so on.

The most typical application of the problem-solution (or need-plan) pattern is in writing proposals or in oral presentations consisting of proposals. This is because any proposal consists essentially of a proposed solution to some problem (or, expressed differently, of a proposed plan to remedy some need). The object, of course, is to secure authorization from management for the proposal to be put into effect. If management is not convinced that the need exists, or that the proposed plan would meet the need to advantage, they are unlikely to approve. For instance, if you wanted to persuade your supervisor to approve a new system of employee appraisal, you would need first to point out the drawbacks of the present system, then show how the new system would be an improvement.

The next most typical application of the problem-solution pattern is in reports—written or oral. This is because any report serves to inform the receiver of the nature of one or more problems, or one or more solutions, or both. If the report focuses only on problems *or* solutions, obviously only part of the pattern would be used.

As a general pattern of organization in business communication, none is more useful than the problem-solution pattern. Through learning to observe and analyze events in our environment in terms of this pattern, we supply meaning at the most basic level. Through using the pattern in our communications, we provide the receiver with an understanding of not only the *what* (the solution), but even more importantly the *why* (the problem underlying the solution); in other words, an understanding of the solution *in light of the problem.* This is important, for we are less likely to propose, and the supervisor is less likely to approve, courses of action which do not advantageously meet a clear need.

Competent utilization of the problem-solution pattern as a basic pattern of organization helps in putting ideas into their most useful perspective. It adds depth to our analysis and enhances both the understanding of the receiver and our own credibility.

Of all possible patterns, the problem-solution is the broadest, most inclusive, most basic. This will become clearer as we examine some of the other common patterns of organization.

Criteria-Application Pattern   On occasion you may be asked to conduct an evaluation and report your results. In writing your report, the criteria-application pattern is the one you should use.

"Criteria" (a plural word; "criterion" is the singular) means the standards by which something is measured. Suppose, for example, as a member of the purchasing department, you are asked to do a report evaluating a new line of desks. Your criteria for the evaluation might relate to their practicality, durability, attractiveness, and cost. The first section of your report would then state and specify what you mean by these four criteria, while the second section would show how each applies to the desk being evaluated. If the criteria are well-established standard criteria fully familiar to your reader, you might simply identify them in the introduction and then use the body of the report for their application.

If it is a comparative evaluation you are making of desks offered by several vendors, you could then use either of two variations of the criteria-application pattern. Briefly outlined, they look like this:

First Variation
I. Criterion 1
  A. Desk A
  B. Desk B
  etc.
II. Criterion 2
  A. Desk A
  B. Desk B
  etc.

Second Variation
I. Desk A
  1. Criterion 1
  2. Criterion 2
  etc.
II. Desk B
  1. Criterion 1
  2. Criterion 2
  etc.

In the above examples, the criteria-application pattern forms the structure of the entire report. In a more extensive report or proposal using the problem-solution pattern, the criteria-application pattern would constitute, in effect, the latter part of the report following the problem stage, when you evaluate the proposed solution or solutions.

Cause-Effect or Effect-Cause   The cause-effect pattern is used for describing any situation and its possible consequences. Thus, in discussing a problem (either to explain it, or to convince the skeptical receiver it exists), we would normally describe the undesirable situation (the cause), then explain the probable consequences (effects). Similarly, in presenting a possible solution to a problem, we would normally first explain the solution, or plan (the cause); then show the probable consequences (the effects). Obviously, these effects could be desirable or undesirable. If we are advocating adoption of the plan, the desirable effects had better outweigh the undesirable!

The effect-cause pattern is commonly used in analyzing a problem (the effect) for its causes. Both patterns focus on the logical, causal relationships between events having chronological sequence. Cause-effect moves forward in time (because any cause naturally precedes the effect). Effect-cause moves backward, because first the effects are discussed, then the causes that led to the effects.

Since causal patterns follow a chronological sequence, using them may seem simple. But actually they can be tricky. Sometimes we may confuse cause and effect, as for instance in analyzing low output in a given department. Are the employees falling down on the job because the supervisor is ineffective, or is the supervisor ineffective because the employees give him or her a rough time? (Chances are it is both.)

In using the effect-cause pattern, a common fault is assigning a single cause when several are present; for instance, blaming part of the system ("our advertising is lousy"), when the whole system is faulty (the entire company is ill managed). In using the cause-effect pattern there is the temptation to predict results beyond what is reasonable. "If only we had a new manual, we'd have no more misunderstanding." It is seldom that simple.

Time (Chronological) Pattern   The time pattern is useful for listing causes in the sequence they occurred in, such as giving historical background, or explaining a procedure (first step, second step, and so forth).

An advantage of the chronological pattern is that it is probably the simplest and easiest for both writer and reader, since this is the pattern we use more often, day in and day out, than any other. But using it introduces potential disadvantages. One is that organizing facts simply in order of occurrence can result in overstressing the unimportant and understressing the important. Amateur travelogues frequently do this. This lack of varying emphasis leads to a second disadvantage: monotony.

Space (Geographical) Pattern   The space pattern is useful for describing a layout of an area (an office, a lab, a new plant site). Its utility in organizing subsections of the problem-solution pattern are thus evident, either in explaining where a problem may be occurring, or explaining a proposed solution to a problem. Like the time pattern, it is simple and easy for both sender and receiver, though it may not always be relevant.

Topical Pattern   The topical pattern is used for discussing any series of topics in a given category—a series of causes, effects, criteria, advantages, disadvantages, and so on. It is the pattern used most frequently in this book, as a review of chapter headings will show. It also is a pattern simple and easy for both sender and receiver. However, like the time pattern, it may distort or obscure the relative importance of some points, since they all tend to be treated as equal, whether or not they are.

Order of Increasing Importance (Indirect Approach)   This pattern is a useful variation of the topical pattern. The difference is that it arranges the topics in order of importance, building to a climax. Since it requires more time to get to the point, it is useful mainly—as already mentioned—in controversial messages where stating the conclusions first could invite rejection, or in oral presentations where a given amount of time is allotted anyway.

Order of Decreasing Importance (Direct Approach)   Like the previous pattern, this also is a variation of the topical pattern. It, too, shows relative importance, but it gets to the main point immediately. For memos, reports, and noncontroversial letters and proposals this is obviously desirable because it conserves time. However, whatever follows tends to be less interesting. In written, noncontroversial messages this is not necessarily a disadvantage. In oral presentations, of course, it would be.

Patterns within Patterns

Our review above of patterns and their uses quite clearly implies that a message may possess not just one pattern but many, and the longer the message, the greater number of patterns. In this respect, it resembles a house: one structural plan for the exterior, another for the room layout, a different furniture arrangement for each room, a special cabinet design for the kitchen, a different arrangement of dishes and food products on each shelf. Thus, a written message of any length may utilize one pattern for the whole, and a different pattern for each section, subsection, paragraph, and even sentence. This concept of patterns within patterns is illustrated at the general level by the following typical structure of a report or proposal:

I. Problem
   A. Spatial pattern to describe area where problem is occurring.
   B. Analysis of problem.
      1. Effect-cause pattern to identify the difficulties and their causes (which could be discussed in a chronological sequence, topical sequence, or order-of-importance sequence).
      2. Cause-effect pattern to point out the consequences if not remedied (which could also be discussed in any of the sequences suggested for discussing the causes).

II. Order-of-decreasing-importance pattern to explain the criteria for evaluating solutions. The criteria and solution stages together use the criteria-application pattern.
III. Solutions (presented in order of increasing importance).
   A. Topical, spatial, or chronological sequence to explain the nature of each possible solution.
   B. Topical or order-of-importance sequence to show advantages and disadvantages of each possible solution.

The above is not intended as the only structure for a report or proposal, but it is typical. It also illustrates why the problem-solution pattern is the most inclusive of all.

The Introduction and Conclusion

The guidelines just offered on planning for clear structure pertain primarily to the body, or main part, of the message. In addition, a message of any length (half a page or more) requires an introduction and conclusion. The introduction serves to prepare the reader or listener as to what is to follow. The conclusion serves to bring into focus what you most want remembered—the *general* ideas of the message.

Because the requirements of effective introductions and conclusions vary with the type of message (letter or memo, report or proposal, or oral presentation), suggestions for planning the introduction and conclusion will be discussed in greater detail in Chapters 10, 11, and 12.

AIDS IN ACHIEVING CLEAR ORGANIZATION

In this section our purpose will be to show techniques—especially outlining—available for planning a message so its organization will be clear.

Planning the Brief Message

The care required in planning and writing a message varies directly with its length and importance; the longer or more important, the greater care is required.

Memos   A departmental memo only three lines long announcing a change in responsibility and title for some staff member will require little planning beyond mentally composing the message. A memo announcing a special meeting may require a bit more to ensure that all bases have been covered as to who, what, why, when, where, and how. This will likely be planned "all in the head," followed by rereading to be certain no point has been omitted or stated unclearly. On the other hand, a special memo from the general manager to all departments announcing a major operations change may warrant at least a rough written outline, followed by careful review to make sure the message is clear and complete.

Letters Letters of more than a paragraph or two may likewise benefit from a simple outline consisting of a short list of topics arranged in appropriate sequence. If the letter is in response to one received, a useful technique is to underline points in the letter being answered, then incorporate these into the list.[15]

Planning Longer Messages

In planning a report or proposal of several pages, or an oral presentation, the use of outlining is a must.

What Outlining Can Do for You Three things that outlining can do for you are these:

1. Save time. Writers who expect to conserve time by skipping the outlining stage invariably waste time instead. After writing a few pages, they discover that their sequence may be faulty, some points overdeveloped, others underdeveloped, some irrelevant, and so on. Then they must start laboriously reworking their material, hoping for better results next time. They are like the backyard carpenter who starts to build a shed, gets it half finished, then discovers he or she must tear it down and start over again. The experienced builder has learned that one gains time in the long run by drawing a plan in advance. The experienced writer knows, likewise, that an outline is a shortcut.

2. Test the soundness of the plan. An outline can tell you, almost at a glance, whether:
    a. your plan is complete
    b. the points are in best sequence
    c. the subpoints are logically related to the points to which they are subordinate
    d. each point is adequately developed
    e. which points need further development

The outline thus allows you to review your "game plan" before you start writing.

3. Secure preliminary feedback from others. If you are presenting the message (either written or oral) by yourself, the outline can be used for securing helpful feedback from colleagues before writing. If you are collaborating, you can (and should) use it for checking with your coauthor before going further. If it is a report which your supervisor must approve, the outline can be used for his or her information and suggestions before writing. Hours or days can be lost by completing the report, only to find you must rewrite it because the boss does not like it.

Steps in Outlining The following steps offer guidelines for each stage in the process of outlining:

1. Set up an idea file.[16] If the message is brief, and you already have stored in your head all the information you need, no file is necessary. For longer messages this is seldom the case.

What should go in your idea file? The answer is, ideas and data from all sorts of sources: casual observation, lab or field tests, completed reports, conversations with others, articles in professional journals, and so on. In addition, you will have thoughts of your own.

An item of special value may be a listing of categories to be included in your report. Such categories may be suggested by reviewing the steps involved in the problem-solution pattern or criteria-application pattern. They could be drawn from reports of a similar nature—test reports, field reports, and so on—to see what topics were included by others. But be sure to use a good model, for if you consult a poor model, you may be misled.

In any case, since few experiences are more frustrating than searching for some piece of information you found two weeks ago then mislaid, all ideas should be placed in your file as soon as you know you may need them. Planning begins with collecting ideas and information, and this should start early.

As a case in point, in writing this text I have been aided immeasurably by having nearly a whole file drawer, built up over the past two or three years, with a separate folder for each chapter and major heading of the entire book. As I came across articles, illustrative materials, or dreamed up ideas of my own that I thought could be useful, I filed these in the appropriate folder. This file has been invaluable. For a shorter project, of course, say a report or proposal of 10–20 pages (or minutes, if oral), a single folder would normally suffice.

One additional suggestion: just as you mark your texts when you study, mark up the materials that you put in your file. Underline, highlight, outline, make marginal notations—anything that will facilitate later review.

2. Write a working outline. This is the outline from which you actually write. Since often it must be revised several times, it would be more accurate to say "outlines." Four steps are generally involved in developing the working outline: listing, grouping, arranging, and revising.

Suppose you are a member of the personnel department and have an idea for improving output per person in the company. You have studied the production data, mulled it over, read articles, reviewed notes from courses in college, and have a folder of ideas. As a result, you feel that adopting some sort of reward system based on positive reinforcement would help solve the problem. "Listing" will be your first step as you plan your working outline. So you jot down, in random order just as they come to you, such points as the following:

    1. Production down over year ago
    2. Supervisors should use praise rather than blame

3. Experience at ABC company
4. Interview with Jones
5. High absenteeism
6. Solution should be acceptable to both workers and company
7. Supervisors should explain better how to do job
8. Low motivation
9. Grievance rate is high
10. Positive reinforcement better than negative reinforcement
11. A reward system would help
12. Dramatic results in other companies
13. Details of plan
14. Scrap rate is high

Note that the random order reflects a "stream of consciousness" style of recording.

After listing these, and perhaps other ideas, you decide on the problem-solution pattern. So "grouping" the ideas is your next step, as follows:

Problem: Nos. 1, 4, 5, 8, 9, 14
Criteria: No. 6
Solution: Nos. 2, 3, 7, 10, 11, 12, 13

On the basis of this grouping you now arrange the points in an outline as follows (note that you have also expanded your original list):

I. Problem: Production is down
   A. Evidence: Production data over last five years
   B. Cause: Motivation is low
     1. Evidence
       a. High absenteeism rate
       b. High grievance rate
       c. High scrap rate
     2. Reason: worker resentment over supervisory tactics; interview with Jones

II. Criteria for good solution
   A. Must increase production
   B. Must not cost more than worth
   C. Must be workable

III. Solution
   A. Based on principle of positive reinforcement
   B. Explanation of plan
     1. Substitute encouragement for criticism
     2. Keep a record of worker performance
     3. Show workers how they can improve performance
   C. Proof of success
     1. Example at ABC company
     2. Statistics from Mallery article

You now have a good working outline, so you can begin writing. However, the odds are that in the process of writing, as new ideas occur and your insights are sharpened, you will revise this outline two or three more times, each revision a refinement over the previous one. And "revising," we said, was Step 4.

3. Write your final outline. The final outline is written *after* the manuscript is complete. This outline serves at least two purposes. First, it provides a final check on such questions as whether each point is adequately developed, or any point is underdeveloped, or the sequence is the best possible. Second, it provides the main and subheadings to be used in the table of contents should there be one.

Mechanics of Outlining   The specific functions of the outline are to identify each point in one's chain of reasoning, show sequence or pattern, and show levels of importance or rank. The following mechanics will aid in achieving these functions:

1. Use symbols and indentation to show sequence and pattern. Suppose your outline includes the following points:

>> economically unsound
>> relatively inefficient
>> high cost
>> low return
>> disadvantages of Plan Y

Note how sequence and pattern, both obscure above, become clear when rearranged and identified in outline form:

>> I. Disadvantages of Plan Y
>>   A. Economically unsound
>>   1. High cost
>>   2. Low return
>>   B. Relatively inefficient

2. Avoid overlap. Make sure that no point covers material that logically belongs to another point. In the version below, observe how points A and B overlap:

>> I. Disadvantages of Plan Y
>>   A. Too expensive
>>   B. Economically unsound
>>   C. Relatively inefficient

"Too expensive" is logically a reason supporting the next point, thus overlapping with it. If further analysis reveals a second reason, revise the outline to the form shown earlier:

>> A. Economically unsound
>>   1. High cost
>>   2. Low return

If analysis does not reveal a second reason, omit "B. Economically unsound."

3. Avoid single subdivisions. If there is an "A" there must be a "B"; if a "1" there must be a "2," and so on. The reason is that a whole cannot be logically subdivided into only one part. In the example above, it would not be logical to reason:

    I. Disadvantages of Plan Y
       A. Too expensive

If there are more disadvantages than one, they should be listed (as they were in the original version above). Otherwise, the point would properly be stated:

    I. Plan Y would be too expensive

However, there is a practice in outlining, quite legitimate, that on the surface *looks* like a violation of this rule. This can occur when the outline includes not only main and subpoints, but support materials as well. In such a case, it is quite permissible to include a single subpoint, because it is not really a subpoint at all, but only an item of specific information supporting the point. For example:

    A. Economically unsound
       1. High cost
          a. Catalogue quotes
       2. Low returns
          a. Example at XYZ company

Or, the above might be written:

    1. High cost (catalogue quotes)
    2. Low returns (ex. at XYZ company)

When the mechanics of proper outlining are observed, the chances are greater that the writer or speaker will fix sharply in his or her own mind a pattern of development, thus heightening the odds that the reader or listener can do likewise.

USE OF HEADINGS AND SUBHEADINGS

Just as the use of outlining aids the writer in achieving clear structure, so the use of headings aids the reader in comprehending the structure.

While the practice for styling headings may vary from one company to another, the system shown here is widely used. In each case, the first letters of principal words are capitalized. The system looks like this:

First Order Heading

    This is a first order heading. It is centered, on a line by itself, and underlined or italicized.

Second Order Heading

This is a second order heading. It is also on a line by itself, and underlined or italicized, but is set at the left margin.

Third Order Heading. This is a third order heading. Like the others, it is underlined or italicized. However, just as a paragraph would be, it is indented and run into the text.

Headings are drawn from and correspond to points in the writer's final outline. When a report or proposal is long enough (five to six pages or longer) to benefit from a table of contents, the table of contents consists normally of the first two levels of headings, with the addition of page numbers.

SUMMARY

1. Clear structure or organization results when the purpose, main and subpoints, sequence, relationships, and use of components are all clear.

2. Clear organization aids receiver understanding and retention. It also saves time for the writer or speaker, increases his or her confidence when giving a talk, and enhances his or her credibility.

3. A basic principle in message construction is to achieve an effective balance between the general and the specific, for too much of either damages the message, and each is needed to complement the other.

4. Because the reader is busy, business messages should normally use the direct approach by presenting the gist of the message at the outset. Exceptions from the reader's point of view to using the direct approach include when the reader is your teacher, or the supervisor wants to check the details him- or herself before looking at the conclusions. Exceptions from the writer's or speaker's point of view include when he or she wishes to "educate" the reader, or is presenting a controversial proposal, or the presentation is oral.

5. The writer or speaker should assume responsibility for providing the pattern of development. Among the more common patterns are problem-solution (need-plan), criteria-application, cause-effect or effect-cause, time, space, topic, order of increasing importance, and order of decreasing importance. A message of any length generally includes patterns within patterns.

6. Use of outlining as an aid in achieving clear organization can help the writer or speaker by saving time, testing the soundness of his plan, and securing preliminary feedback. Suggested steps in outlining include setting up an idea file, writing the working outlines, and writing the final outline. An outline should use symbols and indentation to show sequence and pattern, and should avoid overlap and single subdivisions.

STRUCTURE

7. As an aid to the business reader, appropriate headings and subheadings should be used to identify the main and subsections of the message.

SUGGESTED APPLICATIONS

1. Write a paper of about 300 words in which you analyze the following theme in light of the principles included in this chapter. Begin with an introductory paragraph and end with a concluding one. Organize your analysis clearly, using one or more of the patterns discussed in this chapter. Use headings, and subheadings if appropriate, to make your structure evident.

THE TERROR OF THE NUCLEAR AGE

The year 1945 brought a new era into history with the United States bombing of Hiroshima and Nagasaki. The atomic bombs that were dropped brought the realization to people that they could be destroyed with the push of a button. Never before could one weapon cause so much misery and destruction.

Of course, as soon as the United States built the atomic bomb, the Russians had to build one. Now both countries have large nuclear stockpiles and other nations have also built atomic weapons. That places the entire world in a dangerous situation. If there was a war in which nuclear weapons came into play, the entire world could end up destroyed.

The countries of the world must unite and work toward peaceful applications of atomic energy. They must realize the catastrophe which might occur if there was an atomic war. Meaningful meetings should be set up. From these meetings countries must decide what they are to do if they are to survive in the future.

2. You are a purchasing agent in the Purchasing Department of your company. Recently, one of your vendors, Edwards Spring Co., which has been supplying your company with around 400,000 units of a specially designed spring, has notified you that it can no longer supply the spring in the quantity you need. You have been asked by the Purchasing Director, L. E. Foltz, to investigate other sources and write a report offering recommendations. Your investigation has narrowed the possible choice for a new source to two: American Spring of New Worcester, Inc., and Hurt's Wire and Spring Co.

American Spring is located 700 miles away, has been in business over 50 years, has a good reputation, and can offer the springs at 8.3¢ each. They formerly supplied this same spring to your company, but not since an unpleasant dispute between Mr. Foltz and their sales manager (now retired) about eight years ago.

Hurt's is a new company about three years old, founded by three young graduates from the state university, and located about 50 miles distant. They have had no experience with a spring of this design, but state they can supply it at 9.1¢ per unit.

Using the criteria-application pattern (either variation you think best), write a report to Mr. Foltz evaluating the two sources and offering a recommendation. Use a memo heading as illustrated in Chapter 10 (p. 362).

3. Using the problem-solution pattern, write an analysis of some problem you have observed at school, state and explain three or four criteria you think a good solution should meet, explain two possible solutions, evaluate the two in terms of your criteria, and offer your conclusion or conclusions on what should be done. The paper should be about 300–400 words long.

4. Using the cause-effect pattern, describe some situation or practice you have observed at school that you consider undesirable, and offer your analysis of what the consequences may be unless a change is made. The paper should be around 300–400 words.

5. Using the effect-cause pattern, describe some situation or practice you have observed at school (either desirable or undesirable), and offer your analysis of the causes leading to the situation or practice. The paper should be around 300–400 words.

6. Write a paper of 200–300 words to the instructor of this course in which, using the indirect approach, you argue for a reduction of the amount of work you are being required to do. Use a memo heading (see p. 362).

7. Write a paper as in item 6, but use the direct approach instead.

Regardless of which of the Suggested Applications you do, try to achieve the most effective balance between the general and specific.

NOTES

[1] Raymond A. Rogers, "How to Organize a Research Report for Management," *Technical Communication,* First Quarter, 1973, p. 7.

[2] Rogers, p. 7.

[3] Ernest Thompson, "Some Effects of Message Structure on Listener's Comprehension," *Speech Monographs,* XXXIV (March, 1967), pp. 51–57.

[4] Charles R. Petrie, Jr., "Informative Speaking: Summary and Bibliography of Related Research," *Speech Monographs,* XXX (June, 1963), pp. 79–91.

[5] Ralph G. Nichols, "Listening Is a 10 Part Skill," *Nation's Business,* July, 1957, pp. 56–60.

[6] Harry Sharp, Jr. and Thomas McClung, "Effects of Organization on the Speaker's Ethos," *Speech Monographs,* XXXIII (June, 1966), pp. 182–183.

[7] Wendell Johnson, *People In Quandaries* (New York: Harper & Row, Publishers, 1946), pp. 278–279. Ch. 12, "Language as Technique," is well worth reading for its insights on our discussion of general vs. specific.

[8] College Department, *A Guide for Authors* (Boston: Houghton Mifflin Company, 1974), p. 18.

[9] Rudolf Flesch, *The Art of Readable Writing* (New York: Harper & Brothers, Publishers, 1949), p. 165.

[10] H. W. Hildebrandt, "Communication Barriers between German Subsidiaries and Parent American Companies," *Michigan Business Review,* 25 (July, 1973), pp. 6–14.

[11] J. W. Souther, "Writing Better Reports," *Supervisory Management,* November, 1966, pp. 20–24.

[12] Souther, p. 22.

[13] Souther, p. 22.

[14] For a more complete discussion of the problem-solution pattern, see Roger P. Wilcox, *Oral Reporting In Business and Industry* (Englewood Cliffs, N.J.: Prentice-Hall, Inc., 1967), Ch. 5, "Organizing the Report: The Body," pp. 43–61.

[15] For an informative analysis of the consequences of failing to plan a letter, see Norman B. Sigband, *Communication for Management* (Glenview, Ill.: Scott, Foresman and Company, 1969), pp. 133–134.

[16] This and some other techniques suggested here are developed more fully in L. Clinton Hawes, "Making Technical Writing Easier," *Journal of Technical Writing and Communication,* Vol. 1 (April, 1971), pp. 161–172.

5 EFFECTIVE PARAGRAPHING

FUNCTION OF PARAGRAPHING

DEFINITION OF A PARAGRAPH

GUIDELINES IN FORMULATING THE TOPIC SENTENCE

Understand the Generative Nature of the Topic Sentence

Locate the Topic Sentence at the Beginning of the Paragraph

Phrase the Topic Sentence so It Suggests the Plan of Development

Phrase the Topic Sentence so It Shows the Relationship between That Paragraph and Others

State the Main Idea Clearly and Concisely; Avoid Including Developmental Detail

GUIDELINES FOR DEVELOPING THE TOPIC SENTENCE

Keep the Development Relatively Specific

Stick to the Main Point; Maintain a Sense of Unity

Use Appropriate Methods of Development
        Analysis   Classification   Definition   Description
        Comparison   Contrast   Example
        Statistics   Testimony

Maintain a Sense of Continuity and Coherence

Develop Your Ideas Sufficiently so Your Reader Is Not Left Wondering

Decide on the Appropriate Length for Each Paragraph

Chapter 4 was concerned with the structure, or organization, of ideas in a message; in other words, with planning the blueprint. Chapters 5 through 8 will be concerned with the actual writing. The emphasis throughout will be on achieving clarity—clarity, that is, in the mind of the reader.

Our starting point will be effective paragraphing. The reason for this is that, more than any other single unit of writing, paragraphing puts to use nearly all the principles discussed in Chapter 4:

distinguishing between the general and specific and achieving an effective balance between the two

choosing between the direct and indirect approach

grouping ideas in meaningful patterns

deciding on the appropriate amount of development

Learning to write sentences becomes easier as we master paragraphing, while learning to compose the whole message—whether a simple memo or a complex report—likewise becomes easier.

FUNCTION OF PARAGRAPHING

Paragraphing, if well done, serves several functions. First, it requires writers to think in terms of which are the main and which the supporting ideas, thus forcing them to organize their messages more clearly. Second, it helps readers identify the main and supporting ideas so they can follow the thoughts more readily. Finally, it relieves the monotony of what would otherwise be page after page of unbroken prose.

DEFINITION OF A PARAGRAPH

As pointed out in Chapter 4, the paragraph illustrates clearly the concept of the general and specific and their interdependence on each other. This is because, typically, a paragraph consists of two elements: (a) a general idea, usually expressed in a topic sentence, and (b) the development of the general idea, on a more specific level, in a series of other sentences. For example, consider this item from the *Wall Street Journal* of June 18, 1974:

> China exploded a nuclear device equal in power to a million tons of TNT. The blast, over a Chinese desert area, came only hours after a much smaller test by France in the air over the South Pacific. Neither nation observes the 1963 agreement under which the U.S. and the Soviet Union refrain from nuclear tests in the atmosphere, in space, and under water.

Clearly, this paragraph represents an elaboration of a single topic. If reduced to its simplest terms, the topic might read, "China explodes nuclear device"—the core of the opening sentence (which, since it expresses the main topic, is also the topic sentence). All else in the paragraph consists of detail relating to this topic. Note that each of our two elements is essential to the paragraph. If only the topic sentence were given, the reader's response would likely be, "This sentence doesn't tell me enough. I need to know more." Conversely, if the topic sentence were omitted and only the developing sentences given, the reader would likely ask, "What is the point of all this?"

Before proceeding, we must note two exceptions to our definition. First, not all paragraphs have topic sentences. Sometimes the details so clearly imply the point of the paragraph that a topic sentence seems unnecessary. But this occurs mainly in literary writing—novels, short stories, essays—writing to be read in leisure. Pressures of the work environment on the job typically create such an overriding need for instant clarity that the topic sentence is better retained.

Second, not all paragraphs contain their own development. For example, an opening paragraph (of perhaps but a sentence or two) may serve, in effect, as a topic sentence for a series of succeeding paragraphs. Similarly, a closing paragraph (also consisting of a sentence or two) may serve as a closing sentence for a series of preceding paragraphs. In addition, sometimes the main paragraphs—especially in memos—introduce topics so familiar to the intended readers that little development is needed. Simply stating the information or identifying the point to show the line of reasoning is sufficient.

Aside from exceptions such as the above, our original concept holds: a paragraph is best understood as consisting of (a) a topic and (b) the adequate development of that topic. With this in mind, we shall suggest some guidelines concerning the topic sentence and its development.

GUIDELINES IN FORMULATING THE TOPIC SENTENCE

The following guidelines focus on achieving clarity and readability, two of the primary virtues in business communication.

Understand the Generative Nature of the Topic Sentence

Crosby and Estey speak of the "generative sentence"—a sentence that generates, or raises, "certain questions that will be asked [by the reader] and should be answered."[1] "Most messages," they add, "can be summarized in one sentence, but they cannot be communicated clearly or convincingly without more information."[2] Such is the nature of the topic sentence—hence the need for development as specified above.

To illustrate, consider the generative nature of each of these topic sentences:

> Job motivation today suggests techniques far different from those of a generation ago. [What are today's techniques? What were those of a generation ago? How do they differ?]
>
> One hundred seventeen executives were interviewed for their views on motivating employees. [Who were these executives? Who interviewed them? When? What were their views?]
>
> While problem-solving and decision-making are terms that may overlap, they are not completely synonymous. [In what ways do they overlap? In what ways do they differ?]

A topic sentence, then, should be thought of as one that needs further development to complete the thought introduced.

Locate the Topic Sentence at the Beginning of the Paragraph

In business writing, the topic sentence is preferably located at the beginning of the paragraph; in other words, the direct approach discussed in Chapter 4 should be employed. The rationale for doing so is well stated by Rathbone and Stone:

> Placing the topic sentence at or near the beginning of the paragraph allows your reader to skim through your report. Although he may miss detailed development of main ideas, he will have a good general idea of what the report contains. For the man who reads your report completely, the topic sentence at the beginning of the paragraph serves as "the whole before the parts"—the main idea before the details.[3]

An additional reason is that, in locating the topic sentence early in the paragraph, the writer is forced to consider what *does* belong in the paragraph and what does *not*. The writer provides him- or herself with a cue on how to proceed in developing the topic sentence.

Note how in the following paragraph the opening sentence both conveys the general idea to the reader and supplies the writer with a clear cue for the logical line of development (explaining why "taking several deep breaths before swimming under water is a widespread and dangerous habit"):

> Taking several deep breaths before swimming under water is a widespread—and dangerous—habit, warns the National Safety Council. This practice—called hyperventilation—can block the body's warning signals that tell a swimmer to surface for air. Lack of oxygen then causes a blackout. If not pulled out immediately, the person will inhale water and drown. Survivors report no pain or panic—even a serene feeling. Note, too: Vigorous exercise, such as surface swimming, can cause hyperventilation.[4]

The next example illustrates the same functions of the topic sentence in giving both the writer and reader a sense of direction. The only difference is that the topic is stated in the *second* rather than the opening sentence, but still near enough the beginning to convey the general idea at the outset.

> In the earlier years, any job was considered good enough for most workers. But today's employees are saying that such is not the case anymore. They are clearly dissatisfied with their daily activities. In thousands of interviews over the last several years, it has been found over and over again that a large majority of employees are unhappy with their tasks. They feel underutilized, and they believe they are capable of contributing far more than their jobs either require or allow.[5]

Phrase the Topic Sentence so It Suggests the Plan of Development

Whenever possible, the topic sentence should be phrased so it suggests the plan of development of the entire paragraph—as was done in each of the paragraphs just quoted. Topic sentences such as the following do so even more obviously:

> The United Fastener Company was plagued for several years with problems of absenteeism. [What were these problems?]

> The plan proposed has two main disadvantages. [What are they?]

> Source credibility possesses three main dimensions: trustworthiness, competence, and dynamism. [What does each of these mean?]

Phrase the Topic Sentence so It Shows the Relationship between That Paragraph and Others

When a paragraph is one of a related series, the topic sentence should suggest the kind of relationship between that paragraph and the others. Here, for example, are the topic sentences for a series of four paragraphs discussing employee development within a business organization:[6]

> There are three general categories of activity which can be planned to stimulate individual development. [This paragraph goes on to discuss the first category: work experience.]

> Secondly, development activities can take on a more-or-less formal aspect of specific skill development and training. [Following this topic sentence are four sentences discussing "specific skill development."]

> Third and finally, development may take the more subtle form of a general education type activity. [Four sentences follow on the third category, general education.]

Our Integrated Program for Careers Development utilizes activities in all three of these categories. [This is a one-sentence paragraph which, though brief, performs two functions. It concludes this section of the article and it relates the section to the broader theme of the article, "an integrated program for career development."]

In addition, here are other topic sentences or portions of topic sentences taken from various sources. These sentences clearly link the paragraph they introduce with the paragraph immediately preceding:

Many organizations state that they are already using the job enrichment concept. [Refers to a discussion in the preceding paragraph of the concept of "job enrichment."][7]

The promotion of family planning . . . [Begins a paragraph immediately following a discussion of family planning.][8]

Each of these selected representatives . . . [Refers to individuals identified in the preceding paragraph.][9]

A month and one week after completion of the training program . . . [Refers to a ten-week course of instruction described in the paragraph just before.][10]

State the Main Idea Clearly and Concisely; Avoid Including Developmental Detail

The topic sentence should state only the main idea; specific development should be left to the rest of the paragraph. To the degree that this guideline is ignored, the topic sentence loses its effectiveness in highlighting the main idea of the paragraph. An apparent exception occurs when the main idea is separated from the development of it by a colon. The clause preceding the colon then serves as the topic sentence. An example is seen in the paragraph (p. 99) beginning "The marketing concept encompasses four major elements. . . ."

The following topic sentences illustrate admirably the qualities of clarity and conciseness:

Marketing today is a field in transition.[11]

Nine firms cooperated in the pilot research project.[12]

Now, observe how the effectiveness of these same topic sentences is reduced when reworded to include developmental detail:

Marketing today is a field in transition, since whereas traditionally marketing primarily dealt only with products, the term "product" has gradually been expanded to include services, and the concept of marketing itself has been broadened.

Nine firms, representing a diverse sampling of industry ranging from food processing, shoe manufacturing, pulp and paper to utilities, cooperated in the pilot research project.

In the above examples, the inclusion of developmental details blurs the focus of the topic sentence. Verbosity may also blur the focus; consider the following (deliberately written in a verbose style):

> In the designing of a human motivation system for an employee population, without doubt one of the most fundamental and most critical questions to be considered concerns what sources should be designated to constitute the data base, since whatever choices are made will possess important implications for the long-run usefulness and durability of the system.

A possible reduction of the above could read:

> Designing a system for motivating employees involves careful consideration of how and where to secure preliminary data. [Why this is important can be included in the development.]

Of the above guidelines, the most basic is the first: Understand the generative nature of the topic sentence. The rest of the guidelines help implement the first.

GUIDELINES FOR DEVELOPING THE TOPIC SENTENCE

Clarity and readability—hallmarks of reader-centered writing—are the primary principles underlying the following guidelines on developing the topic sentence.

Keep the Development Relatively Specific

Since our definition of a paragraph included two elements—a general idea and its relatively specific development—it is appropriate that our first guideline reinforce that concept.

Suppose the paragraph above on China's exploding a nuclear device read like this:

> China exploded a nuclear device equal in power to a million tons of TNT. This only shows that China cannot be trusted. Nixon made a mistake in ever recognizing Red China. But perhaps an even bigger mistake was when we exploded the first atom bomb in World War II. Throughout history, mankind has become increasingly destructive. One of these days we'll blow ourselves into self-annihilation and civilization will vanish.

Note that every one of these developmental sentences introduces a new topic, each one itself generating questions that need development. Thus, this "paragraph" is not really a paragraph at all, but simply a collection of topic sentences arranged to *look* like a paragraph. The whole passage consists of statements of about the same level of generality; the concept of specific development is ignored.

Stick To the Main Point; Maintain a Sense of Unity

The pseudo paragraph above possesses a unity of sorts in that each sentence is in some way related to nuclear explosions. But since each sentence introduces a new topic which takes off in a different direction, the unity is far too loose for an effective paragraph.

A more clear-cut violation of unity is seen in a paragraph such as the one below in which the topic sentence states one point but the development talks about another. (This paragraph is one of a series in which the writer explained how he conquered his anxieties while giving an oral report.)

> Another factor which helped reduce my nervousness was the use of visual aids. Explaining a subject such as ventilation systems would be difficult without the use of visual aids. As the saying goes, "A picture is worth a thousand words." Nothing could explain my subject better than a series of diagrams, and I found this device helped convey my ideas better than any other I could have used.

Another violation of paragraph unity occurs when part of the paragraph appears to (or actually does) contradict another part. Consider this example:

> The Omicron Corporation operates on a decentralized basis. The purchasing policies are all controlled by a Director of Purchasing at Central Office.

One is left wondering whether central control of purchasing policies is an exception, or what the relationship may be between the seemingly contradictory statements.

Use Appropriate Methods of Development

Many methods exist for developing a topic sentence. Some of the more common, illustrated below, include analysis, classification, definition, description, comparison, contrast, example, statistics, and testimony. The particular choice of methods given here is relatively unimportant; no claim is made that these are the *only* means of paragraph development. What is important is that each method represents a way of developing a general idea at a more specific level. In practice, of course, the writer may use more than one method in a given paragraph. Which method, or combination of methods, a writer uses will vary with the situation.

Analysis   This means developing a complex idea in terms of its component elements:

> The marketing concept encompasses four major elements: (1) *consumer orientation* (marketing begins and ends with needs of the consumer, not with the goal and objectives of the organization); (2) *social process* (marketing is a social process involving many participants); (3) *integrated effort* (marketing

is a broader concept than selling; it is the integration of marketing research, product conception, promotion, pricing, and physical distribution effort); and (4) *profitable operation* (marketing is concerned with profitability, a prerequisite for viability in the long run, rather than merely generating sales volume). The Louisiana model adopted the spirit of the marketing concept at its inception. Manifestations of its application of the marketing concept are examined below.[13]

Note that in the above paragraph the main idea is contained within the clause preceding the colon. The author could, of course, have written, "The marketing concept encompasses four major elements. These elements are . . ."—but this would have been unnecessarily wordy and cumbersome.

Classification   This is grouping specific elements or data into convenient categories:

> The data in this study were analyzed by grouping the yearly amount of sick leave taken into the following categories: 1 to 9 days, 10 to 19 days, 20 to 29 days, 30 to 39 days, 40 to 49 days, and 50 or more days and by cross-classifying these categories by degrees of formal education, other education, salary, age and seniority.[14]

Definition   This is explaining what a term or concept means:

> As defined in our business, a loss is any thing that does not directly produce a profit. By this definition, stock handling is a loss, since any equipment which simply transports stock takes up "unnecessary" floor space, and floor space is money. Clean-up operations are losses, and although clean-up men are necessary, their salary is put in the losses column. Breakdowns are a major loss, as is personal time or "break" time.

Description   This means telling about something in terms of how it appears or sounds—or however it may be perceived by the senses. Here for example are two paragraphs consisting of descriptive details about the city of Phoenix, Arizona, taken from an article analyzing some of Phoenix's urban problems:

> The desert north of this city has been described as the most beautiful in the world. Giant saguaro cactuses dot the landscape. Paloverde trees blossom in spectacular yellow, and desert hackberry bushes thrive along the washes. Coyotes and road runners dart among boulders.

> Day by day, however, the wild, open desert is being gobbled up by the spreading metropolis of Phoenix. Signs sprout among the mesquite and yucca: "Ironwoods Apartments—Adult Desert Living," or "Saguaro West, a Mobile Home Subdivision—Own Your Own Desert Estate."[15]

Comparison This is focusing on similarities between two or more activities, situations, persons, or the like:

> Golf and high management positions call upon some of the same skills. Both require uncommon degrees of dedication, self-assurance, and the will to win. P. A. Ward-Thomas, the respected British golfing columnist, has written about "the abstracts of judgment, self-discipline and resilience of spirit that enable [great champions] to make the most of good fortune and the best of bad . . . the nervous control that under the severest strain will ensure the preservation of rhythm and timing; the gift of positive thought and the courage to face and overcome the prospect of victory." Obviously, these are not bad qualities for either businessmen or athletes to have.[16]

Contrast This means the emphasis is on differences rather than on similarities. The contrast may be handled in a single paragraph, as it was in the paragraph above (p. 96): "In the earlier years any job was considered good enough for most workers. But today's employees are saying that such is not the case any more." In the following example, the contrast is heightened by discussing in *separate* paragraphs two alternatives open to women seeking careers in management:

> If you decide that, realistically, there are no opportunities and your company is probably not about to become an equal opportunity employer, and the particular working climate is not especially rewarding, your strategy is clear: Move. If the corporate direction is favorable to women and you really love the place, but there is no slot clearly open for you up the road, the challenge for you is to create opportunities, using all you know and can discover about the general goals and forward impetus of the company and about yourself. The alternative is to develop skills more compatible with the openings that do exist.
>
> On the other hand, suppose you decide that there is no place for you to go and that even if there were, the chances are small that you, as a woman, would be given a shot at them—but you still feel this is your work "home." In this situation, you have come to the point of a large, basic decision: How important is it to you, really, to rise? Does making a career for yourself

outweigh the security and satisfaction that bind you to your particular job, your particular company? Where, exactly, does "getting ahead" fit into your whole system of values, and which aspect of the ascent is it that you really prize?[17]

Example This means making use of what Webster's *Eighth New Collegiate Dictionary* defines as "a particular single item, fact, incident, or aspect that is representative of all of a group or type." Using examples is one of the most effective means of presenting an abstract concept so it can be readily understood, identified with, and remembered by the reader. In the following paragraph the writer presents a brief case history to illustrate possible deficiencies of orientation programs for new management personnel:

> Lastly, there was George, a middle-aged physician on the staff of a large metropolitan hospital. Immediately after he was hired, he became deeply involved in his medical duties without bothering to complete his personnel forms, a function routinely included in the hospital's new employee orientation program. He simply did not care much about the organization's personnel programs, other than his own salary of course. Unfortunately, he was fatally stricken by a heart attack soon afterward. Since he did not complete his life insurance enrollment card, his benefits were seriously delayed, and his family suffered unnecessarily.[18]

In the paragraph below a hypothetical example is used effectively to explain the application of a specific hiring procedure.

> Basic tests of ability to perform the tasks required should be administered. For example, if a job requires lifting boxes from a pallet to a shelf 2½ feet high, and each box weighs 100 pounds, applicants should be asked to lift a 100 pound box to a height of 2½ feet. If he can't lift it without strain the candidate is automatically eliminated.[19]

Still another illustration of development by example is seen in the next paragraph in which specific details are cited to show probable effects of more and more people living in multiple-dwelling housing:

> The move toward communal living will result in more professional buying of consumer goods by trained and informed purchasing agents. The apartment corporation's purchasing officer will buy furnishings for the common guest quarters; equipment for the common bowling alleys, tennis courts, golf course, and swimming pool; appliances for the common cleaning, heating, and cooling of the units; equipment and food for

> the preparation of meals in a common kitchen to be delivered to the apartment units or eaten in a common dining room; and all equipment for the game rooms and dancing area.[20]

Statistics   Statistics are numerical data summarizing *numbers* of examples rather than single examples. Single examples are often useful for illustrating or dramatizing a point. But to attempt to *prove* a point through one or two examples results in the fallacy of hasty generalization—bad logic damaging both to the writer's case and his or her credibility. Therefore, a writer may need to present statistics, either to describe adequately a general situation, or to prove that it exists. In the following example, statistics are used effectively to show suicide trends by age groups and ethnic groups:

> Meantime, suicide is rising sharply among young people, from 1,958 in 1951 to 2,319 in 1961 to 5,548 in 1971—and is the second most common cause of death in that age group, after accidents. Researchers claim that perhaps 70,000 to 80,000 young people between the ages of 15 and 24 will attempt suicide in the next 12 months—and 3,500 to 4,000 will succeed.
>
> Black women show an increase of 80 per cent in suicides in the last 20 years. Among Indians, the rate has gone up from 9.8 per 100,000 in 1957 to 11.7 in 1972—and today, among some tribes, the suicide rates is five times higher than the national average. Suicide statistics among Indians show that 70 per cent of all attempts are made by Indian females and 70 per cent of all deaths resulting from suicide occur among men.[21]

A word of caution is in order: Statistics can be tricky and many readers are suspicious of them (remember the familiar saying, "There are lies, damn lies, and statistics"). In using them, therefore, be sure they are accurate and present an undistorted picture. Be sure, also, to make clear the point they are intended to support. Otherwise, your readers may be confused, skeptical, or both. If so, the message you convey may not be the one you thought you were conveying, but rather the message that you are not entirely to be trusted.

Testimony   Using testimony means quoting from others. If a writer is not an expert on the subject, he or she can strengthen his or her credibility by quoting from someone who is. In an article on test marketing, the authors quote from a marketing authority, Henry J. Claycamp, Vice President, Corporate Marketing, International Harvester Company. Note that this is a *direct quotation* (that is, the words of the authority are quoted directly):

> Test markets provide better estimates of consumer response than any pretesting. But, as Claycamp emphasizes, "About all

you can expect from a test market is the answers to the questions that you are asking of it. In other words, one has to be very specific about what one wants from a test market. For this reason, they really are designed only for go/no-go decisions."[22]

If the precise wording of the authority is less critical, the writer may use an *indirect quotation* instead, commonly introduced by "that," not enclosed in quotation marks, and consisting of either the exact wording or a paraphrase of the authority's remarks. Thus:

In a 1937 paper, Dr. Charles Prudhomme, a Washington, D.C. psychiatrist and psychoanalyst, predicted that suicide among blacks would increase in direct proportion to their status change. He is now predicting a skyrocketing of black suicides, especially among males, because of job reversals.[23]

Finally, a writer may simply present a general assertion, then support it by naming sources who concur. From another standpoint, this illustrates development by example as well (that is, examples of authorities supporting the point at hand):

Many companies have management weaknesses because they forget a basic step in finding senior executives. So say three experienced executive search consultants: Edmund R. Hergenrather, Hergenrather & Co., Los Angeles; Bridgford Hunt, The Hunt Company, New York City; and Jack Lawrence, Jack Lawrence & Company, Inc., New York City.[24]

Maintain a Sense of Continuity and Coherence

Continuity is the flow of ideas, the forward movement, from sentence to sentence and paragraph to paragraph; *coherence* is how well a paragraph "sticks together." Consider for example this opening paragraph of a recent article by Lowell Thomas, "Nature's Seven Greatest Wonders":

Back in the second century B.C. when the Hellenistic Writer Antipater selected the "Seven Wonders of the World," he described not one of Nature's marvels, only those that were man-made. But the humbling truth is that even the mightiest of man's creations don't come close to Nature's top handiwork. So, I invite you to consider the works of Nature that I have found most exciting, awesome and inspiring during a lifetime of wandering our planet.[25]

Note what little effort is required to follow the flow of thought from beginning to end. In analyzing this paragraph to discover the reasons, one finds that two devices seem to stand out: reference words and relationship words.

Reference words are those which refer to an earlier idea and serve to carry forward that idea. For example, in the paragraph above:

he	refers back to	Antipater
"Nature's top handiwork"	refers back to	"Nature's marvels"
"works of Nature"	refers back to	"Nature's top handiwork"

Relationship words are those showing such relationships between ideas as chronological sequence, comparison or contrast, or cause and effect. In the above paragraph, for example, "but" clearly points up the contrast between man-made creations and Nature's creations. "So" indicates a causal relationship; in effect Thomas is saying "because Antipater neglected to mention Nature's marvels, I shall do so myself." In addition, note the chronological sequence implied between "back in the second century" of the first sentence and "I invite you to consider the works of Nature that I have found most exciting" of the closing sentence. Indeed, not just mere chronology, but contrast also is indicated by the past tense of what Antipater "selected" and "described" and the present perfect tense of what "I have found."

Thus, both continuity and coherence are well illustrated in this paragraph. To heighten your awareness of the importance of these factors, read the following, taken from a discussion of vocal cues in nonverbal communication:

> Human sensitivity to unpleasant levels of sound is reflected in the present concern with noise pollution. The noises of jet aircraft are not the only disturbing sounds. The person who speaks too loudly often offends others. Most people link volume to certain personality traits; it is commonly thought that an aggressive person speaks in a louder voice than one who is reserved and shy. Volume is not necessarily a function of personality. A person's models as a child can influence his volume level somewhat apart from his personality.

Sounds disjointed and lacking in cohesion, doesn't it? Now read the version as it was actually printed in the text. Note how the inclusion of just the few italicized words, like pieces missing from a jigsaw puzzle, complete the meaning so it does "stick together":

> Human sensitivity to unpleasant levels of sound is reflected in the present concern with noise pollution. *But* the noises of jet aircraft are not the only disturbing sounds. The person who speaks too loudly often offends others. *In fact,* most people link volume to certain personality traits; *thus* it is commonly thought that an aggressive person speaks in a louder voice than

one who is reserved and shy. Volume, *however,* is not necessarily a function of personality. A person's models as a child can influence his volume level somewhat apart from his personality.[26]

Continuity is damaged too, if essential links are omitted in the chain of reasoning. A college student visiting a friend in another state wrote his parents, "It's been so hot here I've had to sleep under an electric blanket." His parents were understandably confused until it was explained to them that because of the heat, the central air conditioning in the house had left the basement guest room, where he was housed, so chilly that his hostess had provided an electric blanket so he could sleep in comfort. In his letter he had unthinkingly omitted a link in the story.

In the same light, consider this example:

> Job enrichment is very much in vogue today. Most of the articles, however, are of a general, nonspecific nature, for studies in this new field have not produced much practical information on how to implement job enrichment programs.

Most of *what* articles? In the version above, the phrase "the articles" implies previous mention of articles that have been published. The original paragraph, from which the above was adapted, makes sense because it includes this missing link:

> Job enrichment is very much in vogue today. Personnel and training journals, industry and trade magazines carry articles on the subject with increasing frequency. Most of these articles, however, are of a general, non-specific nature . . . .[27]

We have spoken of using reference and relationship words, and not omitting links in the chain of reasoning, as if these were magic devices automatically guaranteeing continuity and coherence. However, continuity and coherence must originate in the writer's mind. If the writer's thinking is muddled, no amount of stylistic gimmickry will save him or her. But if one has carefully thought through one's ideas, one's writing will reflect this. The function of whatever devices you use will then serve to aid the reader in perceiving more clearly the meaning inherent in the message.

Develop Your Ideas Sufficiently so Your Reader Is Not Left Wondering

The essence of effective business communication is *reader-centeredness.* No matter how clearly we may understand what we write, if the meaning is unclear to the reader, we have not communicated—not, at least, to the reader's satisfaction.

The parents of a son in college (located over a hundred miles away) returned home one evening after a few hours away to unexpectedly discover this note in the kitchen:

> Mom & Dad
>   I was passing
> through & was here &
> you weren't.
>   Love,
>   Dave

Such a masterpiece of noncommunication is bound to raise more questions than answers: When was he passing through? Why? Where was he headed? Why did he stop—for a meal? Just to say "Hi"? Was he alone? And so on.

The following examples from business reports suffer the same shortcomings:

> Once we got there, we discovered there was not much we could do with the operators or their methods. [*Why?* No explanation is provided.]
>
> One of the disadvantages is that oil usually cannot be piped too far because of insufficient pressure. [How far is "too far"? How much *is* the pressure? How serious a disadvantage is this? Again, there is no explanation.]

It is possible to provide more detail than necessary, but the fault almost always is in providing too little. A classic example is the case of the director of quality control of a foreign auto firm who one day received a telex (a message similar to a cablegram but produced on a teletypewriter) from an American distributor complaining of a wiring defect in the instrument panel. The quality control director examined several vehicles in stock, but finding no defect, sent back a telex requesting more details. The next telex was more specific, but still failed to provide sufficient information. Perplexed, the director called two engineers on his staff to search with him. Giving up after an hour, he shot off a second inquiry, which fortunately brought forth sufficient detail so the defect could finally be found. Without doubt, an extra sentence or two in the original telex could have saved several lost working hours (and in business, time means money), to say nothing of considerable annoyance.

Nor is this example rare. A research administrator has stated that when problems from the field are directed to his attention, more often than not he must first secure additional information before he knows enough of the problem to attempt a solution. Like any competent physician, he must be able to diagnose adequately before prescribing a cure. And a director of labor relations has emphasized that in grievance reports submitted to him by factory supervisors (so he can intelligently seek resolution with union representatives of labor problems in the shop) he wants as much relevant detail as the supervisor can supply. "If a supervisor walked past wearing a red tie and you're in doubt about whether this is relevant, put it in. I can decide for myself whether it is information I need."

Another occasion for providing sufficient development is to make sure the reader understands the reason for a given instruction or course of action. "Don't light a match to see if you have any gas left in the tank" is likely to be less effective than if the reason is added, "You may blow yourself up if you do." Pointing out the consequences (either negative or positive) is an excellent way to emphasize a point and secure cooperation.

At this point you may be wondering whether we haven't forgotten the business reader's demand for time-saving communications. We have not, but bear these points in mind:

1. Messages that require follow-up to be clear do not save time; they waste it.

2. Amount of information must not be confused with wordiness of expression. Busy executives do not object to whatever information is necessary, *provided* it is stated clearly and concisely. They do become annoyed if it is unclear or verbose.

3. The efficiently organized message states the gist at the outset. Readers can then proceed further into the details if they need to.

Frances Christensen, founder of what has been called "the new rhetoric," has rightly said that *"providing the necessary development for an idea makes the difference between self-expression and communication"* [italics mine].[28] The importance of this principle to a reader-centered approach can scarcely be overemphasized.

Decide on the Appropriate Length for each Paragraph

Effective paragraph length is partially a matter of *format* and partially of *content*. As a matter of format, it serves to make the page more inviting by dividing it into sections along the way, thus making the going look easier. Imagine trying to read this or any other text with no paragraph breaks whatever. For a small sample of what it would be like, read the following:

> Jurgen Ruesch, a psychiatrist, and Weldon Kees, a film producer, were two of the first people to devote themselves to a serious study of nonverbal communication in daily experience. They suggest that we express nonverbal messages in one of three languages: sign language, action language, or object language. We are using sign language when we deliberately use gestures to replace words, numbers, or punctuation marks. The gesture can be as simple as the peace sign or the hitchhiker's signal or as complex as the system of signals motorists

use while driving. Ruesch and Kees classify as action language all the movements that we do not use exclusively as signals—walking, running, eating, and so on. Many if not most of these actions are unintentional nonverbal stimuli. For example, if while walking your head droops and your shoulders sag, your posture expresses your mood. If you slam your fist on a table during a stalemated argument, your action conveys anger and frustration very directly. Action language is the principal means of expressing emotion. Object language is the intentional or unintentional display of material things—art objects, machines, clothing, jewelry, and so on. A social worker who appears in a ghetto neighborhood driving a big car and wearing expensive clothes is obviously using the wrong language if he hopes to establish rapport with the residents.

Now compare the unbroken format of the above with the same passage as it was actually printed. What before was a single paragraph has now become four paragraphs. The content remains the same, but the format is vastly more inviting.

Jurgen Ruesch, a psychiatrist, and Weldon Kees, a film producer, were two of the first people to devote themselves to a serious study of nonverbal communication in daily experience. They suggest that we express nonverbal messages in one of three languages: sign language, action language, or object language.

We are using *sign language* when we deliberately use gestures to replace words, numbers, or punctuation marks. The gesture can be as simple as the peace sign or the hitchhiker's signal or as complex as the system of signals motorists use while driving.

Ruesch and Kees classify as *action language* all the movements that we do not use exclusively as signals—walking, running, eating, and so on. Many if not most of these actions are unintentional nonverbal stimuli. For example, if while walking your head droops and your shoulders sag, your posture expresses your mood. If you slam your fist on a table during a stalemated argument, your action conveys anger and frustration very directly. Action language is the principal means of expressing emotion.

Object language is the intentional or unintentional display of material things—are objects, machines, clothing, jewelry, and so on. A social worker who appears in a ghetto neighborhood driving a big car and wearing expensive clothes is obviously using the wrong language if he hopes to establish rapport with the residents.[29]

If we examine the above example from the standpoint of content, we discover that what was shown first as a single unbroken passage naturally divides into the four paragraphs of the second version. First is an opening paragraph introducing three kinds of nonverbal language, then a paragraph apiece for each of the three. So while the format is improved considerably from the paragraphing, the breaks are not arbitrary but governed by content.

How long, then, should a paragraph be? From the point of view of content, it should be long enough to develop adequately its particular topic. From the point of view of format, a better question is: "How long should it *not* be?" Perhaps the best answer is that it should not be so long that it looks uninviting to read. This means, as a rule, at least two or three paragraph breaks per page, thus allowing readers an opportunity to pause and "catch their breath," so to speak.

Expressed differently, a paragraph in business writing should seldom exceed around 150 words; many will run less. When longer, chances are that the main idea can (and should) be subdivided into two or three related ideas and the paragraphs restructured as two or three paragraphs—as in the example just considered.

However, there are exceptions. In certain conditions, paragraphs are characteristically shorter than the suggested 150-word maximum. These include the following:

1. Introductory paragraphs that simply announce topics to be discussed in the ensuing paragraphs. The paragraph introducing the three kinds of nonverbal language is an example.

2. Transitional paragraphs, serving to point up the connection between two major topics. Following is a typical example:

> With these key factors of behavior change in mind—communication, motivation, and trust—let us examine the election campaign at the Apex company.[30]

3. Concluding paragraphs serving to point up the main idea the writer wants the reader to remember. Following is the final paragraph of an article on the use of sick leave by female employees:

> It appears that the employees who took the *least* amount of sick leave were employees under 30 years of age with some business college background, a salary of $250 to $499, and less than 50 months of seniority.[31]

4. Paragraphs in a memo which need little if any development because the topic is already familiar to the reader. Memos of this type are usually announcements or reminders, such as the following:

> SUBJECT: Safety Committee Meeting   DATE: 8/7/74
> TO: Members, Safety Committee

There will be a meeting of the Safety Committee on Monday, Aug. 12, 2-3, in M. Scott's Conference Rm. Purpose: to finalize regulations for the drill press area.

Sharon Jones will also present findings of her investigation on the new Luxor line of safety glasses.

Ann Pohlod

SUMMARY

1. Paragraphing serves several valuable functions in writing. These include (a) requiring writers to distinguish between their main and supporting ideas, (b) helping the reader identify the writer's main and supporting ideas, and (c) breaking the format so the material looks more inviting to read.

2. A paragraph is best thought of as consisting of two basic elements: a main idea, expressed in a topic sentence, and its supporting detail.

3. The topic sentence is the most general sentence in the paragraph and needs further development to complete the thought it introduces. In business writing it should be located at the beginning of the paragraph, and should be phrased concisely to focus clearly on the main idea, leaving the development to the rest of the paragraph. Whenever appropriate the topic sentence should be phrased to suggest the plan of development. If the paragraph is one of a related series, the topic sentence should suggest the nature of the relationship between that paragraph and what has preceded.

4. The development of the topic sentence should be unified and relatively specific. Methods of development include analysis, classification, definition, description, comparison, contrast, example, statistics, and testimony. The development should exhibit a sense of continuity and coherence, and be complete enough for adequate reader understanding. As a rule, a developmental paragraph should not exceed around 150 words. If it is a beginning, transitional, or closing paragraph, or if the purpose is primarily for attention or emphasis, it will seldom exceed 30-40 words. Paragraphs in a memo are also often brief.

SUGGESTED APPLICATIONS

1. The article below appeared in *Time* magazine in the fall of 1974. After reading it, write a paper of 5 to 6 paragraphs taking a definite position on one or more points in the article. Begin with an introductory paragraph, use a different method of development (analysis, classification, and so on) for each of your middle paragraphs, and end with a concluding paragraph.

In the margin at the left of each of the middle paragraphs label, in parentheses, the method of development used for that paragraph. Consciously attempt to apply in the most effective way possible the principles of paragraphing discussed in this chapter.

NOW, THE SELF-CENTERED GENERATION

A new spirit clearly dominates U.S. college campuses as 8.6 million young people begin the fall term this month. Not since the 1950s have students been so pragmatic in their outlook, so highly oriented toward careers and financial security. Deeply worried about an economy that is fraught with future uncertainties, overwhelmingly concerned with preparing for lucrative and satisfying jobs, today's college students can be fairly characterized as the Self-Centered Generation.

Once the draft and the threat of the Viet Nam War ended, American campuses reverted to a normality of sorts. The old political activism and revolutionary fervor have disappeared entirely. Indeed, the shifts in student attitudes and outlook since the late 1960s are so startling that they clearly mark the end of an old era and the beginning of a new one.

"Unwanted Group." The mood is strikingly similar to that of the 1950s Silent Generation, in that today's students are chiefly concerned with their own personal lives. Says Senior Steve Ainsworth, 21, former editor of the *Daily Bruin,* the student newspaper at the University of California at Los Angeles: "The mood is, 'I'm here for me.' The kids are preoccupied with going into the mainstream of economic life."

But the analogy to the 1950s is only partly valid. Studies by Daniel Yankelovich, the public-opinion analyst who periodically surveys American youth, document the fact that the social and moral values that flourished on campus in the 1960s "have grown stronger and more powerful." More liberal sexual mores, a lessening of automatic obedience to established authority and skepticism about the U.S. political process seem to have become fixed characteristics of most American young people.

The overriding influence on student attitudes today is the economy. TIME reporters recently visited two dozen campuses and found that the greatest worry among students is that there will be no jobs for them after graduation. Says Princeton Junior Peter Seldin: "It's depressing to be part of an unwanted group." Moreover, as part of the enduring heritage of the 1960s, students want their careers to provide them with greater self-expression and self-fulfillment as well as high salaries.

That is a significant departure from what young people sought in the 1950s and substantially narrows their future job options.

Students are most interested in preparing for professions like law, medicine and architecture. Claims Senior Judy Wandzilak, 21, of Boston University: "The gut [easy] course is no longer avidly sought. Students can't afford to waste their time and money. They are seeking tangible, not spiritual returns for their investment in a university."

More often than not, freshmen (or "freshpersons" as some feminists solemnly call them) enter college with firm ideas about what courses will prepare them for their chosen careers. Nearly everywhere, chemistry, biology, engineering and business administration classes are packed, while enrollments are dwindling in history, philosophy and the other liberal arts. Quips Tony Peyser, 20, a student in film making at U.C.L.A.: "English is the best prerequisite for unemployment." Black-studies courses are being cut back at some campuses because most black students prefer majors that lead directly to a career.

Young people are approaching their studies with newfound seriousness, crowding into college libraries and competing feverishly for grades. Observes Yale Philosophy Professor Michael Williams, 27: "There's not much goofing off these days." At Brandeis University in Waltham, Mass., close to a third of the 690 freshmen told school officials that they hope to be medical doctors. Shoving matches broke out among some students in the crush to register for premed courses. In one dormitory at the University of Kansas, some 250 students expressed interest in a remedial clinic that aims to raise their grades by improving their reading and study skills; last year only six students wanted to take the optional course.

No Regulations. Inflation has contributed significantly to students' newly sober attitude toward higher education. A year's average tuition and room and board at a private college costs about $3,200; at many schools the total is close to $5,000. "One of the first things the students do is look for part-time jobs," says Eileen Roberson, director of student employment at Simmons College in Boston. Among the most common jobs: waiting on table, manning switchboards and doing research for professors.

Partly because students want to save money, there is a renewed interest in communal living in dormitories as an alternative to more expensive off-campus apartments. Quite a few colleges have abolished most dormitory rules. At Berkeley, says Ben Leifer, 21, a graduate student in public health, "there are virtually no regulations except be discreet, mind your own business and don't bother anyone." Hampshire College in Amherst, Mass., permits students in dormitory suites to choose their own roommates—of whatever sex.

The desire for communal living, as well as the return to normality, has been chiefly responsible for the resurgence of college fraternities and sororities. At the University of California at Berkeley, which gave birth to the student counterculture with the Free Speech Movement ten years ago, the number of fraternities has risen from 24 in 1971 to 28 now; ten others want to reopen chapters that were closed in the 1960s for lack of members.

"Prudes' Palace." At most colleges, the sexual revolution is over; premarital sex and cohabitation among unmarried students are accepted as a matter of course. More recently, students at many campuses have become highly tolerant of homosexual and bisexual behavior. Among the most extreme avant-garde students at Berkeley and Columbia, it has become fashionable to have a homosexual or bisexual experience. On the other hand, at some campuses there has been a noticeable reaction against the new permissiveness. For example, one women's dormitory at the University of Michigan used to be sniggeringly called "Prudes' Palace" or the "Virgin Vault" because men were banned above the first floor during weekdays. This year, however, it has a waiting list of more than 50 coeds.

The student orientation toward jobs has even contributed to the comeback on campus of beer and liquor, since many student fear that a drug arrest might ruin their chances for a successful career. Moreover, they often find alcohol to be cheaper than drugs, which have been hard hit by inflation. At Boston University, Quaaludes have gone from 30¢ a tablet to as high as $3; at the University of Michigan, an ounce of marijuana costs as much as $15, up from $12 last year.

For all their new seriousness, students still blow off steam. They have rediscovered some old fads—panty raids at the University of Michigan and the twist at Houston's Rice University—and some other fancies as well. Among undergraduates at Wake Forest University in Winston-Salem, N.C., rides in large coin-operated clothes dryers are the latest thrill—with the door open or, more dangerously because of the heat, with it closed. Admits Junior Steve Wildey, 20: "It sounds kind of dumb. But after a few beers, it seems like an entirely reasonable thing to do."

Most disturbing for the nation's future, students demonstrate almost no interest in political activities, on or off campus. There are rare exceptions. In 21 states, small numbers of student activists operate public-interest research groups, which lobby for education bills in state legislatures and try to influence state politics. For example, New York's group recently published pamphlet-size political profiles of each of the 60 senators and 150 assemblymen who are running for re-election to the state legislature.

Moreover, many young people still follow and react to big political developments, though not to the rancorous extremes of a few years ago. Not surprisingly, President Ford's promise of limited amnesty for Viet Nam War-era deserters and draft dodgers won him a measure of popularity in campus communities, while his full pardon of former President Nixon produced cries of outrage. On a Sunday evening a student called a talk show in Lawrence, Kans., and suggested that instead of pardoning Nixon, Ford should have urged him to go to Canada.

Afraid to Believe. For the most part, however, students seem unwilling to involve themselves directly in the U.S. political process. A recent survey showed that half of the students polled at the University of Missouri are not even registered to vote. At the University of Kansas, campus Democrats concluded after a poll that large numbers of students did not know that State Attorney General Vern Miller was a candidate for Governor, even though he had gained much notoriety for his flamboyant drug arrests of Kansas students. At the University of Wisconsin, says Tim Tully, 28, a graduate student and veteran radical of the 1960s, "all the activity of late in Madison, political or otherwise, would fit in a shot glass."

Indeed, not even Watergate reignited students' interest in politics. According to Yankelovich, more than six out of ten young people believe that "special interests" run the nation's political machinery. Similarly, George Mihaly, president of Gilbert Youth Research of New York City, recently found that only about 1% of students are thinking of politics as a career. "We know that people and movements are fallible," observes Margie Corbett, 21, a junior at American University in Washington. "We're afraid to believe too much in anything or anyone." Thus the overwhelming majority of students today are far more intent on using their college education as a means of entering the American system than as preparation for reforming it.[32]

2. The "Guidelines in Formulating the Topic Sentence" and "Guidelines for Developing the Topic Sentence" in this chapter are illustrated by examples from business periodicals. In like manner, consult issues from within the past six months of such magazines as *Nation's Business, Harvard Business Review,* and *Fortune* and find other examples that illustrate any five of the "guidelines" presented in the chapter. Write a report in which the body consists essentially of the five guidelines, followed each in turn by the example (quoted verbatim) along with any commentary you wish. For each quoted passage, give credit with a footnote, just as was done in the chapter. Begin with a brief introductory paragraph, and end with a concluding paragraph offering any relevant summary or evaluative comments you wish. Use appropriate main and subheadings throughout.

3. Observing the guidelines given in this chapter for formulating and developing the topic sentence, write a paragraph in which you:

    a. Analyze the elements or attributes of a concept such as "friendship," "love," "hate," "cooperation," "popularity," or "idealism."

    b. Use classification as a means of describing the membership of this class, or your living unit in the dormitory.

    c. Define one of these terms: "deception in advertising," "freedom of speech," "women's liberation," "integration," or "mass transit."

    d. Describe a work area at school (an office, the library, your study desk) or where you are employed.

    e. Compare two people (professors, administrators, students), or two products (cars, stereos, hand calculators).

    f. Contrast two classes you are taking, two personality types, or two ways of doing something.

    g. Use one or more examples to illustrate a general idea, such as a popular saying or proverb.

    h. Use statistics to prove a point (for sources of statistics, ask your librarian; *The Statistical Abstract of the United States,* published annually, is one such source).

    i. Use testimony to support a point. (Any issue of *Newsweek* or *Time* contains dozens of quotations scattered throughout its news stories).

NOTES

[1] Harry H. Crosby and George F. Estey, *Just Rhetoric* (New York: Harper and Row Publishers, 1972), p. 30.

[2] *Ibid.,* p. 107.

[3] Robert R. Rathbone and James B. Stone, *A Writer's Guide for Engineers and Scientists* (Englewood Cliffs, N.J.: Prentice-Hall, Inc., 1962), pp. 7–8.

[4] "News You Can Use," *U.S. News and World Report,* July 1, 1974, p. 65.

[5] Roy W. Walters, "Job Enrichment Isn't Easy," *Personnel Administration/Public Personnel Review,* November–December, 1972, p. 61.

[6] W. J. Palmer, "An Integrated Program for Career Development," *Personnel Journal,* June, 1972, p. 404.

[7] Walters, p. 61.

[8] Adel I. El-Ansary and Oscar E. Kramer, Jr., "Social Marketing: The Family Planning Experience," *Journal of Marketing,* Vol. 37 (July, 1973), p. 1.

[9] Arthur E. Bedeian, "Superior-Subordinate Role Perception," *Personnel Administration/Public Personnel Review,* November–December, 1972, p. 10.

[10] *Ibid.*

[11] El-Ansary and Kramer, p. 1.

[12] Bedeian, p. 10.

[13] El-Ansary and Kramer, p. 2.

[14] Charles N. Weaver and Sandra L. Holmes, "On the Use of Sick Leave by Female Employees," *Personnel Administration/Public Personnel Review,* September–October, 1972, p. 47.

[15] Earl C. Gottschalk, Jr., "Phoenix Area's Sprawl Worries City Planners But Not Its Citizenry," *Wall Street Journal,* June 18, 1974, p. 1.

[16] William Emerson, "Golf Is a Blue-Chip Game," *Fortune,* December, 1973, p. 44.

[17] Jane J. Templeton and Naomi S. Marrow, "Women As Managers," *Personnel,* September–October, 1972, p. 33.

[18] Ted L. Kromer, "New Employee Orientation for Managers," *Personnel Journal,* June, 1972, p. 435.

[19] Walter L. Clarke, "A New Look at the Hiring Procedures," *Personnel Journal,* June, 1972, p. 429.

[20] Robert H. Myers, "Profiles of the Future," *Business Horizons,* February, 1972, p. 11.

[21] "Upsurge in Suicides—and Ways to Prevent Them," *U.S. News and World Report,* July 1, 1974, p. 47.

[22] Jay E. Klompmaker, G. David Hughes, and Russell I. Haley, "Test Marketing in New Product Development," *Harvard Business Review,* May–June, 1976, p. 134.

[23] "Upsurge in Suicides—and Ways to Prevent Them," op. cit., p. 47.

[24] "Position Description: A Key to Finding Good Executives," *Personnel Journal,* June, 1972, p. 450.

[25] Lowell Thomas, "Nature's Seven Greatest Wonders," *Reader's Digest,* July, 1974, p. 121.

[26] Stewart L. Tubbs and Sylvia Moss, *Human Communication: An Interpersonal Perspective* (New York: Random House, 1974), p. 158.

[27] Walters, p. 61.

[28] Quoted from Crosby and Estey, p. 116.

[29] Tubbs and Moss, pp. 143–144.

[30] Dean S. Ellis, Lawrence Jacobs, and Cory Mills, "A Union Authorization Election: The Key to Winning," *Personnel Journal,* April, 1972, p. 247.

[31] Weaver and Holmes, p. 50.

[32] "Now, the Self-Centered Generation," *Time,* September 23, 1974, pp. 84–85. © Time Inc., 1974.

EFFECTIVE SENTENCES

COMPLETENESS

COHERENT STRUCTURE

Faults that Weaken Coherence in Sentence Structure
    Overloading the Sentence   Using Comma Splices
    Mismanaging Modifiers
    Splitting Grammatical Constructions
    Making Vague or Ambiguous References
    Expressing Faulty Relationships
    Switching Point of View or Tense Unnecessarily
    Arranging Ideas in a Confused Sequence
    Using Contradictory Logic

Special Techniques for a More Coherent Structure
    Using a Direct Approach   Using Parallelism

EMPHASIS

Showing Equal Emphasis
    Use Parallelism   Use Coordinate Conjunctions
    Use Semicolons   Use Conjunctive Adverbs

Showing Reduced Emphasis
    Use a Weaker Grammatical Structure
    Locate Less Important Ideas in a Less Emphatic Position
    Use "De-emphasizing" Punctuation

Showing Increased Emphasis
    Use a Stronger Grammatical Structure
    Locate Important Ideas in the More Emphatic Position
    Use Short Sentences   Use Parallelism   Use Repetition
    Use "Emphasizing" Punctuation

APPROPRIATE LENGTH

The Question of Ideal Length

Uses of Sentences According to Length

Sentence Length: Some Closing Comments

CONCISENESS

Examples of Wordiness in Writing

Suggestions for Achieving Conciseness

VARIETY

Variety in Sentence Structure

Variety in Arrangement

Variety According to Function

Variety in Sentence Beginnings

Variety in Length

A Closing Note on Variety

WORD CHOICE

Simplicity

Jargon

Personal Style

    Personal Style in Business Correspondence
    Personal Style in Reports and Proposals
    Personal Style and the Passive Voice
    When to Use a Personal Style
    When to Use an Impersonal Style
    What Pronouns to Use

Triteness

In Chapter 5 we examined the paragraph as a structural unit in writing—a unit consisting of a general idea together with the development of that general idea. In this chapter we shall examine the element paragraphs are made of: sentences.

A *sentence* is the smallest verbal message unit, consisting of words that take on meaning only in the context of other words. Thus, out of context, the isolated words "has," "Catherine," "new," "car," and "a" do not express any meaning. But combining them so they read "Catherine has a new car," does express a meaning. It is true that a single word may express a meaning, but only in the context of other words, as, for example: "Did you write the letter yet?" "No." The "no" in this example has meaning only in relation to the question preceding it.

A more conventional way of defining a sentence is to say that it is a group of words containing a subject and predicate and expressing a complete thought. Although such a definition is acceptable enough, it will not be our primary concern in this chapter. What we *shall* be concerned with is writing sentences that are effective and faithfully reflect the flow of thought and shades of meaning you have in your mind. Although planning the structure of the entire message and the paragraphs comprising it is crucial, it is at the level of the sentence that you either do or do not write well. Unless you can express your ideas in effective sentences, woven together to form effective paragraphs, you can scarcely hope to communicate competently in writing.

What constitutes an effective sentence? Here are seven characteristics that effective sentences in business writing should possess. These seven characteristics will provide the structure for this chapter:

1. Completeness
2. Coherent structure
3. Emphasis
4. Appropriate length
5. Conciseness
6. Variety
7. Effective word choice

Complete sentences in business writing are virtually the norm. A coherent structure (one that hangs together) is an absolute must. Emphasis (signifying the relative importance of ideas) is only slightly less essential. Appropriate length, conciseness, and variety, though important, are secondary. Effective word choice affects the accuracy and readability of the message.

If you can master the techniques to achieve these characteristics, you will enhance both the clarity of your writing and your personal credibility as a writer.

COMPLETENESS

In business writing, a sentence is normally expected to express a complete thought. When the thought is not complete, the result is a sentence fragment, or incomplete sentence, illustrated by examples such as these:

> Only 27 percent availability of the computer system.

Here, "availability" is a subject without a predicate. If written "Only 27 percent availability of the computer system was being used," the sentence is complete.

Another example is:

> Not to mention proprietary items where patents on materials or processes demand that we purchase from single suppliers.

This passage, from a student paper, cannot stand alone, for it consists of only a phrase followed by a *dependent clause* (a clause that depends on further information for the thought to be complete). When joined with an *independent clause* preceding it, the incompleteness is eliminated: "We were depending too heavily on specialized suppliers for essential items, not to mention proprietary items where patents on materials or processes demand that we purchase from a single supplier."

> In order to maintain the flow of materials and reduce the risk of error.

This consists of nothing but a series of phrases (infinitive and prepositional) with no subject or predicate. But it can acceptably be used to introduce a complete sentence: "In order to maintain the flow of materials and reduce the risk of error, the purchasing department must exercise constant vigilance."

The requirement for "completeness" in creative writing allows greater freedom. Here, sentence fragments are often used for expressing the mood of the writer or evoking a mood in the reader. Observe, for example, this passage from Anne Morrow Lindbergh's *Bring Me A Unicorn,* describing a Christmas party attended by Colonel Lindbergh shortly after she had first met him:

> Then dancing. I loved it, in spite of myself, and felt, for a while, un-self-conscious—blessedly so. Music does that, and dancing. It is so heavenly—I glowed with the pleasure of it. Commander Hamilton danced divinely. *He* [Colonel Lindbergh] didn't dance but stood apart and watched—not with envy, but with a kind of dazed pleasure. Grateful, perhaps, to be a silent spectator for a while. But quite dazed.[1]

Of the eight sentence units quoted, three are fragments, skillfully employed. In advertisements, fragments are also frequently used, as in this announcement of a series of radio broadcasts commemorating the Bicentennial:

> On nine weekends over the next year-and-a-half, in 30 different reports each weekend, CBS News Correspondents will talk about America. What it looked like back then. What the founding fathers might think of us today. How Christmas has changed. And our humor. And the people themselves.[2]

But in formal business writing, fragments are seldom if ever used. To be on the safe side, avoid them.

COHERENT STRUCTURE

A requirement as crucial—and difficult—as completeness is *coherent structure*. A sentence possesses coherent structure when the ideas it contains relate logically to each other, are arranged in an orderly pattern, and work *with* each other instead of at cross-purposes; in short, the ideas as expressed make sense—not only to the writer, but to the reader as well. Mastery of the elements of coherent structure is basic to mastery of writing good sentences.

Faults that Weaken Coherence in Sentence Structure

Among the faults that weaken coherence in sentences are these:

- overloading the sentence
- using comma splices
- mismanaging modifiers
- splitting grammatical constructions
- making vague or ambiguous references
- expressing faulty relationships
- switching point of view or tense unnecessarily
- arranging ideas in a confused sequence
- using contradictory logic

Let us examine each of these in turn.

Overloading the Sentence An overloaded sentence is one that is crowded with more ideas than its structure will bear. Like a neat stack of blocks when one too many is added, a sentence tends to fall apart and lose its coherence when it is overloaded. An example of overloading is seen in this sentence:

> Posted on the bulletin board in the supervisor's office would be the number of parts produced for the month, as well as the number of parts expected to be produced, *and* these figures would be updated daily so all the employees, as well as the foreman, would know how their department compared with other departments.

By the time the "and" is reached, the reader needs a break. Omitting the "and" and starting a new sentence with "These figures" would give that break. As it is, the sentence is too unwieldy to hang together tightly. The coherence is weakened and the readability reduced.

From this example, it might appear that overloading is caused by long sentences (62 words in this case). But as we shall see later, sentence length in itself is not the main factor. Structure is. In the example just cited, too many ideas not closely enough related were crowded into one sentence, and the structure (especially at the "and") was too weak for the weight. With a sounder structure the overloading would not have resulted.

Using Comma Splices A comma splice consists of independent clauses joined only by a comma. Consider this example:

> Upon expiration of the period for which full salary is paid, payment will be reduced to an amount equal to 60% of your

> base salary, as indicated in the letter dated 2-26-76, Social Security Disability Benefits awarded are integrated by the company and our insurance carrier.[3]

Note that a period (or semicolon) instead of a comma should be placed after "base salary," and a new sentence begun.

Let us consider another example:

> The third proposed solution was the "Employee Reward" plan, the reward plan was intended to improve employee performance.

Several remedies for strengthening the coherence of this passage are available. The most obvious, perhaps, would be to replace the comma with a period to form two sentences:

> . . . plan. The reward plan . . .

However, since the ideas in the two clauses are closely related, punctuating them as separate sentences fails to suggest this relationship adequately. Although the period remedies the weak connection grammatically, the coherence is not greatly improved. An improved remedy would be to use a semicolon instead:

> . . . the plan; the reward plan . . .

The semicolon forms a stronger bond than does a comma, and is the standard punctuation for joining independent clauses. In addition, since the two ideas are now combined in one sentence, their relationship is more obvious and the coherence thus strengthened.

But this remedy is still not the best. The second clause is worded as if equal to the first (that is, both are independent clauses, grammatically of the same rank). Besides, it repeats "the reward plan" unnecessarily, so is wordier than need be. Consequently, a better remedy would be to convert the second independent clause to one that is dependent, as follows:

> . . . the plan, which was intended . . .

Because of the dependent relationship now introduced, this version draws the two ideas more closely together, so improves the coherence—and the conciseness as well. But for still tighter coherence and greater conciseness, the best remedy would be to reduce the dependent clause to a modifying phrase:

> The third proposed solution was the "Employee Reward" plan, intended to improve employee performance.

The preferred remedy in this example was simple enough: simply delete the four words "the reward plan was." But more important than the particular remedy is understanding the rationale behind it. Knowing both how and why helps make the difference between writing like a rookie and writing like a pro.

We stated above that if independent clauses in a series are short and closely enough related, joining them with commas does not damage the coherence. The classical example is Caesar's introduction to the account of his conquest of Gaul: "I came, I saw, I conquered." A modern counterpart—more prosaic, to be sure—might be, "I examined the claim, I found nothing wrong, I shall not alter my position."

In examples such as these, the shorter and more closely related the clauses, the more appropriate are commas in place of semicolons or periods, since commas more closely connect the related elements. (Thus, because the clauses are shorter, a better case can be made for the commas in Caesar's sentence than in our current-day counterpart.)

Mismanaging Modifiers A *modifier* is a word, phrase, or clause that describes or elaborates on—thus, "modifies"—the meaning of another word, usually a noun, pronoun, or verb. Much of the richness of a sentence is derived from its modifiers. But if they are "mismanaged," the coherence of the sentence can be seriously flawed. Three kinds of mismanagement include misplacing a modifier, leaving a modifier "dangling," and using a "squinting" modifier.

1. Misplacing modifiers. To eliminate confusion, a modifier should be placed next to or near the word it applies to. When misplaced, it weakens the coherent structure of the sentence by disturbing the orderly flow of ideas. The following examples will help illustrate:

> *Misplaced:*   This is done to eliminate a delay in reporting an aircraft that is down *to the control tower*.
>
> *Corrected:*   This is done to eliminate a delay in reporting *to the control tower* an aircraft that is down.
>
> *Misplaced:*   The reason for the probation period is that it is difficult to determine whether a trainee will become a competent operator *during the short period of the training program*.
>
> *Corrected:*   The reason for the probation period is that it is difficult to determine *during the short period of the training program* whether a trainee will become a competent operator.
>
> *Misplaced:*   There was a typewriter alongside the coatrack *that the secretary started to type on*.
>
> *Corrected:*   There was a coatrack alongside the typewriter *that the secretary started to type on*.
>
> *Misplaced:*   This can *only* prevent a few isolated cases.
>
> *Corrected:*   This can prevent *only* a few isolated cases.

"Only," it should be stressed, is one of the most commonly misplaced modifiers. To avoid misplacing it, put it directly *before* the word or phrase it modifies.

2. Dangling modifiers. A verbal phrase (such as, "working steadily," "to be certain," "sitting at my desk"—note that "working," "to be," and "sitting" are all verb forms; hence, the term, "verbal") has, of course, no subject of its own. Lacking one, it grammatically modifies the subject of the main clause it precedes. If it also *logically* modifies this subject, no problem arises. For example:

> *Working steadily,* I completed the job by 4:00.
> *To be certain,* we should consult the legal staff.
> *Sitting at my desk,* I saw the boss walk into my office.

But if these modifiers fail to modify the subject logically as well as gramatically, they are said to "dangle," since there is no logical connection. For example:

> *Working steadily,* the job was completed by 4:00.
> *To be certain,* the legal staff should be consulted.
> *Sitting at my desk,* the boss walked into my office.

Logic tells us that it was not the job that was "working steadily," the legal staff that wanted "to be certain," nor was the boss "sitting at my desk" when he or she walked into my office!

Clearly, a dangling modifier damages sentence coherence, since it expresses an illogical relationship. The sentence fails to hang together properly.

3. Squinting modifiers. A *squinting modifier* looks in both directions at once, but the reader has no way of being sure which direction the writer intended it to look. Again the coherence suffers. Examples of squinting modifiers are seen in these sentences:

> Parker has said *repeatedly* his department excels. [Has Parker said this repeatedly or does his department excel repeatedly?]
>
> The foreman stated *around 10:30* the situation began to worsen.

Depending on the intended meaning, the first sentence could be revised, "Parker repeatedly has said that his department excels" or "Parker has said that his department excels repeatedly." Likewise, the second sentence could be rewritten, "The foreman stated that the situation began to worsen around 10:30" or "The foreman stated around 10:30 that the situation began to worsen." Corrected, the weakened coherence is repaired.

Splitting Grammatical Constructions Certain grammatical constructions belong together, and normally should be written that way, just as a modifier should normally be placed near what it modifies. When such constructions are split, the sentence tends to lose coherence.

Split infinitives are a common example. For instance, "Wilson tried *to more fully comprehend* the implications of the problem" is better written

"Wilson tried *to comprehend* more fully the implications of the problem." Likewise, "Miss Scott hoped *to* with distinction *handle* the assignment" should be written "Miss Scott hoped *to handle* the assignment with distinction."

When verbs consist of two or more words, normally they should not be split either. Thus, "I *was* early in the week *asked* to investigate the case" should be "I *was asked* early in the week . . ." or "Early in the week I *was asked* . . ." But again, exceptions may apply, the most common being the insertion of a negative in the verb. Examples of this are: "The attempt *did* not *succeed*" or "Because the patient *was* barely *breathing,* the doctor was called back in the room." Another exception may result from giving a modifier special emphasis by locating it within the verb form, as "While Apex has *occasionally* let us down, over the years they have built a reputation for dependability." Splitting an infinitive may be justified similarly, as in "Visitors are requested to *please* use the visitors' parking lot." While infinitives and verbs sometimes may be split advantageously, the general rule cautions against splitting without a good reason.

Still another case of splitting that can strain coherence results from separating the subject unduly from its verb. The following examples illustrate what could be the unfortunate result:

> In this report, I shall relate an intriguing grievance that *I,* through the advice of my supervisor, *decided* to read.
>
> Beyond these, the *failure* to work directly with a child on his writing, to help the class write a group composition, to provide the encouragement needed, and to properly recognize [*to recognize properly?*] differences in children's abilities and interests *indicate* a lack of proper teacher guidance and direction.[4]

Note that in this sentence the distance between subject and verb is so great that the writer forgot that the subject was singular, and used a plural verb, so together they read "The failure indicate"!

Incidentally, while some might argue that the basic weakness of this sentence stems from its length (45 words), it would be more accurate to say instead that the weakness derives from faulty structure. If restructured to begin, "Beyond these, a lack of proper teacher guidance and direction is indicated by the failure to work directly . . . ," this sentence would offer little difficulty to either the reader or writer.

Separating elements that normally belong together may weaken the structure of the sentence. The practice should be exercised with caution.

Making Vague or Ambiguous References   A pronoun, of course, is a marvelously convenient device in writing, since it eliminates the need for clumsy, unnecessary repetition of whatever noun it stands for. Consider, for instance, the following: "Ms. Barrett has completed the report Ms.

Barrett was asked to write, and Ms. Barrett plans to give Ms. Barrett's report to Ms. Barrett's supervisor this afternoon." Substituting a "she," an "it," and a "her" would get rid of the clumsy repetitions completely: "Ms. Barrett has completed the report she was asked to write, and plans to give it to her supervisor this afternoon."

However, useful as pronouns are, and simple to use as they may seem to be, they can nevertheless damage sentence coherence badly if the reader is not clear what noun they stand for. Consider this example:

> As of today there are no requisitions in Crib 3 for any of these cutters. Where are they?

On reflection, you probably can decipher that "they" refers to requisitions, not cutters. But, as reader, you should not *have* to decipher at all; the reference should be clear at first reading. Here are additional examples:

> *Ambiguous:* This is a program in which employees turn in suggestions and are paid for them if *they* are adopted. [The *employees* are adopted?]
>
> *Ambiguous:* A new employee needs to familiarize him- or herself with the department and what part he or she will play in it. *It* will allow him or her to observe the methods, forms, and processes used daily. [This is especially confusing because of the uncertainty whether the "It" beginning the second sentence has the same referent as the "it" at the end of the first.]
>
> *Improved:* In order to familiarize him- or herself with the department and what part he or she will play in it, a new employee should observe the methods, forms, and processes used daily.
>
> *Ambiguous:* Brown disliked his boss because he thought he was undependable.
>
> *Clear:* Brown disliked his boss because the boss seemed undependable. Or: Brown disliked his boss because the boss thought Brown undependable.
>
> *Vague:* To have a successful career at my plant, one has to learn how *they* do things.
>
> *Improved:* To have a successful career at my plant, one must learn the "rules of the game" used there.

Using pronouns with vague or ambiguous references is an easy trap to fall into. *You* know what you mean; but, of course, it is not to yourself you are writing. The reader is someone else, and unless the meaning is clear to him or her, you are failing to communicate effectively. The trick in part is to avoid the trap to begin with. Even more, it is to proofread from the point of view of the reader and revise as necessary to eliminate possible confusion.

Expressing Faulty Relationships   Another barrier to sentence coherence is failing to bring out clearly the proper relationships among ideas in the sentence. Relationships commonly existing among ideas include comparison, contrast, cause-effect, continuation, illustration, chronological sequence, and others. The way in which such relationships are shown is by use of such terms as "similarly," "however," "therefore," "furthermore," "for example," "second," and the like.

To the extent that the relationship is misleading or not even stated (when it is not clearly obvious) coherence is strained, readability impeded, and the probability of falloff increased. Note how failure to indicate precise relationship reduces the effectiveness of these sentences:

> The project was successful; *however,* an evaluation was attached.

Since no actual contrast exists here, the "however" confuses. A more accurate wording would be: "The project was successful, as can be seen from the attached evaluation."

In the following example, the connective "and" is not so much misleading as inadequate.

> In order to meet schedules as set forth by our project office, we urgently need to supplement existing diazo equipment. *And* I recommend the purchase of a new Revolute High Speed Diazo Printer at a cost of about $5000.

"And," is a useful connective to link ideas having a simple relationship with each other—"bread and butter," "Joe and his brother," "snowy and slippery." But when a relationship exists in which one idea depends on another, such as a cause-effect relationship, "and" hardly fills the bill. In the example above, the causal relationship would be better expressed:

> In order to meet schedules as set forth by our project office, we urgently need to supplement existing diazo equipment. *Therefore,* I recommend . . .[5]

Similarly, the sentence "Mrs. Truesdell is an accountant *and* has been with the firm nine years" would be better expressed, "Mrs. Truesdell is an accountant *who* has been with the firm nine years."

Even weaker coherence results when an "and" is used to join ideas having no relationship whatever with each other, as in this sentence from a high school book report: "So Jacob and Henrietta were married, and electricity was discovered"! (Or, perhaps as reader, I was too obtuse to perceive the proper relationship.)

Sometimes the relationship is obscured—thus the coherence weakened—when the word or phrase denoting the relationship is not strategically placed. The word "but," for instance, should be placed between the two ideas being contrasted. This sometimes could mean beginning a sentence with "But," since the idea being contrasted was expressed in the sentence preceding. In like manner, to indicate the next idea in a series, sentences often begin with such words as "first," "lastly," "furthermore," or "finally." In the following example, the chronological sequence is obscured by the date in the second sentence being located at the end:

> The project was initiated April 23, 1974, by Mr. Sasaki, Plant Engineer. I was brought into the project *in January of this year.*

If the date phrase were located at the beginning of the sentence—"In January of this year I was brought into the project"—the flow of ideas would be smoother and the coherence strengthened. In addition, the pronoun "I," relatively unimportant in this sentence, would be removed from its position of prominence. (If, however, "I" is the important point of the second sentence, the sentence should be left as is.)

At other times the relationship is weakened through the omission completely of the relationship term. Compare, for instance, these two versions of the closing sentence of a paragraph on the nature of the exit interview.

> These are the essential points to be remembered in conducting an exit interview.
>
> These, *then,* are the essential points to be remembered in conducting an exit interview.

Clearly, the "then" suggests a summing up which is not implied in the earlier version. The version lacking the "then" would serve well as the topic sentence of an opening paragraph; the version with the "then," as the concluding sentence—or, as the topic sentence of a concluding paragraph.

Making clear the relationship among ideas, then, is an essential requirement for effective coherence. If the relationship term is inappropriate, poorly placed, or omitted altogether, the sentence coherence is less strong.

Switching Point of View or Tense Unnecessarily Still another assault on sentence coherence results from switching the point of view or tense unnecessarily. Note, for example, how the switching back and forth in this passage interferes with bringing into focus the point of view (whether "you" or "he") from which the sentence is written:

> *You* must score high on a written exam. . . . If *you* come in as an apprentice . . . It will take four years if *he* works only five days a week. If *he* gets overtime it will require less. As a

trainee, *you* must complete 275 hours of school work and eight years of work on the job, no matter how many hours and days *he* may work per week.

In the following example, the point of view switches illogically from describing what was done to giving the reader directions what to do:

> Sound level readings were taken as near as possible to the center of each bay. A B & K Sound Meter type 2209 *was used*. If the sound level is continuous (less than 2 decibels fluctuation), *record* only the average reading.

In the example below, the switch is in tense, again illogical and unnecessary:

> The men usually *worked* in gangs of two or three, but sometimes they *work* alone or in larger groups. The foreman *will give* the men their job assignments at the beginning of the shift.

If there is sound reason for the switch, no harm to the coherence results. Thus, in a memo you might say: "Mr. Peterson prefers that when people see him they make an appointment. So your odds of having your talk with him will be better if you call his secretary in advance." Here, the switch from "they" to "you" and from present tense ("make") to future tense ("will be") is logical. But when switches are needless and illogical, they place a strain on coherence.

Arranging Ideas in Confused Sequence   Since coherence depends on an orderly pattern, the coherence is hurt when ideas are unfolded in a disordered pattern—as in the following example:

> *Confused order:*   Conducting the survey involved deciding on the questions we actually would use, after first collecting as many questions as we could, then analyzing the responses once we had them tabulated.
>
> *Clear order:*   Conducting the survey involved collecting as many questions as we could, deciding which questions we actually would use, then tabulating and analyzing the responses.
>
> *Confused order:*   Total manufacturing time for the deluxe bracket was .3 of an hour, and 15 minutes for the standard bracket. [Here the coherence is further affected by comparing tenths of an hour with minutes.]
>
> *Clear order:*   Total manufacturing time for the deluxe bracket was .3 of an hour, and for the standard bracket, .25 of an hour. [or, "for the deluxe bracket was 18 minutes, and for the standard bracket, 15."]

An example of "disorder" recently appeared in a Christmas note from a personal friend: "Dan goes to Japan Dec. 29th to come back with Miko [his Japanese wife, who had gone earlier to visit her parents] and see his in-laws." Obviously, Dan would see his in-laws *before* he returned, though the sentence indicates otherwise. Such an error in a personal note (even an informal personal memo on the job) is perfectly understandable and excusable. But in a business letter or a more formal communication, errors of this kind should be caught and corrected before the final draft goes out.

Using Contradictory Logic   Just as a confused sequence can detract from the coherence, so may contradictory logic. Lt. Gov. Warren Knowles of Wisconsin made a practice for years of collecting examples of fractured logic he overheard from fellow politicians. Here are a few:

> This will tie the hands of former Common Councils for the next 30 years.
>
> He was absolutely right to a certain extent.
>
> There's just one more thing I forgot to overlook.

While such remarks are entertaining to read, they illustrate violations of coherence. Logically speaking, they fail to hang together.

In Review

A strong coherent structure is a prime requisite of an effective sentence. Among the faulty practices weakening coherence are the following, all discussed above:

> Overloading the sentence
> Running sentences together
> Mismanaging modifiers
> Splitting grammatical constructions
> Making vague or ambiguous references
> Expressing faulty relationships
> Switching point of view or tense unnecessarily
> Arranging ideas in a confused sequence
> Using contradictory logic

Clearly, avoiding such practices is essential to improving your writing.

Special Techniques for a More Coherent Structure

One means of assuring a coherent sentence structure is to avoid faults such as those above. Two additional techniques especially helpful in bringing about a clear structure are (a) the direct approach, and (b) parallelism.

Using a Direct Approach   If readers must read to the end of a lengthy sentence to be sure of the main idea, the coherence, in their minds, is unclear. Though the ideas presented may relate perfectly to each other, their relationship cannot be discerned except by the reader's looking back. But if the main idea is presented at the beginning, how the specifics are related can be grasped immediately. By way of illustration, compare the readability of the sentences in each of the following pairs. In the indirect version, the main idea comes last; in the direct version, it comes first.

> *Indirect:* Time taken by the employee for incidental activities at the beginning of each shift, before and after lunch, and at the end of the day is included in this category.
>
> *Direct:* This category includes time taken by the employee for incidental activities at the beginning of each shift, before and after lunch, and at the end of the day.

In the example above, not only is the coherence strengthened by using the direct approach; it is also strengthened by eliminating the separation between the subject and verb ("time . . . is included" in the first version vs. "category includes" in the second).

> *Indirect:* In terms of content, the candidate, the company and the job, the interviewer, the interviewing process, and the pleasantries are five types of information that tended to be discussed in the interviews.
>
> *Direct:* In terms of content, five types of information tended to be discussed in the interviews: (a) the candidate, (b) the company and the job, (c) the interviewer, (d) the interviewing process, and (c) the pleasantries.[6]

For longer sentences (say over 25–30 words) the direct approach helps considerably in promoting a sense of coherence that the reader can grasp at once.

Using Parallelism *Parallelism* means expressing similar ideas in similar word structures. Whenever there are similarities in ideas, these similarities stand out more clearly when they are expressed in similar (that is, parallel) grammatical constructions. Parallelism may involve using single words, phrases, dependent clauses, main clauses, or whole sentences, as illustrated here:

> *Nouns:* I have notified Rogers, Emerson, and Underwood.
>
> *Adjectives:* The project has been rejected because it would be unnecessary, expensive, and impractical.
>
> *Prepositional phrases:* "government of the people, by the people, for the people."

Verbal phrases: Constructing the questions, conducting the survey, and tabulating the results took about a month. Or: It took about a month to construct the questions, conduct the survey, and tabulate the results.

Dependent clauses: Because the design is faulty, because the production is costly, and because customer acceptance has been sluggish, the Handy-Dandy Fixit-All has been dropped.

(In the last example, the repetition of "because" highlights the cause-effect relationship. For greater conciseness, though with a corresponding loss of emphasis on the causal relationship, this sentence could be written: "Because the design is faulty, the production costly, and customer acceptance sluggish, the Handy-Dandy Fixit-All has been dropped." The parallelism remains; the coherence is not affected; only the emphasis on "because" is reduced.)

Main clauses: Labor approves, management approves, the government approves; thus the prospect for success appears good.

Whole sentences: In past years, taking inventory has been a slow, time-consuming job. This year, the new procedure allowed us to finish in less than half the time.

Note how in the last example the parallelism would be lost, the contrast obscured, and the coherence lessened if the second sentence were to read, "The new procedure used this year allowed us to finish in less than half the time."

All the examples above illustrate parallel construction. To illustrate the concept more fully, here is how the above examples might read if the principle of parallelism were ignored. Your own ear will tell you, I believe, how the loss of parallelism reduces the coherence and readability.

Rogers and Emerson have been notified; also Underwood.

Because the project is unnecessary it has been rejected. It would cost a great deal, while its impracticality would be another disadvantage.

. . . government deriving its authority from the people instead of the rulers, with the officials being elected by the people, and having as its aim the welfare of all.

The questions first had to be constructed. Then we conducted the survey. Finally the results were tabulated. About a month was required for all this.

We have dropped the Handy-Dandy Fixit-All. One reason was the faulty design. It also cost too much to produce. Besides, the customers were sluggish in accepting it.

Labor has said it approves; approval has also been indicated by management, and government has issued its OK, too. Thus the prospect for success looks good.

From studying the above good and poor examples, you can doubtless see that improved coherence and readability are not the only gains from using parallelism. Emphasis is improved through ideas being brought into sharper focus. Conciseness likewise benefits, since fewer words usually are required.

In your writing, therefore, look for legitimate similarities in ideas, then seek to express the similarities in parallel constructions. While parallelism is not the only tool used by skilled writers, it is one of the most useful. Learn to use it well.

Coherent Structure: A Summing Up

In judging a house, a basic question is, "How well is it built? Is the structure sound?" The same basic question applies to a sentence. This concern is primary, and if the answer is negative, the fault must be remedied. Once it is sound, we then can proceed to other concerns—emphasis, variety, and the others—concerns which, though important, are nonetheless secondary. On the other hand, we must not regard these qualities as unrelated, for they all interact with each other.

EMPHASIS

We have already seen in Chapter 4, "Structure," that the ideas in messages possess varying levels of importance. This concept applies to sentences as well as to a paragraph or a whole report. Some sentences, it is true, contain but a single idea ("The survey is finished") or two or more ideas of equal importance ("The survey is finished and the report is begun"). Many sentences, however, contain ideas of unequal importance ("Rounding the corner, he saw the turned-over truck"). Whatever the case, the writer's job is to express ideas so the reader can readily grasp their relative importance. If the reader misjudges the writer's intent as to which ideas are important and which unimportant, communication falloff will result.

For minimizing falloff concerning relative importance of ideas, we shall consider techniques concerning three conditions: showing equal emphasis, showing reduced emphasis, and showing increased emphasis.

Showing Equal Emphasis

Showing equal emphasis implies the presence of a compound construction (that is, two or more words, phrases, or clauses of equal rank). Since this is the case, the only question is, How do you show the equality? Techniques include the use of parallelism, coordinate conjunctions, semicolons, and conjunctive adverbs.

Use Parallelism   We have already discussed parallelism as a tool of coherence in helping to provide a clear structure. But by definition, parallelism is also a tool for showing equal emphasis, since ideas that are parallel are also equal. Thus, the use of parallelism signifies that equality. A quick review of the examples above illustrating parallelism will readily demonstrate this point.

Use Coordinate Conjunctions   Coordinate conjunctions are used for joining elements of equal rank, whether words, phrases, dependent clauses, or independent clauses. The seven coordinate conjunctions—"or," "nor," "for," "and," "but," "yet," "so"—are illustrated in these examples.

> *Words:*   labor *and* management; tired *but* happy
>
> *Phrases:*   to be *or* not to be; out of one crisis *and* into another
>
> *Dependent clauses:*   after Mazzatenta finishes his speech, *but* before Sawyer begins his
>
> *Independent clauses:*   sales have increased, *yet* the future remains uncertain; Diaz has not given her approval, *nor* is she about to do so; Wong was reluctant to sign, *for* he had not forgotten the earlier hassle; absenteeism remains high, *so* the special reports will still be required.

Use Semicolons   When independent clauses within the same sentence are not joined with a comma and coordinating conjunction, a semicolon must be used. (An exception, noted earlier, is when the clauses are brief and closely related, as in the "I came, I saw, I conquered" type.) In each of the examples just given, the comma and coordinating conjunction could be replaced by a semicolon: "Sales have increased; the future remains uncertain," or "Diaz has not given her approval; she is not about to do so"; and so on. Although there are other differences, as we shall see later, either way the two clauses would have equal emphasis.

Use Conjunctive Adverbs   Since a semicolon by itself does little to indicate the relationship between independent clauses (except that they *are* independent, and equal), the writer may wish to follow the semicolon with a conjunctive adverb (an adverb used as a conjunction or "joining" word). Common examples include "however," "furthermore," "therefore," "consequently." Thus, one could write, "Sales have increased; *however,* the future remains uncertain," or "Diaz has not given her approval; *furthermore,* she is not about to do so."

When the coordinate elements are independent clauses, it makes little difference, from point of view of equal emphasis alone, whether the clauses are set off by a comma and coordinate conjunction, a semicolon alone, or a semicolon and conjunctive adverb.

But there are other considerations: How explicit should be the relationship between the two clauses? How formal a style does the situation require? If the relationship is self-evident, the semicolon alone is preferable, as in "Sales have declined sharply; the future looks bleak." This construction is more concise, more compact, more direct. If the relationship would be more effective if stated explicitly, then either a coordinate conjunction (preceded by a comma) or a conjunctive adverb (preceded by a semicolon) must be used.

Now the question becomes one of formality. Stated broadly, commas are more casual and informal; semicolons more deliberate and formal. Commas give a lighter touch; semicolons a heavier. Thus, the semicolon (with or without a conjunctive adverb) tends to give the *entire expression* (as opposed to either of the clauses alone) increased emphasis. To illustrate, compare once again "Diaz has not given her approval; furthermore, she is not about to do so" with "Diaz has not given her approval, nor is she about to do so." Which style is preferable would depend on the writer's intent and the nature of the situation. But a whole series of sentences with semicolons would make for stiff, heavy reading.

Showing Reduced Emphasis

Not all ideas in a sentence are equally important; indeed, the reverse is more often the case. How, then, may an idea be given *less* emphasis? We suggest three ways:

Use a Weaker Grammatical Structure   The principle involved here is that the grammatical structure in which an idea is expressed should correspond to the importance of the idea. A dependent clause normally suggests less emphasis than an independent clause, a phrase less than a dependent clause, and a word less than a phrase.

For example, let's say you have two ideas you wish to combine in one sentence: "Tubbs was the best qualified candidate" and "he received the appointment." For merely expressing a causal relationship, you could join them with "so" or "therefore" (including, of course, the comma or semicolon). But if you wish to reduce the emphasis on *why* he received the appointment, an appropriate means would be to express it as a dependent (or "subordinate") clause—a process known as *subordination*. The result, a *complex sentence* (one independent clause plus one or more dependent clauses), would then read: "Since Tubbs was the best qualified candidate, he received the appointment." Or you could say, "Tubbs, who was the best qualified candidate, received the appointment." In this version, "Tubbs," being now part of the independent clause, is still emphasized, but his qualifications remain de-emphasized.

To carry this process a step further, you could reduce the emphasis on Tubbs's qualifications still more by replacing the dependent clause with a phrase: "Tubbs, being the best qualified candidate, received the appointment," or "Tubbs, the best qualified candidate, received the appointment." If his qualifications seemed unimportant to mention, you could write simply, "Tubbs received the appointment"; or, more simply yet, "Tubbs was appointed."

In applying this principle of placing the less important idea in the weaker grammatical structure, naturally you would want to be certain which idea actually *is* less important. Otherwise, you could end up with a case of misplaced emphasis like this:

> The driver was distracted by a miniskirted blonde, thus losing control of his car and being killed.

(If you can't decide how to correct this example, ask your teacher. If your teacher can't decide either, perhaps he or she should not be teaching this course. Definitely he or she should never drive a car!)

Locate Less Important Ideas in a Less Emphatic Position The most emphatic position in a sentence is normally at the end, the next most emphatic at the beginning, and least emphatic in the middle.

To illustrate this, the sentence "Since Tubbs was the best qualified candidate, he received the appointment" could as easily be written: "Tubbs received the appointment because he was the best qualified candidate." In either version, the less important idea (that he was the best qualified candidate) is de-emphasized by being expressed in a dependent clause. But in the second version, the less important idea, though still in a dependent clause, is given a slight bit more emphasis by being placed in the more emphatic position at the end.

Which arrangement is better? Probably the first (beginning "Since Tubbs . . .") because the less important idea is de-emphasized two ways: (a) being expressed in a dependent clause, and (b) being located in a less emphatic position. However, the context could favor the reverse. If the sentence preceding the statement about Tubbs were to read, "Aiken was not even considered; Hillary's qualifications were unimpressive," then you might well continue with "Tubbs received the appointment because he was the best qualified candidate." In this situation, beginning the sentence with "Tubbs" continues the parallelism and heightens the contrast between him and his competitors.

To illustrate the location factor again, consider this sentence:

> Without doubt, one of the most important reasons we are losing ground in owner loyalty is loss of contact with customers, in my opinion.

Note that what is probably the least important idea in the sentence ("in my opinion") occupies the most emphatic position, while the most important idea ("loss of contact with customers") is buried in the middle.

If we revise this sentence according to the principle of emphasis by location, it would read:

> Without doubt, one of the most important reasons, in my opinion, that we are losing ground in owner loyalty is loss of contact with customers.

Here the main idea is moved to the end, the most emphatic position, while the least important idea, "in my opinion," is now buried in the middle. Indeed, the "in my opinion" is so nonessential, it could easily be omitted altogether.

In shorter sentences, locating the main idea at the end is especially effective for building to a climax. In longer sentences, starting with the main idea is usually preferable, since it provides a clear, direct opening to which subsequent ideas may be related.

Use "De-emphasizing Punctuation" Two marks of punctuation often used to denote reduced emphasis are parentheses and commas.

By definition, parentheses are used for setting off parenthetical expressions—material not essential to the main thought, but inserted to amplify or explain it. The following examples seem self-explanatory:

> Engineering drawings (both the wash-off and mylar types) are now processed by hand.

> During the last five years a new type of microscope, the *scanning electron miscroscope* (SEM) has been reaching prominence.[7]

> It was only by coincidence that the senior author of this article was caught in the middle of such a campaign. (The names of both the company and union have been changed.)[8]

Commas, like parentheses, may also be used to set off information not essential to the meaning, but inserted to amplify or explain. One such use is in punctuating *nonrestrictive clauses* (or "nonessential" clauses—nonessential, that is, for identifying what they refer to). These are typical examples:

> The chief metallurgist, who graduated from Michigan State University, has been with the company many years. [Note that "who graduated from Michigan State University" is not essential for identifying who the chief metallurgist is.]

> Your application, which reached us last week, is now being reviewed.

Observe, however, that if the clause is *restrictive,* or essential for identifying what it refers to, it may not be set off by commas as if it were parenthetical. (Note the difference between the examples above and those following: "The metallurgist who wrote that report [as opposed to some other metallurgist] is not the one I was thinking of," or "The letter that you sent me last week [as opposed to your letter this week] made no mention of the problem.")

Commas also are used to set off *appositives* (phrases offering incidental information), as shown below:

> The chief metallurgist, Mr. Jack LaBelle, has been with the company many years.
>
> Suzanne Baird, vice-president in charge of sales, is now in Europe on business.

The question now arises, if either parentheses or commas may serve to set off explanatory, nonessential information (thus indicating reduced emphasis), how can you be sure which to use? The answer is a matter of judgment. In general, the more parenthetical or nonessential the information, the more appropriate to use parentheses; the less parenthetical, the more appropriate to use commas. By noting in your reading when parentheses and commas are used to punctuate explanatory information, you can develop a feel for when to use which.

Showing Increased Emphasis

For showing increased emphasis, some of the most obvious means include simply reversing the techniques suggested above for indicating reduced emphasis.

Use a Stronger Grammatical Structure As a general principle, this means that to show increased emphasis you could use a phrase instead of a word, a dependent clause instead of a phrase, or an independent clause instead of a dependent clause. In the last instance, the independent clause could be the main clause of a complex sentence, or it could be the whole sentence (thus indicating more emphasis still).

To extend this principle further, a single sentence set off as a separate paragraph gives more emphasis than if used at the end of a paragraph. Compare, for example, these two versions:

> During the past 15 years, we have been providing precision circuits of high quality to EDL. However, especially during recent months, as our equipment has deteriorated, so too has our ability to perform. As a matter of fact, since our most recent equipment failure, a good deal of EDL circuit work has been subcontracted. We want that work. We have the precision camera; we have the technical competence. All we need is a good contact printer. I urge your approval of this new equipment so that we may once again perform in a manner that is beneficial to EDL and RSC.

Below is the same passage, but with the final sentence in a paragraph by itself. Note the increased emphasis:

> During the past 15 years, we have been providing precision circuits of high quality to EDL. However, especially during recent months, as our equipment deteriorated, so too has our ability to perform. As a matter of fact, since our most recent equipment failure, a good deal of EDL circuit work has been subcontracted. We want that work. We have the precision camera; we have the technical competence. All we need is a good contact printer.
>
> I urge your approval of this new equipment so that we may once again perform in a manner that is beneficial to EDL and RSC.[9]

Locate Important Ideas in the More Emphatic Position   Instead of burying the most important idea in the middle of the sentence, locate it at either the beginning (if a longer sentence), or the end (if a shorter sentence). The examples given above to illustrate reduced emphasis serve to illustrate increased emphasis as well.

Use Short Sentences   Similar to gaining emphasis through a one-sentence paragraph is gaining it through using a short sentence. Suppose, for example, you are proposing a switch to computerized procedure in mailing monthly newsletters. You could conclude your memo with a sentence like this, "Because (reason 1, reason 2, etc.), the time to consider computerization, I feel, is now." Or, you could instead use two sentences. The first would summarize the reasons; the second would emphasize the urgency: "The time, I feel, is now." Without doubt, the six-word concluding sentence would give increased emphasis to the idea of "now."

Use Parallelism   Earlier we stated that parallelism indicates equality among a series of ideas. This is true. But parallelism also gives increased emphasis to the whole series of ideas within its immediate context. To illustrate, note first the lack of parallelism in the following paragraph:

> The installation of a terminal at the No. 1 Dock would eliminate the need for the general foreman to enter the parts information in Building 90, thereby saving approximately one hour per day. A portion of the load on Building 90 would be relieved, since installing a terminal would allow the receipt of purchased parts at Store #1. Also, the need to store parts on the dock until they receive zone tags would be eliminated.

This paragraph gives three benefits resulting from the installation of a terminal; however, without parallelism, they fail to stand out. Compare now the following version of the same information (in which the italics are used only to point up the parallelism):

> The installation of a terminal at the No. 1 Dock would provide three benefits. *It would eliminate* the need for the general foreman to enter the parts information in Building 90, thereby saving approximately one hour per day. *It would allow* the receipt of purchased parts at Store #1, thus relieving the load on Building 90. Finally, *it would eliminate* the need to store parts on the dock until they receive zone tags.

This version may be given further emphasis by the insertion of numerical symbols:

> The installation of a terminal at the No. 1 Dock would provide three benefits: (1) eliminate the need for the general foreman to enter the parts information in Building 90, thereby saving approximately one hour per day; (2) allow the receipt of purchased parts at Store #1, thus relieving the load on Building 90; and (3) eliminate the need to store parts on the dock until they receive zone tags.

Finally, through changing the format so the points are shown in a vertical list, we can give these benefits greater emphasis still:

> The installation of a terminal at the No. 1 Dock would provide three benefits:
>
> 1. Eliminate the need for the general foreman to enter the parts information in Building 90, thereby saving approximately one hour per day.
>
> 2. Allow the receipt of purchased goods at Store #1, thus relieving the load on Building 90.
>
> 3. Eliminate the need to store parts on the dock until they receive zone tags.

Because of the high degree of emphasis created, the format of a numbered list is commonly used for stating the conclusions and recommendations in a formal report or proposal. As a matter of fact, the final version above was taken from a formal report. Such a format as shown here (arranging points in a vertical list) would normally be used only for introducing a series of ideas to be elaborated upon, or for summarizing a series of ideas already elaborated upon. The most common exception would be in listing a series of points too self-evident to need elaboration, such as "Ten Reminders in Using Firearms."

Incidentally, if a series of points is given, a general statement introducing the ideas *must* precede the list. Otherwise, there is no way of being sure what general topic the ideas relate to.

Use Repetition Repeating a key word or phrase is a potent technique for giving emphasis.

In the passage below, a concluding paragraph from an article on emotional aspects of purchasing in the steel industry, the idea of "fear" receives intense emphasis through repetition of the word (eight times in one brief paragraph):

> Out of all this comes one overriding general conclusion: that fear is one of the major influences in industrial buying. Fear of displeasing the boss. Fear of making a wrong decision. Fear of committing the company to substantial outlays. Fear of making a mistake. Fear of losing face with the boss or with one's associates. Fear of losing status. Fear, indeed, in extreme cases, of losing one's job.[10]

Incidentally, since the passage just cited consists of a series of parallel structures ("Fear of . . . ," and so on), it might seem that this example illustrates no more than another instance of parallelism. But parallelism refers to use of the same grammatical structure for a series of similar ideas; repetition refers to repeated use of a key word or phrase. While it is true that the parallelism heightens the effect, the greater emphasis results from the repetition of the word "fear." In fact, the emphasis becomes so great that the author's meaning is perhaps overstated; substituting the word "concern" might, in overall effect, have been more accurate. Parallelism and repetition may be employed together, as above, but the presence of one does not necessarily mean the presence of the other. Indeed, most of the examples of parallelism given in this chapter do *not* use repetition.

Since repetition is such an emphatic device, it should be used only where strong emphasis is warranted. Used carelessly, repetition can easily exaggerate the importance of an idea. One common instance of such overemphasis results from beginning a series of sentences with "I," as shown here:

> I chose to write about this topic because I found it very interesting. I was given an assignment with both the responsibility and authority to do what was necessary to complete the job. I had to rely on my own judgment and personal responsibility, as well as depending on and working with heads of other departments. I also found it interesting to work with the man on the line.

The repetition of "I" in this passage (especially at the beginning of each sentence) focuses undue attention on the writer (inappropriate in this instance), while detracting from the emphasis that should have been focused on the writer's activities instead.

Anytime we begin a series of phrases, clauses, or sentences with identical wording, we need to be very sensitive to whether we have overemphasized an idea beyond whatever emphasis it deserves. In short, we should avoid repeating the same word (or a similar word) when this gives undue emphasis to what may be a relatively unimportant idea. Examples of such clumsy overemphasis are seen here:

> Certain psychological factors operating within the interview must be *understood* to *understand* how bias arises.
>
> For *example,* the *example* . . .
>
> Thus, instead of *being* a means of *being* original . . .
>
> . . . this principle applies *likewise. Likewise,* a similar principle to remember . . . [Repetition of "principle" is appropriate, since this is a key word in the line of reasoning, but repeating the "likewise" is not warranted.]

Such ineffective repetition, which may easily creep into a first draft, should be eliminated in the revision.

Use "Emphasizing" Punctuation   Just as some marks of punctuation reduce emphasis on ideas, so other marks of punctuation increase emphasis. Chief among these are underscoring or setting in italics in print, dashes, and capital letters.

1. Underscoring. Underscoring (or underlining, shown in print by italics) is the punctuation device perhaps used most commonly to show emphasis. Following are common examples:

> It appears that the employees who took the *least* amount of sick leave were females under 30 years of age.[11]
>
> They send supervisors and managers to classes to study motivation theory, see a few films, and, in many instances, gain a good foundation of knowledge, but *they fail to make any actual changes in the jobs.*[12]

Underscoring, while useful, should be employed sparingly, or the result may resemble an adolescent's diary: "The band was *great,* and my date was just *incredible.* The evening *couldn't* have been *more beautiful* . . . ," and so forth. Showing emphasis through subordination and location, as described above, is normally preferable to relying on underscoring.

2. Dashes. Like parentheses and commas, dashes may be used to set off ideas. Such ideas are, however, those that the writer seeks to emphasize rather than de-emphasize, and the dashes indicate this difference. Observe their use in these examples:

> It's not outer space—but inner space—that most interests research scientists of the Edsel B. Ford Institute for Medical Research.[13]

> Today, the problem of management succession is much more complex, but some of the situations—and some of the faulty judgments—of the 12th century seem to have survived.[14]
>
> This is only the beginning of some startling changes that will be forthcoming in the years ahead in our "people" or human relationships—a sort of preview of the future.[15]

Dashes, like underscoring, should be used discreetly. The dash is a legitimate device in writing, but it ought not to be used as a substitute for commas, semicolons, colons, and periods. A careful writer knows when to use dashes—and when not to.

3. Capital letters. The reference here is not merely to capitalizing a word, but to typing or printing an entire word or passage in capitals. In formal reports, the title on the title page is normally in caps: "CYLINDER LINER REWORK." Similarly, warnings are commonly in caps.

> CAUTION: FLAMMABLE. KEEP AWAY FROM HEAT OR FLAME.
>
> WARNING: Keep this and all medicines out of reach of children.

But again, capital letters used for emphasis should be used sparingly. They do serve to emphasize, but typing an entire memo or report in caps (as sometimes is done) overdoes the emphasis to the point that total emphasis results in no emphasis at all.

APPROPRIATE LENGTH

How long should a sentence be?

Since around the time of World War II this question has figured prominently among teachers and practitioners of business writing. The popular trend has been toward brevity. The leading apostle of brevity (in sentences) has been without doubt Rudolf Flesch. In his book, *The Art of Plain Talk,* he advises, "Try to keep sentences under twenty words, certainly under twenty-five words," while the ideal length, he believes, is 17 words.[16] The longer the sentence, runs the argument, the less readable it becomes—and certainly there can be no quarrel with the high priority placed on readability.

The Question of Ideal Length

If we could settle on some magic number—17, 25, or whatever—the question could be put painlessly to rest. But such a solution is too simple, as the following two examples will illustrate.

The first example is a relatively brief sentence pulled from a report on an employee alcoholism recovery program:

> The objective of this effort is to help employees who became afflicted with alcoholism and established a system of early categorization. [21 words]

Because of faulty structure (revealed especially in the uncertainty as to the subject of "established," plus the confusing switch in tense), this sentence, though brief, is baffling to read.

The second example is more personal. It comes from a letter I wrote several years ago declining (with regrets) an invitation to attend an informal reception honoring a superintendent and his wife who had been teachers of mine in the small town I grew up in. Not until some time later did I realize that the main paragraph of the letter consisted of just two sentences, one 416 words long, the other six. This is the paragraph:

> Your invitation has, however, stirred up a host of nostalgic memories of years ago that have been entertaining me in my off moments since last night: the old, square, red brick school sitting on the hill waiting patiently for us every morning; the sight of a long-legged, red-haired superintendent and history teacher striding vigorously past Menno Schafer's orchard up the sidewalk to school, with his conspicuously shorter English-teacher wife alongside, hustling furiously to keep up; studying *Evangeline* in 8th grade English and deciding privately that I could probably write something like that as well as Longfellow; the innumerable spelling bees our class held, not just in English but in other classes as well, and challenging every other grade, 7th through 12th, and never being beaten; the "banquet" for our parents at the end of 8th grade held up in the old "Assembly Hall" when the fuse blew, leaving us in total darkness for 20 minutes, and Bert Linsley laughing like mad at the "class poem" I wrote and recited about a "close shave" an imaginary dog of mine had—a theme not precisely what Mrs. Lange had in mind when she asked me to write the poem; the softball game between us and the 7th grade that never was completed and left me feeling sad because I knew we'd *never* find out who really won; the "baseball game" in Michigan Civics under Mr. Lange in which the pitches were questions from the text and each right answer was a hit but each miss was a strike; the inauguration "banquet" in history class on March 4, 1929, when Bud Sebright played the role of Calvin Coolidge and no one could take a bite of his sandwich except when Cal did (I was Herbert Hoover, I recall); the diary of spring vacation that Marian Calkins read in class when we were back in school, ending philosophically with "Like all good things, this, too, came to a close"; genial Henry Ellinger

keeping the floors swept up; our raising the devil in Mr. Klitzke's agriculture class; attending basketball games in the windy, barn-like upstairs at the old boat factory—also skating parties and even class plays up there; the Chevrolet the Langes took on a trip west and brought back badly dented from a heavy hailstorm; walking the cinder path with you to and from school past John Glascott's depot, then across the footbridge and past Herb O'Meara's "Greatest Store on Earth" and Charlie Smith's barbershop—and so on. Didn't realize how much I'd forgotten.

The longer of the two sentences contains more than 24 times the "ideal" 17-word length Flesch proposes. But is it difficult to read? Judge for yourself.

As these two examples suggest, word count by itself is no sure guide to readability. The question of length is better answered in an article, "Brevity Isn't Everything," in which the author, Louis Foley, cites a highly respected French scholar, François Richaudeau, on this point:

> He [Richaudeau] finds that "the problem of the ideal length" of a sentence is a false problem. Mere length is of only secondary importance. Readability is more importantly determined by *structure*. Given from the start a clear plan as a whole, with subordinate clauses joined by appropriate connectives, a really long sentence can be read with perfect ease.[17]

The same point is reinforced in an article by Mary Bromage, "Sentences That Make Sense," in which she declares, "length and structure . . . must be applied together, not separately. It is length in relation to structure which produces or reduces clarity."[18]

The importance of structure in relation to length explains why in this chapter we examined "Coherent Structure" thoroughly before tackling "Appropriate Length." Several times in that section we showed how the readability of a sentence was noticeably increased when the structure was corrected; and when this was accomplished, length in itself was no problem. Consistent with this approach is the following advice offered by Bromage:

> Parallelism, enumeration, agreement, clear antecedents—all these and other stylistic means are needed to make long sentences work. Modifiers must be properly placed. Consistency in point of view must be maintained. Tenses must be kept in sequence. Relationships like cause and effect must be logically established. Emphasis must be selectively located.[19]

Each of these "stylistic means" has received explicit treatment in this chapter.

If word count is not a sound guide to sentence length, what is? By way of answer, let us point out the special uses and limitations of various sentence lengths.

Uses of Sentences According to Length

The most obvious use of the longer sentence is for grouping or combining ideas, as seen in my 416-word sentence, in which every item consists of some event remembered from junior high school days. Grouping is equally well illustrated in the example given earlier of parallelism listing the benefits of "installing a terminal at the No. 1 Dock" (a sentence containing nearly 70 words). Such sentences are useful especially for previews and summaries. But it should be stressed that such sentences require a direct approach; that is, the general idea to which the specifics relate *must* be stated clearly at the outset as a kind of hook to hang the succeeding details onto.

Medium-length sentences (roughly 10–25 words) excel in expressing relationships among ideas. Here, for example, is a sentence from the *Wall Street Journal:*

> Because most of the new communities have no employment base, new roads must be built linking them to Phoenix. [19 words][20]

Between the two ideas presented in this sentence (one for each clause) are expressed three relationships: (1) the first idea is less important than the second (as indicated by its being written as a dependent clause), (2) the first idea is the cause of the second (as indicated by the word *because*), and (3) the two ideas are closely related (as indicated by their being combined in one sentence). Writing these two ideas as separate sentences could express the causal relationship satisfactorily, but not the other two relationships.

For expressing complex relationships, the short single-clause sentence is severely limited. On the other hand, the long multiclause, multiphrase sentence is too cumbersome.

As for the very short sentence (ten words or less), its best use, as already implied, is for emphasis. Since the most emphatic locations in a paragraph (as in a sentence) are at the beginning or end, one would expect to find short sentences at either of these two locations. The six-word sentence closing my paragraph of school memories is a typical example. Other examples are frequently found in short, opening topic sentences, as pointed out in Chapter 5, on paragraphing.

It should be stressed that the striking effect of short sentences derives as much from contrast as from brevity. Using nothing but short sentences would be choppy, but an occasional short sentence, well placed, can point up an idea remarkably well.

Sentence Length: Some Closing Comments

Out of curiosity, I checked the word count of the first 20 sentences (not including illustrative examples) in this section, "Appropriate Length." To my surprise, the average was 17.75 words per sentence. The shortest sentence contained 3 words, the longest 38. My own average (for these 20 sentences, at least) is virtually identical with Flesch's "ideal length"!

But more important than striving for some ideal length is understanding two basic principles: (1) the function of a sentence determines how long it *should* be; (2) its structure determines how long it *can* be—and remain readable. If you keep in mind these two principles and master their use, you probably need not worry about sentence length per se. Chances are it will take care of itself.

CONCISENESS

Strunk, in his justly famous *The Elements of Style,* laid down as a cornerstone of good writing: "Omit needless words":

> Vigorous writing is concise. A sentence should contain no unnecessary words, a paragraph no unnecessary sentences, for the same reason that a drawing should have no unnecessary lines and a machine no unnecessary parts. This requires not that the writer make all his sentences short, or that he avoid all detail and treat his subjects only in outline, but that every word count.[21]

Making "every word count"—avoiding verbosity—is what conciseness means. Though conciseness is a factor in sentence brevity, the two are not identical. A 60-word sentence can be concise and a 10-word sentence verbose. Achieving conciseness (and indirectly brevity) is our concern here.

Examples of Wordiness in Writing

The following examples of wordiness, with suggested revisions, should help provide a feeling for the problem of conciseness:

Original: To obtain this check, a request for samples is sent to the manufacturer. This form is shown in Figure 4. This is done by the purchasing office. [27 words]

Improved: To obtain this check, the purchasing office requests samples from the manufacturer (Fig. 4). [14 words]

Original: I was introduced to the program and during my experience with it I learned the in-depth operations of the selection procedure. [21 words]

Improved: During my experience with the program, I learned the in-depth operations of the selection procedure. [15 words]

Original: Some of the Suggestion Department's functions include the following: the gathering of all employees' suggestions, the routing of various suggestions to different departments, and the investigation of suggestions that have been submitted. [32 words]

Improved: Some of the Suggestion Department's functions include gathering employees' suggestions, routing suggestions to different departments, and investigating suggestions that have been submitted. [22 words]

In these three examples, the suggested revisions contain only 64 percent as many words as the original. Translated into time, this means that only 64 percent as much time should be needed for reading the revised versions, and if it turns out that the shorter versions are also simpler to comprehend, even more time may be saved. Projected over the work week of a busy executive, such time-saving may be significant. Certainly it will be welcome!

Suggestions for Achieving Conciseness

How does one achieve conciseness? No simple solution exists, but here are some suggestions:

1. Become aware of our natural tendency to be wordy. We all tend to think, talk, and write verbosely—simply because formulation of ideas is a difficult process, and seldom are we able to express the first time precisely the meaning we would like to.

2. Become convinced of the virtue of conciseness. This may require reversing your habits, for often in school students are assigned to write themes of a specified length (500, 1,000, 2,000 words, or whatever). Chances are by now you have become a real expert at padding! This may win you grades in class, but it ill prepares you for business or the professions. Make no mistake about it: on the job, conciseness is much more welcome than wordiness. (This does not mean being incomplete in developing your ideas; only being concise while being complete.)

3. Avoid redundancies (extra words repeating the same idea). Examples of obvious redundancies include "descended down," "10:00 a.m. in the morning," "triangular in shape," "consensus of opinion."

4. Avoid using a phrase where a single word will suffice. Common examples include:

due to the fact that	for	because
in order to	for	to
in the near future	for	soon
by means of	for	by

5. Use a colon instead of an introductory phrase. For instance, instead of writing:

> Two objections to the proposal were raised by the comptroller. These objections were, first, that the cost is out of line, and second . . .

write:

> Two objections to the proposal were raised by the comptroller: (1) the cost is out of line, and (2) . . .

Or, instead of writing:

> The arguments all boiled down to one issue. That issue was cost.

write:

> The arguments all boiled down to one issue: cost.

6. Avoid the gerund-preposition combination where a participle alone will suffice. This practice, found all too often in student papers, is illustrated in the sentences above on the Suggestion Department: "*The gathering of* suggestions" for "gathering suggestions"; "*the* investigation *of* suggestions" for "investigating suggestions." However, if "investigating" were preceded by another "ing" word—"*following* investigating suggestions"—you might want to write "following the investigation of suggestions" to avoid the awkwardness of two successive "ing" words.

7. Avoid repeating words if the meaning is clearly implied. For example, in the sentence, "I was introduced to the program and during my experience with it I learned . . . ," the second "I" can be safely omitted. Similarly, in the sentence earlier in this chapter, "A careful writer knows when to use dashes—and when not to," to add "use them" (so the final phrase would read "and when not to use them") would have been unnecessary. Likewise, in "We can do the job as well as they," the meaning is complete enough without adding "can" after "they."

8. Avoid repeating phrases unnecessarily. Several pages earlier you read this paragraph:

> For expressing complex relationships, the short, single-clause sentence is severely limited. On the other hand, the long multiclause, multiphrase sentence is too cumbersome.

My original draft of this paragraph reads as follows:

> The short, single-clause sentence is severely limited for expressing complex relationships. On the other hand, the long multiclause, multiphrase sentence is too cumbersome for expressing complex relationships.

In this instance, the revision (first version above) produced several gains:

a. It is more concise ("for expressing complex relationships" is used only once).
b. It states the general topic ("expressing complex relationships") at the outset.
c. It heightens the contrast between short and long sentences (by placing these two ideas closer together).

9. Relentlessly revise. Effective writing seldom occurs on the first draft. The revision just cited is only one of hundreds I could cull from writing this book. Sometimes, for sake of clarity, the revision may result in more words, but more often in fewer; and often, as just seen, in other improvements as well.

One authority, when asked the secret of good writing, replied, "Revise, revise, revise." There is much truth in this advice. One gain is usually conciseness.

VARIETY

H. J. Tichy, a widely respected authority on business and technical writing, has declared: "Dull paragraphs of sentences formed in one mold are as depressing as the vista presented by a typical cheap housing development—hundreds of houses all the same size, all with the same architectural plan." [22]

To illustrate, imagine reading a report in this style:

> The union represents the workers by means of a shop committee. The committeemen are chosen from among the workers by periodic elections. The various committeemen represent, after the election, specified districts within each plant. The districts are made up of various departments within the plant. The borderlines of each district are set up in each local contract between management and the union.

Bored yet? If not, you have a remarkably high tolerance for monotony.

Variety is to style as flavoring is to food. One caution, however: in striving for variety, avoid variety for its own sake. To illustrate, a child may recite a poem in a sing-song pattern, thus introducing variety (in pitch inflection), but detracting from the mood and meaning. Similarly, in writing, variety *can* be inappropriate. The most common instance is when parallelism is being used, for parallelism requires an *un*varied pattern to achieve its effect. Although, as a rule, variety aids readability, variety should never be allowed to interfere with clarity or accuracy.

How achieve variety in writing? A number of ways are available: through structure, arrangement, sentence function, sentence beginnings, and sentence length.

Variety in Sentence Structure

As to structure, sentences may be classified in four categories: *simple, complex, compound,* and *compound-complex.* A series of sentences having all the same structure—unless deliberately so written for emphasis—becomes monotonous. Thus mixing the types introduces variety. Examples of each type are given below.

Simple, consisting of a single independent clause:

> For Charlotte, N.C., the federal aid is considered especially timely.[23]

> The nation's cities soon will start drawing on the biggest pool of transit money in history—nearly 12 billion dollars—to revitalize their floundering local transportation systems.

Complex, consisting of one independent and one or more dependent clauses:

> If we can't somehow resolve this problem, we'll have to cut service and increase fares.

> We'll have to cut service and reduce fares if we somehow can't resolve this problem.

> If we can't somehow resolve this problem, we'll have to cut service and increase fares, which would be a last-resort measure.

Compound, consisting of one or more independent clauses:

> Federal operating subsidies will not make up for that loss, but they would help.

> Federal operating subsidies will not make up for that loss; however, they could help.

> This new law represents only a start; we need more dollars to get the job done; furthermore, the Federal Government must make a total commitment.

Compound-complex, consisting of two or more independent clauses along with one or more dependent clauses:

> A boost in bus fares has been suggested, but there is wide disagreement on whether this would increase revenues or drive away riders and put Metro deeper into the hole.

Variety in Arrangement

In terms of arrangement of ideas, sentences may be classified as *periodic* or *loose.* The periodic sentence uses the indirect approach, in that the main idea is not completed until the end of the sentence. The loose sentence uses the direct approach by stating the main idea at the outset, then adding additional information. Mixing the two results in greater variety than relying on either exclusively. But again, the variety must be appropriate to the situation. For a brief sentence, the periodic sentence is often preferable, since delaying the main thought till the end creates suspense and adds emphasis. But for longer sentences, stating the main thought at the beginning (thus using the loose construction) is usually preferable to avoid placing too great a strain on the reader in remembering the details before the main thought is reached. Examples of the two kinds of sentences are given here.

Periodic (main thought delayed until end of sentence):

> Once considered a detriment because areas around stations became run down, such systems are getting a new image.
>
> Such systems, once considered a detriment because areas around stations became run down, are getting a new image.

Loose (main thought stated at the outset, followed by additional information):

> Such systems are getting a new image, although once they were considered a detriment because areas around stations became run down.

Variety According to Function

According to function, sentences may be classified as *declarative, imperative, interrogative,* or *exclamatory*. The declarative sentence makes a statement; in business writing, which tends to be factual and informative, nearly all sentences are declarative. The imperative sentence gives a direction, suggestion, or command. The interrogative sentence asks a question; in business writing, questions—when used—serve typically as transitions or attention-getters, often at the beginning of a paragraph. They may also appear in quoted dialogue. The exclamatory sentence expresses surprise or strong emotion; it is seldom used in business writing except in quoted dialogue. The following are examples:

> *Declarative:* Houston, Dallas and Omaha all hope to cut fares.
>
> *Imperative:* Look at the job from all angles.[24]
>
> *Interrogative:* Can it be finished?
>
> *Exclamatory:* Jones replied, "I'll get even with you!"[25]

Variety in Sentence Beginnings

Although the most standard way of beginning a sentence is probably to start with the subject ("A *boost* in bus fares has been suggested") a wide variety of ways is available, as illustrated here:

> *Verb:* Says B. R. Stokes, executive director of the American Public Transit Association, an industry trade group, "The private and public transport industry . . ."

Infinitive phrase: *To end* the frustration of people trying to get bus information, the Chicago Transit Authority has expanded its answering service and employs many operators who speak foreign languages.

Participial phrase: *Beginning* this week, Americans can buy, hold, and trade gold bullion for the first time since Franklin Roosevelt banned private ownership of the yellow metal 41 years ago.[26]

Conjunction: *Or,* if a community's buses or rail-transit cars need replacing, the Government will pick up 80 percent of the tab.

Conjunctive adverb: *However,* this belief does not seem to be shared by their subordinates.[27]

Adverb: *Currently,* there are 35.4 miles of Metro under construction.

Adverbial phrase: *By the 1980s,* this city and its suburbs in Virginia and Maryland are supposed to be linked by a 98-mile Metro system, the largest single mass-transit construction project ever undertaken.

Variety in Length

As mentioned earlier, various sentence lengths have different uses. Most sentences run 20 words or less. Occasionally a short sentence of half a dozen words, or a longer one of perhaps 30–40, offers a welcome change of pace. But a steady fare of all the same length becomes deadening.

A Closing Note on Variety

Variety, though important, must not be permitted to interfere with coherent structure or emphasis—either within or between sentences. Yet these need not interfere with variety. Structure can be sound without sacrificing variety; emphasis, well used, helps create variety. Although variety, like color, is of secondary importance, it is often the difference between writing that is lifeless and writing that has life.

WORD CHOICE

As explained in Chapter 2, there is no way to convey ideas directly—only indirectly through symbols. In sentences, the symbols are words (and punctuation). Thus, word choice in writing is of utmost importance. To serve faithfully, words must meet two criteria: (a) express accurately our thoughts, both through denotation and connotation, and (b) elicit accurate interpretation by the receiver of our thoughts.

Although the meaning is affected by other factors—structure and emphasis especially—an inescapable part of the meaning depends upon the words themselves. Thus, the student who wrote "considered *singularly*" when "separately" was meant, or "I had to *improvise*" when "compromise" was meant, chose words unable to meet the criteria of accuracy either in expression or interpretation.

Four aspects of word choice we shall consider here are *simplicity, jargon, personal style,* and *triteness.*

Simplicity

Margaret Mead, the eminent anthropologist, was once asked in a public appearance, "To what do you attribute the fact that you have been famous for so many years?" Her reply, in essence, was, "When I wrote my first book [*Coming of Age in Samoa,* 1928] many years ago, I was so bold as to write in a style that the ordinary person could understand."

Apparently, fellow social scientists have not profited from her example. British sociologist Stanislav Andreski has criticized his colleagues for what he calls "ponderous restatements of the obvious." His choice example of "nebulous verbosity" is a passage whose point is that for attaining one's goals one needs intelligence, skills, and knowledge. But this simple point is concealed in thick layers of verbiage as follows: "Skills constitute the manipulative techniques of human goal attainment and control in relation to the physical world, so far as artifacts or machines especially designed as tools do not yet supplement them. Truly human skills are guided by organized and codified knowledge . . ." and so on.[28]

By way of contrast, consider this passage from *The General Theory of Relativity* by Albert Einstein: "I am standing in front of a gas range. Standing alongside of each other on the range are two pans so much alike that one may be mistaken for the other. Both are half full of water. I notice that steam is being emitted continuously from one pan, but not from the other . . ."[29] At this point we shall break in, since our interest here is not in the theory of relativity but in simplicity of style.

Perhaps you're surprised that someone of Einstein's stature should write this simply. Or perhaps that's the point. When writers become concerned with making an impression, their focus on the subject becomes blurred, and shows it. Einstein, not being concerned with impressing, could focus more simply on his ideas, thus *think* more clearly, and in turn *write* more clearly.

Readers appreciate writing that uses a clear, simple style.

Jargon

Jargon refers to the specialized language of a trade or profession. Even students use jargon ("I hope to comp out of Bio. Sci. next term"—that is, to take and pass a comprehensive examination which will excuse the student from having to take a course in biological science). Here are other typical examples from business reports:

> The GR-70 dip was dropped on cast date 126 and replaced with a dip GEN.
>
> The half width of the 99th percent K-S confidence band is 1.39% for the MIC distribution and 2.62% for the CAL distribution.

Should jargon be used or shouldn't it? In view of the advice given just above on simplicity, you might expect the answer to be an automatic "no." But the answer is not that easy; it depends on who the reader or readers will be.

If you *know* that the intended recipients will understand the jargon, by all means use it. It would be ridiculous, for instance, for a medical lab report addressed to a physician to be written in layman's language. But if the recipients include even *any* to whom the jargon might present a barrier, either avoid the jargon completely, or use what you must, but take care to define it immediately.

An exception, however, applies to longer reports or proposals. Here, the boss up the line reads typically only the opening pages (title page, abstract, table of contents, introduction, conclusions, recommendations). In these sections jargon should be carefully avoided. But in the detailed discussion following, jargon may be safely used (with appropriate definitions where necessary), since ordinarily this will be read only by other specialists in the subject. The opening sections, however, should be clear to *any* intended reader, whatever his or her background.

In few situations in business writing is the reader-centered concept more apparent than in deciding when to or not to use jargon. This principle is further illustrated by a recommendation from a metallurgist in a manufacturing plant. The original draft reads as follows:

> Subject: Titanium Anode Baskets for Tin Plating
>
> Currently we are having control problems in tin plating which result in varying degrees of too much plate, too little plate, dark plate, and rough plate. This stems from the difficulty in maintaining consistent electrical contact with the lightweight anodes which are needed when pistons are plated with the domes out of the bath. Considerable plate stripping and replating is necessary, more work on anode control is needed, and the bath composition varies because of the anode imbalance further aggravating the problem.
>
> Tests have been run showing that titanium anode baskets in conjunction with ball tin anodes can be used to eliminate the problem. A permanent positive electrical connection can be made between the baskets and the buss bars. Anodes are replenished simply by dropping the tin balls into the baskets to keep them full. Contact between the balls and baskets occurs under the solution and no chance of corroded electrical contact

exists. This procedure, in addition to correcting current problems, also eliminates the need for specially casting the tin anodes on steel strips and facilitates procuring and handling the anodes.

The cost of the anode baskets to equip the Model 71 bath is $5,000. The writer strongly recommends your approval of this purchase to correct the aforementioned problems.

The difficulty was that the recommendation was addressed to the general superintendent and the purchasing agent. For them, the explanation was too technical (and too detailed); it did not speak their language. So the recommendation was revised with the intended readers in mind. The new version reads:

Our current tin plating problem of too heavy plate, too light plate, dark plate, and rough plate has cost Detroit Diesel approximately $460.00 per month in reworking costs, downtime, and unnecessary maintenance.

Tests using titanium anode baskets with ball tin anodes show that the technical difficulties responsible for the problems can be eliminated with these baskets. Baskets to handle Model 71 production will cost $5,000. Your approval of this purchase is strongly recommended.[30]

Note that in the revised version, most of the technical explanation was replaced by one magic phrase, "$460.00 per month." This is reader-centered language!

Personal Style

A lingering controversy over the years concerns how personal should be one's style in business writing; in other words, whether it is acceptable to use personal pronouns and nouns, or whether personal views and references should be hidden from sight. Traditionally, the view has been largely the latter.

To explore this question more fully, we shall look at the practice both in business correspondence and in reports and proposals, then offer some guidelines on when to use personal style and when not to.

Personal Style in Business Correspondence At one time business correspondence was typically formal, stilted—and impersonal. Had you lived in the early 1900s, you might have found in your mail a letter like this:

Mr. James A. Weir
Purchasing Agent
Argon Company
Kansas City, Kansas

Dear Sir:
  Yours of the 15th received and wish to acknowledge receipt thereof. It is requested in your letter that samples of Part #617

be sent for inspection before an order is placed. In compliance with said request, six (6) samples are being shipped under separate cover. I remain

Yours truly,
Ronald O. Wolcott

This style is now as outdated as horse-drawn milk wagons. In business correspondence today great emphasis is placed on a more natural, informal, personal approach—sometimes summed up as the "You Approach." Thus, the above letter, if written today might read:

Mr. James A. Weir
Purchasing Agent
Argon Company
Kansas City, Kansas 66102

Dear Jim:

Thanks for your letter of the 15th asking that we send you some samples of Part #617 to inspect before you place an order. We are happy to do this, and are sending six samples immediately under separate cover.

If we can be of further help, please get in touch.

Sincerely,
Ronald O. Wolcott

Why this change in style? Apparently it reflects a shift from a "business is business" philosophy to one that says "people are people." As we shall see in Chapter 10, letters are the one form of business (aside, notably, from advertisements) aimed at readers outside the organization. There is thus less opportunity for establishing face-to-face the positive relationship needed for effective communication. Therefore, more care must be taken in writing letters to cultivate and sustain this relationship. Thus, the importance of the personal approach and informal tone.

Personal Style in Reports and Proposals In reports and proposals, the attitude toward a personalized style has traditionally been negative. The argument appears to rest mainly on two assumptions: (1) reports and proposals should be objective, and (2) a personal style—especially one using "I"—reduces objectivity. Both assumptions warrant scrutiny.

In the main, the first assumption—that reports and proposals should be objective—is sound. However, as we shall see in Chapter 11, at times the writer's opinions—in the form of interpretation of data, conclusions, or recommendations—are called for. And opinions, when offered, should be identified as such. This may be done by use of the headings "Conclusions" or "Recommendations," which automatically imply that opinions are being offered. Opinion may—and often is—expressed in the passive voice: "It is thought," "It is suggested," and so on. Or, the opinion may be quite directly expressed in a personal style: "In my opinion," "I suggest," "I recommend," and so forth.

This leads to the second assumption, that a personal style reduces objectivity. This assumption does not necessarily hold. For example, to say "I discovered three errors" is just as objective as to say "Three errors were discovered." Besides, it is more informative, for it identifies *who* discovered the errors.

To carry this a step further, here are two sentences—one with "I," one without—in which the sentence with the "I" is, in fact, *more* objective (in spite of the "I," not because of it).

> I saw that she had red hair.
>
> She is beautiful.[31]

The first is a simple statement of fact, expressing an objective observation. The second is clearly nothing more than the writer's opinion. To someone else she might be ugly!

Personal Style and the Passive Voice We mentioned the passive voice above as one means of expressing opinion. The *passive voice* refers to the grammatical construction in which the subject is the receiver of the action as compared to when the subject is the doer and the voice is *active*. (For example: "Several solutions *were discussed*" vs. "*We discussed* several solutions.") Obviously, the passive voice is more compatible with an impersonal style, and the active voice more compatible with a personal style.

Now, the passive voice is a perfectly proper verb form to use—when appropriate; in other words, when the interest is on what happened rather than on who or what caused it to happen. For example, from a test report on the cooling system of a particular model automobile is this sentence: "The taxi was driven from New York City to Lockport (460 miles) on Tuesday, September 23." In the context of this report, it is completely beside the point *who* did the driving.

However, indiscriminate use of the passive, with no regard to whether it is appropriate, tends to result in such drawbacks as these:

1. Less informative. As stated above, "Three errors were discovered" (passive voice) is less informative than "I discovered three errors" (active voice).

2. Less dynamic. Because the doer is either de-emphasized or omitted altogether when the passive voice is used, the passive is less dynamic than the active. For example:

> *Passive:* It is believed that a 3% increase in sales will occur.
>
> *Active:* We believe that a 3% increase in sales will occur.

3. *Less concise.* Frequently (though not always), use of the passive voice is more wordy. Compare, for instance, the following:

> *Passive:* It is sometimes found that a billing error is made by our clerk. [13 words]
>
> *Active:* Sometimes our clerk makes a billing error. [7 words]

4. *Less natural.* H. J. Tichy relates an amusing incident in which she had been late for an appointment with a foreign-born engineer who had recently learned English. When she apologized for her lateness, he replied, "It is nothing. A cigarette was smoked and a book was read while waiting." A student of mine who had had the "virtue" of the passive voice impressed strongly on him by his supervisor at work, turned in as a class assignment a report containing such strained expressions as these:

> To gain knowledge of the area, time was spent becoming familiar . . .
>
> It was directed to his attention that the one proposal . . .
>
> It was needed to confer with Mr. Jones . . .

No wonder that English critic V. S. Pritchett in a letter to the *New York Times Book Review* of May 10, 1959, deplored the passive voice as creating "the bureaucratic impression that things 'were done' and that nobody 'did' them."

Speaking more broadly, the abstract of Cohen's article, "A World Without People" (from which the passage above by Einstein was quoted), says bluntly:

> We shall never improve the general quality of technical and scientific writing until it is liberated from the unwritten rule that prohibits the use of personal pronouns. . . . Many of our problems in technical writing—verbosity, obscurity, pomposity, awkwardness, and a dozen other ills—could be relieved or eliminated if writers would accept the idea that personal pronouns are as much a natural part of communicating ideas on paper as they are in talking.[32]

When to Use a Personal Style By now you may have concluded that the main point of this discussion has been to forget tradition and adopt a personal style in all your writing. More accurately, the main point has been to ignore the traditional bias against using a personal style at all in business communication. Each style—personal and impersonal—has its proper place. The purpose here will be to offer some guidelines on when to use which. (Since some of the guidelines have been implied already, little more than a reminder will be necessary here.)

The following are some of the occasions in business communication when the personal style is probably preferable:

1. To express personal warmth and directness—especially important for promoting a positive relationship with your reader. Cohen refers to impersonal writing as "turning your back on a person when you speak to him."[33] Flesch expresses it this way:

> Keep a running conversation with your reader.... Translate everything into *you* language. "This applies to citizens over 65" = "If you're over 65, this applies to you."

As already noted, the relationship factor is especially important in correspondence. It may also be important in memos on the job for expressing appreciation, commending an employee, announcing attainment of a departmental goal, and the like.

2. To identify the doer—the person or persons responsible for the action. This is especially appropriate for giving credit where credit is due; also for assuming personal blame. For example:

> Mr. Bacon moved that the meeting be postponed one week. [From the minutes of a meeting]
>
> Ms. Stevens is especially to be commended for her role in the project.
>
> The reason the shipment was late was that I overlooked sending in the order on time. [This is assumed to be from an interdepartmental memo, and is preferred to "The shipment arrived late because the order was not sent in on time," which may sound too much like a cover-up that in the long run can do more harm than good to one's credibility.]

3. To express opinion. As stated above, opinions—when the writer is qualified to give them—may have a rightful place in a report. When this is true, they should always be identified as such, and to say "In my opinion" or "I propose" may be the simplest way of doing this.

In general, the more informal the situation and the more relevant the relationship factor between writer and reader, the more personal the style may be—and the livelier and more natural it will seem.

When to Use an Impersonal Style Situations in which it may be preferable to be impersonal include the following:

1. When the doer is not important to the purpose of the message, as in the example above of the taxi driver on the test run.

2. When it is desirable to avoid finger-pointing. "A misunderstanding seems to have arisen" is certainly preferable to "You failed to understand my directions." Likewise, it is preferable to write "Objections were raised concerning the feasibility of the project," when the objections themselves are more important than who raised them, and no purpose is served by focusing attention on personalities instead of on issues.

3. When the personal style would sound self-important. A freshman I once taught wrote a memo to the dean (as a class assignment) proposing certain changes in class scheduling procedure. Of nine sentences in the memo, seven began with "I." You can imagine that had the dean actually received this memo he might easily have reacted, "Who is this self-important young upstart trying to tell *me* how to run this place!" (Of the seven "I's," several could have been omitted through slight revision, and the others played down by relocating them inside the sentence.)

4. When the boss is biased against the personal style. In Chapter 3 we saw that the manager-as-communicator sometimes has his or her pet biases. One of the most common of these is a blind bias against personal pronouns in formal reports, coupled with a strong preference for the passive. When this is the case, you may try educating the manager if you can. But if he or she remains unbudged, you then must decide how important it is to comply or rebel—or seek a new boss (which hardly seems that urgent). At least, *you* have some sound guidelines, so you need not impose bad biases on others when you have employees reporting to you.

What Pronouns to Use   When using pronouns, here are a few guidelines to observe:

1. If you wish to refer to yourself, the simplest terms to use are "I" or "my." But if you wish to sound less personal or to downplay the "I," using "the writer" may be preferable. Thus:

> I feel that *x* brand is as good as *y*.
>
> In my opinion, *x* brand is as good as *y*.
>
> In the writer's opinion, *x* brand is as good as *y*.

However, avoid using "we" to refer only to yourself, as in "We request our vacation be scheduled July 2 through July 20." (How many of you are taking the vacation?)

2. If you wish to refer to yourself and one or more associates, or to the company in general, or to yourself and the reader, "we" or "our" are appropriate. For example:

> As a result of our investigation ["our" referring to you and the others in your group, who have already been identified, perhaps in the introduction to the report], we recommend that . . .
>
> We [meaning the company] appreciate your calling this problem to our attention.
>
> We [meaning you and the reader] can feel proud of the recognition we have received.

3. If you wish to refer to the reader, simply use "you" or "your"; thus:

> In your letter of April 17 . . .
> When you reach Third Avenue, turn left.

But avoid the indefinite "you" if the "you" does not realistically apply to the reader. For instance, "You turn the main valve two turns to the right, then you record the pressure" would be appropriate if giving directions to someone who actually will be operating the equipment, but not if addressed to someone who will not be, such as someone in higher management. (Most likely, in giving directions, the "you" would be omitted entirely.)

Triteness

Triteness refers to using worn-out expressions. When first coined, such expressions caught on because they seemed a good way to say it—whatever the "it" may have been. But because they were so effective, they became overused, and through overuse lost their originality. Instead of being a means of expressing originality, they become a substitute for originality. It is better, then, to avoid them; to use language that best represents your particular ideas in the terms most meaningful to the reader.

Examples of common trite expressions include:

> as luck would have it
> equal to the occasion
> none the worse for wear
> the whole can of worms
> when all is said and done
> the last straw
> straight from the shoulder
> combine business with pleasure
> hanging in the balance

Timeworn expressions such as these are better avoided. If one's language sounds stale, one's thoughts are likely to sound stale as well.

SUMMARY

1. Although planning the structure of the message and the paragraphs comprising it is crucial, it is at the level of the sentence that a person either does or does not write well.

2. Sentence effectiveness may be measured in terms of seven characteristics: completeness, coherent structure, emphasis, appropriate length, conciseness, variety, and word choice.

3. Of the seven characteristics, coherent structure is the most important. An effective sentence must contain ideas that hang together, relate logically to each other, are arranged in an orderly pattern, work with instead of at cross-purposes with each other; in short, that make sense to the reader. In achieving sound structure, it is important to avoid sentence faults that weaken it, and to use writing techniques that strengthen it.

4. In sentences that contain more than one idea, it is essential to indicate whether the ideas are of equal importance or which ones should be given increased or reduced emphasis.

5. Appropriate sentence length is best understood in terms not of some "ideal" length but rather of the special functions that sentences serve. Longer sentences are best for grouping or combining ideas, medium length for expressing complex relationships, and short ones for emphasis.

6. Assuming that the meaning is complete, the structure sound, and the relative importance of ideas made clear, conciseness is a hallmark of good writing. It is a factor in sentence length, and contributes to readability.

7. Although never an end in itself, variety does relieve monotony and add flavor, thus contributing significantly to readability. Variety may be achieved through differences in sentence structure, type, and length.

8. Word choice is critical in influencing the fidelity with which ideas are expressed and interpreted. Among considerations in word choice are simplicity, personal (or impersonal) style appropriate to the situation, and freedom from triteness.

SUGGESTED APPLICATIONS

1. Write a critical analysis of a term paper you have submitted in some other course. As a basis of your analysis, use the seven characteristics of effective sentences developed in this chapter. Organize your paper as follows:

Introduction (around 50–75 words): Inform your reader (the instructor of this course) of the nature of the term paper assignment and the topic you wrote on. Include a preview of the pattern of organization you will use in your critical analysis.

Analysis (around 300–400 words): Focus on (a) the characteristics you feel you were satisfactory or strong in, and (b) the characteristics you find need definite improvement. In this section, be specific; cite sentences or passages from your paper illustrating ambiguous references, faulty parallelism, wordiness, or whatever the fault may be, and show exactly how you would revise them to eliminate the fault.

Conclusion (around 30–60 words): Sum up your strengths and the main areas that need improvement. Try to be objective and fair to yourself.

Use headings and subheadings to indicate clearly the main and subtopics of your paper. Proofread *carefully* before handing in the paper to be sure it says clearly what you want it to say, and is free from misspellings, grammatical errors, and so forth. Type, or write in ink, as your instructor may direct. (Note: your instructor may prefer different word numbers than those suggested above.)[34]

2. Write a comparative evaluation of two or three letters to the editor appearing in a daily paper. (Suggested length: 400–500 words.) Base your evaluation on one or more of the seven characteristics of effective sentences developed in this chapter, choosing those you feel most relevant to the particular letters. Use headings and subheadings to indicate clearly the main and subtopics of your paper. Proofread carefully before handing the paper in to be sure it says clearly what you want it to say, and is free from misspellings, grammatical errors, and so on. Type, or write in ink, as the instructor directs. Attach the letters, mounted on standard size typing paper, at the end of your evaluation, and indicate by footnote the name, date, and page of the newspaper from which the letters were taken.

3. Improve, according to the category and directions indicated, each of the following:

COMPLETENESS

Sentence Fragments. Add—either before, within, or at the end of the example—whatever will serve to complete the thought logically and produce a complete sentence:

1. Of all the candidates
2. And forever
3. When the bills have all been paid
4. Although the dean was not in and the assistant dean was unwilling to offer a decision
5. To supervise fabrication follow-up men in procuring all trim components and materials to support seating development within the requirements of Corporate Master Training

COHERENCE

Overloading. Improve the readability of the examples below by dividing them into shorter length sentences easier to read. Add whatever phraseology is necessary to ensure a smooth style:

6. The managerial responsibilities embrace an hourly production work force of 705 persons, 84 maintenance personnel,

and 45 salaried individuals of various grade levels, all of whom are involved in producing cores made from sand, such as one might find on lake shores.

7. All bills for payment which must fulfill audit requirement number one, as explained above, are received by messenger, inter-company mail, or U.S. mail, at an average rate of approximately 2,000 daily, but it is physically impossible to perform a 100 percent rate audit and still conform to commission regulations.

8. One man, who joined us six years ago as a management trainee after having been assigned to me for a period of one year following an expression of desire to work in the Production Control Department, has been a personal source of pride to me.

Comma Splices. Rewrite each of the following to remove the comma splice:

9. As supervisor of freight payments for the ABX Corporatin, I must not only ensure that our processing meets the above requirements, in addition, I must be sure they meet certain internal requirements.

10. Usually a hand rework is required on the detail part in order to salvage the material, this again becomes my responsibility to provide the necessary equipment.

11. My thoughts right now are not very clear, I assume that no matter what is transmitted to paper, it will invariably be criticized in some manner or other.

Mismanaging Modifiers—Misplaced. Revise each of the folowing by relocating the misplaced modifier so it clearly refers to what it is supposed to:

12. Miss DuClerq is only a secretary to Mr. Grossmeyer.

13. Report any other defects or mechanical damage to the people in the finished product.

14. Loose blouses which some women wear around punch presses are hazardous.

Mismanaging Modifiers—Dangling. Revise each of the following so the introductory phrase modifies the subject of the sentence logically as well as grammatically:

16. Arriving early for my interview, the Personnel Office was not open.

17. Swearing thunderously, the office almost shook with the boss's anger.

18. Driving cautiously, the dangerous intersection was approached.

Mismanaging Modifiers—Squinting. Revise each of the following so it is clear what the modifier in the middle of the sentence refers to:

19. Jackson has opposed often giving praise to the workers.
20. Vicki reported excitedly the inspector began to shout.
21. Posavetz stated late in the week the production was behind schedule.

Split Grammatical Construction. Revise each of the following so the subject and verb or the two elements of the infinitive are not ineffectively separated:

22. On my next assignment, I shall try to with greater attention to detail complete all phases of the job.
23. Your letter seems to unnecessarily, unfortunately, emphasize what Mrs. Pionk is already painfully aware of.
24. The reason for an initial planning session followed by the three-page questionnaire with in-depth interviews with selected respondents and finally a written report based on the interviews, plus a computer analysis of the questionnaires is that this is the method found to be most effective.

Vague or Ambiguous References. Revise each of the following so it is unmistakably clear what the pronoun refers to:

25. Wisner, after discussing the dispute between Allen and Kline, could see that his directions were unclear.
26. Ann wondered whether the schedule was complete and the reservations made. This was mainly what worried her.
27. I am trying to catch up from a work overload plus a slight case of flu, which is why I felt I should skip the meeting.

Faulty Relationships. Revise each of the following so the relationship between ideas is made more clear:

28. July has been a disappointing month for sales, and morale has remained high.
29. Both Susanne and Paul have proven very satisfactory in their new assignments; however they will soon be considered for promotion.
30. John Kelley is a salary administrator, yet has been with the company 13 years.

Switching Point of View. Revise each of the following so the person's point of view the sentence is written from remains consistent:

31. I soon learned that Harris was undependable; then it isn't long before you discover that not many of the others are either.
32. To use the office copier, it is necessary first to turn on the

switch to let the machine warm up. The operator should meanwhile check to see that there is an adequate supply of paper. If the red warning light comes, call Mrs. Amboy to correct whatever is wrong.

33. A new employee should first be certain he understands the foreman's directions, since you can really get off to a bad start by lousing up your first job. Probably it will take you two or three days to learn the routine. Once he has mastered the routine, however, he will experience a feeling both of satisfaction and letdown.

Switching Tense. Revise each of the following so the tense remains consistent throughout the sentence:

34. When Jason walked into my office I was busy on the telephone. Then he breaks in without even an apology and demands that I loan him ten dollars.
35. The questionnaire responses will sometimes arrive at the rate of 10–15 a day. We processed them promptly and report on the results.
36. Ms. Easton was so elated with her success that she actually starts dancing around the office.

Ideas in Confused Sequence. Revise each of the following so the sequence of ideas is as easy as possible for the reader to follow:

37. In planning your trip, it is useful to find out what clothes to take. Motel and airline reservations are other factors; also what reports and correspondence you will need. Wonderland Travel Agency will handle reservations for you, including a rental car if you need one.
38. Lunch will be followed by your meeting with Dr. Travaglini; Dr. Carlson will meet with you 11–12; and Ms. Harrison and Dr. Marshall at lunch.
39. Following your meeting with Mr. Brundle, you should give Mrs. Slater a ring. Your first appointment, of course, is with Mr. Farrington.

Using a Direct Approach. Revise each of the following so the main idea is presented at or near the beginning of the sentence:

40. Collecting money for registrations and program materials (including giving receipts for all monies received) and taking roll are among your duties at the beginning of the first meeting.
41. Determining brand preferences and knowledge of competing brands, also learning their buying habits, then securing

their reactions to the sample advertisements are the major topics for your session with the consumer research panel.

42. "Entirely diagreee," "Sometimes disagree," "No opinion," "Sometimes agree," and "Always agree" are the five response categories for use in the questionnaire.

Parallelism. Revise each of the following so each of the series of similar ideas in the sentence(s) are expressed in similar grammatical constructions:

43. The proposed dress design was preferred by 56 percent of the women over 40. Thirty-one percent of the women disliked it. "No opinion" was the response of the remaining 13 percent.

44. Woldraw has been absent an average of two days a week during the past two months. His work performance has been generally poor. Four times the past month he came to work intoxicated.

45. It is recommended that:
   a. A new MNX copier be purchased.
   b. In order to control use of the copier, that the company issue keys to selected personnel for operating the copier.
   c. Issuance of a policy statement governing use of copiers.

Equal Emphasis—Coordinate Conjunctions. Use any of the seven coordinate conjunctions ("or," "nor," "for," "and," "but," "yet," "so") to construct a sentence from each of the following pairs of ideas so each pair is given equal emphasis:

46. Wittkowski and Riethmiller both approve
   the problem remains unsolved
47. Miss Fischer has refused to OK it
   we may as well abandon the notion
48. Gail was eager to participate
   she remembered the success she had enjoyed last time

Equal Emphasis—Conjunctive Adverbs. Write sentences from the ideas presented in problems 46–48, using in each case a semicolon and conjunctive adverb (such as "however," "consequently," "furthermore," or "therefore") to indicate equal emphasis between the ideas. Number these sentences 49–51.

Reduced Emphasis—Weaker Grammatical Structure. Use a weaker grammatical structure (phrase or dependent clause) to reduce the emphasis on one of each of the pairs of the ideas in 46–48 above. Note that in so doing, you are at the same time increasing the emphasis on the other idea. Number these sentences 52–54.

Reduced Emphasis—Less Emphatic Location. Rewrite each of the following to reduce the emphasis on the italicized expression by relocating it in a less emphatic position in the sentence:

55. *I* now am responsible for supervising training activities in the Northeast Region.
56. An organization consists of a number of people who are interdependent on each other, require coordination, and must communicate with each other, *according to Haney.*
57. Tables and figures (or illustrations) are two categories under which graphics *may be discussed.*

Reduced Emphasis—De-emphasizing Punctuation. Use either commas or parentheses to set off secondary ideas in the following sentences. Note that the more parenthetical the idea, the more appropriate to use parentheses instead of commas.

58. Mr. Mallis who travels frequently is a competent executive.
59. The concept of credibility see Chapter 9 is more important than most people realize.
60. The American Business Communication Association ABCA held its 1975 convention in Toronto.

Increased Emphasis—Use of Underlining or Italics. Copy each of the following sentences, underlining the word or phrase you feel should receive special emphasis. (Note that in printed material italics would usually be used instead of underlining.)

61. Today's organization demands communication competency at a higher level than ever before.
62. The key to the art of managing, according to Theory Y, is the ability to trust appropriately.
63. Let us examine the communication issue.[35]

Increased Emphasis—Use of Dashes. Copy each of the following sentences, inserting a dash or pair of dashes to give added emphasis to the word or phrase you feel should receive added emphasis; insert commas where needed.

64. The computer people have a phrase for it GIGO Garbage In Garbage Out.
65. The French however tend to say "Jean sais sage!" be wise.

66. Words are just so many meaningless sounds "X" and "Y" and "Zalunke" until someone gives them a meaning.[36]

Appropriate Length—Shorter Sentences. Rewrite each of the following by breaking them into shorter sentences for increased readability. Eliminate unnecessary verbiage as appropriate.

67. Our present shortage of personnel may be stressed to its utmost limit by sending Mr. Dequindre to Detroit, and provided this problem still exists at the time of the training program, we may be forced to withdraw one service representative from the field.

68. The costing phase is very critical because of lack of information, so we believe that if the ECR costing developed by the cost-estimating section were made by utilizing its cost engineers' team in cost estimating instead of waiting for information, the ECR's could be analyzed in a go-no-go decision approach (based on profitability), and could be accelerated and timed, the items of major importance would then have their action re-emphasized.

69. While we are, of course, extremely concerned about the considerable delay in obtaining the required spare parts for your vehicle, a situation which is created by the recent strike in the United States, we want to assure you that we have traced your order and are doing everything possible within our power to obtain the parts within the next coming days.

Appropriate Length—Longer Sentences. Rewrite each of the following passages so the ideas are combined smoothly into longer sentences. Note that in the revision, some ideas will be de-emphasized by being expressed as phrases or dependent clauses:

70. Paragraphing aids readability. Paragraphing is partially a factor of format. It is also partially a factor of content. As a factor of format it serves to make the page appear more inviting. It does this by dividing the page into clearly identifiable sections. This results in breaks along the way. These breaks make the going look easier.

71. Credibility refers to trust. It is the trust the reader has in the writer. Or it may be the trust the listener has in the speaker. This trust results from the reader's perception of the writer's expertise. This trust may also result from the listener's perception of the speaker's expertise. The trust may also result from the confidence the reader has in the integrity of

the writer. Or the trust may result from the confidence the listener has in the integrity of the speaker.

72. I work at the Jakeda Corporation. We build Wedfrisats, Janmarips, and Jusepters. This is an assembly plant. We do not manufacture any parts. All we do is put components together. This results in the finished product.

Conciseness—Elimination of Unneeded Words. Revise each of the following to eliminate the unnecessary words. (In some instances whole ideas may be omitted because they are unnecessary.)

73. Digital indexes will be included on some 1979 Jusepters, but there will also be some models without the digital indexes.

74. It is the general consensus of opinion that production of Janmarips will be substantially and significantly increased as a result of combining the two operations together.

75. In the misunderstanding of the meaning of another person, it is very important to remember that in all probability the causes are many and varied.

76. Jeanne was given the responsibility and she handled it well.

77. Our salespeople show as much initiative as theirs do.

Conciseness—Use of Colons. Substitute a colon where appropriate to reduce the number of words in these examples:

78. In reducing communication falloff three approaches may be used. These approaches are (1) establish a good personal relationship, (2) formulate the message carefully, and (3) utilize feedback from the receiver.

79. One factor is more important in persuasion than any other. That factor is *adapting to the need of the persuadee.*

80. The Jakeda Corporation is planning to introduce three new models in 1978. These three models are the Oretana, Calorida, and Minnada.

Word Choice—Personal Style. Rewrite the following passage to reduce the overemphasis on "I":

81. I have chosen as the topic for my report, "Artificial Visual Environments." I shall discuss the reasons as to why and how we artifically illuminate our environment. I shall begin with the human eye and how it functions under different colors and intensity of light sources, along with other variables in the process of seeing. I shall conclude by discussing the recommended illumination levels and how they are calculated.

82. I spent three hours with the Director of Reliability, Mr.

Ashbury, then I was taken on a tour of their facilities. I then met with Mr. Hoyt, Director of Sales and Marketing, discussing some questions I shall talk over with you when I return.

Word Choice—Passive to Active. Rewrite the following passage, making use of personal pronouns and the active voice whenever such changes would seem natural and appropriate:

83. It was expressed that there existed a need for rearrangement of the layout of the blueprint area, since numerous complaints have been received concerning the crowded conditions. To gain knowledge of the area, time was spent becoming familiar with the operations in the area. It was directed to the attention of the writer that a major source of irritation was the inconvenient location of the files. Upon examination, it was determined that this had resulted in part because an aisle had to be maintained through the center of the area, since it had been directed by the fire chief that without this aisle safety regulations would be violated. In order for the investigation to be completed, it was necessary to confer with Mr. Sample, the Director of Planning.

Word Choice—Trite Expressions. Rewrite each of the following to express the italicized idea in less trite phraseology:

84. Anyone who works for Ms. Medalia soon finds that it's *all work and no play.*
85. Mr. Allerind prefers to have jobs completed on time, but if they're not, he seems to feel that it's *better late than never.*
86. Those conclusions in Cohen's report must be taken with a *grain of salt.*
87. *When all is said and done,* the sales force has *put on a stellar performance.*
88. If you start asking questions about the scrap problem, you'll *open up a whole can of worms.*
89. Lee's report contains *more than meets the eye.*
90. Grant's bullheadedness, together with the workers' stalling, just *creates a vicious cycle.*

4. By paging through such magazines as *Business Week, Harvard Business Review, Management Review, Nation's Business, Newsweek,* and *Time,* find examples of sentence variety according to the categories given below. In the paper you hand in, show the number (as listed below), state the label, copy the sentence (using quotation marks), and show the source. For example:

    1. Simple: "It was only a matter of time." *Business Week,* August 15, 1975, p. 36.

Variety in Sentence Structure
1. Simple
2. Complex
3. Compound
4. Compound-complex

Variety in Arrangement
5. Periodic
6. Loose

Variety According to Function
7. Declarative
8. Imperative
9. Interrogative
10. Exclamatory

Variety in Sentence Beginnings
11. Verb
12. Infinitive phrase
13. Participial phrase
14. Conjunction
15. Conjunctive adverb
16. Adverb
17. Adverbial phrase

Variety in Length
18. Five words or less
19. Thirty words or more

NOTES

[1] Anne Morrow Lindbergh, *Bring Me A Unicorn* (New York: The New American Library, 1972), p. 81.

[2] From an advertisement for the CBS Radio Network, *Time* Magazine, January 27, 1975, p. 59. Copy reprinted courtesy CBS/Broadcast Group, Advertising and Design Department.

[3] Adapted from a letter by Gail F. King. Used with permission of the author.

[4] This example is cited in Louis Foley, "Brevity Isn't Everything," *The Journal of Business Communication,* Vol. 12 (Fall, 1974), pp. 30–34.

[5] From a memo by Albert O. Pardoe, Raytheon Service Company. Used with permission of author.

[6] Calvin A. Downs, "A Content Analysis of Twenty Selection Interviews," *Personnel Administration/Public Personnel Review,* Sept.–Oct., 1972, p. 28.

[7] J. H. L. Watson, "The Scanning Electron Microscope," *Henry Ford Hospital Medical Journal,* Vol. 21, No. 2 (Nov. 2, 1973), pp. 75–78.

[8] Dean Ellis, Lawrence Jacobs, and Cory Mills, "A Union Authorization Election: The Key to Winning," *Personnel Journal,* April, 1972, pp. 246–254.

[9] From a memo by Albert O. Pardoe, Raytheon Service Company. Used with permission of author.

[10] From Hector Lazo, "Emotional Aspects of Industrial Buying," in *Dynamic Marketing for a Changing World,* Robert S. Hancock (ed.), Proceedings of the

43rd National Conference of the American Marketing Association, American Marketing Association, Chicago, 1960, pp. 258–265.

[11] Charles N. Weaver and Sandra L. Holmes, "On the Use of Sick Leave by Female Employees," *Personnel Administration/Public Personnel Review,* Sept.–Oct., 1972, pp. 46–50.

[12] Roy W. Walters, "Job Enrichment Isn't Easy," *Personnel Administration/Public Personnel Review,* Sept.–Oct., 1972, pp. 61–66.

[13] "A 3-D View for Science," *Henry Ford Hospital Review,* Vol. 21, No. 2 (Summer, 1973), pp. 10–11.

[14] Thomas M. Meade, "Executive Promotions: Does Familiarity Breed Oversight?" *Personnel,* September–October, 1972, pp. 45–58.

[15] Charles W. Bartells, "Why Change Hourly Employees to Salary?" *Personnel Journal,* June, 1972, pp. 439–441.

[16] Rudolf Flesch, *The Art of Plain Talk* (New York: Harper & Brothers Publishers, 1946), pp. 38–39.

[17] Foley, pp. 30–34. The French source is François Richaudeau, *La Lisibilité* [Readability], Centre d'Etude et de Promotion de la Lecture, Paris, 1969.

[18] Mary C. Bromage, "Sentences That Make Sense," *The Journal of Accountancy,* May, 1967, pp. 56–60.

[19] *Ibid.,* p. 58.

[20] "Phoenix Area's Sprawl Worries City Planners But Not Its Citizenry," *The Wall Street Journal,* June 18, 1974, p. 1.

[21] William Strunk, Jr. and E. B. White, *The Elements of Style,* 2nd ed. (New York: The Macmillan Company, 1972), p. 17.

[22] H. J. Tichy, *Effective Writing for Engineers, Managers, Scientists* (New York: John Wiley & Sons, 1967), p. 242.

[23] Unless otherwise noted by additional footnotes, the examples illustrating variety are from two articles, " 'Last Hope' Effort for Transit: Where 12 Billions in Aid Will Go" and "Another Victim of Inflation: Washington's Subway," *United States News and World Report,* Dec. 23, 1974, pp. 42–44.

[24] "Position Description: A Key to Finding Good Executives," *Personnel Journal,* June, 1972, pp. 450–451.

[25] From a grievance report by a supervisor to the Director of Labor Relations.

[26] "Get Ready! Get Set! Gold!" *Time,* January 6, 1975, p. 84.

[27] Arthur Bedeian, "Superior-Subordinate Role Perception," *Personnel Administration/Public Personnel Review,* November–December, 1972, p. 9.

[28] "Science or Sorcery?" *Time,* September 25, 1972, p. 71.

[29] Quoted from Gerald I. Cohen, "A World Without People," *IEEE Transactions on Engineering Writing and Speech,* Vol. EWS-12 (October, 1969), p. 79.

[30] Jack E. LaBelle, "Communications" (unpublished). Used with permission of the author.

[31] Cohen, p. 80.

[32] Cohen, p. 79.

[33] *Ibid.*

[34] This assignment is adapted from one described by Wayne Baty, Arizona State University, in the *American Business Communication Bulletin,* March 1974, pp. 20–22.

[35] These examples are adapted from William V. Haney, *Communication and Organizational Behavior,* 3rd ed. (Homewood, Ill.: Richard D. Irwin, Inc., 1973).

[36] *Ibid.*

7 GRAMMAR, PUNCTUATION, AND WORD USAGE

ABBREVIATIONS	177
Academic Degrees	178
Dates and Places	178
Familiar Abbreviations	178
Manuscript Abbreviations	178
Titles	179
AGREEMENT	179
Subject-Verb	179
Pronoun-Antecedent	183
CLAUSES	184
Independent Clauses	184
Dependent Clauses	185
COMPARISONS	185
Degree of Comparison	186
Illogical Comparisons	186
Inequivalent Comparisons	186
Comparing Absolutes	187
Incomplete Comparisons	187
CONJUNCTIONS	187
Coordinate Conjunctions	187
Correlative Conjunctions	188
Subordinate Conjunctions	188
NUMBERS	189
When to Use Figures	189
When to Use Words	190
When to Use a Combination of Words and Figures	191
Miscellaneous Guidelines	192
PLURALS	192
POSSESSION	194
Using Apostrophes	195
Using Possessive Pronouns	196
Using the Possessive Form with Gerunds	196
PREPOSITIONS	196
PUNCTUATION	197
Apostrophes (')	198
Brackets ([ ])	198
Capitalization	198
Colons (:)	203
Commas (,)	204
Dashes (—)	208
Ellipses (. . .)	209
Exclamation Points (!)	209
Hyphens (-)	209
Parentheses (( ))	211
Periods (.)	212
Question Marks (?)	213
Quotation Marks (" "; ' ')	214
Semicolons (;)	216
Underlining (___) and Italics	218
SPELLING	219
VERB TENSE	220
WORDS—CONFUSED AND MISUSED	222

Chapter 7 is the handbook chapter of the text. It is intended to help you with the fine points of being clear and correct in your writing. It's your guide to answering the often encountered question: "Which is the right way to write it?" Serious use of the chapter can increase significantly both your competence and confidence in writing, and as a result enhance your image in the eyes of your readers as a writer who is literate and who takes pride in his or her work.

This is not a chapter to be read like the others in this text, but to be referred to—often—like a dictionary. As a start, glance first through the chapter outline; then consult some topic you feel unsure of. Make it a habit to refer to this chapter regularly; the more often you use it, the easier you will find using it and the more valuable it will become. If you use it enough, you will find it the most practical in the entire text. It's up to you.

ABBREVIATIONS

In using abbreviations, consider whether they will be (a) clear to the reader, and (b) appropriate to the occasion. The more limited the readership and the more informal the occasion, the more freely one may use them; the more extensive the readership and more formal the occasion, the less freely.

For example, an engineer might leave this note on his or her secretary's desk:

11-4-75
5:15

Jennifer,
    Lv for L. G. on UA741, 7:45 a.m. Back for IMA dinner tomorrow night. Please have rough draft of ASME report on met. app. in gear ratios typed; will want to look it over Th. a.m.

T.

This memo is intended for one person: Jennifer. Jennifer will have no trouble deciphering that the memo is from her boss, Thomas Newton, that he is leaving for LaGrange, Illinois, on United Airlines flight 741, that IMA is the Industrial Mutual Association, and that the desired report is on metric applications and is to be submitted to the American Society of Mechanical Engineers. The abbreviations, as used in this memo, are therefore entirely satisfactory.

But if Thomas Newton is writing a section for the annual stockholders' report (a formal report to a diverse readership), he will avoid any abbreviations not generally understood and accepted. However, he may write "American Society of Mechanical Engineers (ASME)" the first time, and use "ASME" after that.

Trouble spots encountered in using abbreviations include the following:

Academic Degrees Academic degrees are usually abbreviated: B.A., M.A., D.V.M. Use either the title or degree; not both:

> *Incorrect:* Dr. Duane Murphy, D.V.M.
>
> *Correct:* Dr. Duane Murphy *or* Duane Murphy, D.V.M.

Dates and Places In formal writing, spell the name completely: Tuesday, February, Tremont Street, Colorado, Los Angeles. The more informal the occasion, as in routine correspondence or informal memos, the more acceptable it may be to abbreviate: Tue., Feb., Tremont St., Colo., L.A. The Post Office Service now approves shortened abbreviations of states in envelope addresses—but *only* if the zip code is included: California, CA; Colorado, CO; Texas, TX; Ohio, OH.

Familiar Abbreviations If an abbreviation is familiar and acceptable to the expected reader, use it. Examples: C.P.A. (Certified Public Accountant), CIA, USSR. However, be certain the abbreviation may not convey a different meaning for some readers. For instance, "USA" may mean "United States of America" or "United States Army." In Michigan, "U of M." means "University of Michigan," but in Minnesota it means "University of Minnesota."

Manuscript Abbreviations Manuscripts for college term papers, business reports or proposals, or articles for publication often use special abbreviations. Among the more common are these:

&	and (not used in formal writing except when part of a corporate name: Wm. C. Roney & Co.)
cf.	compare
ch. (chs.)	chapter (chapters)
col. (cols.)	column (columns)
ed. (eds.)	editor (editors); edition (editions)
e.g.	for example
et al.	and others (as in referring to a lead author and the coauthors: Sanchez, et al.)
etc.	and so forth (often misused as a vague, catch-all term; should be used sparingly)
f. (ff.)	and the following line or page (lines or pages)
fig. (figs.)	figure (figures)

i.e.	that is
illus.	illustrated
l. (ll.)	line (lines)
no. (nos.)	number (numbers)
p. (pp.)	page (pages)
rev.	revised
sic	precisely as quoted (confirms an expression or spelling that might be questioned as, "The letter was headed, 'Los Angeles, Calfornia [sic].'" Note that sic is enclosed in brackets.)
vol. (vols.)	volume (volumes)

Titles

Mr., Mrs., Ms., and Dr. are properly abbreviated *only* when followed by a proper name:

Incorrect: The Dr. was in practice over 40 years.

Correct: Dr. Leighton was in practice over 40 years; *or* The doctor was in practice over 40 years.

Titles such as Reverend, Major, the Honorable, and President are customarily written out, but may be abbreviated if the initials or name is included:

Incorrect: Rev. Geske, Maj. Sobey

Correct: The Reverend Geske, Major Sobey, The Rev. W. A. Geske, Maj. Albert Sobey

AGREEMENT

As emphasized in Chapter 6 in the section, "Coherent Structure," elements in a sentence must agree grammatically. If a subject is singular, the verb also must be singular. If a noun is plural, any pronoun used later to refer to the noun must be plural; or if the noun is feminine the pronoun must be feminine. And so on.

Lack of agreement weakens the sentence structure, reduces readability, and detracts from writer credibility.

The most important pairs of elements requiring agreement are subject-verb and pronoun-antecedent.

Subject-Verb

Some conditions always require a singular verb, some always a plural verb, and some depend on the particular situation. All three conditions will be covered by the following guidelines:

Single Subjects Single (as opposed to compound) subjects, when singular, require singular verbs; plural subjects require plural verbs:

>The *attorney agrees* with our position.
>The *attorneys agree* with our position.

Intervening Phrases An intervening phrase between subject and predicate does not alter the rule just stated:

>The attorney, one of several consulted, *agrees* with our position.
>
>The *attorney,* as well as other business and professional leaders, *agrees* with our position.
>
>The *attorneys,* along with the vice-president, *agree* with our position.
>
>*Helen Johnson,* not Cecil Stackpole nor Robert Carter, *is* the originator of that proposal.

Indefinite Pronouns: Singular The following pronouns are singular; therefore, when any of them is used as a subject a singular verb must be used:

anybody	each	everyone	neither	someone
anyone	either	everything	one	something
anything	everybody	neither	somebody	

>*Everybody does* as he or she pleases. (Note: "Everybody does as *they* please" would be wrong.)
>
>*Neither* of the bids *was* accepted.

Indefinite Pronouns: Plural The following pronouns are always plural; therefore, they require plural verbs: "both," "few," "many," "several":

>*Both* of the men *are* overpaid.
>*Few* of the alternatives *were* feasible.
>*Many* of the votes *were* invalid.
>*Several* of the women *have been promoted.*

Indefinite Pronouns: Singular or Plural The following pronouns may be either singular or plural, depending on the meaning they express: "all," "any," "none," "some." Often the meaning (whether singular or plural) is indicated by a prepositional phrase following the pronoun:

>*All* that remains *is* to sign the contract. ("All" represents a "collective idea"—see below—in this sentence.)
>
>*All* of the officers *are* completely in favor.

> *Is any* of that policy still in force?
>
> *Any* of the men *are* free to leave.
>
> *None* of the birthday fund *is* left.
>
> *None* of the mistakes *are* serious. (Also correct—indeed preferred in formal writing: "*None* of the mistakes *is* serious," meaning literally, "No one of the mistakes is serious.")
>
> *Some* of the lumber *is* usable.
>
> *Some* of the workers *were* furious.

Relative Pronouns   A relative pronoun introduces a dependent clause. The most commonly used relative pronouns are "who," "which," and "that." The verb following a relative pronoun is singular if the antecedent (the noun the pronoun stands for) is singular; plural if the antecedent is plural:

> Any *license* that expired March 31 *is* invalid.
>
> All *licenses* that expired March 31 *are* invalid.
>
> Knapp is the *delegate* who *was* chosen.
>
> Knapp is one of the *delegates* who *were* chosen.
>
> Knapp is the only *one* of our delegates who *was* invited to speak. (Note how "the" identifies "one" as the antecedent of "who.")

Compound Subjects   Two or more subjects joined by "and" or "both" require a plural verb:

> *Richetto* and *Zima* are co-authors.
>
> Both *Falen* and *Adams* have been hired.

Compound subjects joined by "or," "nor," "either . . . or," or "neither . . . nor" require that the verb agree with the subject that is *nearer* the verb:

> Either Jackson or his *representative is* coming.
>
> Either Jackson or his *representatives are* coming.
>
> Neither the lawyers nor their *client is* at fault.
>
> Neither the lawyers nor their *clients are* at fault.

Collective Ideas   Sometimes a compound subject stands for a collective idea which is singular in meaning, thus requiring a singular verb:

> *Fifteen thousand* down and *$450* per month *is* too much to pay.
>
> *Lucasse and Sons is* an insurance agency.
>
> *Directing* the campaign while *attending* to his regular duties at the same time *is* too much to expect.

Collective Nouns Collective nouns refer to groups of people or things. Common examples include:

audience	faculty	majority	most	rest
board	family	minority	number	some
committee	group	more	plenty	variety

When the collective noun refers to the group as a unit, the verb is singular:

> The *audience was* attentive throughout.
> The *committee was* appointed only last week.
> A *majority is* required for passage of the motion.

When the collective noun refers to the members of the group as individuals, the verb is plural:

> The *faculty are* just now arriving. (The members are arriving individually, not as a group.)
> The *board are* in complete agreement.
> A *minority* of the committee *were* opposed.

Sometimes if a prepositional phrase intervenes between a collective noun and its verb, the object of the preposition influences the verb:

> *Most* of the time *is* well spent.
> *Most* of the opponents *were* present.
> A *lot* of attention *was* given.
> A *lot* of the men *were* dissatisfied.

If "number" is preceded by "the," the verb is singular; if it is preceded by "a," the verb is plural:

> The *number* of protesters *is* small.
> A *number* of *objections* were raised.

Admittedly, the question of whether a collective noun is singular or plural can be confusing. The guidelines just offered should help resolve most questions. If not, another approach is to revise the sentence to avoid using a collective noun as subject. Thus, instead of writing:

> The *group are* unanimous.

write:

> *Members* of the group *are* unanimous.

Beginning a Sentence or Clause with "There" or "Here" In a sentence or clause beginning with "there" or "here," whether the verb is singular or plural depends on the subject which follows:

> There *is* but one *candidate* for the position.
> There *are* four *requirements* to be met.
> Here *are* the *forms* you asked for.

Beginning a Sentence or Clause with "It" "It" at the beginning of a sentence or clause always takes a singular verb:

> *It has* only one advantage.
> *It has* at least three advantages.

Pronoun-Antecedent

Agreement in Number A pronoun must agree in number (singular or plural) with its antecedent (the noun or pronoun it stands for). The rules just given for determining whether a subject takes a singular or plural verb also apply in determining whether a pronoun should be singular or plural:

> *Single noun:* *Carson* filed *her* complaint yesterday.
> Credit is due both the *superintendent* and *his* deputy.
>
> *Intervening phrase:* One of the cartons fell from *its* shelf.
> Nearly *all* of the committee voiced *their* disapproval.
>
> *Indefinite pronoun:* *Somebody* is careless in *his* or *her* work.
> *Everybody* was enthusiastic in *his* response.
>
> *Compound subjects:* *Hoffman* and *Thornton* have completed *their work*.
> Neither Spencer nor her *associates* would give *their* approval.
> Neither Knittel nor McMonagle regrets *his* decision.
>
> *Collective nouns:* The administrative *committee* gave no reason for its action.
> The labor relations *committee* can never seem to agree among *themselves*.

Agreement in Gender A pronoun must also agree with its antecedents in gender (masculine, feminine, or neuter). Little problem arises when the gender of the antecedent is clear-cut (*Hill* gave *his* approval; *Marie* expressed *her* opinion; the *policy* has lost *its* effectiveness).

When the antecedent is (or could be) both masculine and feminine, the solution is less obvious. "Each seminar *participant* should bring *his* or *her* notebook" sounds cumbersome. It might sound simpler to write, "Each *participant* should bring *his* notebook," but if some of the participants are female, this version would be inaccurate. "All *participants* should bring *their* notebooks" would be more acceptable.

On the other hand, "Either the *father* or *mother* must give *his* or *her* consent" is less easy to revise. "Either the *father* or *mother* must give *his* consent" alters the meaning, as does "Either the *father* or *mother* must give *their* consent" (which is grammatically unacceptable as well, especially in formal writing). The sentence could be completely revised to "A statement giving consent must be submitted by either the father or mother"—although this is less natural and direct. So perhaps the original version, ". . . give his or her consent" is the best choice in this case. It is instances like this that most writers would as soon avoid.

CLAUSES

A clause is a group of related words containing a subject and predicate. A phrase, by comparison—which is also a group of related words—does *not* contain a subject and predicate. To illustrate:

Clauses	*Phrases*
although I feel well	into the office
whenever you come	has been lost
I shall always be grateful	to be sure

Understanding clauses is important to writers for at least four reasons. It aids them in (a) combining ideas more effectively in a sentence, (b) showing reduced emphasis to less important ideas and increased emphasis to more important ideas, (c) achieving more pleasing variety in sentence structure and length, and (d) using commas and semicolons with greater skill. (In this connection, see "Emphasis" in Chapter 6 and "Commas" and "Semicolons" in this chapter.)

Independent Clauses

Clauses may be either independent or dependent. An *independent clause* may serve by itself as a simple sentence, or—combined with other clauses—as part of a complex or compound sentence. It is called independent because grammatically it does not depend on anything else to express a complete thought. In the following examples the independent clauses are italicized.

Simple Sentences (consisting of a single independent clause):

> *Jenkins protested.*
> Shouting angrily, *Jenkins protested.*
> *Jenkins protested, but too meekly to do any good.*

Complex Sentences consist of one independent clause and one or more dependent clauses. In the following examples, the portions *not* italicized are all dependent clauses:

> *Jenkins walked out* before the meeting ended.
> Before the meeting ended, *Jenkins walked out.*
> *Jenkins,* who arrived late, *left in a hurry.*

Compound Sentences consist of two or more independent clauses:

> Jenkins walked out; Hamel remained.
>
> Hamel remained, but Jenkins walked out.
>
> Jenkins walked out; however, Hamel remained.
>
> Jenkins is opposed; Ferguson is opposed; Green and Black also are opposed—the scheme is doomed to defeat.

Dependent Clauses

A *dependent clause* normally begins with a subordinating word or phrase which keeps it from being independent; sometimes the subordinating word is omitted, as in "I know the young woman [whom] you referred to." Grammatically it depends on the rest of the sentence for its thought to be completed.

Dependent clauses may serve in three different ways: as adjectives, adverbs, or nouns. In the following examples, the dependent clauses are italicized.

Adjective Clauses describe or identify a noun or pronoun:

> The gentleman *who just spoke* was Dr. Cutler. ("who just spoke" identifies which gentleman.)
>
> The lady *whose fender you dented* is Mrs. Harrington.
>
> That woman to *whom you were just introduced* has a Ph.D. in nuclear physics.
>
> The man *that I marry* will have to be the holder of at least one college degree.

Adverbial Clauses explain how, when, where, or why:

> *After inventory is finished,* I'll have a little more time.
> Your idea may be great, *although I'm not convinced.*
> I did it this way *because I supposed that's how you wanted it.*

Noun Clauses serve the function of a noun:

> *That Mayberry is upset* is of little concern to me. ("That Mayberry is upset" serves as the subject of "is.")
>
> I'm upset because of *what you just said.* ("what you just said" serves as object of the preposition "of.")
>
> *Whoever is unhappy* may withdraw if he or she wishes. ("Whoever is unhappy" serves as the subject of "may withdraw.")

COMPARISONS

In business writing we frequently must compare (show similarities between) one person, product, or event with another. In order for the comparison to be correctly understood, it is necessary that certain guidelines be observed.

Degree of Comparison

For comparing *two* of anything, use the *comparative* degree:

> Dwight is a *slower* worker than George.
> Prices rose *faster* in 1974 than in 1973.
> Plan B is *more* expensive than Plan A.
> Jacobs is a *less* effective supervisor than Berry.

For comparing *three* or more things, use the *superlative* degree:

> Dwight is the *slowest* worker in the department.
> Prices rose *fastest* following the Arab oil embargo.
> Plan B would be the *most* expensive of them all.
> Jacobs is the *least* effective supervisor we have.

Avoid using the comparative degree where the superlative should apply, and vice versa:

> *Wrong:* Dwight is the *slower* worker in the department. (This would be correct if there are only two people in the department. If there are more than two, the adjective must be "slowest.")

> *Wrong:* Plan B would be the *most* expensive of the two. (It could be "most" only if three or more plans were being compared.)

Illogical Comparisons

Avoid making comparisons which are illogical:

> *Wrong:* Our line of cosmetics is *better* than any on the market. (Illogical because it says that our line is better than any on the market, including our own.)

> *Right:* Our line of cosmetics is better than any *other* on the market; *or:* Our line of cosmetics is the *best* on the market.

> *Wrong:* Our line of cosmetics is the best of *any* on the market. (Illogical because it says that our line is better than itself.)

Inequivalent Comparisons

Whatever is being compared must be of the same class:

> *Wrong:* The *prices* of X company are lower than Y *company*. (Wrong because "prices" are being compared with a "company.")

> *Right:* The *prices* of X company are lower than *those* of Y company.

> *Right:* John's raise was greater than Joe's. (Acceptable because it is clearly implied that the word "raise" follows "Joe's.")

Comparing Absolutes

Certain adjectives have no degrees of comparison because they represent absolutes. A common example is "circular"; a figure is either circular or it is not. We cannot say that one figure is "more circular" than another; we can only say "it is *more nearly* circular."

Other common examples of absolutes include:

appropriate	impossible	square
complete	parallel	unique
correct	perfect	wrong
dead	pregnant	
identical	right	

Sentences illustrating correct use of absolutes include the following:

Johnson's guess *was more nearly correct* than was Adams'. (But not, "Johnson's guess was more correct.")

The assignment proved almost *impossible*. (It would be incorrect to say, "*more impossible* than we expected.")

The two paintings are identical. (Not "exactly identical.")

She is *unique in more ways* than anyone else I know. (Not "more unique," because "unique" means "one of a kind.")

Incomplete Comparisons

Avoid omitting words so the comparison is incomplete, leaving the reader unsure of what is being compared:

I like Peterson *better* than Holmes. (Not clear whether this means "I like Peterson better than Holmes does," or "I like Peterson better than I like Holmes.")

We paid Tucker more than Pierce. (Not clear whether this means "We paid Tucker more than we paid Pierce" or "We paid Tucker more than Pierce paid him.")

CONJUNCTIONS

Conjunctions (words that connect other words or groups of words) may be classified as *coordinate, correlative,* and *subordinate*.

Coordinate Conjunctions

Conjunctions that are coordinate join elements of equal rank. Since coordinate conjunctions ("or," "nor," "for," "and," "but," "yet," "so") have already been discussed in Chapter 6, "Effective Sentences," as a means of showing equal emphasis, we shall not deal further with them here.

Correlative Conjunctions

Correlative conjunctions are those used in pairs: "both . . . and," "either . . . or," "neither . . . nor," "not only . . . but also." Rules to remember:

1. Correlative conjunctions should be followed by elements of the same class:

> *Right:* **Both** the sales manager *and* his assistant are out of town. (Each conjunction is followed by a noun: "manager" and "assistant.")
>
> *Wrong:* Haines likes *neither* to record data *nor* writing reports once the data is recorded. ("Neither" is followed by an infinitive; "nor" by a gerund.)

2. Use "either-or" and "neither-nor" only when no more than two persons or ideas are involved:

> *Wrong:* *Either* Tom, Dick, *or* Harry can do the job.
>
> *Right:* Tom, Dick, *or* Harry can do the job; *or:* The job can be done by Tom, Dick, *or* Harry.

3. As noted earlier in this chapter under "Agreement," when "either . . . or" or "neither . . . nor" are used to join the elements of a compound subject, the verb must agree in number with the nearer subject:

> Either White or his *men are* mistaken.
> Either the men or *White is* mistaken.

Subordinate Conjunctions

A subordinate conjunction begins a dependent clause and indicates that the clause is subordinate (that is, expresses a meaning that the writer wishes to emphasize less than he or she does the idea expressed in the main clause). Common examples include "although," "since," "before," "after," "if," "unless," and "whether":

> *Although* profits are down, our confidence remains firm.
> Maloney reached his decision *after* he received the notice.

In formal writing, use "if" to introduce a condition or requirement that must be met. If no condition is involved, use "whether" or "that":

> *Right:* *If* the weather clears, the flight will leave on time. (That is, the flight will leave on time on the condition that the weather has cleared.)
>
> *Wrong:* It is not clear *if* Crosby will sign. (Wrong because no condition is stated.)
>
> *Right:* It is not clear *whether* Crosby will sign.
>
> *Right:* It is not clear *that* Crosby will sign.

In informal writing (such as informal memos or letters), the distinction between "if" and "whether" is not necessarily observed. Thus, in an informal memo the sentence, "It's not clear if Crosby will sign," would be acceptable. However, "whether" or "that" is still preferred.

NUMBERS

Since figures are easier to read than words, as a rule use figures in business writing. However, there are special cases in which words are commonly used instead (although such cases vary from one company, one industry, one profession to the next—any of which may follow its own set of practices, sometimes as laid down in a rule book of its own).

When to Use Figures

Use figures rather than words in the following conditions:

1. In statistical tables, purchase orders, and similar forms.
2. For numbers 11 or over (for numbers ten or under, use words):

    The personnel department now numbers 11.

    January sales amounted to 16,149 units. (*But:* Jackson reported that *three* candidates have applied for the position.)

3. For all numbers *in a series,* whether over ten or under:

    We have purchased 12 chairs, 4 tables, 1 serving cart, and 16 sets of silverware.

4. Addresses (except number one):

    547 Riverview Dr., Apt. B-2

    Columbus, Ohio 43202

    1700 West Third Avenue or 445 East 5th Street (use Third or 5th depending on the local practice, as indicated, for example, on the letterhead)

    But:

    One Beacon Street (not 1 Beacon Street)

5. Dates: August 26, 1939

    26th of August, 1939
    1 September 1939 (military style; commas are omitted)
    Your letter of January 6

6. Decimals: 30.5 inches $4.8 million   .0045
7. Dimensions:

    8½ x 11 paper or 8½ by 11 paper
    2- by 2-inch slide projector

8. Money:
a. When dollars are expressed in even amounts, omit the decimal and double zero: $76 (not $76.00).
b. When a series of dollar amounts include both dollars and cents for some, include the decimal and double zero for the others.

$$\begin{array}{r} \$\ 76.76 \\ 69.00 \\ \underline{51.87} \\ \$197.63 \end{array}$$

c. In a report or proposal, amounts over one million are often expressed thus:

$1.3 million $4.75 billion
$263 million $23 billion

d. Cents may be expressed in a variety of ways:

$0.41 $.41   41¢   41 cents (but not .41¢)

9. Pages: page 21, p. 21, pp. 21–27 (not pp. 21–7 for 21–27, or pp. 318–19 for 318–319)
10. Percentages:

47%, 47 percent (except at the beginning of a sentence, when the number should be spelled out, "Forty-seven percent")

11. Ratios: The odds were 2-to-1 in favor of Breakaway.
12. Time with a.m. or p.m.:

11 p.m.   11:35 p.m.
11 P.M.   11:35 P.M. (capitals used in headings)

But:

eleven o'clock   eleven thirty-five o'clock
eleven o'clock in the evening

When to Use Words

In addition to exceptions already noted (numbers "ten" or under, number "One" in an address, "cents" as optional for ¢, and time when followed by "o'clock"), use words to express numbers in the following situations:

1. Beginning of sentences:

Unacceptable: 7 houses were sold during July.
Correct: Seven houses were sold during July.

If the number is large, it is far better to locate it within the sentence and use figures:

Cumbersome: Four thousand eight hundred twenty-three requests were processed last month.

Preferable: The number of requests processed last month was 4,823.

2. Round numbers: Round numbers representing approximations (or sometimes exaggerations); however, words such as "around" or "about" may be used with figures to express approximations:

> The crowd was estimated at eight hundred to nine hundred.
>
> Mr. Whittaker must have warned you a hundred times about this.
>
> About 40 telegrams have been received.

3. Ordinal numbers (that is, numbers indicating order):

> eleventh day of the month (not 11th day)
> second edition
> Twenty-Third Psalm

When to Use a Combination of Words and Figures

1. When a sentence contains two series of numbers side by side, use words for one series and figures for the other:

> There are fourteen 2 × 4's on the order.
>
> The starting lineup includes two 7-footers.
>
> We have two desks available at $195, seven at $245, and four at $295.
>
> We need 400 two-by-three-inch name tags.

However, if more than two series of numbers are involved, use a table:

Quantity	Item	Size	Price	Total
400	Name tags	2 × 3	.03	$12.00
24	Poster cards	24 × 30	.06	1.44

2. When it is important for a number not to be mistaken, use both words and figures. This is especially true of legal and financial documents, specifications, and bids:

> Seventy-six and 76/100 dollars ($76.76)
>
> Fourteen dollars ($14.00)
>
> Eighteen dollars and ninety-two cents ($18.92)
>
> Please send seven (7) grinding wheels. (Customary in many business firms, though the practice may seem unnecessary.)

But

> The typewriter cost $495. (No need to use both figures and words.)

Miscellaneous Guidelines

1. In a table, align columns of Arabic or Roman numerals on the right. Align decimal numbers according to the decimal point:

I	345	2954.207
II	2,780	3.2616
III	4	.0059
IV	14	12.1714
V	181	.806

2. In identifying numbers expressed in figures, observe the following practices:

   No. 354 (not: Number 354)

   Rm. 3-332 or Room 3-332 (Not: Room No. 3-332)

   Calculator #4M96 4801 (Use # for "number" only for serial numbers, stock numbers, and the like.)

3. For writing the plural of figures, see the next section, "Plurals."

PLURALS

Guidelines to cover nearly all questions concerning plurals are shown below. For questions not covered, consult a dictionary, where the abbreviation "pl" indicates the plural form:

1. Form the plural of most words by adding *s*:

   book books   card cards   cupful cupfuls
   nation nations   tablespoonful tablespoonfuls

2. If adding the *s* forms an extra syllable, add *es* (except for words already ending in *e*, like house):

   church churches   box boxes   bus buses (or busses)
   Tubbs Tubbses   Jones Joneses

3. For nouns ending in *y*:
   a. If the *y* is preceded by a vowel, add *s*:

   boy boys   money moneys (sometimes monies)

   b. If the *y* is preceded by a consonant, change the *y* to *i* and add *es*:

   army armies   body bodies   century centuries

4. For nouns ending in *o*:
   a. If the *o* is preceded by a vowel, add *s*:

   patio patios   studio studios

b. If the *o* is preceded by a consonant, either learn the correct form or check the dictionary, since no standard rule can be applied:

    dynamo dynamos   Filipino Filipinos   piano pianos
    echo echoes   Negro Negroes   potato potatoes
    tomato tomatoes

5. For nouns ending in *f,* either learn the correct form or check the dictionary, since no standard rule can be applied.

  a. Some words ending in *f* form the plural with *ves*:

    half halves   knife knives   thief thieves

  b. Other words ending in *f* form the plural by simply adding *s*:

    belief beliefs   proof proofs   roof roofs

6. To form the plural of compound words:
  a. As a rule add *s* at the end:

    All-American   All-Americans
    attorney general   attorney generals
    high school   high schools

  b. If an earlier word in the compound expression is clearly more important, add the *s* to it:

    attorneys-at-law
    daughters-in-law
    vice-presidents-elect

7. A few nouns have the same form whether singular or plural:

    fish (but fishes for   politics
      different varieties)   scissors
    headquarters   sheep
    mathematics   trousers
    means

8. A few nouns form the plural by using older English plural forms:

    brother brethren (church)   child children   ox oxen
    foot feet   man men   tooth teeth

9. For words borrowed from foreign languages:
  a. As a general rule, use the foreign plural form for formal scientific writing; for writing informally or to nonspecialists, use the English form:

	Foreign Plural	*English Plural*
antenna	antennae	antennas
appendix	appendices	appendixes

	Foreign Plural	*English Plural*
criterion	criteria	criterions
formula	formulae	formulas
index	indices	indexes
radius	radii	radiuses

However, the longer a foreign word is used in English, the more likely the English plural will be regularly used (e.g., "bonuses," "encyclopedias," "plateaus"). On the other hand, "alumnus" still forms the plural "alumni" (masculine) and "alumna" (feminine).

b. Change *is* to *es* for certain nouns of Latin or Greek origin:

analysis	analyses
basis	bases
crisis	crises
diagnosis	diagnoses
thesis	theses

10. When needed to prevent confusion, use an apostrophe before the *s* to form the plural in the following situations. However, if no confusion will result, the apostrophe becomes optional:

   a. Figures: six 7's (or 7s); the 1980's (or 1980s)
   b. Symbols: the t's; avoid the &'s
   c. Letters: too many I's; five a's
   d. Abbreviations: Ph.D.'s; VFW's (VFWs); if the abbreviation uses periods, it should also use an apostrophe to form the plural (U. of M.'s football team).
   e. Words used as words: four "however's" (or "howevers") in one sentence. (But do not use the apostrophe to form any other plurals; it shows possession instead.)

POSSESSION

As a general rule (with some exceptions explained below), show possession as follows:

1. To show that something belongs to an object:
   a. Use "of" ("the front of the building," not "the building's front")
   b. Use the impersonal possessive pronoun, "its"—not "it's," which means "it is"—("that policy has long since lost *its* effectiveness"; "The Ramshackle Inn has increased *its* patronage.")

2. To show that something belongs to a person:
   a. Use an apostrophe ("Helen's office"; "Joe's desk")
   b. Use a personal possessive pronoun ("her office"; "his desk")

Using Apostrophes

1. For words not ending in *s* (whether singular or plural), show possession by adding *'s*:

    Al's office
    John's father-in-law's boss
    the man's stubbornness
    somebody's misunderstanding
    our mother-in-law's hobbies
    the men's room

2. For words (singular or plural) that do end in *s* (or with an *s* or *z* sound), show possession by adding either an apostrophe or *'s,* whichever you feel sounds bettter:

    the cactus' bloom
    the waitress' uniform
    Mr. Jones's illness
    Mrs. Thomas' new job
    Miss Hernandez' application
    Robert Jaycox' record
    the cactus's bloom
    the waitress's uniform
    Mr. Jones' illness
    Mrs. Thomas's new job
    Miss Hernandez's application
    Robert Jaycox's record

3. To show joint ownership, make the last word in the series possessive:

    Swift and Patterson's office
    Milton and Davis's proposal
    Adele, Jackie, and Lauri's proposal

4. To show separate ownership, make each word in the series possessive:

    physicians' and surgeons' supplies
    Swift's and Patterson's offices
    Wagoner's, Stevens', and Curtis's donations

5. To show possession for a noun followed by an appositive, use the apostrophe with the appositive:

    This is Mr. Sharp, the chief engineer's, invention.
    This is the chief engineer, Mr. Sharp's, invention.

6. To show possession for a noun at the end of the sentence when what is possessed is understood, simply use an apostrophe with the possessive noun:

    Apex's program is less expensive than Zilch's.
    That idea was Tony's.

7. For company and organizational names, omit the apostrophe if the company or organization omits it:

    Stokes Steel Treating Company
    Stirlings Furniture
    Steve's Heating and Plumbing
    Larry's Refrigeration and Appliance Service
    Northern State Teachers College

8. For periods of time or sums of money, use the apostrophe just as with nouns referring to people:

a moment's notice	April's rainy weather
yesterday's weather	Monday's poor attendance
two weeks' pay	two dollars' worth
a month's leave of absence	four cents' difference

9. Caution: Do *not* use an apostrophe when possession has already been shown by a possessive pronoun:

> *Wrong:* the home of the Smith's
>
> *Right:* the home of the Smiths (*or:* the Smith's home)

Using Possessive Pronouns

1. Do not use an apostrophe with a possessive pronoun:

> *Wrong:* our's, her's, his', their's, it's (which means "it is")
>
> *Right:* ours, hers, his, theirs, its

(However, a nonpossessive pronoun does use an apostrophe to show possession: e.g., *one's, another's, anybody's.*)

2. Use a possessive pronoun to avoid awkward or ambiguous use of the apostrophe:

> *Awkward:* The employee who received the award's car was stolen.
>
> *Acceptable:* The car of the employee who received the award was stolen.

Using the Possessive Form with Gerunds

Gerunds are verbs ending in *ing* and used as nouns. Any noun or pronoun standing before a gerund must be in the possessive form:

> *Wrong:* I hope you don't mind *me* calling this to your attention.
>
> *Right:* I hope you don't mind *my* calling this to your attention.
>
> *Wrong:* Mr. *Stone* calling in the police was a mistake.
>
> *Right:* Mr. *Stone's* calling in the police was a mistake.

PREPOSITIONS

Prepositions are words showing relationship between a noun or noun equivalent and another part of the sentence. For example: "the thermostat *on* the wall"; "I am tired *of* working." "On" indicates a relationship between "wall" and "thermostat"; "of" indicates a relationship between "working" and "tired."

1. End the sentence or clause with a preposition if it seems natural; (this is the current-day advice as opposed to the traditional rule never to end a sentence or clause with a preposition):

> *Awkward:* *Upon* whatever regulation Ware is basing his case, he will have a hard time establishing it.
>
> *Improved:* Whatever regulation Ware is basing his case *upon,* he will have a hard time establishing that case.
>
> *Optional:* To whom am I speaking?
>
> *Optional:* Whom am I speaking to? (Or, informally, "Who am I speaking to?")

2. Avoid using double prepositions where one will do, as:

in back of	for	back of
in order to	for	to
off of	for	off

3. When two words are linked prepositionally to the object of the phrase, use two prepositions if usage requires:

> *Wrong:* We are grateful yet suspicious *of* Tuttle's unexpected legal maneuver. (Wrong because one would say "grateful *for,*" not "grateful *of.*")
>
> *Right:* We are grateful *for* yet suspicious *of* Tuttle's unexpected legal maneuver.
>
> *Wrong:* Mackin participated and profited *from* the stock sharing program.
>
> *Right:* Mackin participated *in* and profited *from....*
>
> *Right:* Rogers was both talented and interested *in* music.

PUNCTUATION

Punctuation in writing performs a function similar to that performed in speaking by using pauses, pitch, variety, or vocal stress. Punctuation is the writer's way of helping the reader more accurately interpret the meaning intended.

The punctuation devices considered here are:

apostrophes	hyphens
brackets	parentheses
capitals	periods
colons	question marks
commas	quotation marks
dashes	semicolons
ellipses	underlining or italicization
exclamation points	

Apostrophes (')

Apostrophes are used for three purposes:

1. To show possession. Used primarily to form the possessive of names of people or names referring to people. See "Possession" above for a more detailed coverage.

2. To form the plurals of figures, symbols, letters, abbreviations, and words used as words. See "Plurals" above (No. 10) for a more detailed coverage.

3. To indicate letters omitted in contractions (acceptable in informal writing; not usually in formal writing):

> won't (will not)   can't (cannot)
> shan't (shall not) you're (you are)
> isn't (is not)   who's (who is; not to be
> it's (it is)   confused with "whose")

Similarly, in informal writing, apostrophes may be used to indicate numerals omitted in calendar years, as "the late '50's" (1950's).

Brackets ([ ])

Brackets are used almost exclusively to enclose explanatory material in a quoted passage. They should not be confused with parentheses, which are used to enclose explanatory material in one's own writing. Consider these examples:

> "Role playing is a means of putting two or more people in a stimulated [simulated?] situation."

> "If that means putting him out on the golf course, shoulder your portable gear and go out there. [For more on portable TV systems, see p. 44—Ed.]"[1]

> "Many [executives of General Products, Inc.] are displeased with the results."

> Wrote Lucius MacDonald, "When I was 37 [actually he was 43], I was promoted to the position of executive vice-president."

Capitalization

Besides being used at the beginning of sentences, capital letters serve two additional purposes: (a) to emphasize by calling special attention to whatever is capitalized, or (b) to indicate status or respect.

Capital letters are generally used as illustrated in the following situations, arranged below alphabetically:

1. Addresses:

>Mr. Maurice Ramsey
>16686 Whitcomb St.
>Detroit, MI 48823

>Mr. Nemi Jain
>Department of Communication
>University of Wisconsin
>Milwaukee, WI 53201

2. Brand names:

>Bulova   Kodak (but not Kodak Film; should
>Xerox   be Kodak film)
>Coca Cola (or Coke)

3. Complimentary closes in letters (note that only the first word is capitalized):

>Sincerely,   Yours truly,
>Sincerely yours,   Truly yours,

4. Directions, when used to refer to geographical sections, are capitalized:

>the South
>the Midwest
>the Far East

(Note: When used only to indicate a direction, such words are not capitalized; thus, "Cincinnati is south of Columbus"; not "Cincinnati is South of Columbus.")

5. Graphic aid references:

>The cost of living has risen steadily since then (Fig. 4).

>Earnings classified according to occupation show sharp differences (Table 2).

6. Headings and subheadings. Headings and subheadings in reports, etc., use capitals just as do titles of books, articles, and the like. Capitalize the first and last words, all important words, and longer prepositions:

>Six Approaches to Selling
>Analogy with the News Media
>Social Needs Within the Group

7. Historical periods or events:

>the Industrial Revolution   The Great Depression
>the Elizabethan Age   the Korean Conflict

8. Hyphenated words. In hyphenated words containing proper nouns or proper adjectives, capitalize only the proper noun or adjective:

>un-American (unless part of a proper name, as "the House Un-American Activities Committee")
>
>English-speaking countries

9. Names referring to family relationships when used with the person's name or in place of the name. (Exception: When preceded by a possessive word, the relationship name is not capitalized unless followed by the name of the person as well; note "his uncle" and "his Uncle Fred" below):

>Uncle Fred
>his uncle
>his Uncle Fred
>This was the advice Father gave me.
>This was the advice my father gave me.
>He was accompanied by an older brother.

10. Organizations, clubs, societies, etc.:

>American Cancer Association
>First Presbyterian Church
>Southern Illinois University
>Department of Communication Arts and Sciences
>Kiwanis Club
>United States Chamber of Commerce
>Society for the Prevention of Cruelty to Animals

11. Outlines—the first word of each point:

>II. Criteria for a good solution
>   A. Must increase production
>   B. Must not cost more than worth
>   C. Must be workable

12. Proper nouns and adjectives. A proper noun names a particular person, place, thing, event, or institution as opposed to a common noun, used to name classes of persons, places, things, events, or institutions. A proper adjective is derived from a proper noun:

Proper	*Common*
President Gerald R. Ford	a president
Prof. John Mariotti	a teacher
Idaho	a state
New Orleans	a city
Amazon	a river
Equitable Life Assurance	a company
the French people	citizens
he spoke Chinese	he spoke a foreign language

13. Religious references:

>   God   Allah   Thou
>   the Lord   Buddhism   Messiah
>   in His name Christianity the Koran

14. Salutations in letters:

>   Dear Miss Johnson:
>
>   My dear Mr. Nielsen: (when preceded by "my," "dear" is not capitalized. "My dear ____," incidentally, is usually considered more formal than simply "Dear ____," thus conveying less personal warmth.)

15. Sentences—first word of. Capitalizing the first word of a sentence is perhaps the most familiar rule of capitalization, but two special cases not so widely understood are these:

    a. Capitalize the first word of a direct quotation whether a sentence, dependent clause, or phrase. A direct quotation is one that states, in effect, "Jones said, '. . . .'"

    > Mr. Dewey stated: "We shall have no comment until tomorrow morning."
    >
    > "We shall have no comment until tomorrow morning," stated Hawkins. "At that time we'll issue a complete statement."

But:

>   "We shall have no comment," Hawkins stated, "until tomorrow morning."
>
>   Wendell's response to his foreman was, "When I get ready."
>
>   Ms. Kostiuk's reply was, simply, "Yes."

    b. Capitalize the first word of a sentence or phrase following a colon when the sentence or phrase is fairly long:

    > Here is a partial list of their faults as I noted them: Too much abstraction, not enough concrete detail; too many data, not enough interpretation; failure to define key terms.

If the material following the colon is arranged vertically in a tabular list, capitalize the first word in each item, just as in an outline:

>   Here is a partial list of their faults as I noted them:
>
>   >   Too much abstraction, not enough concrete detail
>   >   Too many data, too little interpretation
>   >   Failure to define key terms.

If the list of items following the colon is not long, the first word may be left uncapitalized. What constitutes "long" becomes a matter of the writer's judgment. In the above example "long" is 18 words; in the example below, "not long" is six:

> Maslow classifies human needs in five categories: physiological, safety, affection, esteem, and self-actualization.

16. Subjects in a curriculum. Capitalize the titles of specific courses, but not the name of a general subject area (unless it is a language):

> He is enrolled in Business Law for Engineers next term.
>
> He has taken several courses in business law.
>
> Everyone should take speech.
>
> We recommend that you take Speech 101.
>
> Anyone planning to do business in Latin America should learn Spanish.
>
> Professor Perez teaches Spanish 304 this term.

17. Table of contents. The title "Table of Contents" is usually typed in all capitals: TABLE OF CONTENTS. Use of capitals in topics listed within the table of contents varies depending on the preference of the publisher, editor, company, or typist. One common practice is to use all capitals for chapter headings, and capitals for the important words and longer prepositions in topic headings within the chapter:

3.	DESCRIBING A MECHANISM	31
	Outline for Description of a Mechanism	33
	The Introduction	33
	Description	35[2]

A second common practice is similar, the sole difference being that in chapter headings only the important words are capitalized, just as in the topic headings:

6.	Leadership Communication	147
	What Is Leadership?	148
	Determinants of Leadership	149
	Types of Leadership	151[3]

A third practice, less common, is to capitalize the important words in the chapter headings, but only the first word in topic headings:

46.	Writing Good Themes	223
	Choosing an interesting subject	223
	Limiting the subject	224[4]

18. Time—days of the week, months, and holidays (but not seasons):

> Friday   Fourth of July
>
> May   autumn

19. Words preceding figures and letters (except for "page"):

Figure 4 Appendix A
Table 2 Exhibit 13
Chapter 9 page 83

Colons (:)

General Function Colons are used generally to introduce or announce an idea, series of ideas, or a direct quotation. The statement preceding the colon arouses an expectation of what is to follow; the material following the quotation completes the idea and fulfills the expectation:

> Research shows one consistent finding: women are more readily swayed than men.[5]
>
> Credibility is composed of three factors: trustworthiness, competence, and dynamism.
>
> The marketing concept encompasses four major elements: (1) *consumer orientation* (marketing begins and ends with the needs of the consumer, not with the goals and objectives of the organization); (2) *social process* (marketing is a social process involving many participants); (3) *integrated effort* (marketing is a broader concept than selling; it is the integration of marketing research, production conception, promotion, pricing, and physical distribution effort); and (4) *profitable organization* (marketing is concerned with profitability, a prerequisite for viability in the long run, rather than merely generating sales volume).[6] (Note that the statement preceding the colon performs the function of the topic sentence of this paragraph, even though grammatically the entire paragraph consists of one sentence.)
>
> In his book, *The Managerial Mind,* David Ewing says: "The main commitment of the managerial mind is to the organization."[7]

However, quotations are not always introduced by a colon, as in this example: Wendell Johnson wrote a well-known book, *People in Quandaries,* in which he referred to "theoretical articles . . . pitched on very high levels of abstraction, and . . . very dry indeed to most people."[8]

A similar use of the colon for introducing an idea is when that idea serves as "proof" for the statement preceding the colon. Consider these examples:

> Jones is a magnificent musician: he can play the theme from *The Sting* on a dulcimer.
>
> Ruth is a fine organizer: she organized the election campaign for Ms. Barnes.

Note that in all the examples above illustrating the "introducing" use of the colon, the statement preceding the colon is—and must be—an independent clause. Thus, you should not use a colon in such a sentence as: "Three engineering schools I considered attending were: Massachusetts Institute of Technology, Rensselaer Polytechnic Institute, and General Motors Institute." Grammatically, this is like writing, "My home town is: Rockwood, Illinois."

Special Functions   Besides being used for the general functions given above, colons also are used for certain special functions:

1. To punctuate a salutation in a letter:

>   Dear Sir:
>   Dear Miss Pituch:
>   Dear Robert:

(However, in personal correspondence—also in business correspondence if you know the recipient well—you may use a comma instead: "Dear Kathy,"; "Dear Bob,". And Europeans, even in formal business correspondence, use a comma rather than a colon, as "Dear Mr. deGraffenried,".)

2. To separate a subtitle from the title of a paper, an article, or a book:

>   *Human Communication: An Interpersonal Perspective*
>   "Social Marketing: The Family Planning Experience"

3. To punctuate the word "Attention" on an envelope or in a letter:

>   Attention: Steve Cenko

4. To punctuate the elements in a memo heading:

>   SUBJECT: Vacation Preferences   DATE: February 3, 1975
>   TO: Merle DeMoss   FROM: Duane McKeachie

5. To separate the writer's (or dictator's) initials from the typist's initials at the end of a business letter:

>   CTS:dl

6. To separate hours from minutes and minutes from seconds:

>   12:28   2:04:17

Commas (,)

General Uses   Nearly all commas serve one of the following five uses:

1. To separate independent clauses joined by conjunctions (either coordinate conjunctions—"or," "nor," "for," "and," "but," "yet," and "so"—or correlative conjunctions—"either . . . or," "neither . . . nor," and "not only . . . but also"):

> Either the order must be filled by the 20th of the month, or we will lose the contract.
>
> The regulations we agreed on last fall have proven impractical, so we had better find another way of dealing with the problem.
>
> The cost of energy is unlikely to go down, and we had better get used to that fact.
>
> Neither proposal would solve our problem, nor does any other solution appear likely in the near future.
>
> Brandt worked days preparing his case, yet when he met the committee they turned him down flat.

(Exception: If the clauses are short, contain no other punctuation, and would not be misread, the comma may be omitted. Example: "It rained and it poured." But as a general rule, the comma should be used.)

2. To set off names of people directly addressed:

> Mr. Hildebrandt, I appreciate your thoughtfulness.
> As I've told you before, George, we cannot let this continue.
> What are you waiting for, men?

3. To set off introductory words, phrases, or clauses preceding an independent clause:

> However, there is little likelihood that Congress will approve such a bill this year.
>
> Therefore, I urge all of you to cooperate fully.
>
> In the beginning, we had high hopes for the success of the project.
>
> After their bitter disagreement, they never seemed to work together closely.
>
> To summarize, I feel that the main causes appear to be indifference on the part of some and hostility on the part of others.
>
> Considering the circumstances, I feel that Solecki has performed exceptionally well.
>
> Upon reviewing Phelps' analysis, I'm inclined to agree with his conclusion.
>
> Although the first quarter was slow, sales have been gradually improving.
>
> Whenever I hear that excuse, I'm generally not much impressed.

4. To set off words, phrases, or clauses which explain parenthetically or interrupt the main train of thought:

> There is little likelihood, however, that Congress will approve such a bill this year.

> I urge all of you, therefore, to cooperate fully.
>
> I feel, considering the circumstances, that Solecki has performed exceptionally well.
>
> Lynch, not Patterson, is the man you're looking for.
>
> Mr. Henderson, the Manager of Manpower Development, has just announced a new program in quality control.
>
> Mrs. Wilson, who is our Supervisor of Alumni Relations, will not be back until next week.

(Note: If the explanatory expression is necessary to identify the person or thing being referred to, commas must *not* be used, as "The Mrs. Wilson in Alumni Relations [as opposed to some other Mrs. Wilson] will not be back until next week."; or, "Our appointment which was scheduled for May 18 [as opposed to any other appointments on other dates] has been canceled." If the sentence were punctuated, "Our appointment, which was scheduled for May 18, has been canceled," the sentence would mean that there was only one appointment, and the phrase, "which was scheduled for May 18," is included only to provide incidental information rather than to identify which appointment was canceled.)

5. To separate words or phrases in a series:

> Lela, Lila, Lola, and Lulu are all being considered for promotion.
>
> This policy will apply to production, accounting, shipping, receiving, purchasing, sales, and advertising.
>
> When you meet with Sawyer, you'd better have along your correspondence file on the F-12 model, the new design completed by Oliveira last week, and the test report of March 19.

(Note: There has been some tendency toward omitting the comma after the next-to-last item, so the example above would read ". . . sales and advertising." But since this introduces some ambiguity as to whether—in this case—"sales and advertising" are one or two departments, it is safer to use the comma after every item in the series except the last.)

Special Uses   In addition to the five general uses given above, there are some special situations in which commas are used:

1. To punctuate dates:

> The reception will be Thursday, June 19, at 6:30 p.m.
>
> That policy took effect March 1, 1975, and was superseded by our present policy on October 1, 1976. (A comma appears on

both sides of the year unless the year is at the end of the sentence.)

But:

That policy took effect 1 March 1975 and was superseded by the new policy on 1 October 1975. (Military usage; no commas required.)

2. To punctuate geographical place names:

The Bairds moved from Flint, Michigan, to Columbia, Missouri, in the summer of 1975.

Glendale, Oregon, is located north from Medford.

3. To punctuate numbers of four digits or more except numbers referring to accounts, dates, insurance policies, pages, post office boxes, street addresses, telephones, and zip codes:

6,238	21,928,490
422,809	288,325,475,001

4. To punctuate salutations in informal letters (either personal letters or business letters to personal friends):

Dear Marjorie,   Dear Don,

5. To indicate that one or more words understood have been omitted:

To err is human; to forgive, divine.

The bid from Aronson & Sons was $48,761.27; the bid from Schumacher, $42,699.72.

6. To prevent possible or probable misunderstanding:

Misleading: To Eva Marie is a saint.
Clear: To Eva, Marie is a saint.

Misleading: Below the machine operators worked steadily on.
Clear: Below, the machine operators worked steadily on.

Misleading: After bathing Miss Farquhat felt completely refreshed.
Clear: After bathing, Miss Farquhat felt completely refreshed.

7. To introduce dialogue or a quotation:

What Mrs. Dooley said was, "He better not be late again."

To quote Professor Bettinghaus, "The charismatic leader is one whose ability or persuasion and leadership seems to transcend any of the usual abilities that individuals seem to possess."[9]

Dashes (—)

Dashes may be classified as *internal* (consisting of a pair of dashes setting off material within a sentence), or *end* (setting off material at the end of a sentence).

1. Internal dashes are used for two purposes:
    a. To set off ideas representing an abrupt interruption or change of thought the writer wishes to emphasize or point up:

    > The sales manager seemed vague—in fact, downright evasive—about any promises he had made.

    > Tompkins' past two blunders are enough—in fact, more than enough—to question his suitability for promotion.

    b. To set off an appositive (explanatory statement) having internal punctuation:

    > The chairman of the committee, Joe Flor, said the report will be ready in two weeks. ("Joe Flor" is an appositive without internal punctuation, so is correctly set off with commas.)

    > Four members of the committee—Bett, Mackela, Stormzand, and Weller—expressed doubts that the report would ever be finished.

2. An end dash sets off, and thus emphasizes, information that adds to, sums up, or perhaps contradicts the main idea just preceding. Unlike a colon, which points the reader ahead by introducing the completion of an unfinished thought, a dash points back to the thought just expressed:

    > Jenkins always listens carefully to whatever his advisers tell him—and then goes ahead and does just as he pleases. (This could also be written ". . . tells him, and then goes ahead and does just as he pleases," but the emphasis would be lost.)

    > Bright gold, deep maroon, forest green—these are the popular shades this season.

Compare either of these two examples with such a sentence as this, in which the proper punctuation is a colon: "Professors Crosby and Estey are highly regarded for their two recent texts in English: *College Writing* and *Just Rhetoric*."

Special cautions in using the dash include these:

1. Avoid using dashes indiscriminately in place of commas, semicolons, or parentheses. Dashes serve particular purposes, as described above, and should be reserved for these purposes.

2. Form a dash on the typewriter by using two hyphens with no spaces between the hyphens nor between the hyphens and the words on either side: "Harlow and Cook—both appointees of Wood—were quick to disagree on this point." In longhand, make the dash about twice as long as a hyphen.

Ellipses (...)	An ellipsis ("ellipses" is plural) is an omission in a quoted passage. The ellipsis is shown by three periods (with a space between each if typed). If the ellipsis occurs at the end of the sentence, a fourth period is added to indicate end of sentence:

> "Our data suggest the following public portrait of the shy person. He or she is almost always silent . . . . He frequently avoids eye contact . . . . He avoids taking action . . . ."[10]
>
> ". . . the nonshy person believes that external events cause shyness . . . ."
>
> "Shyness quietly intrudes upon the lives of many people . . . who never become leaders even when they might be the most qualified to do so."

When readers encounter an ellipsis, they have a right to assume that the writer has not distorted the meaning of the passage by what he or she omits. Note, for instance, the reversal in meaning if the last passage above were to be written like this: "Shyness quietly intrudes upon the lives of many people . . . who . . . become leaders. . . ."

Exclamation Points (!)	An exclamation point is used to express strong emotion, such as surprise or protest. It is used more commonly in fiction or essays than in business writing, as:

> "How he struggled!"
>
> "Kathryn's father advanced toward her in cold rage. 'Get out!' he thundered."

In business writing, in which the subject matter seldom involves such strong emotions, exclamation points are less appropriate and are seldom used. A special case in which the use of exclamation points might be appropriate is a report by a supervisor of a dispute with one of his or her workers in which he or she quotes the worker directly. For instance, "Heinze replied, 'I'll be damned if I will!'" The purpose of the direct quotation in such a report is to convey more accurately the tone of the dispute so the director of labor relations can better represent management in the arbitration that follows.

Hyphens (-)	The hyphen is used to link two or more words, prefixes to a word, or two parts of a word when the whole is considered as one word. Conditions requiring a hyphen include the following. (Note that in each example, saying the phrase aloud helps greatly to indicate where the hyphen belongs.)

1. Need for clarity:
   a. To prevent ambiguity:

>   Mrs. Larkin is a great aunt. (An aunt who is "great.")
>   Mrs. Larkin is a great-aunt. (An aunt of one of my parents.)
>   A rear engine-mount.
>   A rear-engine mount.

  b. To avoid misleading the reader:

>   recover (my self-confidence)
>   re-cover (the sofa)

2. Compound adjectives:
   a. An adjective of two or more words *preceding* a noun is hyphenated:

>   An up-to-date version.
>   A once-in-a-lifetime experience.

   b. If the compound adjective comes *after* the noun, the hyphens are usually omitted:

>   This version is up to date.
>   Such an experience occurs once in a lifetime.

   c. If the first word in the compound adjective is an *-ly* word, the hyphen is omitted:

>   An overly negative response.   A well-written letter.
>   A harshly critical review.   A badly written letter.

3. Compound nouns:

>   son-in-law
>   attorney-at-law
>   six-year-old

(Note: Numerous words have gone through three stages of development: (a) two separate words, (b) a hyphenated word, and (c) a single word. Examples include: "basket ball," "basket-ball," "basketball"; "brief case," "brief-case," "briefcase." Thus the practice concerning any given case may vary from one generation to the next.)

4. Numbers; fractions, and numbers twenty-one through ninety-nine require hyphens when written out:

>   three-fourths
>   five-eighths
>   thirty-four
>   one hundred thirty-four

5. Officer, name of in an organization:

>   secretary-treasurer
>   executive-secretary

6. Page numbers:

>pp. 12–13
>pp. 372–381

7. Prefixes:

>anti-American
>ex-convict
>pro-German
>self-analysis

(Note: It is customary, to use a hyphen when the last letter of the prefix and the first letter of the main word are the same: "anti-intellectual," "pre-eminent," "re-entry," "semi-independent"; but, "cooperate"—although co-operate is acceptable.)

8. Time span:

>1916–1929
>16-20 years

9. Word breaks at end of line:
   a. Break the word at the end of a syllable:

   >regis-trar (not "regist-rar")
   >symp-tom (not "sympt-om")

   b. When breaking a word at a double consonant, break *between* consonants, not after:

   >accom-modate (not "accomm-odate")
   >stop-ping (not "stopp-ing")

   c. Avoid breaking after or before a single-letter syllable:

   >elev-en (not "e-leven")
   >cupo-la (not "cupol-a")

(Note: In deciding where to hyphenate a word, a dictionary is the only safe authority.)

Parentheses (())   Whereas brackets (see above) enclose explanatory comments in material quoted from others, parentheses enclose incidental information inserted in one's own writing. Unlike dashes (see also above), which emphasize the material they set off, parentheses tend to de-emphasize—to indicate that the material is only "parenthetical." The following examples are typical:

> The meeting will be held in the usual place (Room 207) at 1:30–3:00, Thursday, May 15.

> The entire department (except Fogle, who was on vacation) was on hand for the ceremony.
>
> The revised layout (Fig. 4) had several advantages over the old one.
>
> The lay-off procedure described above (see p. 9) was felt by some to need a few changes.
>
> The founder of the company was Arnold Schumann (1871–1944).

A special use of parentheses is to enclose numbers or letters when listing items in a series:

> The recommendation was reviewed in terms of the following criteria: (1) manpower requirements, (2) equipment requirements, (3) employee acceptance, and (4) internal control.

Note, however, that if the items are listed vertically, the more common practice would be to punctuate the numbers or letters with a period—simpler to type, and less cluttered in appearance:

> The recommendation was reviewed in terms of the following criteria:
>
> 1. Manpower requirements
> 2. Equipment requirements
> 3. Employee acceptance
> 4. Internal control

Periods (.)

Periods are used in the following situations:

1. At the end of a sentence that makes a statement:

    > Sales were up slightly in March.
    >
    > The new Director of Advertising will be Mary Diaz.

2. At the end of a sentence consisting of a request or command:

    > Next, press the starter buttons with both hands.
    >
    > Please check all doors before leaving tonight.
    >
    > Will you please respond at your earliest convenience. (Even though worded as a question, this statement is equivalent to a polite request. If the writer really is raising a question, as in "Can you let us know how you feel about this?" a question mark should be used.)

3. After most abbreviations:

    > c.o.d.   Mr.   S.E.
    > col.   pt.   yd.

(Notable exceptions include initials identifying government agencies: FCC, FHA, USDA.)

4. After initials in a person's name:

>A. Maxwell McCloud
>Helen M. Ash
>T. A. Koliopoulos

5. To indicate omissions in quoted material (see "Ellipses" above).

6. After a number or letter identifying an item in an outline or in a series of items vertically listed. As an example, note the period after each number, 1–6, in this discussion on "Periods." If the item following the number or letter is a complete sentence, it should be followed with a period. If it is a word, phrase, or dependent clause, the period is often omitted—but the writer should be consistent in either omitting or not omitting.

Question Marks (?)

Question marks are used in the following situations:

1. At the end of a sentence which asks a question:

>What can be done?
>What are the alternatives?

2. After each questioning utterance in a sentence:

>How many times have we heard that excuse? fifty times? a hundred?
>
>Someone (was it Holmes? Redwick?) evidently leaked information to the press.

3. To indicate parenthetically that something is uncertain or questionable:

>The main author of the book is Dr. Paul Watzlawiak (Watzlawick?).

What this really says is, "I'm not sure of the correct spelling and do not consider it important enough at this point to look it up." This practice is usually acceptable in informal memos or letters, but in writing in which it *is* important to be correct, the writer should take pains to be so and avoid casual use of the question mark as above. However, if the information is simply not available, use of the question mark in parentheses is fully acceptable in formal as well as informal writing, "Archimedes (287?–212 B.C.) is credited with the invention of both the screw and the lever."

>The success (?) of our promotional campaign should be analyzed closely.

Quotation Marks
(" "; ' ')

The following guidelines pertain to the use of quotation marks:

1. Double quotation marks indicate material quoted verbatim from someone else:

> According to Ronald L. Goldfarb, a practicing attorney: "Our prison system does not work. We waste over a billion dollars a year to continue a system that has not undergone fundamental re-evaluation in 200 years."[11] This is but the opening statement of a damning case Mr. Goldfarb launches against America's present system of prisons.
>
> Goldfarb refers to "squalid and terrifying confinement among hardened criminals."[12]
>
> Grotts called the incident "disgusting . . . debasing."

2. Single quotation marks indicate a quotation within a quotation:

> Said McCormick, "The first I knew we had trouble was when I heard someone scream 'Help.'"
>
> Goldfarb added, "I asked whether he thought psychiatrists made a big difference in prisons. He said, 'No. We spend 99 percent of our time dealing with institution-induced anxieties, and never get to the problems that got the guy into prison in the first place.'"[13]

3. Punctuation introducing a quotation varies with the length of the quotation:

   a. If the quotation is very short, no special punctuation is needed:

> The guard called "Halt" twice, then fired.

However, even though the quotation is very short, a comma or colon may be used to increase emphasis:

> When I asked Mary when she would have the job done, she replied, "Today."
>
> Mr. Stone's reaction could be summed up in one word: "No!"

   b. If the quotation is moderately short, a comma generally is used:

> Goldfarb concludes, ". . . I still believe we should seriously consider tearing down most prison walls."[14]

   c. If the quotation is long (especially if more than one sentence) or introduced formally, a colon is more likely to be used:

> Commenting on the scope of the prison problem in this country, Goldfarb has this to say: "Presently in the U.S. there are about 5000 city and county jails, 400 state and Federal prisons, plus innumerable local lockups, work houses, camps, farms,

> ranches, and detention centers. On an average day we confine about 1.3 million offenders in these places. . . . And all these prisoners in all these prisons only breed more crime."[15]

4. Longer quotations may be set off from the text by indenting eight spaces from the left margin and single spacing. This additionally indented, single-spaced format indicates by itself that the material is quoted, so no quotation marks are needed. If the quoted passage itself contains a quotation, double quotation marks are used instead of single.

Instead of the block form, as described above, regular indentation and spacing may be used, just as for shorter quotations. In this case, double quotation marks are used, and any internal quotation would be punctuated with single quotation marks. If the passage runs more than one paragraph, each paragraph would begin with double quotation marks, but only the final paragraph quoted would end with them.

5. Quotation marks are used to indicate slang terms:

> "A third direction for reform . . . would call for keeping but improving what the convicts call 'sweet joints.' "[16]

> He suffered what drug addicts sometimes call a "bummer"—an adverse reaction to drugs.

6. Quotation marks may be used to indicate words used as words:

> You have too many "I's" in your letter.
> You tend to overuse "well."

(Note: Underlining or italics in printed material may also be used for the same purpose: "You have too many *I's* in your letter." In fact, underlining is more commonly used for this purpose, and usually is preferable. It is "cleaner" in appearance, and less ambiguous, since quotation marks primarily denote quoted material.)

7. Quotation marks are used to indicate titles of chapters or other divisions within books, or titles of articles, short stories, or other features within periodicals. (See "Underlining and Italics" below, concerning punctuation of titles of books and periodicals.):

> An important chapter in Kepner and Tregoe's *The Rational Manager* is Chapter 7, "Finding the Cause."

> "Theory Y in Practice" is the title of Part Two of McGregor's book, *The Human Side of Enterprise*.

> An excellent review of business writing principles is found in John Fielden's article, " 'What Do You Mean, I Can't Write?' " (Note the single quotation marks within the double quotation marks. This is because Fielden's title itself is a quotation.)

> Congratulations on your letter in "The Public Letter Box" of yesterday's *News-Gazette*.

(Note: Do not place quotation marks around the title on the title page or at the head of your own paper unless your title is itself a quotation, as in the Fielden title just cited. Quotes are necessary in the text itself when you refer to your title—in a paragraph, footnote, or bibliography in the paper or elsewhere.)

8. End punctuation used with quotation marks varies:
   a. Commas and periods always go *inside* the end quotation mark:

   "Date with Dignity," was the way the ad began.

   "I don't give a damn," the operator shouted, "whether we get this job out today or next week."

   b. Colons and semicolons always go *outside* the end quotation mark:

   Snodgrass began what he called his "Advice to Young Fellers": "When I began as shipping clerk here 45 years ago . . ."

   Goldfarb emphasizes that, "Now, when the public seems ready for correctional reform, it is especially important to move carefully"; he adds, "Neither the get-tough . . . nor the treatment-in-prison approach will . . . work."[17]

   c. Question marks and exclamation points belong inside if part of the quotation; outside if not:

   Miller inquired, "How many are dissatisfied?"
   Did Miller really ask, "How many are dissatisfied"?

(Note: In the second example, only one question mark is used, even though two questions are asked. This sentence would *not* be punctuated: Did Miller really ask, "How many are dissatisfied?"?)

Semicolons (;)

A semicolon provides a less definite break than a period, but a more definite break than a comma. The most common use of semicolons is that of separating independent clauses under the following conditions:

1. When the writer wishes to show a closer relationship between clauses than would be implied by a period:

   Acceptable: Few of us enjoy knowing we have failed; indeed, much of our reward comes from knowing we have performed well.

   Acceptable: Mrs. Allen favors expanding the service; Miss Grimes is opposed. (However, if the writer wished to emphasize Miss Grimes's opposition, he or she could write the second clause as a separate sentence: "Mrs. Allen favors expanding the service. Miss Grimes is opposed.)

Not recommended: China exploded a nuclear device equal in power to a million tons of TNT; the blast, over a Chinese desert area, came only hours after a much smaller test by France in the air over the South Pacific.[18] (The reason a semicolon is not recommended here is that the first clause, ending "two tons of TNT," serves as the topic sentence for the paragraph. This relationship is blurred if a semicolon is used instead of a period.)

2. When the two clauses are not joined by a coordinate conjunction ("or," "nor," "for," "and," "but," "yet," "so"):

Sales are down; costs are up.

Sales are down; moreover, costs are up. ("Moreover" is a conjunctive adverb, which, when used between clauses must be preceded by a semicolon.)

Sales are down; costs up. (In the second clause the verb "are" is understood. In other words, not all words need be included in the second clause provided they are understood to be present.)

3. When the two clauses are joined by a coordinate conjunction, but one or both clauses contains internal punctuation—usually commas:

Schroeder reasoned, pleaded, threatened, and exploded; but it was all to no avail.

Price's performance has been irregular; yet, considering the stress he has been under, it's surprising his performance has been as good as it has.

Besides separating independent clauses, two other uses of semicolons include:

1. Separating items in an enumeration unless the items are very brief or contain no internal punctuation:

The most common use of semicolons is that of separating independent clauses under the following conditions: (1) when the writer wishes to show a closer relationship between clauses that would be implied by a period; (2) when the two clauses are not joined by a coordinate conjunction; and (3) when the two clauses are joined by a coordinate conjunction, but one or both clauses contain internal punctuation—usually commas.

2. Preceding an expression such as "for example" that is used to introduce a series of items in a sentence:

Various steps could have been taken to prevent the disaster; for example, the controls could have been checked more thoroughly; the alarm should have been tested periodically; and the first sign of danger should have been reported promptly. (Note: If the "for example" were omitted, the list would be introduced with a colon instead of a semicolon. Better yet, a period would be placed after "the disaster," and a new sentence begun with "the controls.")

Underlining (———) and Italics

Underlining, or underscoring (shown in print by italics), is used for a number of reasons:

1. To identify phrases, words, letters, or figures referred to as such:

> Some of the expressions useful for showing relationships between ideas include *however, therefore, on the other hand,* and *in other words.*
>
> Do you realize that you've begun three sentences in a row with *But?*
>
> *Receive* is spelled with *e* before *i; relieve* with *i* before *e.*
>
> All I recall is that the number ended with four *7's.*

2. To identify the titles of books, periodicals, newspapers, plays, movies, works of art, and names of ships, planes, and trains. (See "Quotation Marks," item 7, above for use of quotation marks to indicate titles of other divisions of publications.):

> Tubbs and Moss, *Human Communication: An Interpersonal Perspective,* contains an especially useful section, Chapter 12, "Enhancing Interpersonal Relationships."
>
> Two periodicals recommended for anyone planning to enter management are *Fortune* and *Harvard Business Review.*
>
> The November 1971 issue of *Psychology Today* contained a provocative article, "Group Think," of special interest to anyone in decision making.
>
> *Death of a Salesman,* by Arthur Miller, is considered by some as the finest American play of the twentieth century.
>
> Da Vinci's *The Last Supper* is possibly the best known painting of all time.
>
> The sinking of the *Titanic* in 1912 has been well described in the book, *A Night to Remember.*

3. To identify foreign words and phrases not yet naturalized into English. (Consult a dictionary when in doubt. Some dictionaries contain a section called "Foreign Words and Phrases."):

GRAMMAR, PUNCTUATION, AND WORD USAGE

>The Finnish word for soap seller, *saippuakauppias,* reads the same backward as forward.[19]
>
>The *par avion* on your letter from France simply means "by airmail."

4. To emphasize an idea:

>The key elements in bringing about behavior change are *communication, motivation,* and *trust.*
>
>They do not act because they lack *trust.*[20]

(Note: Although underlining is useful for emphasizing ideas, it should be used sparingly. Stated in extreme terms, if *everything* were underlined, *nothing* would be emphasized—by underlining, that is.)

SPELLING

Faulty spelling afflicts many. To illustrate, here is a list of misspelled words chosen randomly from a recent batch of college term papers written by students in a freshman class:

adminisrate	desparate	quidelines
arrise	develope	recieve
bullentin	droped	superintendant
catagories	factorys	truely
convience	it's (its)	to many (too many)
corportation	occuring	varibles
corportion	profesor	verry

The problem arising from poor spelling is seldom one of confusing the reader. It is doubtful that any of the misspellings in the list above—especially in the context of a sentence—would cause much loss of meaning. But such misspellings would create "noise" by distracting the reader's attention from the message itself. Worse yet, poor spelling brands the writer—unfairly, perhaps—as illiterate, with consequent damage to his or her credibility.

The importance of correct spelling in the business world was revealed "When a number of business leaders were asked to list the types of instruction that they wished were given to all college students, [and] spelling led all the suggestions."[21]

So what is the solution? One seemingly simple solution in business is "leave it to the secretary." But while sometimes this may work, in general it is a notoriously unreliable solution. She or he may spell no better than you. Even if she or he does, one's secretary is often too busy to do more than type what she or he sees.

The best answer is careful proofreading. If someone else does the typing, the longhand manuscript should first be proofread, then the finished copy from the typist proofread just as carefully. Of the misspellings listed above, probably two-thirds are typographical errors which the students could—and should—have caught by themselves. (How else account for "quidelines"?). Students who habitually give attention to their spelling should have caught most of the others as well.

Indispensable, of course, is a dictionary. This could be a standard, general-purpose dictionary, or a special spelling dictionary such as one of the following:

Lewis, Norman, *Dictionary of Correct Spelling,* Funk & Wagnalls Co., Distributed by Thomas Y. Crowell Co., 666 Fifth Avenue, New York, N.Y. 10019.

Miller, Shirley M. (ed.), *Webster's New World Thirty-Three Thousand Word Book,* revised edition, 1971, Wm. Collins & World Publishing Co., Inc., 2080 W. 117th St., Cleveland, Ohio 44111.

VERB TENSE

To indicate time—past, present, and future—English uses three tense forms: simple, progressive, and perfect:[22]

	Simple	*Regular*	*Irregular*
	Present	I talk	I see
	Past	I talked	I saw
	Future	I shall (or will) talk	I shall (or will) see
	Progressive		
	Present	I am talking	I am seeing
	Past	I was talking	I was seeing
	Future	I shall (or will) be talking	I shall (or will) be seeing
	Perfect		
	Present	I have talked	I have seen
	Past	I had talked	I had seen
	Future	I shall (or will) have talked	I shall (or will) have seen

(Regular verbs form the past tense and past participle by adding *ed:* "walked," "have walked." Irregular verbs form the past tense and past participle by changing the root vowel: "swam," "swum.")

Guidelines to assist in deciding which tense to use include these:

1. In general, use the simple tense form to express present, past, and future action:

> I *question* your use of this term. (Present action.)
>
> Miss Hampton *was married* last summer. (Past action.)
>
> You *will* probably *hear* from Brown by the end of the week. (Future action.)

2. In general, use the progressive tense to express action in progress:

    > I *am working* on the budget this week. (Action currently in progress.)
    >
    > The nurse *was administering* a shot when the doctor walked in. (Action in progress at some time in the past.)
    >
    > You *will be hearing* more about Gibbs' plan in the future. (Action that will be occurring in the future.)

3. In some cases, simple present or progressive present may also refer to past or future:

    > I *enjoy* bowling. (Refers to past, present, and future.)
    >
    > In his book, *The Young Executives*, Guzzardi *describes* the drive for achievement of these men. (Statements about the contents of books and articles generally use the present tense. However, when the past is clearly being referred to, the past tense is used, as "In an article in the *Harvard Business Review* in 1961, Robert McMurry *declared* . . .")
    >
    > Sharpe *leaves* for Israel tomorrow. (Simple present tense, future action.)
    >
    > I *am writing* Renshaw later in the week. (Progressive present tense, future action. However, use of the simple present or simple progressive tense to express future action is relatively informal. The more formal expression would be "Sharpe *will leave* for Israel tomorrow"; "I *shall write* Renshaw later in the week.")

4. Use the present perfect tense to express action completed at the present time:

    > I *have concluded* that the cost is too great.
    >
    > Miss Gronski *has completed* the first stage of her investigation.

5. Use the past perfect tense to express action completed before some specific time in the past:

    > Borey *had* already *left* before you arrived.
    >
    > I *had supposed* before reading the report that Simpson was the only one involved.

6. Use the future perfect tense to express action that will be completed by or before some specific time in the future:

> By the time you return from your vacation, I *shall have completed* the reorganization.
>
> Tonjia Moore *will have been* with us three years next August 19.

WORDS—CONFUSED AND MISUSED

Words used incorrectly impede clear communication. The following are words which give trouble to many writers:

accept—except "accept" means "to receive"; "except" means "not including":

> I *accept* your apology.
> Everyone was invited *except* Theresa.

adapt—adopt "adapt" means "to adjust"; "adopt" means "to accept or put into effect":

> I'm having trouble *adapting* to the new school.
> We *adopted* the new system in June.

advice—advise "advice" is the noun; "advise" is the verb:

> Your *advice* is excellent.
> The doctor *advised* me to take it easy.

affect—effect "affect" means "to influence"; "effect" means (a) "a result" or (b) "to cause to happen":

> This is bound to *affect* your chances.
> One good *effect* will be less dissatisfaction.
> Leas was able to *effect* a reconciliation.

all ready—already "all ready" means "all prepared"; "already" means "by this time":

> Is everyone *all ready* to begin?
> The semester is *already* half over.

all right—alright Only "all right" is correct. "Alright" is no more acceptable than "alwrong."

all together—altogether "all together" means "in a group"; "altogether" means "completely":

> The men are *all together* in their opposition.
> This assumption is *altogether* wrong.

amount—number "amount" refers to "quantity"; "number" means "a sum of units":

The *amount* of enthusiasm is encouraging.
A large *number* of replies has been received.

and etc.   "etc." means "and so forth" (from Latin *"et cetera"*); "and etc." means "and and so forth," and therefore is incorrect:

> *Incorrect:*   We manufacture nuts, screws, bolts, *and etc.*
>
> *Correct:*   We manufacture nuts, screws, bolts, etc.
>
> *Repetitive:*   We manufacture such equipment as nuts, screws, bolts, etc.
>
> *Correct:*   We manufacture such equipment as nuts, screws, and bolts.

apt—liable—likely   "apt" means to "possess aptitude"; "liable" means "subject to adverse consequence"; "likely" means "probable":

> Jane is an *apt* candidate to become our next personnel director.
> You are *liable* under the law.
> Sales will *likely* pick up after Labor Day.

bad—badly   "bad" is an adjective; "badly" an adverb:

> *Incorrect:*   I feel *badly*. (unless you mean your sense of touch is defective)
>
> *Correct:*   I feel *bad* about your demotion.
>
> *Correct:*   He plays the stock market *badly*.

balance—remainder   Use "balance" to mean "remainder" only when referring to financial records:

> *Incorrect:*   Harms will be gone the *balance* of the month.
> *Correct:*   Harms will be gone the *remainder* of the month.
> *Correct:*   Your checking account shows a *balance* of $405.72.

being that—being as how   Both expressions are incorrect for "since" or "because":

> *Incorrect:*   *Being that* (or *being as how*) you're so happy with our product . . .
>
> *Correct:*   *Since* (or *because*) you're so happy with our product . . .

beside—besides   "beside" means "near"; "besides" means "in addition":

> She sat *beside* me at the staff meeting.
> *Besides,* we had lunch together.

between—among "between" is used with two; "among" with more than two:

> I'm sorry for the disagreement *between* you and me.
> The estate was divided *among* the heirs.

can—may (could—might) "can" means "able to"; "may" means "have permission to"; "could" is the past tense for "can"; "might" is the past tense for "may," but is also used to express a possibility or probability in the past or present:

> I *can* call anytime after 3:00.
> You *may* finish later if you wish.
> I *could* have completed it yesterday if I had known.
> They *might* not have known of the arrangement.
> You *might* get an appointment later in the week.

cannot—can not "cannot" and "can not" both mean the same, but "cannot" is the preferred form.

capital—capitol "capital" is a city; "capital" may also be money; "capitol" is a building; "Capitol" is the building in which the United States Congress meets:

> Richmond is the *capital* of Virginia.
> Webster Printing Co. is short of *capital*.
> I shall meet you at the *capitol* at 10:00.
> The *Capitol* is at the end of Pennsylvania Avenue.

casual—causal "casual" means "informal"; "causal" refers to a cause:

> Dress will be *casual*.
> Jumping to conclusions is a common fallacy in *causal* reasoning.

combine into one "into one" is redundant (i.e., duplicates meaning already expressed, as in "7:00 a.m. *in the morning*") in this phrase:

> *Incorrect:* The dean plans to *combine* the three departments *into one*.
> *Correct:* The dean plans to *combine* the three departments.

complement—compliment "complement" refers to that which "completes"; "compliment" is a "praising remark":

> Joan's friendliness *complements* very well her husband's shrewdness.
> I *compliment* you on your success.

consensus of opinion "of opinion" is redundant after consensus:

> *Incorrect:* It is the consensus *of opinion* . . . (or, worse, "general consensus of opinion")
>
> *Correct:* It is the *consensus* . . .

continual—continuous "continual" means "repeatedly"; "continuous" means "without ceasing":

> He is *continually* complaining about his back.
>
> The bell rang *continuously* for 45 minutes.

council—counsel "council" is an advisory group; "counsel" is an adviser or some advice:

> The City *Council* meets Monday evening.
>
> Mr. Rosiello is *counsel* for the defense.
>
> Johnson offered some very wise *counsel*.

data—criteria—memoranda—phenomena These are all plural words (although through common usage "data" is becoming acceptable as a singular word in informal communication, as "Is there enough *data* on hand?"). The standard singular forms are "datum," "criterion," "memorandum," and "phenomenon."

differ from—differ with Something differs *from* something else; one person differs *with* another:

> Harry's approach *differs from* (or "is different from") Joe's. (Note: "different than" would be incorrect.)
>
> Harry and Joe seldom *differ with* each other on policy.

disinterested—uninterested "disinterested" means "lack of self-interest"—hence, impartial or objective; "uninterested" means "not interested":

> A judge is expected to be *disinterested*.
>
> Stoebick appeared quite *uninterested* during the entire presentation.

disorganized—unorganized "disorganized" means "loss of organization where it formerly existed"; "unorganized" means "not organized yet":

> The society *disorganized* several years ago.
>
> The office looked completely *disorganized*.
>
> Since the workers were *unorganized,* there was little they could do.

enthuse "enthused" should not be used for "enthusiastic":

> *Questionable:* Norton was *enthused* over the offer.
> *Correct:* Norton was *enthusiastic* over the offer.

explicit—implicit "explicit" means "clearly stated"; "implicit" means "implied":

> My instructions on this assignment were *explicit*.
> *Implicit* in his request was a demand for more money.

farther—further "farther" refers to distance; "further" to amount:

> We had already driven *farther* than I expected.
> Any *further* demands are certain to be rejected.

fee—honorarium—salary—stipend—wage "fee" is a price paid for professional services; an "honorarium" is a payment for services where custom forbids a price to be set; "salary" refers to payment for a given period of time; a "stipend" is a modest salary or allowance, especially to graduate students, for services rendered and to take care of living expenses; a "wage" is a payment based on hours worked or units produced:

> The lawyer's fee was $2500.
> The speaker received an honorarium of $150.
> Timko's current salary is $18,950.
> Your stipend for next year as graduate assistant will be $3200.
> Our electrician's starting wage is $5.75 an hour.

good—well "good" is an adjective; "well" is usually an adverb (telling how), but is an adjective when referring to one's health:

> *Incorrect:* He types *good*.
> *Correct:* He types *well*.
> *Correct:* I feel *good*. (I have a good feeling.)
> *Correct:* I feel *well*. (I am not feeling ill.)

hanged—hung "hanged" refers to death by hanging; "hung" means "suspended" or "fastened without support from below":

> The prisoner was *hanged* at dawn.
> That picture is *hung* too high.

if—whether In formal writing, "if" introduces a condition to be met; "whether" suggests uncertainty. In informal writing or conversation, the distinction is often ignored:

> *Less acceptable:* I'm not sure *if* I can attend. (No condition is stated.)
>
> *Correct:* I'm not sure *whether* I can attend.
>
> *Correct:* *If* I can attend, I'll let you know. (Means: "On the condition that I can attend, I'll let you know.")

imply—infer "imply" means to suggest without openly stating; "infer" means to draw a conclusion from what someone else has said or done:

> Your letter *implies* that you're not very interested.
> I *infer* from your letter that you're not interested.

in—into "in" refers to being within something (location); "into" means "going from outside to inside" (direction):

> São Paulo is located *in* Brazil.
> That door leads *into* the shipping area.

incredible—incredulous "incredible" means "unbelievable"; "incredulous" means "unbelieving" or "skeptical":

> Taylor's sales record throughout July was *incredible*.
>
> Even when shown the proof, the boss remained *incredulous*.

inter—intra "inter" is a prefix meaning "between"; "intra" is a prefix meaning "within":

> interpersonal   intrapersonal
> intercollegiate intramural

irregardless "irregardless" means literally "not regardless" and should not be used:

> *Incorrect:* He left *irregardless* of my advice.
> *Correct:* He left *regardless* of my advice.

its—it's "its" is the possessive; "it's" means "it is":

> The fad has lost *its* appeal.
> *It's* too bad your letter arrived late.

kindly Use "please" instead of "kindly":

> *Less acceptable:* *Kindly* send me your address.
> *Preferable:* *Please* send me your address.

kind of—sort of These should be used only when "type" can be substituted. They should not be used as substitutes for "rather" or "somewhat":

> *Correct:* What *kind of* arrangement did you decide on?
> *Incorrect:* I'm *sort of* confused about the sick leave procedure.

lay—lie "lay" (present tense) means "to place something"; "lay" may also be the past tense of "lie," which means "to rest in a horizontal position":

> *Lay* the wrench on the bench. (present tense)
> I already *laid* it there. (past tense)
> I *have* always *laid* it there. (present perfect tense)
> *Lie* down for awhile. (present tense)
> I *lay* down this morning for awhile. (past tense)
> Rose *has lain* down and gone to sleep. (present perfect tense)

lend—loan In formal writing, "lend" should be used as a verb; "loan" as a noun:

> I am asking that you *lend* me $10.
> Such a *loan* would be appreciated.

less—fewer "less" preferably applies to degree or amount; "fewer" to numbers (thus applies only to plural nouns or pronouns):

> I am *less* hopeful now than before.
> I have *less* money now than yesterday.
> *Fewer* people are in attendance. (Not "less people.")

loose—lose "loose" means "not tight"; "lose" means "to misplace":

> Your tie is *loose*.
> Don't *lose* your checkbook.

majority—plurality "majority" means "one or more over half the votes cast"; "plurality" means "less than a majority but more votes than anyone else received":

> Huber won by a *majority* of 5204 to 3777.
>
> Conklin received 39 votes, Shriver 31, and Stark 27. Therefore, Conklin won by a *plurality*.

moral—morale "moral" refers to questions of right and wrong; "morale" to mood or spirit:

> Lying is usually a *moral* question rather than a legal one.
> The *morale* of the department is skyhigh.

new innovation A redundancy, since an "innovation" *is* new:

> *Incorrect:* Our honor system is a *new innovation*.
> *Correct:* Our honor system is an *innovation*.

party—person "party" should not be used for "person" except in legal papers:

> *Incorrect:* Higgenbotham is the *party* you're looking for.
> *Correct:* Jonas Higgenbotham, the *party* of the first part . . .

personal—personnel "personal" refers to a person; "personnel" to a group of employees:

>This problem is *personal* between my doctor and me.
>Leslie is a secretary in the *Personnel* Department.

plus—besides "plus" should not be used in place of "and" or "besides":

>*Incorrect:* I enjoyed the convention; *plus* it gave me a bit of a vacation.
>
>*Correct:* I enjoyed the convention; *besides,* it gave me a bit of a vacation.

precede—proceed "precede" means "to go in front of"; "proceed" means "to begin" or "to continue":

>You will *precede* me in the procession.
>Ailes *proceeded* to cross-examine the witness.
>Please *proceed* with your story.

precedence—precedent "precedence" means "higher priority"; a "precedent" is "a practice already established":

>Reverend Updike felt that moral law should take *precedence* over civil law.
>
>We've followed the *precedent* for years that the chairman serves two terms.

principal—principle "principal" as a noun means a sum of money or the chief officer for a school, or it may be an adjective meaning "the most important"; "principle" means "a basic idea":

>The interest on your *principal* is $24.17.
>
>Miss Bensett was the *principal* of Holly High School for many years.
>
>One of the *principles* of Freudian psychology is that the subconscious exerts a profound influence on one's behavior.

proved—proven "proved" should be used as a verb; "proven" as an adjective:

>The scheme *proved* unworkable.
>It is a *proven* conclusion.

reason is because A redundancy, since "reason" and "because" are both "why" words. Say "the reason is that":

>*Incorrect:* The *reason* he resigned is *because* he was angry.
>*Correct:* The *reason* he resigned is *that* he was angry.

It is useful to remember that "is" (or any other form of the verb "to be") can be completed correctly only by a verb, a noun, an adjective, or a location:

>Jones is *leaving* early.
>Marianne is a *leader*.
>The comptroller will be *upset*.
>The clients are *here*.

refer—refer back A redundancy, since *re* means "back":

>*Incorrect:* The chairman *referred back* to the minutes.
>*Correct:* The chairman *referred* to the minutes.

respectively—respectfully "respectively" means "in turn"; "respectfully" means "with respect":

>Pleasure Boy, Blue Haze, and Greased Lightning placed first, second, and third *respectively*.
>
>I *respectfully* ask that the fine be reduced.

semiweekly—biweekly (monthly, annually, etc.) "semiweekly" means "twice a week"; "biweekly" means "every two weeks":

>The *Campus Gazette* is published *semiweekly*.
>The board meets *biweekly,* or twice a month.

set—sit "set" means "to place something," and always has an object; "sit" means "to rest on one's bottom" (usually in a chair):

>*Set* the beer over here. (present tense)
>
>I *set* it over there last time. (past tense)
>
>I *have* always *set* it over there. (present perfect tense)
>
>Please *sit* down. (present tense)
>
>I *sat* for two hours. (past tense)
>
>I *have* never *sat* in a more uncomfortable chair. (present perfect tense)

their—there—they're "their" is a possessive pronoun; "there" means "in that place"; "they're" is a contraction for "they are":

>*Their* contract has expired.
>Please move the desk over *there*.
>*They're* not used to being treated that way.

try to—try and "try to" is the preferred form. For instance, "I'll *try and* finish by tonight" means literally, "First I'll try, then I'll finish." Say "I'll *try to* finish by tonight."

up   Avoid unnecessary use of "up" following a verb:

> *Incorrect:*   They ate *up* all the ice cream.
> *Correct:*   They ate all the ice cream.
>
> *Incorrect:*   Let's divide *up* what's left.
> *Correct:*   Let's divide what's left.

(However, there are exceptions, as "John is trying hard to live *up* to his father's reputation.")

vital   "vital" refers to something necessary for existence; it should not be used to refer to something merely "important":

> *Incorrect:*   Martin's presence at the meeting is *vital*. (Not correct unless the meeting will be a complete loss if he is not there.)
>
> *Acceptable:*   Martin's presence at the meeting is urgent. (Or, "It is urgent that Martin attend the meeting.")

where—that   "where" should not be used in place of "that" to introduce a clause:

> *Incorrect:*   I see *where* you will be attending the convention.
> *Correct:*   I see *that* you will be attending the convention.

where—when   Do not use "where" or "when" to introduce a definition:

> *Incorrect:*   A lending library is *where* they rent books at a given charge per day.
> *Correct:*   A lending library is a library that rents books at a given charge per day.
>
> *Incorrect:*   A laryngectomy is *when* the doctor removes the larynx.
> *Correct:*   A laryngectomy is surgical removal of the larynx.

who—whom (whoever—whomever)   "who" (or "whoever") is the subject; "whom" (or "whomever") the object:

> *Who* has any questions?
>
> *Whoever* has any questions should remain a few minutes.
>
> I would like to see *whoever* has any questions. ("Whoever" is still subject; the whole clause, "Whoever has any questions" is the object of "to see.")
>
> That is the man of *whom* I spoke.
>
> With *whom* are you going?
>
> *Whom* are you going with? (In informal situations, such as conversation or casual memos, this sentence would ordinarily be "*Who* are you going with?")

Who's—whose "who's" means "who is"; "whose" is a possessive:

Who's that strange looking gentleman?
He's the man *whose* wig was stolen.

REVISION EXERCISES

Rewrite correctly each of the following sentences in which you find an error of the category under which the sentence is found. After each sentence, place in parentheses the number of the page from this chapter on which the rule is given. Consult a desk-size dictionary if necessary. If the sentence contains no errors, write, "Sentence OK."

Abbreviations

1. Dr. Harlan Hanes, M.D., has joined TRA as company physician.
2. Sam, let's get together for coffee after the meeting Tue. a.m.
3. McKinnon, Herbst, & Witherspoon is opening a new office in Miller's Mall.
4. Several companies quote much lower prices; eg., Mahoney Products.
5. Gen. Mgr. Pierce, Superintendent Elliott, and Chief Engr. Forbes have all approved the plan.

Agreement

6. All the sales representatives, especially Green, agrees that the policy should be changed.
7. Ray Page, as well as Lee Davis and Alma Friess, is concerned that the mistake not be repeated.
8. Everyone in our department are agreed that something must be done.
9. Several of the supervisors, especially Mrs. Gibson, seems unhappy with the new procedure.
10. Any of the women is eligible to apply.
11. Susanna is the only salesperson from our company who was honored.
12. Neither Lee nor his assistants seem concerned.
13. Neither his assistants, nor Lee himself, seem concerned.
14. Andersen & Newman are a well-known consulting firm.
15. The audience were enthusiastic.
16. The number of complaints are very few.
17. Everybody arrived early with their families.
18. Neither Ramsey nor Flowers were willing to give their consent.
19. Cheryl had her report completed ahead of time.
20. Each couple in the Mr. and Mrs. Club must pay his dues by October 15.

Clauses and Phrases Copy each statement and place after it in parentheses (Clause) or (Phrase) to indicate whether it is a clause or a phrase:

21. after they arrive
22. early in the morning the rain began
23. the box hidden behind the door in the storage room
24. Frank protested

Sentence Types Copy each sentence and place after it in parentheses (Simple), (Compound), or (Complex) to indicate which type of sentence it is.

25. After only two years, Pinder & White, the newest competitor in the market, has taken the lead.
26. After only two years, Pinder & White, which is the newest competitor in the market, has taken the lead.
27. Although often discouraged, Hazel continued the research.
28. Although she was often discouraged, Hazel continued the research.
29. Tabor completed the course; however, Ball dropped out after two sessions.
30. Tabor completed the course, but Ball dropped out after two sessions.
31. However you figure it, the answer is always the same.

Comparisons

32. Linda is the more conservative of the three.
33. If it's George and Isabel Hansen you're referring to, Isabel is by far the most congenial.
34. Our new design is more advanced than any on the market.
35. Your report is more complete than mine.

Conjunctions

36. Woodcock enjoys both tennis and golfing.
37. Neither Emily, Grant, nor Harriet is well-qualified for the job.

Numbers

38. Your bill comes to $112.00.
39. Wronsky received 54% of the vote.
40. 42 workers came in late.
41. Headley & Sons has moved from 349 First St. to 1 Johnson Avenue.
42. For the new office we shall need eight desks, 16 bookcases, 12 filing cabinets, and two conference tables.
43. If you will look on pp. 478–9 of our catalog, you will see that our prices range from .51 to .87¢ per unit.

44. If I've told you once, I've told you 100 times not to omit the date from this form.
45. The luncheon meeting is scheduled for 12:30 p.m. o'clock.

Plurals

46. Copy each word below and after it write its plural form:

but	headquarters	dynamo	moose
a	son-in-law	company	Gibbs
4	chairman-elect	valley	handful
parenthesis	Negro	latch	U. of W.

Possession

47. Philmont is displeased with our office's appearance.
48. The company has improved it's reputation considerably.
49. Harper's job seems secure enough, but that of Harris appears doubtful.

Apostrophes

50. I'll meet you in the ladie's sportwear department.
51. The secretaries' March meeting has been cancelled.
52. Mr. Lopez' records are here, but Mrs. Lopez's file has disappeared.
53. Lange's and Korver's proposal is a good one.
54. Lange's and Korver's proposals are good ones.
55. That was Mrs. Bell's, the chief supervisor's, idea.
56. Tomorrow's attendance should be higher than today's.

Possessive Pronouns

57. Caron's is OK, but our's is better.
58. Anybody's guess is as good as mine.

Possessive Form with Gerunds

59. I thought that Millicents asking that particular question was astute.
60. Your having to wait a full hour was bad enough, but Raker then giving you the cold shoulder was inexcusable.

Prepositions

61. About what are you so upset?
62. Please hand me the folder from off of the floor.
63. Marge was both interested and doubtful about David's suggestion.

GRAMMAR, PUNCTUATION, AND WORD USAGE

Punctuation

64. Who's coat is that?
65. It's Helen's; she must have forgotten it.
66. "Mr. and Mrs. Wigbrink must be having martial (marital?) difficulties."
67. Very Truly Yours, James Bradley
68. Our sales territory extends as far South as Macon, Georgia, which as you know is south of Atlanta. The rest of the south is covered by our Miami office.
69. Customs have changed radically since the Victoria era.
70. My Aunt Olive taught english for many years.
71. My Father never took much interest in me, but mother was the great inspiration of my life.
72. Both Christianity and Judaism claim many adherents in this country, but buddhism and hinduism very few.
73. My Dear Miss Hoover:
74. "After the board meeting," Morris added, "We'll be able to announce the results."
75. Guidelines to cover some of the questions concerning plurals are shown below:
    a. form the plural of most words by adding *s*.
    b. if adding the *s* forms an extra syllable, add *es*.
    c. change *is* to *es* for certain nouns of Latin or Greek origin.
76. The dismissal of a company president is rare: and usually unexpected.
77. My reply to Mr. Seitel is this: "The postal service may have made some improvements, but it still needs more effective management."
78. Man is the only animal that blushes—or needs to. (Mark Twain)
79. Michigan State University, Purdue, and Ohio State University, all founded as land-grant colleges, have had long rivalries in football.
80. Mrs. Wisner bought a gold locket for Marianne Davis and Josephine Weir bought one for Linda Thorpe.
81. Miss Wingelmire please be seated.
82. After forty-five minutes of wrangling the committee finally settled down to business.
83. Even though sales have been sluggish so far, I still feel the future looks bright.
84. Alec who was wearing a green tie that morning looked especially sharp.
85. Virginia the sales analyst will be on vacation next week.
86. Our medium line of filing cabinets comes in black, light and dark green, grey, tan, yellow and brown.
87. After January 10, 1977 the Empire line will be discontinued.
88. Because of the unsightly ink blob, I'll have to ask you to resign the certificate.

89. To Smead's sarcastically-worded comment, Davis replied philosophically, "It's all-in-a-lifetime."

90. Woodbridge N. Ferris (founder and president until his death in 1928) was the subject of the principal address.

91. Four alternatives were open to us:
   (a) Continue with the present equipment another year.
   (b) Contract some of the work to an outside firm.
   (c) Cut back on services.
   (d) Purchase additional equipment.

92. Who raised that question, why did he raise it, how serious is it?

93. In a recent interview, Studs Terkel refers to a steelworker, Mike. "Every once in awhile," says Terkel, "he wants to commit an act of sabotage just to prove he exists. Every now and then, he takes a hammer and punches a dent into a big steel ingot. He says, "That dent, I made it. *I made that dent!*" He commits an act of sabotage just to prove he exists."[23]

94. Crime in the Suites is an article by Joel Seligman that appeared in the June 1976 issue of MBA: Master in Business Administration.

Word Usage

95. Thoresen excepted the explanation with some skepticism, but wondered what the affect would be of combining the two regulations into one.

96. I am deeply effected by your generous complement.

97. This announcement pertains to whomever has been with us less than five years.

98. I see where Williams is going to try and complete the drawings this week.

99. They felt that there claims should take precedents over ours.

100. It has been proven beyond doubt that the reason is because the Personal Department ignored the advise of the Executive Counsel.

101. If you will refer back to the minutes of the last bi-weekly meeting (i.e., the second meeting this week), you will see where the consensus of opinion was that the wage for the keynote speaker should not exceed $300.00.

102. The further west you travel, the farther you will be effected by how enthused the people are over our new delicious snack, Nibbly-New.

103. I imply from your advise that you think I do not handle my accounts good enough.

104. It seemed quite implicit from the judge's rambling remarks that he was proceeding in a quite disinterested manner.

105. I'm wondering if I can use the telephone for long-distance calls.

106. Ever since the office rearrangement, there has been continuous friction between Flughaven, Bentsen, and Shortley.

107. Irregardless of what you say, it seems incredulous to me that Lester would have spoken to his boss so disrespectively.

108. If you will loan me your calculator, I promise not to loose it.
109. Bates and Croshaw's personnel feud has been solved, plus the moral of the department has risen farther than ever before.
110. Quigley felt sort of tired, so he decided to lay down for the balance of the afternoon.

NOTES

[1] Jack Hilton, "Boss on Camera," *Training,* April, 1975, p. 52.

[2] Steven Pauley, *Technical Report Writing Today* (Boston: Houghton Mifflin Company, 1973), p. iii.

[3] Arnold E. Schneider, William C. Donaghy, and Pamela Jane Newman, *Organizational Communication* (New York: McGraw-Hill Book Company, 1975), p. v.

[4] Floyd C. Watkins, William B. Dillingham, Edwin T. Martin, *Practical English Handbook,* 4th ed. (Boston: Houghton Mifflin Company, 1974), p. xv.

[5] Stewart L. Tubbs and Sylvia Moss, *Human Communication: An Interpersonal Perspective* (New York: Random House, 1974), p. 278.

[6] Adel I. El-Ansary and Oscar E. Kramer, Jr., "Social Marketing: The Family Planning Experience," *Journal of Marketing,* Vol. 37 (July, 1973), p. 1.

[7] David W. Ewing, *The Managerial Mind* (New York: The Free Press, 1964).

[8] Wendell Johnson, *People in Quandaries* (New York: Harper & Row, Publishers, 1946), p. 278.

[9] Erwin P. Bettinghaus, *Persuasive Communication* (New York: Holt, Rinehart, and Winston, Inc., 1968), p. 117.

[10] This and the following two passages are from Philip G. Zimbardo, Paul A. Pilkonis, and Robert M. Norwood, "The Social Disease Called Shyness," *Psychology Today,* May, 1975, pp. 69–72.

[11] Ronald L. Goldfarb, "American Prisons: Self-Defeating Concrete," *Psychology Today,* January, 1974, p. 20.

[12] Goldfarb, p. 20.

[13] Goldfarb, p. 88.

[14] Goldfarb, p. 89.

[15] Goldfarb, p. 20.

[16] Goldfarb, p. 22.

[17] Goldfarb, p. 89.

[18] Adapted from *Wall Street Journal,* June 18, 1974, p. 1.

[19] Quoted in *Reader's Digest,* April, 1975, p. 142, from *The Leslie Frewin Book of Ridiculous Facts.*

[20] These two examples are taken from Dean S. Ellis, Lawrence Jacobs, and Cory Mills, "A Union Authorization Election: The Key to Winning," *Personnel Journal,* April, 1972, p. 247.

[21] Harry H. Crosby and George F. Estey, *Just Rhetoric* (New York: Harper & Row Publishers, 1972), p. 263.

[22] For the plan of this discussion of verb tense I am indebted to Watkins, Dillingham, and Martin, p. 22.

[23] "Studs Terkel Loves His Work, But He Says You Don't," *MBA: Master in Business Administration,* June, 1976, pp. 41–44.

# USING GRAPHIC AIDS

BASIC CONSIDERATIONS

KINDS OF IDEAS BEST PRESENTED GRAPHICALLY

CLASSIFICATION OF GRAPHIC AIDS

TABLES

Advantages in Using Tables

Kinds of Tables

    Formal Tables   Informal Tables

FIGURES

Graphs

    Line Graphs   Bar Graphs
    Circle Graphs
    A Closing Word on Tables and Graphs

Photographs

Diagrams

Flow Charts

Organization Charts

Models

Maps

CHECK LIST FOR PLANNING GRAPHIC AIDS

PLACEMENT OF GRAPHIC AIDS

Chapter 4, "Structure," discussed the concept that some ideas in a message are general while others are specific, with the general expressing the main point of the message and the specific providing the developmental detail. In the chapters on paragraphs and sentences we dwelt at length on various ways of being specific—all of them verbal. But not all ideas can be explained adequately through words alone. Sometimes illustrations or graphic aids must be used. As the familiar Chinese proverb has put it, "A picture is worth a thousand words." At least, in some instances, it is.

Let us suppose you have become interested in sailing, and in a book on the subject you encounter this passage:

> A mariner's compass . . . is designed to give a navigator, at a glance, his boat's correct heading relative to the direction of the magnetic north. The compass' prominently displayed dial, called the compass card, is plainly marked with directions expressed in degrees, and is usually illuminated for night steering. . . .
>
> Inside a compass . . . are gimbals and a counterweight to keep the card level when the boat tilts. The card—and the attached magnets aligning it with the earth's magnetic field—balance on a pivot. The housing is filled, through an opening sealed by a plug, with a clear, highly refined kerosene. The fluid buoys up the card, reducing pivot friction, and damps the oscillations caused by vibration. A flexible diaphragm beneath lets the fluid expand and contract with changes in temperature. Corrector magnets in the base aid in adjusting the compass after its installation.[1]

Although the second paragraph gives specific details, you would still, without a doubt, have great difficulty visualizing a compass. But a diagram such as Figure 8.1 would aid immensely.

BASIC CONSIDERATIONS

The example above illustrates two important points concerning graphic aids: (a) a graphic aid provides understanding that words alone cannot give, and (b) a graphic aid is only an aid, not a substitute; seldom can it do the job by itself. Put differently, when words alone are insufficient, graphic aids should be used, but graphic aids require verbal explanation to be clear—sometimes to clarify specifics, and always to point out the general idea of the aid. Graphic aids support words; words support graphic aids.

Another consideration is that whether an aid should be used depends on the situation. If the reader is already familiar with the subject, an aid is superfluous. For instance, in a memo to the engineer who designed this compass, a diagram such as the above would hardly be needed, unless to call attention conveniently to a particular feature of the compass. To a traveler, a map is a highly useful graphic aid, but if he or she is already familiar with the territory, the map isn't necessary.

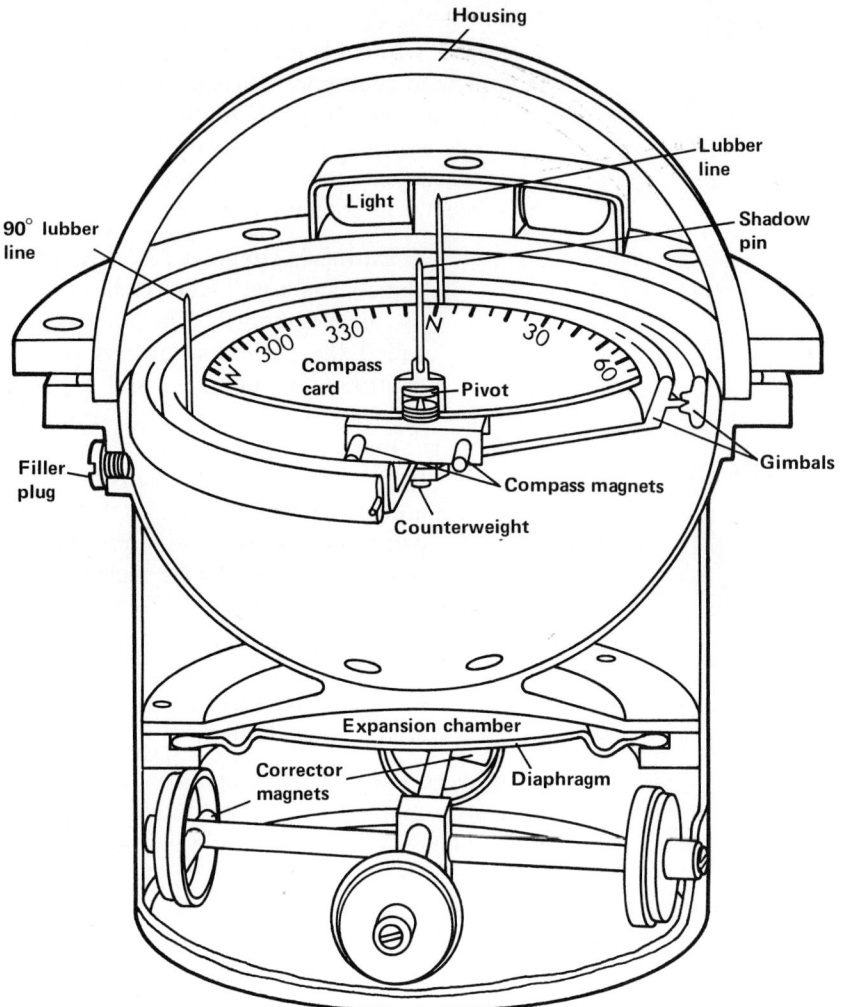

FIGURE 8.1 Diagram of a Mariner's Compass. (*Navigation,* Time-Life Books, New York, 1975, p. 84. Artist, Roger Metcalf. Redrawn.)

Another situation in which readers would not need a graphic aid (even if they're not "familiar with the territory") arises when it would serve no useful purpose. For example, one's address in a letter need not be accompanied by a photo of one's home or workplace; the recipient of the letter hardly needs to know what the sender's place of business looks like to be able to address an envelope in return. On the other hand, if a salesperson has a 1:30 appointment with a prospective client at an unfamiliar location, a map showing how to reach the client may make the difference between a sale and no sale. Graphic aids, although invaluable if relevant, should not be used unless relevant.

KINDS OF IDEAS BEST PRESENTED GRAPHICALLY

Not all ideas can meaningfully be illustrated with graphic aids; a sentence acknowledging receipt of a letter is a case in point. The kinds of ideas best adapted to being explained graphically include these:

Statistical data (as in tables and graphs)
Descriptions of what something looks like (as in photographs or diagrams)
Procedures (as in diagrams or flow charts)
Organizational relationships (as in organization charts)
Abstract relationships (as in models)
Locations (as in maps, photographs, or diagrams)

CLASSIFICATION OF GRAPHIC AIDS

In discussing graphic aids, it will be convenient to take them up under the two generally accepted, broad categories of *tables* and *figures,* with subcategories as follows:

Tables: Formal and informal
Figures: Graphs, photos, diagrams, flow charts, organization charts, models, and maps

This list, while not necessarily all-inclusive, does represent virtually all the graphic aids likely to be used in business writing.

TABLES

Tables consist of data (usually statistical, though not necessarily so) arranged systematically in rows and columns—that is, in tabular form. The standings (as in baseball or football) shown daily on the sports page are a common example.

Advantages in Using Tables

Organizing data into tables has advantages for both the writer and reader. From your own standpoint as writer, it assists greatly in understanding the data yourself. Suppose, for example, you have conducted a survey concerning drug use by students in your school. You would find that organizing the survey data in tabular form would enable you to see more clearly which drugs are being used most frequently and which least, which students (classified, for example, by class level, scholastic level, or sex) are the heaviest users and which the lightest, and so on.

From the reader's standpoint, being able to see the data arranged in a table as opposed to straight text enables him or her also to grasp the

FIGURE 8.2 Example of Data Arranged in Tabular Form[3]

TABLE I Homicides and Suicides: Number and Rate, 1930–1960

Year	Homicides		Suicides	
	Number	Rate[a]	Number	Rate[a]
1930	10,473	12.4	18,323	21.6
1940	8,329	8.6	18,907	19.5
1950	7,942	7.3	17,145	15.7
1960	8,464	7.0	19,041	15.7

[a]Per 100,000 population 16 years old and over

Source: U.S. National Center for Health Statistics, *Vital Statistics of the United States*, annual.

material more readily. Compare, for example, Figure 8.2 with the following paragraph:

> According to the annual, *Vital Statistics of the United States*, published by the U.S. National Center for Health Statistics, in 1930 there were 10,473 homicides in the United States, which was at a rate of 12.4 per 100,000 population, and 18,323 suicides at a rate of 21.6. In 1940 the number of homicides was 8,329, a rate of 8.6, and 18,907 suicides, a rate of 19.5. In 1950 there were 7,942 homicides at a rate of 7.3 and 17,145 suicides at a rate of 15.7. And in 1960 the number of homicides was 8,464 at a rate of 7.0 and 19,041 suicides at a rate of 15.7.[2]

However, the same information is included in both examples. For instance, the first three columns of the top line tell the reader that "In 1930 there were 10,473 homicides, or 12.4 per 100,000 population 16 years and over." But not only is the information now easier to grasp, it is more interesting as well, for the presence of the table interrupts the sameness of the solid flow of prose, making it more visually appealing.

Kinds of Tables

Tables are commonly classified as formal and informal. The characteristics of each and differences between them are given below.

Formal Tables While some tables in business writing are informal, most are formal. This means that they are numbered, have a title, and are sometimes enclosed in a border with lines separating columns and headings. The terminology and layout of a formal table are illustrated in Figure 8.3.

A formal table with the headings and data supplied is shown in Figure 8.4.

In designing a formal table, guidelines to keep in mind include the following:

1. A formal table should be numbered and given a title (except that if there is only one table, the number is omitted). The reason is so the table

USING GRAPHIC AIDS

FIGURE 8.3
Elements and Their
Arrangement in a
Formal Table

TABLE I   Model Table

Stub Heading	Multiple Column Heading		Single Column Heading	Single Column Heading
	Subheading	Subheading		
Line Heading	Datum[a]	Datum	Datum[b]	Datum
Line Heading				
Subheading	Datum	Datum	NA	Datum
Subheading	Datum[c]	Datum[c]	Datum	Datum
Totals	Column Total	Column Total	Column Total	Column Total

[a]Footnote
[b]Footnote
[c]Footnote
Source:

FIGURE 8.4   Example of Formal Table with Headings and Data Supplied

TABLE II   Employment, Sales, and Profits

Plant	Employees		Sales	Profits
	Professional	Clerical		
St. Louis	647[a]	1,011	$ 8.91[b]	$ 992,100
Minneapolis				
Plant 1	486	902	7.14	806,300
Plant 2	112[c]	198[c]	2.22	248,450
Totals	1,245	2,111	$18.27	$2,046,850

[a]Includes technicians
[b]In millions
[c]April 1–December 31
Source: King Cole Novelties Annual Report, 1976.

can be readily identified and located, especially if a List of Illustrations is included with the Table of Contents. Numbers identifying tables are more often shown in Roman numerals (Table I, Table II) as opposed to numbers identifying figures, which are always shown in Arabic numerals (Figure 1, Figure 2).

The title itself should be long enough to be accurate, yet not so long as to be cumbersome. For example, "Homicides and Suicides" gives too little information, while "Number and Rate of Homicides and Suicides from 1930–1960 in Which 'Rate' Means per 100,000 Population 16 Years and Older" gives too much. If the title must run more than six or eight words, it should be divided into two or more lines with each succeeding line being preferably somewhat shorter than the one above. Thus:

Production and Sales of Numerex Calculators
1970–1976

is preferable to

Production and Sales of Numerex Calculators: 1970–1976

The location of the number and title of tables is at the top, as shown in the examples, whereas for figures the location is below. However, in informal reports and proposals (see Chapter 11), it is permissible to locate the number and title at the bottom for both figures and tables.

2. The table should be enclosed in a border or frame, although often the left and right sides of the frame are omitted (as in most of the tables shown here). Although practice varies, as a rule the number and title of the table are placed above the top border rather than within it.

3. The vertical lines between columns may be omitted if the columns are sufficiently far apart that they do not appear to run into each other. If the lines are omitted, the table appears less cluttered. Figure 8.5, for example, is a simple table in which vertical lines between columns would be superfluous. The more columns of data the table includes, the more likely that vertical lines will be needed to keep the columns separate.

FIGURE 8.5 Simple Table in Which Vertical Lines Between Columns Would Be Superfluous

TABLE I Number of Supervisors by Level

Levels of Supervision	T_1[a]	T_2[b]
Foremen	159	142
General Foremen	46	47
Superintendents and General Superintendents	29	23
Total	234	212

[a]*June, 1972*
[b]*January, 1974*

Source: Robin Widgery and Gary Richetto, Maslow's Theory: Support for the Notion of Hierarchy, *unpublished manuscript, 1975. Used with permission of authors.*

4. Figures in a table may be rounded off, depending on how accurate the data must be. In a table showing mileage between cities, for instance, the distance from Columbus, Ohio, to New York City may be safely rounded off from 558.6 to 558, or even 560. But a table listing hand calculators by dimension should be accurate to probably ¼″.

5. Arabic numerals in a column should be aligned on the right, and decimal numbers aligned according to the decimal point:

```
     5      352.0566
    13       23.4223
 1,079         .0029
   641        4.5
```

6. The data in a table may consist of words or symbols as well as of statistics. A typical example is the table from an article in *Consumer Reports:* Figure 8.6.

A reader consulting this table can discover rather easily that, according to tests conducted by *Consumer Reports,* the Zenith stereo phonograph, model E547W, has an excellent tone quality, good freedom from flutter, very good to excellent pickup tracking ability, a vertical tracking force of 2.7 grams which can be adjusted by the user, and good to very good freedom from rumble.

Occasionally a table may consist entirely of words, as shown in Figure 8.7.

7. "NA," as shown in Figure 8.3, means "information not available." Three periods (. . .) or three hyphens (- - -) may be used for the same purpose.

FIGURE 8.6 Table Using Combination of Word Symbols and Statistics

Low-cost Stereo Phonographs: Performance Characteristics

	Tone quality	Freedom from flutter	Pickup tracking ability	Vertical-tracking force (grams)[a]	Freedom from rumble
ZENITH E547W	E	G	VG-to-E	2.7	G-to-VG
CLARINETTE II 131192	F	VG	VG	6.5	G
GENERAL ELECTRIC P380A	G	F-to-G	P	7.0	G
ZENITH E543W	G	F	P-to-F	6.0	VG
LLOYD'S F689	F	F	G	5.0	F-to-G
ZENITH E540L	F	F-to-G	F	6.0	P
PENNEYS Cat. No. 3192	F	P-to-F	G	4.7	VG
WARDS Cat. No. 6034	F	F	P	6.5	G-to-VG
SEARS Cat. No. 3255	P-to-F	F	F-to-G	5.0	G-to-VG
CLARINETTE I 131191	F	P	G	6.7	F
GENERAL ELECTRIC V935	P-to-F	F	P	7.2	G-to-VG
WARDS Cat. No. 911	P	P	P	7.0	VG

[a]*As received; can be adjusted by user (see story).*
Key: E, *Excellent;* VG, *Very Good;* G, *Good;* F, *Fair;* P, *Poor*

Source: "Low-Cost Stereo Phonographs," Consumer Reports, *November, 1974, p. 788. Copyright 1974 by Consumers Union of the United States, Inc., Mount Vernon, N.Y. 10550. Reprinted by permission from Consumer Reports, November, 1974.*

FIGURE 8.7 Table Consisting Entirely of Words

TABLE V Relevant Roles for Research Analysis

Role	Characteristic
User	The person most directly involved in the consumption (or use) of the product or service of interest
Buyer	The individual who actually makes the purchase
Decision maker	The person who decides that the satisfaction of needs requires a purchase and has the authority to direct the expenditure of funds
Influencer	A person who, by word or action, deliberately or not, exerts some influence on the decision to buy, the actual purchase, and the use of some product or service

Source: *Gerald Zoltman and Philip C. Burger,* Marketing Research Fundamentals and Dynamics. *(Hinsdale, Ill.: The Dryden Press, 1975), p. 142.*

8. The data should be arranged in some kind of order. For example, in the homicide-suicide table (Figure 8.2), the arrangement is chronological; in the table on number of supervisors (Figure 8.5), by level of supervision; and in the table on stereos (Figure 8.6), by order of overall quality. Other variables by which data may be arranged include cost, size, and alphabetical order.

9. As the examples above indicate, totals are included only if relevant. If they are included, they may be located in a row at the bottom (as in Fig. 8.4), or—for extra emphasis—in a row at the top just above the first line heading (see Figure 8.8).

From this table the reader can see at a glance that in 1960 the United States government paid $702 million to agriculture, and that the annual payments reached a high point in 1972 of $3,961 million.

10. Footnotes in a table differ in three ways from other footnotes: (a) they are typically designated by letters rather than by numerals; (b) they give explanatory information rather than citing a source; and (c) they are located within the border of the table instead of at the bottom of the page.

11. The source of data in a table is identified by the word "Source." Generally this information is located at the bottom of the table, below the footnotes (if there are any), and within the border.

Informal Tables   Unlike formal tables, informal tables are not numbered, titled, nor set off with lines. Following are two examples of informal tables. The first example is taken from the opening page of a fascinating book published by the United States Bureau of Census in 1967, the year our population reached 200 million. Under the heading, "Who Are We?" appears this information:[3]

FIGURE 8.8   Table with Totals Shown in a Line at the Top

No. **1030.** Government Payments to Farms, by Type: 1960 to 1973 [In millions of dollars]

Item	1960	1965	1967	1968	1969	1970	1971	1972	1973
Total	702	2,463	3,079	3,462	3,794	3,717	[1]3,145	[1]3,961	2,600
Conservation	223	224	237	229	204	208	173	198	115
Soil Bank	370	160	129	112	43	2	—	—	—
Sugar Act	59	75	70	75	78	88	80	82	75
Wool	51	18	29	66	61	49	69	110	65
Feed grain	—	1,391	865	1,366	1,643	1,504	1,054	1,845	1,173
Wheat	—	525	731	747	858	871	878	856	467
Cotton	—	70	932	787	828	919	822	813	705
Cropland adjustment	—	—	85	81	78	76	67	52	—

— Represents zero.
[1]Includes miscellaneous programs, not shown separately.
Source of tables 1028–1030:   U.S. Dept. of Agriculture, Economic Research Service, *The Farm Income Situation,* July 1974.

About 102 million of us are females.
        98 million   males.
        19 million   under 5 years of age.
        19 million   over 65 years of age.
      175 million   white.
        25 million   not white.
        91 million   married.
        11 million   widows or widowers.
      120 million   old enough to vote.
         6 million   in college.
        50 million   in other schools.
        33 million   white collar workers.
        27 million   blue collar workers.
         9 million   foreign born.
      125 million   "city" dwellers.
        33 million   home owners.
      123 million   church members.

The second example is taken from a text on market research:

Suppose we gave a group of housewives a test consisting of 10 true-false questions designed to measure their knowledge of our product. The results of the test were:

Housewife	Number of Correct Answers
A	5
B	8
C	9
D	4
E	7[4]

In neither of these informal tables did the writer feel it necessary to give the information the amount of emphasis that a formal table would have provided. Yet the tabular format does cause the figures to stand out more than would be true if they were presented in a straight prose arrangement. Thus, informal tables share with formal tables the advantage of giving added emphasis when desired, besides breaking up the page for increased visual appeal.

What the informal table does *not* do—because it has no number nor title—is allow the table to be included in a list of illustrations. Furthermore, it gives less emphasis than does the formal table (although this is a limitation only if the information *should* be emphasized more).

Tables—mainly formal, but sometimes informal—play a useful, widespread role in business writing. From the discussion just completed, you should be able to decide for yourself when to use a table and whether it should be formal or informal.

FIGURES

Figures (sometimes referred to as "illustrations") refer to any graphic aid except a table. They include graphs, photos, diagrams, flow charts, organization charts, models, and maps.

Graphs

Graphs, like tables, are used for presenting statistical data. The chief difference is that, whereas tables present specific facts more accurately, graphs convey the general idea more quickly and vividly.

The first step in constructing a graph is to arrange the data in a table—even if only a rough table for your own use. The kind of idea that is usefully conveyed by a graph can be decided only when the data have been organized in tabular form. Some tables, of course, do not contain data that can be usefully depicted in a graph at all. The table listing performance characteristics of low-cost stereo phonographs (Fig. 8.6) is one such example; the table of relevant roles for research analysis (Fig. 8.7) is another. But other times the data suggest trends, relationships, comparisons, or proportions that a graph can convey. Then you decide what kind of graph to use: line, bar, or circle.

Line Graphs   Line graphs are used primarily for showing *trends* over a period of time or relationships between two or more phenomena.

FIGURE 8.9   Line Graph with Single Plot Line

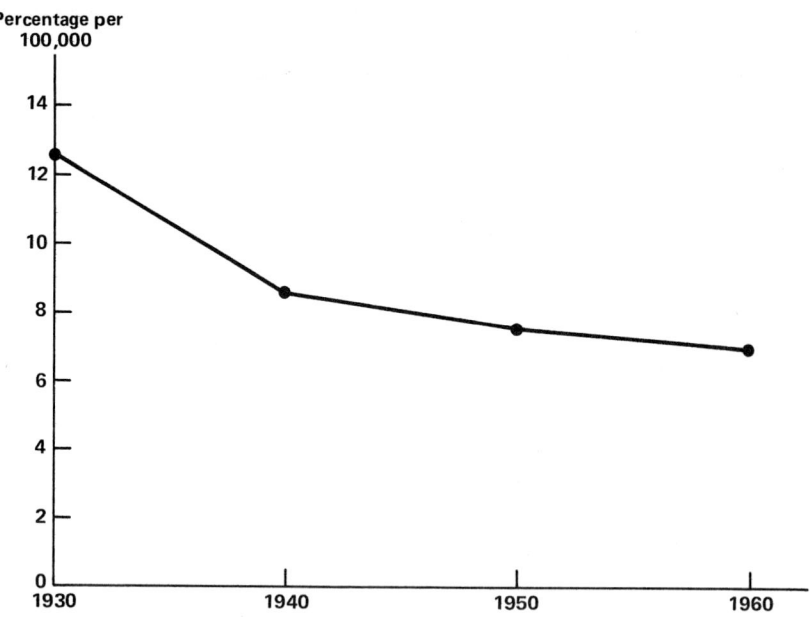

Fig.1. Decrease in Homicide Rate: 1930-1960
   Source: U.S. National Center for Health Statistics, *Vital Statistics of the United States,* annual.

Suppose, for example, upon studying the data in the homicide-suicide table, that you would like to highlight the point that between 1930 and 1960 the homicide rate declined. You might then draw a graph like the one in Figure 8.9.

Note that while this does not include the precise data of the table (Fig. 8.2), it does emphasize much more vividly the downward trend from nearly 13 per 100,000 in 1930 to fewer than 8 per 100,000 in 1960.

Or, perhaps you wish to show that both the homicide and suicide rate declined during those years. You could, of course, construct a second graph. However, to show the *comparative* rate of decline more effectively, as well as in less space, you could simply add a second plot line to the same graph. Note, though, that in so doing you must alter the vertical scale to accommodate values nearly twice as high for the suicide rate (Figure 8.10).

Sometimes, instead of a decline or increase of two or more variables,

FIGURE 8.10 Line Graph Showing Two Plot Lines Roughly Parallel

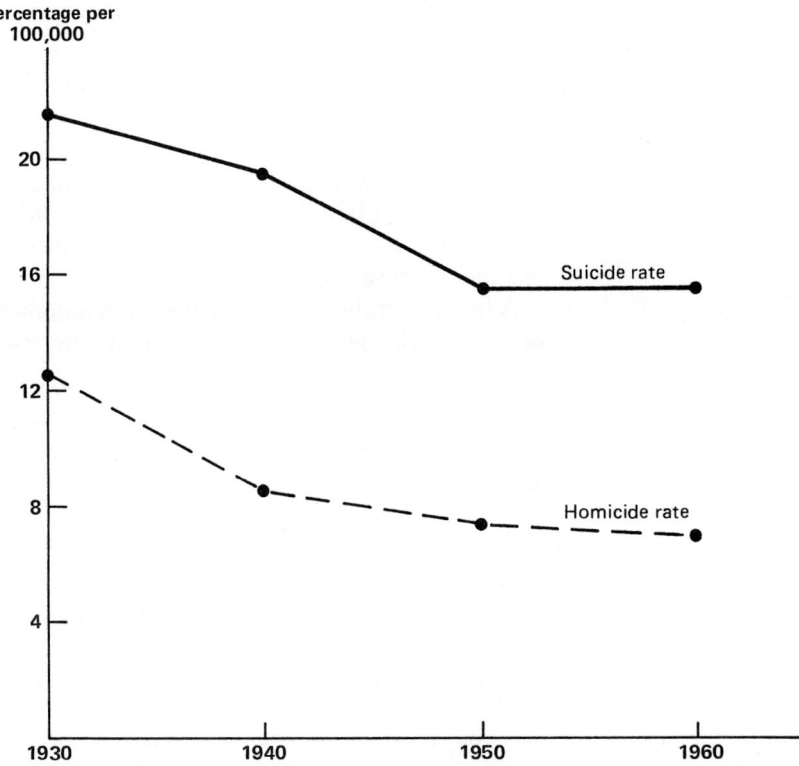

Fig. 2. Decrease in Suicide and Homicide Rates: 1930-1960
Source: U.S. National Center for Health Statistics, *Vital Statistics of the United States,* annual.

FIGURE 8.11 Line Graph with Plot Lines Showing Increase in One Condition and Decrease in the Other

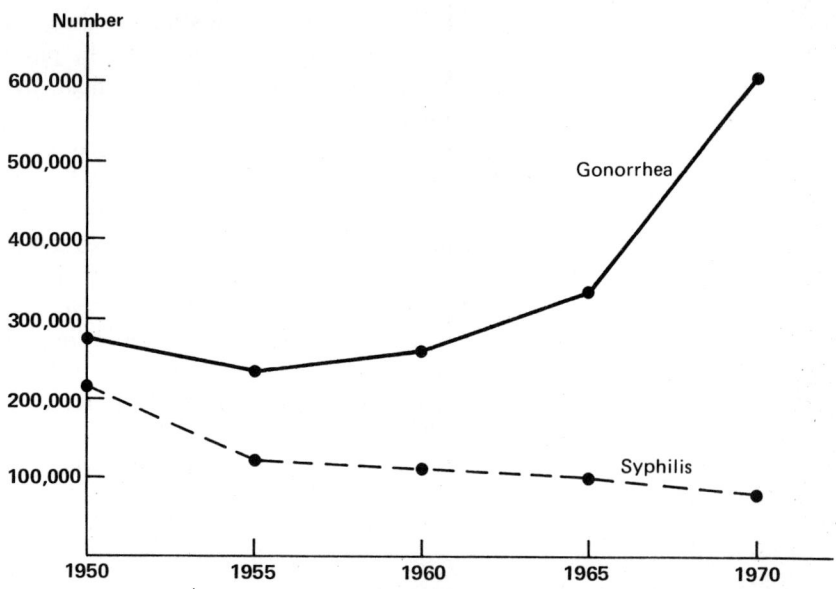

Fig. 3. Civilian Cases of Venereal Disease Reported: 1950-1970
Source: *Statistical Abstract of the United States,* 1973, p. 82.

the data may show an increase in one and a decrease in the other. The two graphs in Figures 8.11 and 8.12 show variations in this phenomenon. Note that in each graph, one line is solid, the other broken, thus helping to distinguish between the two.

A line graph, like a table, consists of a number of elements, all but one of which (the grid) are illustrated in the examples just given. These elements are:

1. Two scales: one a vertical scale showing *amount* (dollars, pounds, production, population, etc.); the other a horizontal scale showing, usually, *time* (years, months, days, hours, etc.).

2. Two axes, one for each scale: a vertical axis known as the *ordinate* and a horizontal axis known as the *abscissa*. The scale on the ordinate represents one or more dependent variables (quantities which vary depending on changes in an independent variable), while the scale on the abscissa represents the independent variable. In the homicide-suicide example, the homicide and suicide rates are the dependent variables, while the passage of time between 1930 and 1960 is the independent variable. Expressed differently, the suicide and homicide rates vary with the passage of time rather than the passage of time varying with the change in these rates.

In the following example, the independent variable is a factor other

USING GRAPHIC AIDS

FIGURE 8.12 Line Graph Showing Plot Lines Crossing Each Other

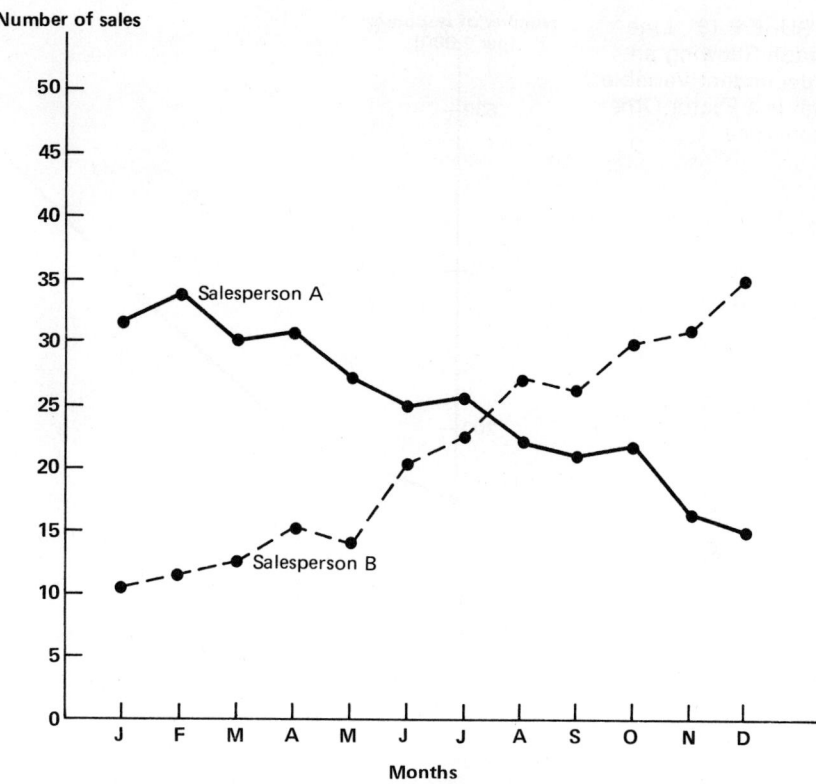

Fig. 4. Comparative Sales, 1976: Salesperson A and Salesperson B

than time. Suppose that you are in the subscription department of a magazine publisher and have compiled data on the number of subscribers who renew their subscriptions depending on the number of notices they receive. In this instance, the independent variable is the number of notices; the dependent variable, the number of renewals. A graph showing the relationship between these two variables might look like Figure 8.13.

In this graph the point is made quite clear that the number of responses increases for the first three notices; after that additional notices produce little further response.

3. A *plot line* or *curve* that represents the data. If more than one plot line is shown, the lines should be readily distinguishable from each other. Different colors may be used if the material will be professionally printed (which presupposes an important document—such as a stockholder's report—intended for a wide readership). But if the material will be duplicated on a copier, broken-line patterns should be used instead, since color

FIGURE 8.13 Line Graph Showing an Independent Variable that Is a Factor Other than Time

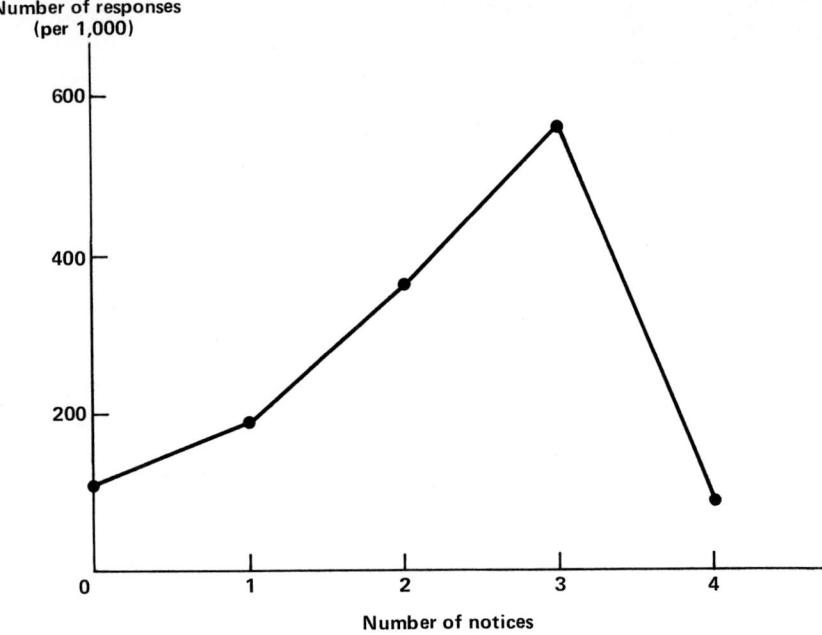

Fig. 5. Number of Responses in Relation to Number of Notices

will not show up on the copies anyway. Using differing patterns becomes especially important if the lines are close to each other or cross each other.

4. Values. The values are shown on the two axes and vary according to the data involved. In each of the graphs above the values are either labeled or clearly implied: years, number of suicides per 100,000, number of responses, number of notices.

5. Grid. The grid consists of the network of uniformly spaced lines created when the scale marks (usually called stub lines) are extended both horizontally and vertically across the graph. In each of the examples above, the grid has been omitted. If the graph last given above were to include the grid, the result would look like Figure 8.14.

Probably the grid lines help the reader to some extent in determining the amounts represented by the plot line. But since the shape of the plot line remains the dominant feature, while the grid lines often distract as much as they assist, they frequently are omitted.

In planning a line graph, several rules should be kept in mind:

1. The spaces formed by the grid lines (or that would be formed if grid lines were used) should be square or nearly so. Overexpanding or over-

FIGURE 8.14 Line Graph Showing Grid

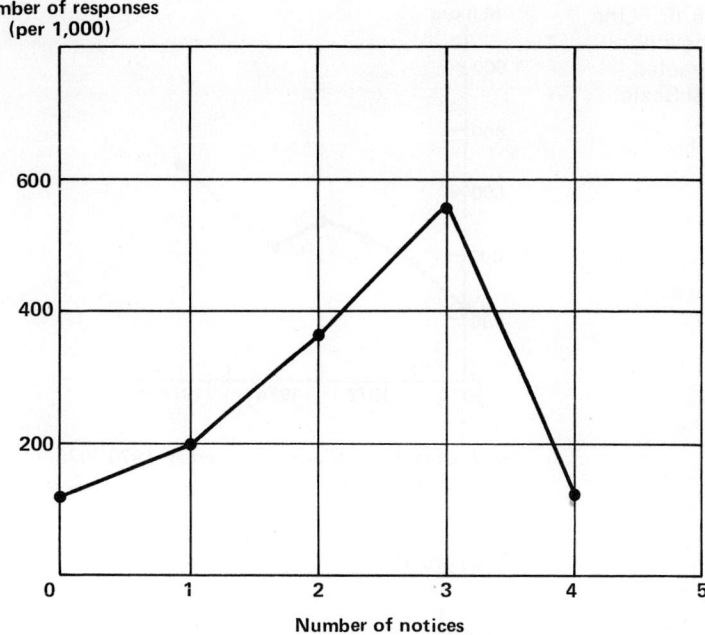

Fig. 6. Number of Responses in Relation to Number of Notices

contracting either scale can be grossly misleading, as shown in Figures 8.15 and 8.16, each depicting the same set of data.

2. The vertical scale should normally begin with zero to avoid creating an inaccurate visual impression, as in Figure 8.17. This graph is misleading for two reasons. It gives the impression that the profits in 1972 were about

FIGURE 8.15 Line Graph Showing Overexpanded Horizontal Scale

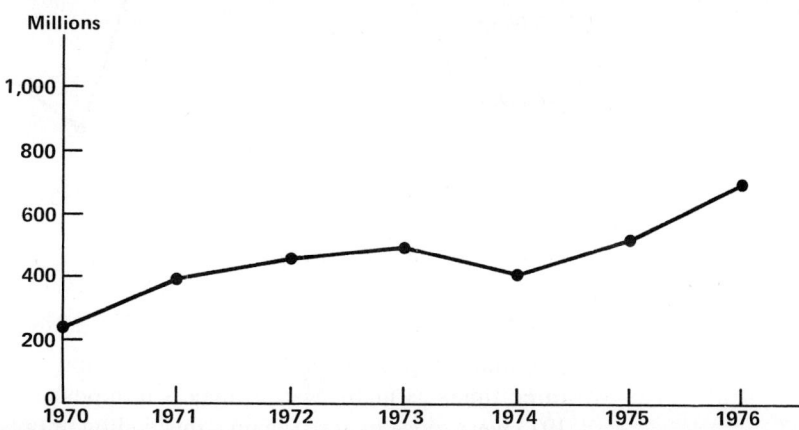

Fig. 7. Gross Sales, King Cole Novelties, 1970-1976

FIGURE 8.16 Line Graph Showing Overcontracted Horizontal Scale

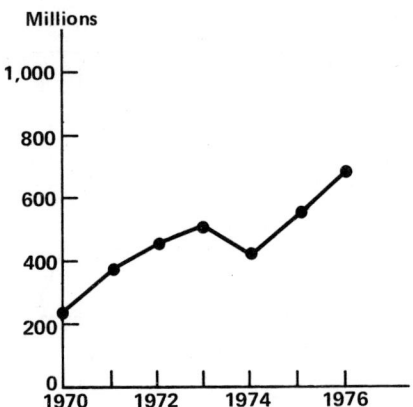

Fig. 7. Gross Sales, King Cole Novelties, 1970-1976

FIGURE 8.17 Line Graph Showing Vertical Axis Not Beginning at Zero

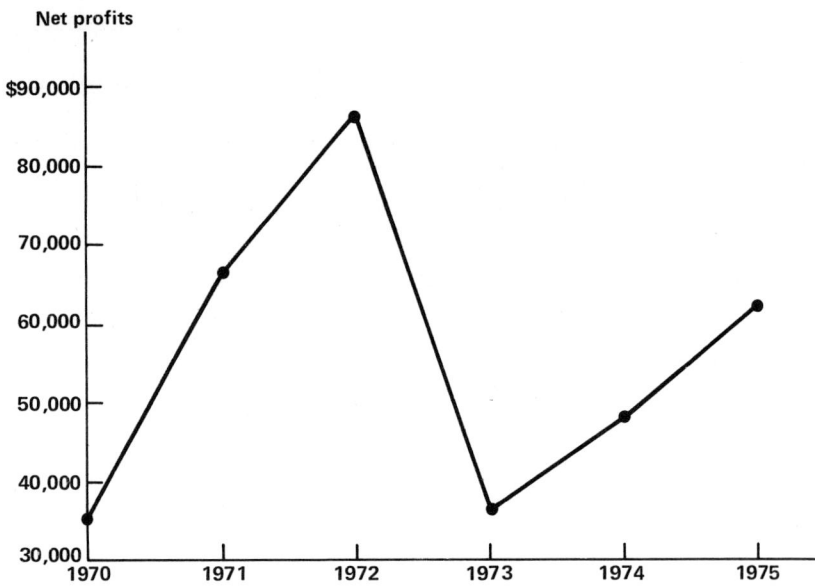

Fig. 8. Net Profits, King Cole Novelties, 1970-1975

ten times as great as in 1970 and 1973, when actually they were less than three times as high. Also, it makes it appear that the profits in 1970 and 1973 were close to zero, again a misleading impression. If including all the increments on the scale between zero and the lowest usable point is unwieldy, a jagged line should be inserted to represent the omission (see Figures 8.17 and 8.18).

USING GRAPHIC AIDS

FIGURE 8.18 Line Graph Showing Jagged Break between Zero and Lowest Usable Value on Vertical Scale

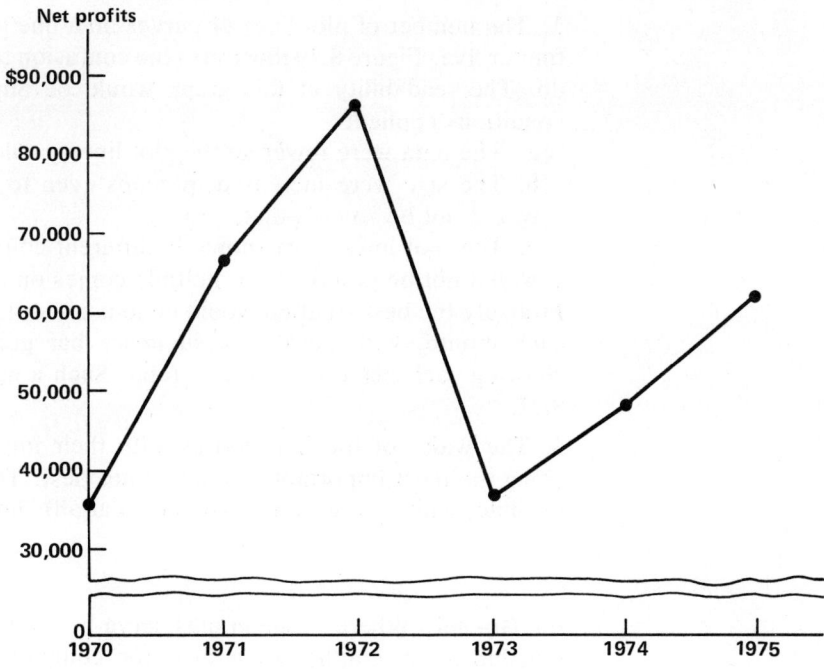

Fig. 8. Net Profits, King Cole Novelties, 1970-1975

FIGURE 8.19 Line Graph with Too Many Plot Lines for Clarity

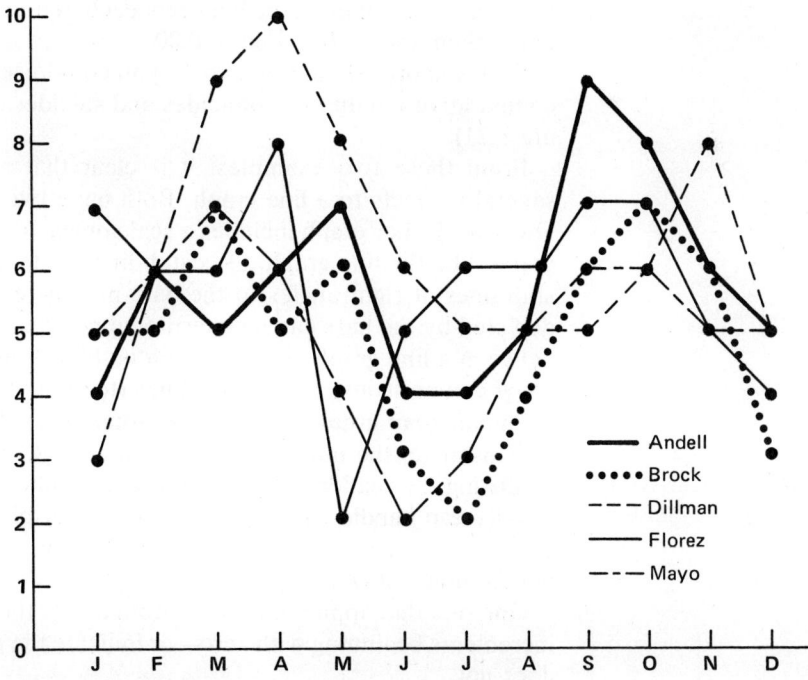

Fig. 9. Projects Completed per Month by Staff Member

3. The number of plot lines or curves on a line graph should not exceed four or five. Figure 8.19 illustrates the confusion that can result when they do. The readability of this graph would be improved if the following conditions applied:
   a. The data were fewer so the plot lines would be less crowded.
   b. The size were increased, perhaps even to full page so the details would not be so crowded.
   c. The plot lines were shown in different colors (though this solution would not be practical for multiple copies on an ordinary copier).

Probably the best solution would be to use a series of bar graphs, one for each month, with perhaps a summary bar graph for the entire year showing each person's year-end total. Such a graph is shown in Figure 8.22.

4. The width of the lines varies with their importance. The plot line, being the most important, should be heaviest. The axes should be intermediate, while the grid lines (if shown at all) should be quite faint.

Bar Graphs Whereas line graphs serve best for showing trends or relationships, bar graphs serve best for comparisons. To return to the homicide rate for 1930–1960, let's say you decide that rather than emphasizing the trend during the 30-year period, you would like instead to point up the comparison between each ten-year interval. Your graph might then appear like Figure 8.20.

Furthermore, should you wish, you could use a bar graph to show the comparative number of homicides and suicides for each given year (Figure 8.21).

From these two examples, it is clear that a bar graph is similar in several respects to a line graph. Both have two axes. Often (though not always), the bar graph includes a scale on each axis. And as a rule the bar graph, like the line graph, uses stub lines instead of a grid—although the stub lines at right angles to the bars may be extended so the quantities depicted by the bars can be interpreted more easily. The chief distinction between a line graph and bar graph is the use of the bars themselves (to show comparisons) rather than lines (to show trends).

Planning bar graphs is simpler in some ways than planning line graphs. For instance, the number of bars that a single graph can handle without confusing the reader is greater than the number of lines that a line graph usually can handle. Also, there is no danger of distorting the interpretation, as in a line graph, as a result of the spaces formed by the grid lines not forming squares.

One rule that applies equally to both is that the scale should show equal increments beginning with zero—or indicate the gap with a jagged line if it does not.

FIGURE 8.20 Vertical Bar, or Column, Graph Showing Comparisons on a Time Scale

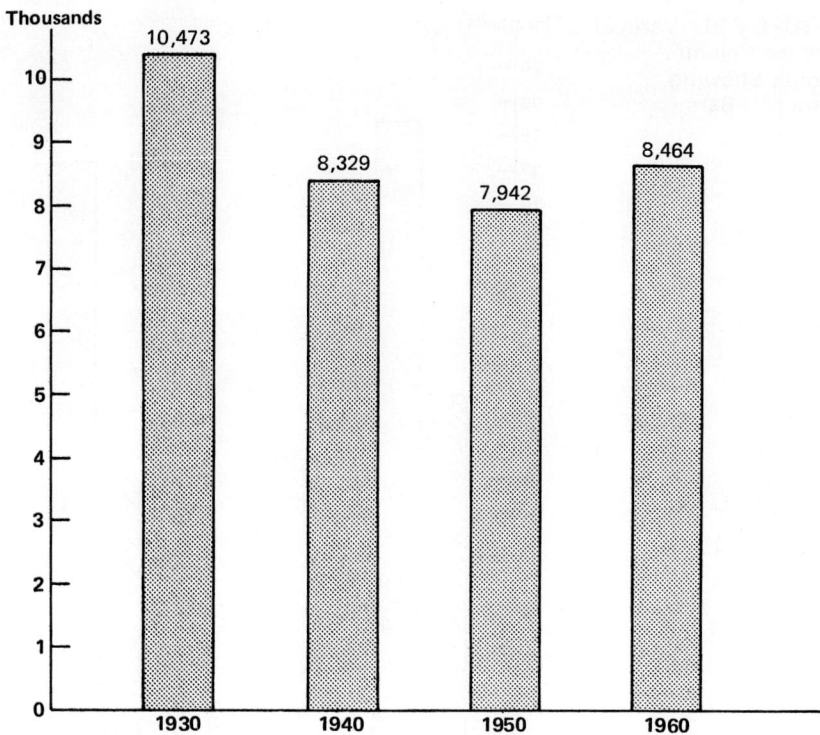

Fig. 10. Number of Homicides: 1930-1960
Source: U.S. National Center for Health Statistics, *Vital Statistics of the United States,* annual.

There are a few guidelines not relevant to line graphs that apply to bar graphs specifically. One is that the space between bars should be of a different width than the bars themselves. Another guideline concerns whether the bars should be horizontal or vertical (if vertical, the bars are often called *columns* and the graph a *column graph*). Put briefly, the bars should be horizontal if:

1. They compare data for a single segment of time (as opposed to comparing the data over a period of time).
2. They represent length or distance, such as the stopping distance of an automobile at different speeds.

On the other hand, the bars should be vertical if:

1. They compare data over a period of time (as in Figure 8.20), so the time scale can be located on the abscissa, as in a line graph.
2. They represent height, as in a graph showing the world's tallest skyscrapers.

FIGURE 8.21 Vertical Bar, or Column, Graph Showing Grouped Bars

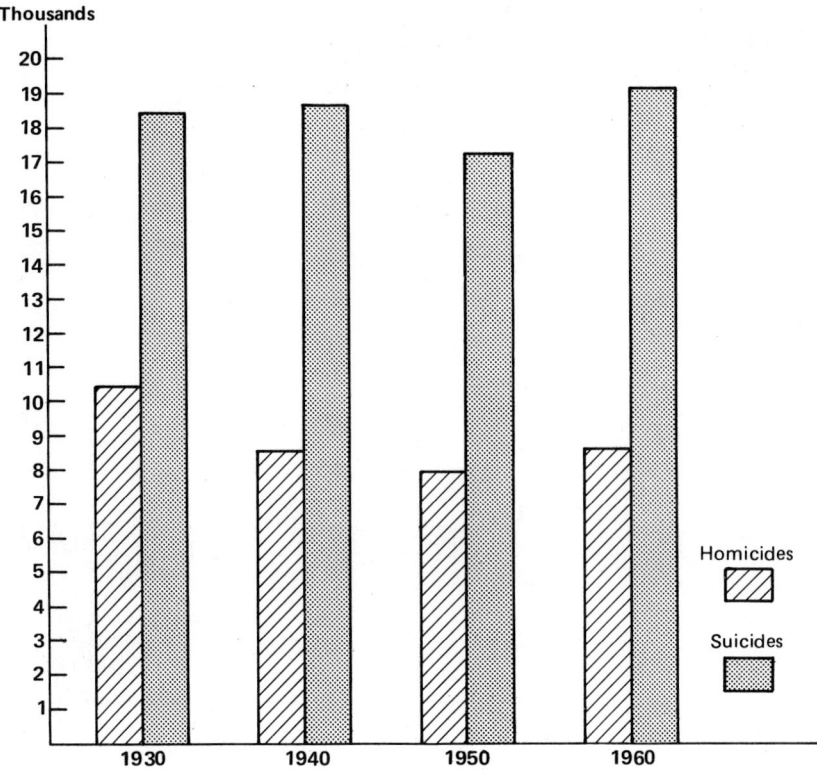

Fig. 11. Number of Homicides and Suicides: 1930-1960
   Source: U.S. National Center for Health Statistics, *Vital Statistics of the United States,* annual.

Otherwise, whether the bars are horizontal or vertical is a matter of preference.

Another guideline, applicable especially to bar graphs, is that the bars should be arranged in some kind of order: numerical, chronological, order of decreasing importance, or some other.

We have already seen in Figure 8.20 the use of single vertical bars (columns) to compare data over a period of time, and in Figure 8.21 the use of grouped bars or columns for the same purpose. Further illustration of the use of bar graphs follows:

1. Horizontal bar graph to compare data for a single segment of time (Figure 8.22). Note the use of the extended stub lines to facilitate identifying the number of projects completed by each person. Note, also, that the bars are arranged in descending order of tasks completed. The data, incidentally, are the same as those shown for January in Figure 8.19 (a line graph).

USING GRAPHIC AIDS

FIGURE 8.22
Horizontal Bar Graph
Comparing Data for a
Single Segment of
Time

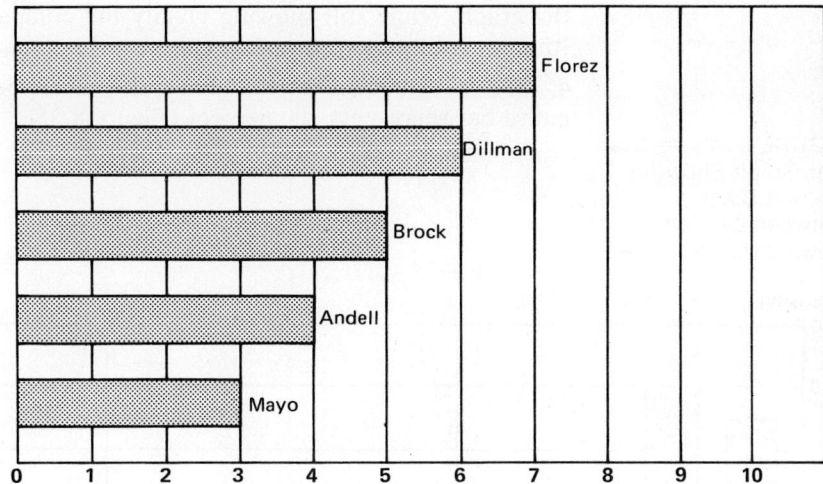

Fig. 12. Number of Projects Completed During January by Research Department

2. Horizontal bar graph showing negative and positive values (Figure 8.23). Although this example uses horizontal bars, it could be drawn to use vertical bars just as well, very much as an ordinary household thermometer shows values below and above zero.

3. Use of jagged break to indicate missing values in the scale (Figure 8.24). The break makes it possible to reduce considerably the height of

FIGURE 8.23 Bar Graph Showing Negative and Positive Values

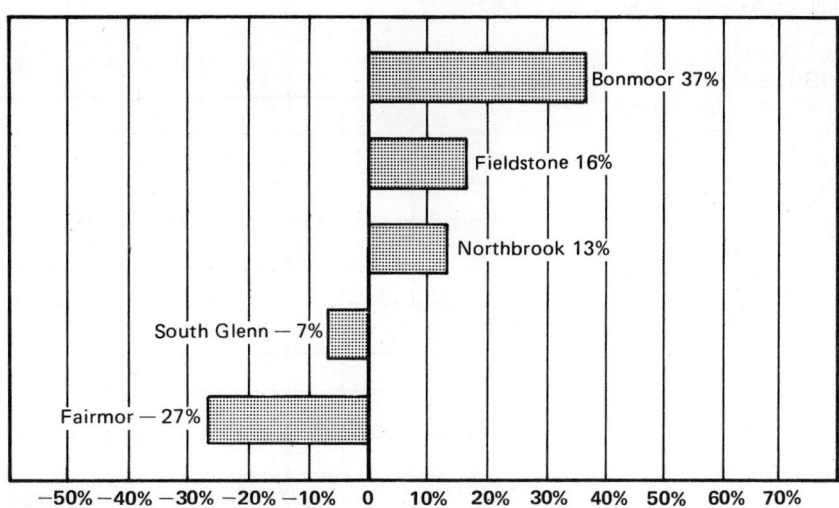

Fig. 13. Percentage of Decrease or Increase in March Sales as Compared with February Sales, by Retail Outlet

the graph, while still showing vividly the comparison from one quarter (three-month period) to the next.

4. Use of segmented horizontal bars to indicate percentages, in which the entire bar represents 100 percent (Figure 8.25).

FIGURE 8.24 Vertical Bar Graph Showing Jagged Break between Zero and Lowest Usable Value

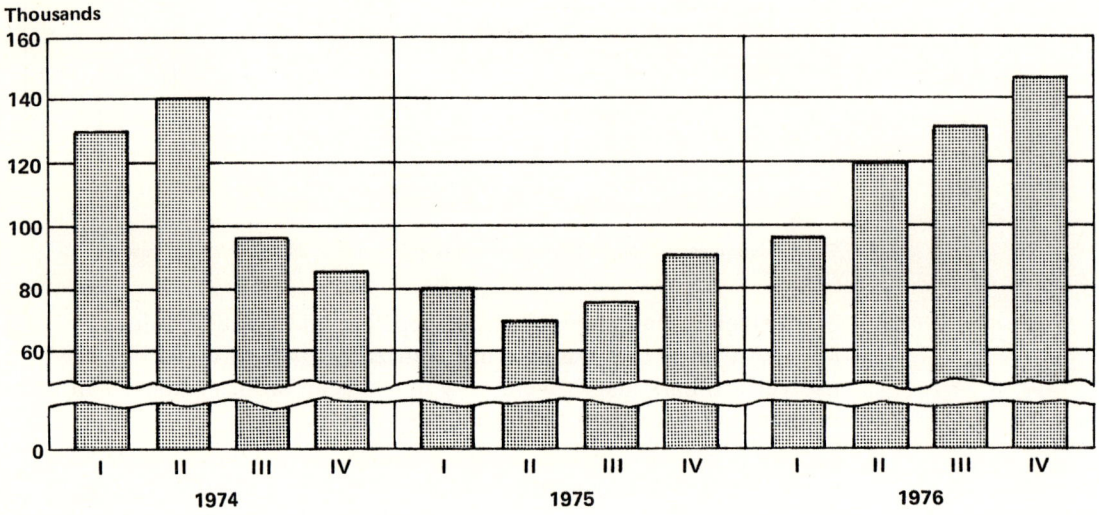

Fig. 14. Number of Units Produced Per Quarter

FIGURE 8.25 Horizontal Bar Graph Using Segmented Bars to Indicate Percentage

Fig. 15. Percentage Distribution of Labor Grievances by Department and Shift: 1974

**FIGURE 8.26
Horizontal Segmented
Bar to Show
Percentages**

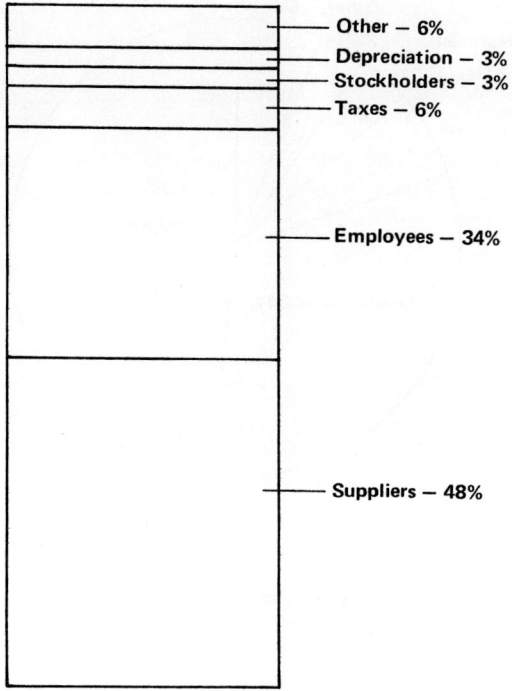

Fig. 16. How King Cole Novelties Spent Its Revenues During 1976

5. Use of a single segmented bar to show percentages of a whole (Figure 8.26). This bar is drawn horizontally because the labels can then be shown more easily; however, the bar could be drawn vertically if desired. Although a bar may be used to show parts of a whole, circle graphs—described below—are much more commonly used.

Circle Graphs Circle graphs (often called "pie charts") are used for depicting parts of a whole. The circle, of course, represents the whole, and each segment (or slice of the pie) a part. Often the part is expressed in percentages or fractions; or, if the whole represents a sum of money, each part as a rule stands for number of cents in a dollar.

The data shown in Figure 8.26 could also be shown in a circle graph as in Figure 8.27.

An alternative way of showing the same information, in terms of cents instead of percentages, is illustrated in Figure 8.28.

Guidelines to keep in mind in designing a circle graph include these:

1. Include a label and value (such as percentage or cents) with each section, located either inside the circle (if room) or outside (if not room).

FIGURE 8.27 Circle Graph Showing Percentages of the Whole

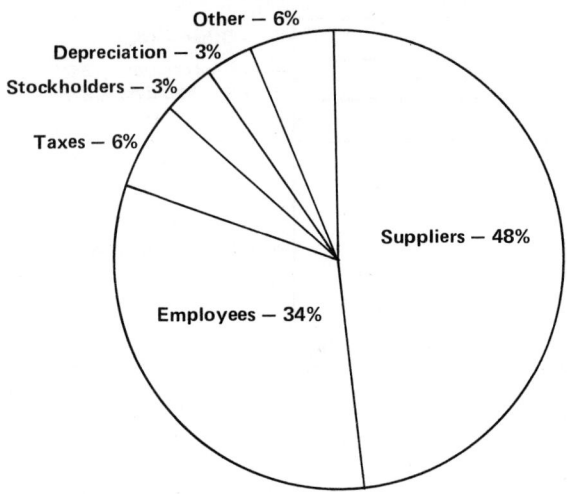

Fig. 17. How King Cole Novelties Spent Its Revenues During 1976

FIGURE 8.28 Circle Graph Showing Cents in a Dollar

Fig. 18. How King Cole Novelties Spent Each Dollar of Its Revenues During 1976

2. If there are several categories too small to represent individually, group them together in a single section labeled "Miscellaneous" or "Other."

3. Begin the largest section at the 12 o'clock position and arrange the remaining sections in descending order according to size—except that "Miscellaneous" or "Other" should be last, even though it may be larger than the section preceding it.

4. If the circle is large (four to five inches), it will look less bare if each section is shaded in a different design. But if it is small, the shading may give it a heavy, cluttered look. Different colors, instead of shading, are often used if the graph is to appear in a printed publication.

A Closing Word on Tables and Graphs Any body of statistics in business writing should always be presented in tabular or graphic form. To gain proficiency in tables and graphs—since this discussion provides only a general introduction—you should do at least these two things:

1. Become actively aware of their value and widespread use in presenting statistical data. One excellent way of developing such awareness is to start observing their use in business publications. Such a magazine, for example, as *Business Week* (without a doubt available in your library) includes virtually dozens of attractive tables and graphs in each issue. (Note, however, that unlike reports and proposals on the job, magazines do not necessarily follow the guidelines presented above concerning the use of numbering and titles.)

2. Start constructing your own tables and graphs. A pencil, ruler, compass, and protractor (and, oh yes, an eraser!), along with a little imagination and patience, are about all you need.

Photographs

Photographs may be used in business writing for a number of reasons. One reason may be visual appeal. For instance, an annual report to stockholders by a manufacturing company will almost certainly contain numerous photographs in color of the firm's latest products. Similarly, a recent report to taxpayers by a county park board featured on nearly every page enchanting scenes of recreational facilities and people using them.

A quite different purpose is served when a photograph is included as evidence to demonstrate the existence or nature of some problem. Such a use is illustrated in the following correspondence from the director of reliability and quality control of one firm to his counterpart in an overseas firm. In his letter, the reliability director stated: ". . . we have received the first shipment of transmission parts, damaged due to water penetration into the individual packages and envelopes. To better visualize the effect and cause, we are attaching photographs showing the severity of the damage." As can be seen (Figures 8.29 and 8.30), the accompanying photos (the first showing the crate before opening; the second, the contents of the crate after opening) convey the message far more realistically than could any verbal description.

A similar purpose is served by using photographs to explain a situation to someone with a different language background. The same director of reliability and quality control referred to above has found it expedient when describing a problem in overseas correspondence to include photo-

FIGURE 8.29
Photograph Showing
Damaged Carton.
(Stefan Bogar. Used
with permission.)

FIGURE 8.30
Photograph Showing
Damaged Contents of
Carton. (Stefan
Bogar. Used with
permission.)

FIGURE 8.31
Photograph Showing Location of Rust. (Stefan Bogar. Used with permission.)

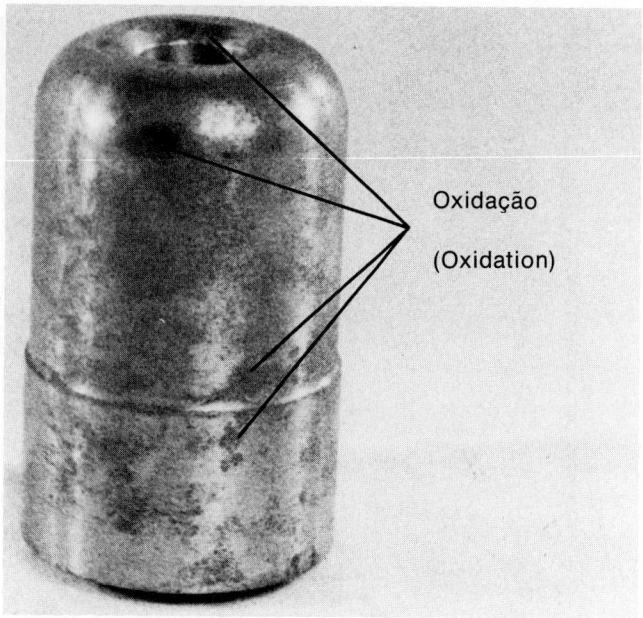

graphs showing what the problem is—in this instance, the problem was rust, as illustrated in Figure 8.31.

The great advantage in using photographs is their realism and authenticity. However, they do have limitations. One is that, although a competent photographer can reduce this possibility, photographs may offer distractions through including irrelevant detail. For instance, a photograph of a new model motorcycle in action may attract more attention to the clenched-teeth expression on the face of the rider than to the bike itself.

A greater limitation is that photographs reveal only surface features. It is because of this that diagrams are often more useful in business writing than photographs.

Diagrams

A diagram is a line drawing that shows appearances and relationships and is used for explaining rather than representing photographically. Diagrams have the advantage over photographs of showing only what the artist wants to call the reader's attention to. They can also be adapted more closely to the reader's level of understanding.

Some of the possibilities in using diagrams are shown in the following examples:

1. Diagram to show outward appearance (Figure 8.32).
2. Cutaway diagram (Figure 8.33).
3. Series of diagrams showing varying conditions of wear (Figure 8.34).

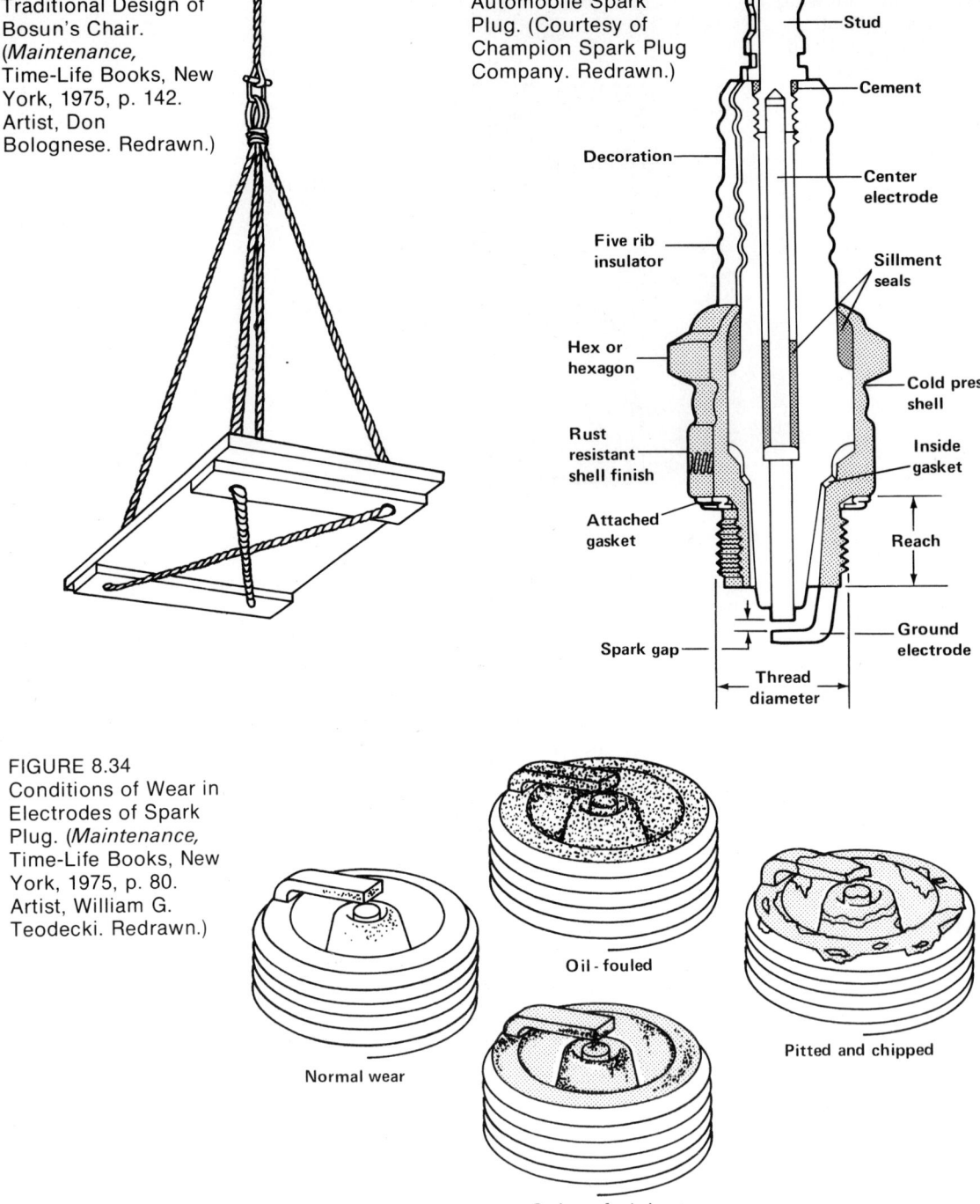

FIGURE 8.32 Traditional Design of Bosun's Chair. (*Maintenance*, Time-Life Books, New York, 1975, p. 142. Artist, Don Bolognese. Redrawn.)

FIGURE 8.33 Automobile Spark Plug. (Courtesy of Champion Spark Plug Company. Redrawn.)

FIGURE 8.34 Conditions of Wear in Electrodes of Spark Plug. (*Maintenance*, Time-Life Books, New York, 1975, p. 80. Artist, William G. Teodecki. Redrawn.)

FIGURE 8.35
Functional
Components of a
Lawn Sweeper.
(*Owners Guide,* The
Parker Sweeper
Company, 1971, p. 4.)

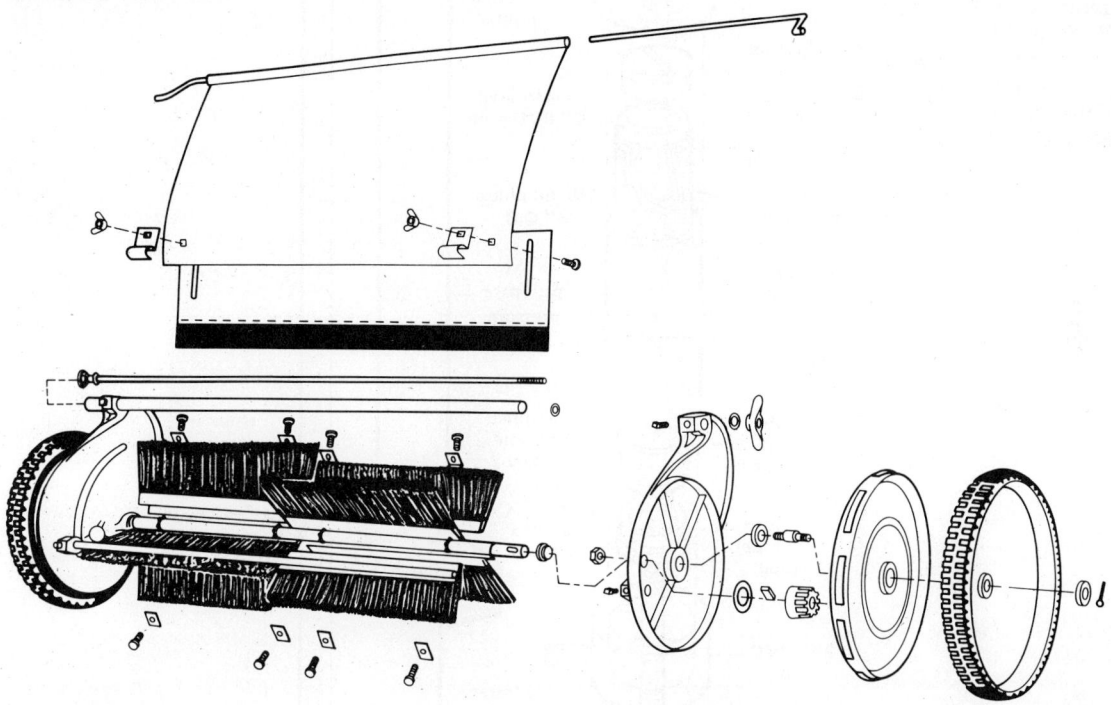

4. Exploded diagram, in which, for easier identification, the components are shown separated from each other (Figure 8.35).

5. Exploded diagram alongside a diagram showing the external appearance (Figure 8.36).

6. Show-through diagram, allowing the viewer to "see through" the exterior to internal components (Figure 8.37).

7. Schematic drawing showing the operation of an electronic device (Figure 8.38).

8. Series of diagrams explaining a procedure (for filling an opening in a boat deck left by a broken screwhead). It should be emphasized that the explanation in the text accompanying these diagrams makes clear the points that the diagrams illustrate (Figure 8.39).

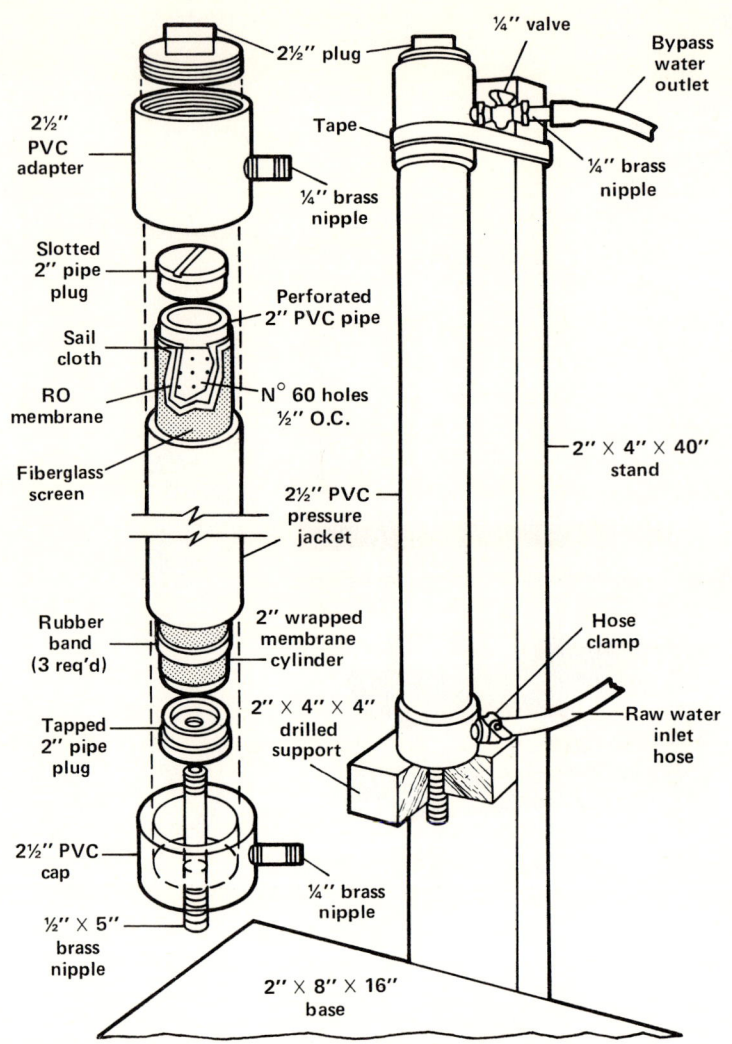

FIGURE 8.36
Pressure Jacket Showing Internal Parts. (Richard Day, "Reverse-Osmosis Water Improver," *Popular Science,* January, 1973, p. 103. Reprinted from *Popular Science* with permission. © 1972, Times Mirror Magazine, Inc.)

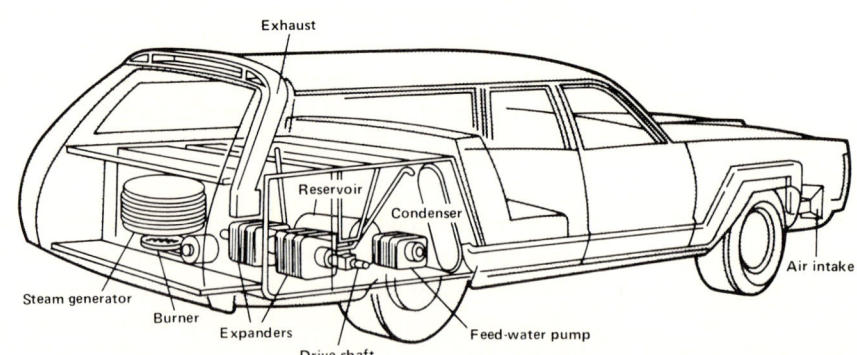

FIGURE 8.37
Suggested Installation of the KROV Steam-Power System. (E. F. Lindsley, "New KROV Engine Boosts Hope for Steam Cars," *Popular Science,* June, 1973, p. 92. Reprinted from *Popular Science* with permission. © 1973 Times Mirror Magazine, Inc.)

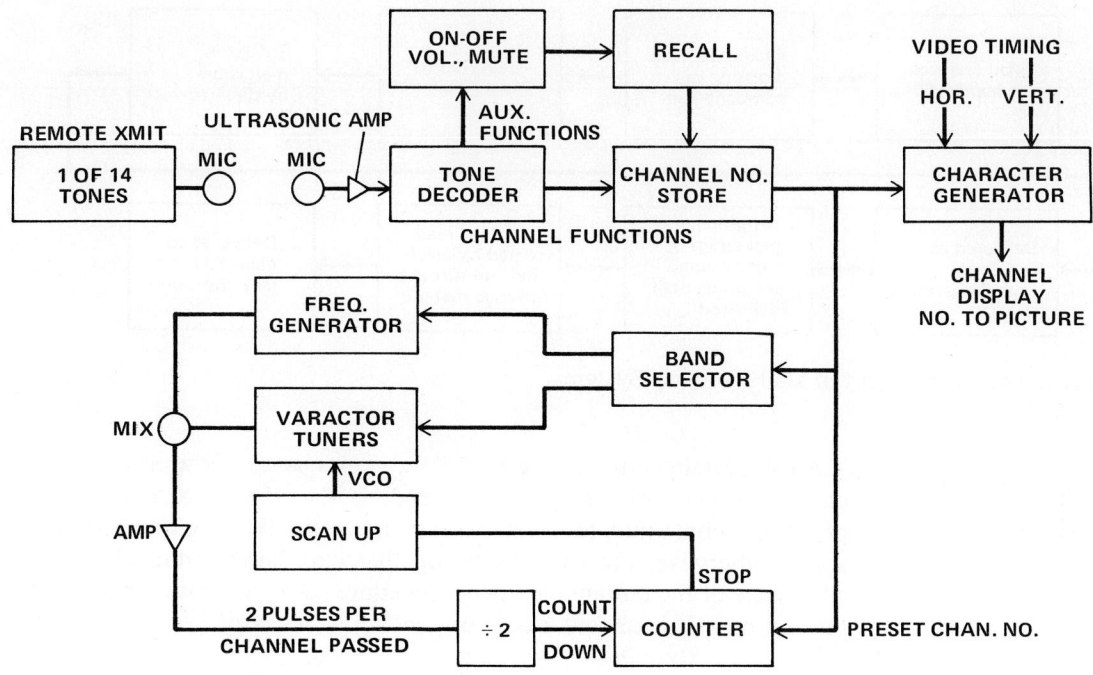

FIGURE 8.38 Digital Tuner for TV. (William J. Hawkins, "Magnavox Does It: Digital TV with Instant All-Channel Control," *Popular Science,* August, 1974, p. 38. Reprinted from *Popular Science* with permission. © 1974, Times Mirror Magazine, Inc.)

FIGURE 8.39 Procedure for Filling Hole Left by Broken Screwhead. (*Maintenance,* Time-Life Books, 1975, p. 41. Artist, Roger Metcalf. Redrawn.)

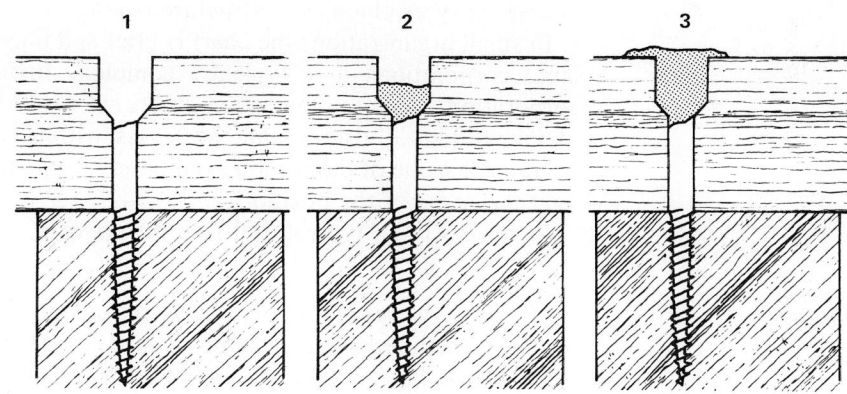

Flow Charts

As their name implies, flow charts depict by means of a chart, or diagram, the flow of steps in a procedure. Instead of the steps being named in a list, they are stated briefly in a series of squares or rectangles joined by arrows showing the direction of flow. Figure 8.40 is an example of a simple flow chart describing the mail handling system for an organization of several hundred employees.

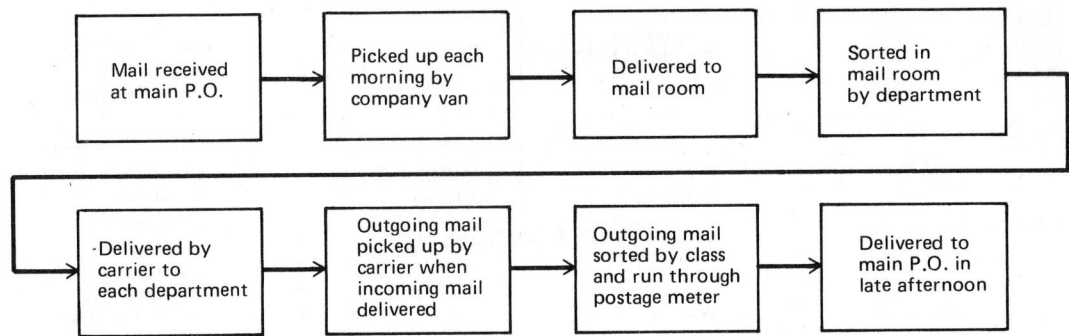

FIGURE 8.40 Flow Chart of Mail Handling System

An especially effective use of flow charts is to show a set of two charts—one describing a present procedure, the other a proposed simpler procedure containing fewer steps. Assuming that the proposed change is sound otherwise, the two charts together can demonstrate vividly the advantage of the streamlined new procedure over the more cumbersome present one. It is almost a case of "seeing is believing."

Organization Charts

An organization chart looks much like a flow chart, but its purpose is different. What it does is to show the positions of formal authority in an organization and the relationship of each position to the others. Organization charts naturally vary from one organization to another; and, of course, vary as changes in structure occur.

In small organizations the chart is brief and uncomplicated, whereas in large corporations it is typically complex. In fact, in the very large corporations, many organization charts are needed to show the structure of the various divisions and the levels within each division. In some charts, the name of the person occupying the position is shown; in others, only the name of the position.

Figure 8.41 is a typical, but simple, example.

Models

A model (in the sense used here) is also similar to a flow chart, except that instead of depicting a physical procedure or system, it depicts an abstract set of ideas. The communication model in Chapter 2 is an example, as is the Real World–Verbal World model in Chapter 11. Figure 8.42 is a model showing steps for implementing change in the work climate of industrial organizations.

Note that these models (as are any models—for instance, a model airplane) are greatly simplified in relation to what they represent. Their function is to point up essential features of whatever they illustrate, usually a process.

USING GRAPHIC AIDS

FIGURE 8.41
Organization Chart,
Jakeda Corp.

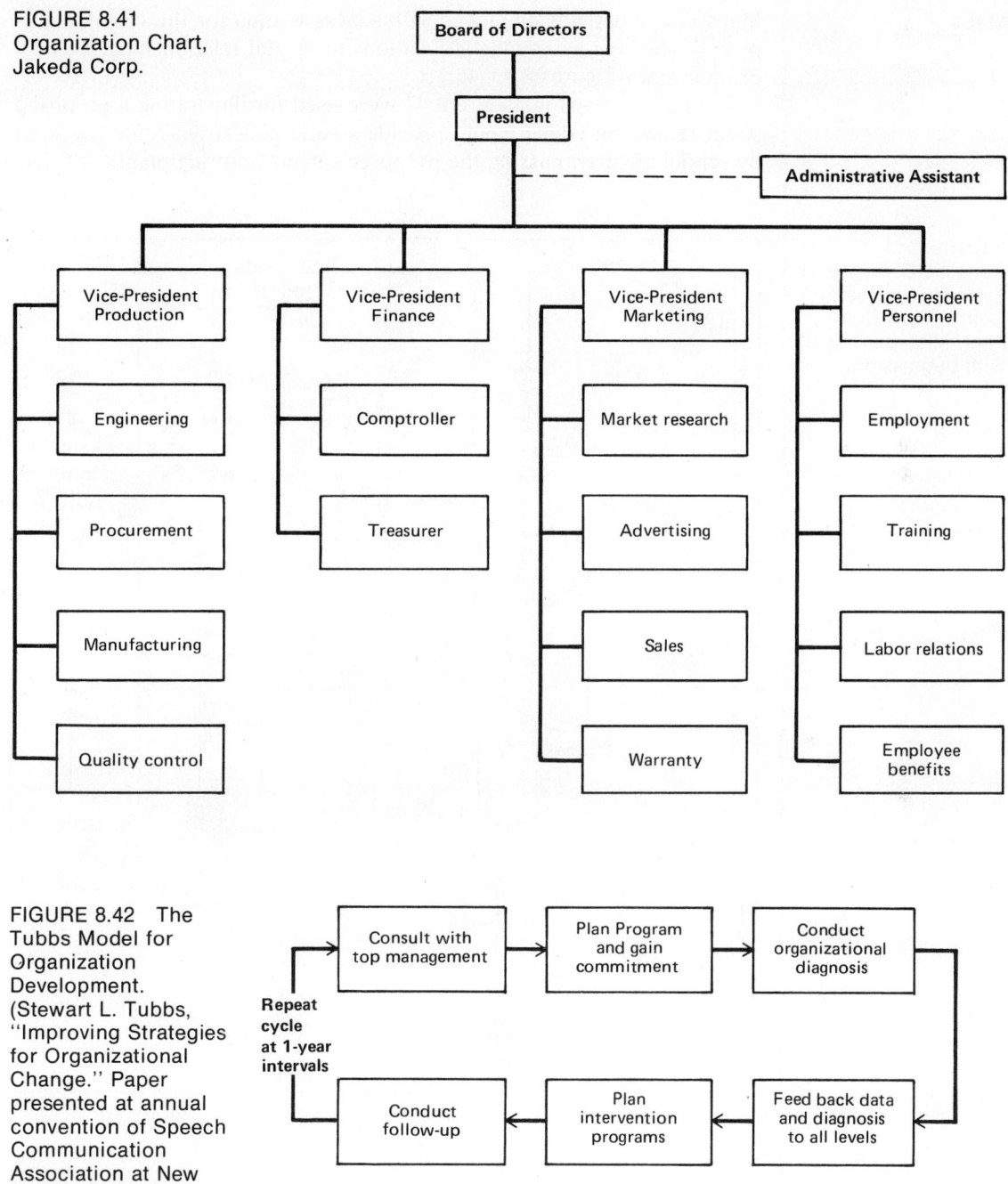

FIGURE 8.42 The
Tubbs Model for
Organization
Development.
(Stewart L. Tubbs,
"Improving Strategies
for Organizational
Change." Paper
presented at annual
convention of Speech
Communication
Association at New
York, 1973, p. 8. Used
with permission.)

Maps

Maps are sometimes employed in business writing for the obvious purpose of showing geographical locations or spatial relationships. Typical examples are Figures 8.43–46.

The pair of maps in Figure 8.47 were used for illustrating a proposed street relocation which would provide a safer pedestrian route followed by school children passing the proposer's manufacturing plant.

FIGURE 8.43
Genesee County Park System. (Genesee County Park Board, Flint, Michigan. Used with permission.)

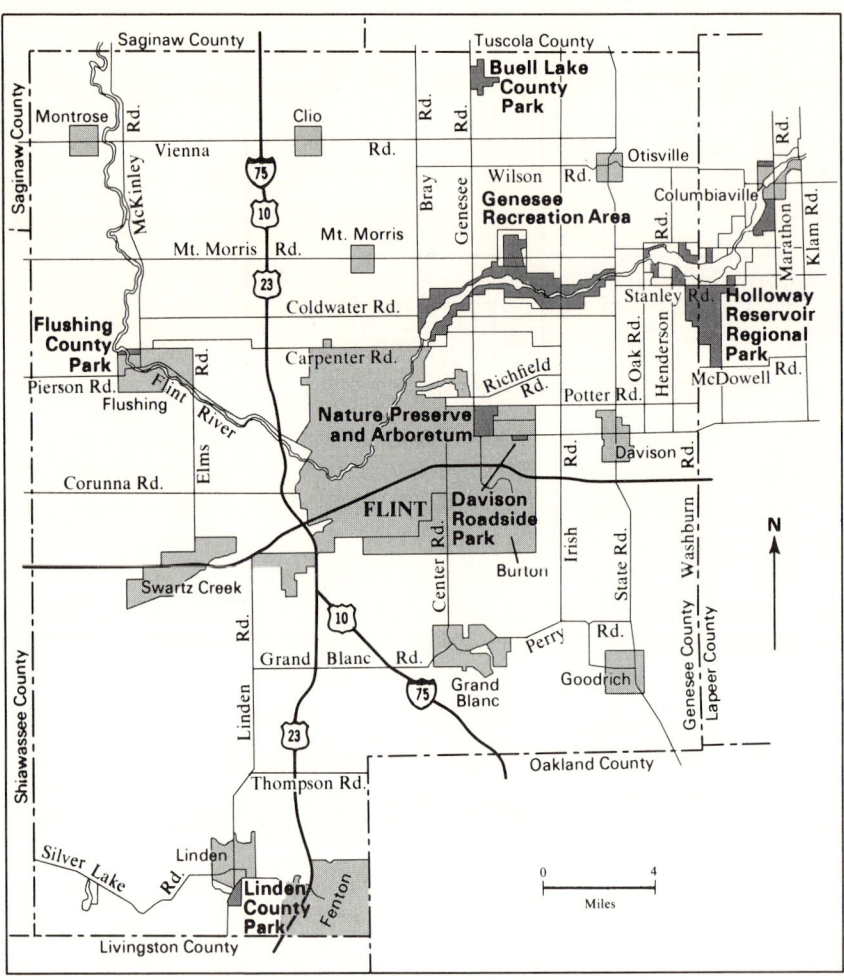

USING GRAPHIC AIDS

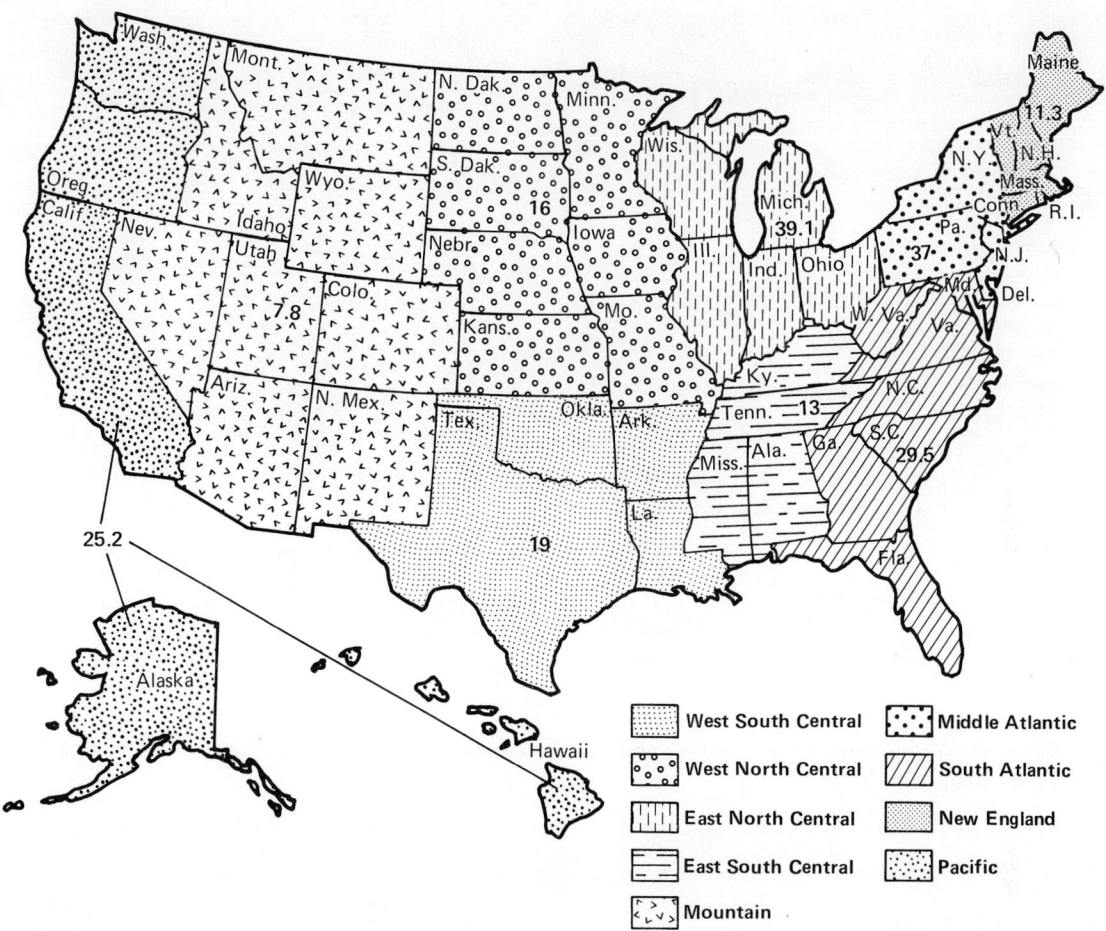

FIGURE 8.44 Population of United States by Geographic Division, 1967. (*200 Million Americans*, U.S. Department of Commerce, Bureau of the Census, November, 1967, p. 28.)

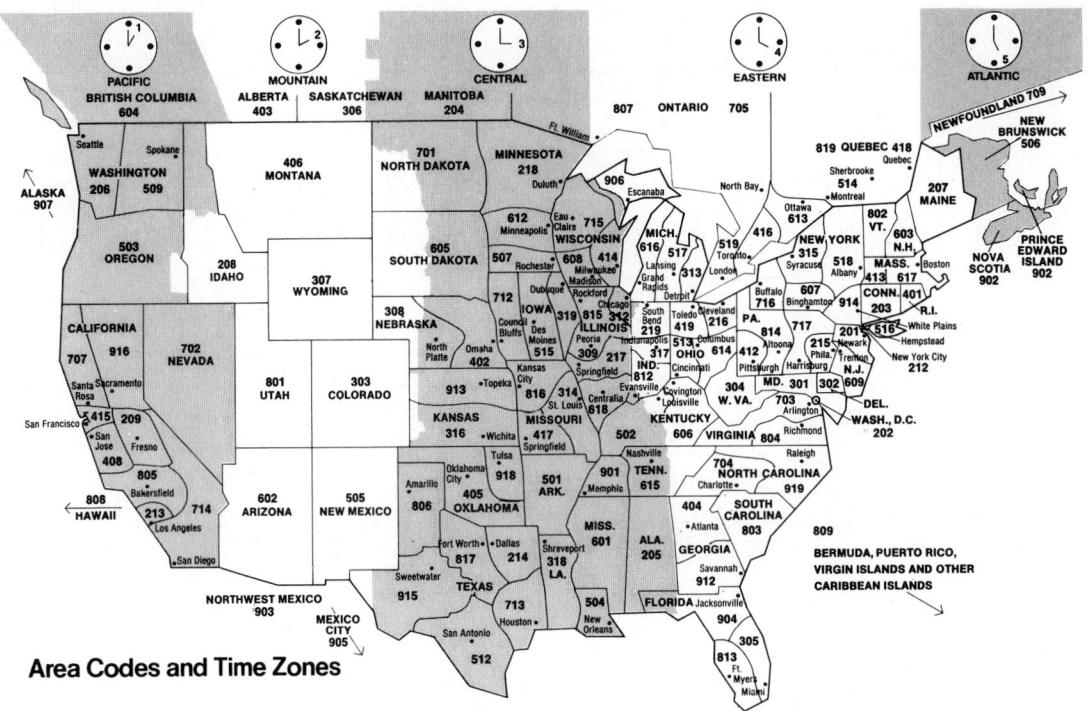

FIGURE 8.45 Telephone Area Codes and Time Zones in the United States. (New England Telephone. Used with permission.)

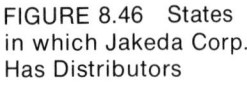
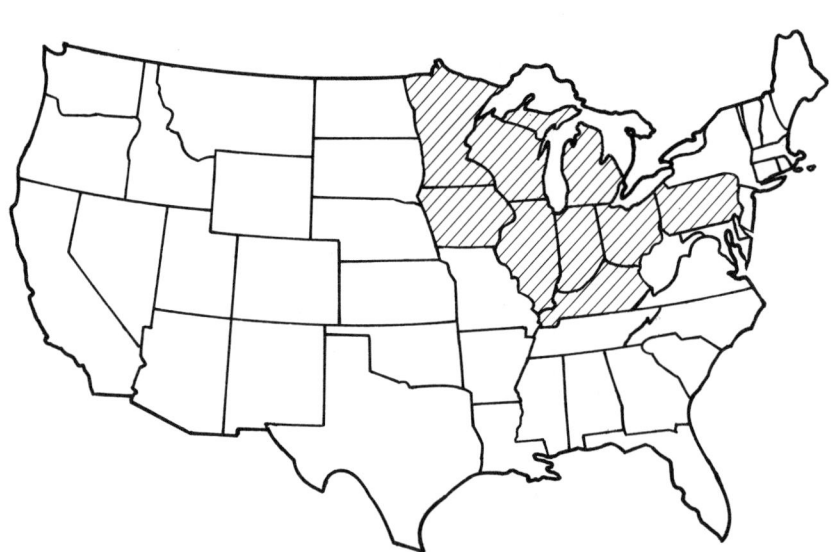

FIGURE 8.46 States in which Jakeda Corp. Has Distributors

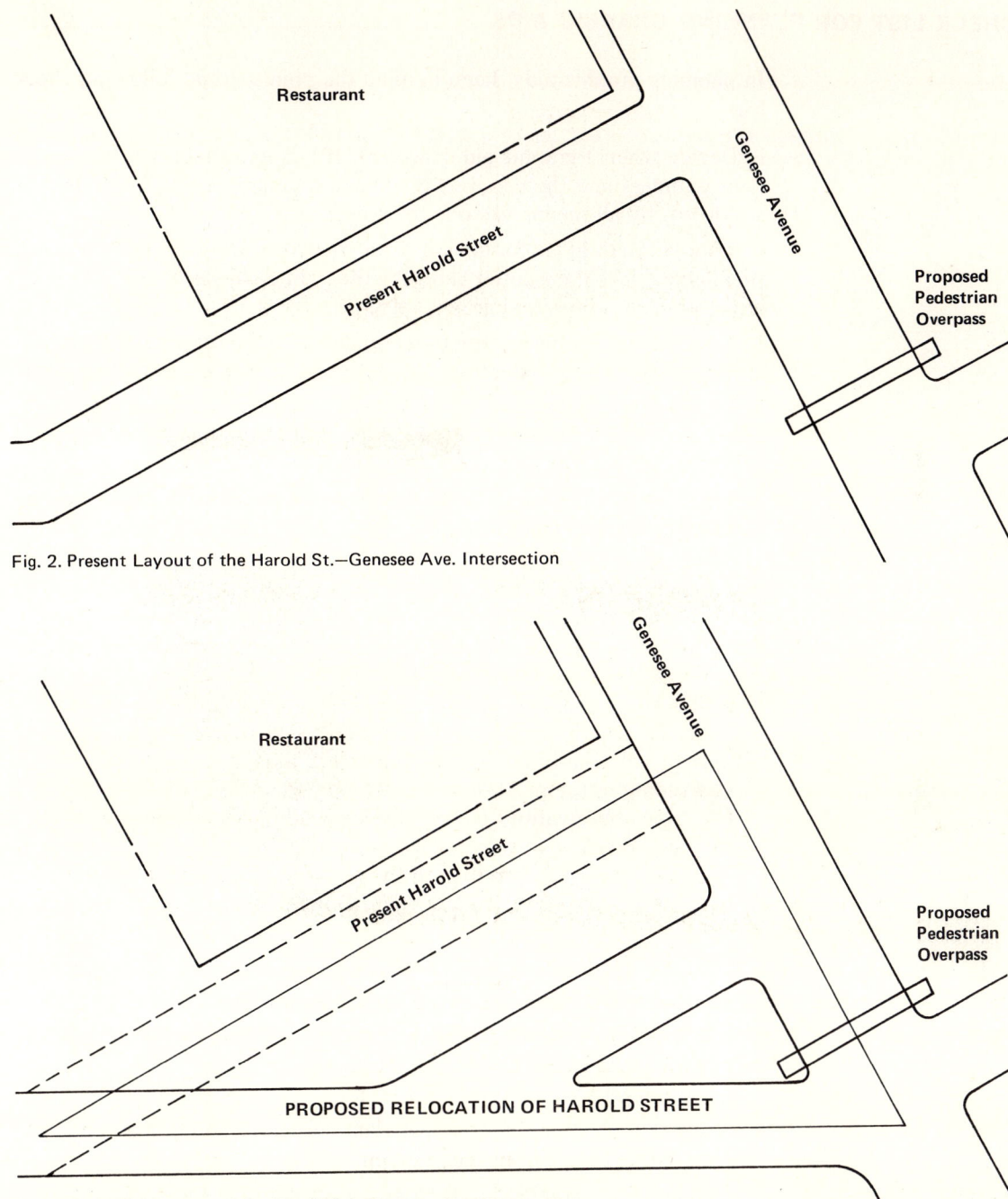

FIGURE 8.47 Maps Used for Illustrating Proposed Street Relocation. (James R. Frahm. Used with permission.)

CHECK LIST FOR PLANNING GRAPHIC AIDS

In planning graphic aids, keep in mind the points in the following check list:

1. Decide when a graphic aid is needed. If it is important that the reader clearly understand the detail involved and a graphic aid will help him or her do so, by all means use one (or more).

2. Choose the right aid for the job. From the coverage in this chapter, you should be able—like a golfer choosing the right club—to determine which of the array of tables and graphs to select.

3. Keep the aid simple and uncluttered. Adapt to the reader's understanding and interest—consistent, of course, with the purpose of the message.

4. Design the aid large enough so the reader need not squint to make out details, but avoid using space wastefully; a line graph need not require a full page if one 2×3 inches in size will suffice.

5. If the table or figure is larger than page size, possibilities for dealing with the problem include:

    a. Using a narrower margin than for the text (but still leave at least one-half to three-quarters of an inch minimum).
    b. Using smaller size type (12 characters per inch instead of 10).
    c. Reducing the illustration on a copier (some copiers will reduce material by as much as 50 percent).
    d. Turning the illustration sidewise (but be sure the top of the table or figure is toward what would be the left side of the sheet when held upright, and the bottom toward the right side).
    e. Folding in the illustration accordion-style.
    f. Using abbreviations (especially for headings in a table)—as long as they will be clear to the reader.
    g. If a table, continuing it on the next page (but only if it is more than a page to begin with; if it is *less* than a page, locate it on a single page only).

6. Enclose each table or graph in a border (unless it is an informal table)—but avoid if possible running into the margin.

7. Use a series of simple tables or graphs rather than trying to cram too much into one illustration. (This is another possible solution if the illustration is too big.)

8. Number each page (in the upper right corner as usual) that contains a graphic aid, even if there's no text on the page.

9. Number each graphic aid (unless it's an informal table). In a formal report or proposal (see Chapter 11), tables are traditionally identified by Roman numerals at the top; figures by Arabic numerals at the bottom, and the two series are numbered separately (Table I, Table II, etc.; Fig. 1,

Fig. 2, etc.). However, if the report or proposal is informal, Arabic numerals and titles at the bottom may be used with both tables and figures.

PLACEMENT OF GRAPHICS

Graphic aids should be located for the convenience of the reader. The following guidelines will aid in achieving this objective:

1. If the table or figure occupies less than a page, include it within the text on the page where it is referred to immediately following the first reference—or on the next page if necessary.

2. If the aid is a full page, place it on the left side opposite the page where the prose explanation is located, or on the page immediately following the prose explanation.

3. If it is relevant only in a general way and does not make any particular point in the text, put it in the appendix.

SUMMARY

1. Graphic aids, in the form of tables and figures or illustrations, are often more effective than words alone for explaining or supporting ideas. However, graphic aids seldom suffice by themselves; almost always they require verbal explanation to be clear.

2. Kinds of ideas best developed graphically include statistical data, descriptions of what something looks like, explanations of procedures, organizational relationships, abstract relationships, and locations.

3. Tables consist of data arranged in columns and rows with appropriate headings and labels. Tables have the advantage over straight prose that the data is in a more readable form, and the advantage over graphs of being usually more precise and complete.

4. Figures, or illustrations, refer to any graphic aid not a table. Figures include graphs, photos, diagrams, flow charts, organization charts, models, and maps.

5. Line graphs are best used for showing trends, bar graphs for showing comparisons, and circle graphs for showing parts of a whole. Graphs are less useful than tables for presenting precise and complete data, but more useful for presenting the "general picture" at a glance.

6. Photos have the advantage of being able to depict appearances realistically, but the disadvantage of being limited to what the camera can see (including details that may be irrelevant or distracting).

7. Diagrams, though less realistic than photos, are more versatile. Diagrams may be used to show not only outward appearances, but also

cutaway, exploded, or show-through views or schematic representations of selected components of a system.

8. Flow charts show steps in a procedure; organization charts show positions of formal authority in an organization and the relationship of each position to the others; models (in the sense used here) show relationships among abstract ideas; and maps show geographical or spatial relationships.

9. In planning graphic aids, the writer must determine when an aid is appropriate and what kind of aid would be best adapted to the need. Aids should be simple and uncluttered, large enough to be comfortably legible, and located for the maximum convenience of the reader.

SUGGESTED APPLICATIONS

1. Using a questionnaire that you distribute to the members of a particular group, such as this class, secure data that will enable you to construct three different bar graphs depicting such information as the following:

    a. Major fields of study or interests of this group.

    b. Political preferences (or lack of).

    c. Religious affiliations (or lack of).

    d. Views on one or more current controversial issues (local or national) of your choice, using a five-point scale such as "Agree completely," "Agree somewhat," "No opinion," "Disagree somewhat," and "Disagree completely."

2. Using the data from your survey, convert the numbers to percentages and construct circle graphs to correspond to your bar graphs.

3. Construct an informal table showing the academic departments in your school and the chairperson of each department. Precede the table with an appropriate identifying statement.

4. Construct a formal table showing the information given below concerning the Jakeda Corporation:

Employees: 1945, professional-14, nonprofessional-104; 1950, professional-68, nonprofessional-685; 1955, professional-128, nonprofessional-1279; 1960, professional-189, nonprofessional-2013; 1965, professional-256, nonprofessional-2732; 1970, professional-282, nonprofessional-3022; 1975, professional-260, nonprofessional-2860.

Gross sales: 1945, $918,000; 1950, $7,780,000; 1955, $20,105,000; 1960, $42,230,000; 1965, $89,100,000; 1970, $105,700,000; 1975, $109,800,000.

Net profits: 1945, $110,160; 1950, $933,600; 1955, $2,412,600; 1960, $5,067,600; 1965, $10,692,000; 1970, $12,684,400; 1975, $13,176,000.

5. Using the same data concerning the Jakeda Corporation, construct line graphs showing the following growth trends:
   a. Number of employees, differentiated by professional and non-professional
   b. Gross sales
   c. New profits

6. Consulting such sources of statistical data in your library as the *Annual Abstract of Statistics, Business Statistics, The Official Encyclopedia of Sports, Statistical Abstract of the United States, Statistical Yearbook of the United Nations,* or *World Almanac* (most of which are issued annually), choose one or more subjects of interest to you and construct:
   a. A line graph
   b. A bar graph
   c. A column graph
   d. A circle graph

On each graph identify the source; for example, Source: *Statistical Yearbook of the United Nations,* p. 856.

7. Draw a diagram showing the layout of an office, office area, or lab area at your school.

NOTES

[1] *Navigation,* Time-Life Books, New York, 1975, p. 84.

[2] Source of data: *Statistical Abstract of the United States,* 1973, p. 149. These data are also used in a number of graphs in this chapter.

[3] *200 Million Americans,* U.S. Department of Commerce, Bureau of the Census, November, 1967, p. 7.

[4] Gerald Zoltman and Philip C. Burger, *Marketing Research: Fundamentals and Dynamics* (Hinsdale, Ill.: The Dryden Press, 1975), p. 429.

THREE BEING PERSUASIVE

PERSUADING YOUR READER OR LISTENER

WHAT WE MEAN BY PERSUASION

THE THREE FACTORS OF PERSUASION: AN OVERVIEW

ADAPTING TO THE RECEIVER'S NEEDS

The Maslow Hierarchy in Persuasion

The Consistency Principle
    The Basic Premises of the Consistency Principle
    Using the Consistency Principle in Persuasion

The Common Denominator: A "Good Decision"

PERSUADING THROUGH CREDIBILITY

Interrelationship of the Three Persuasive Factors

What We Mean by Credibility

Variables of Credibility
    The Receiver   Subject Matter   Time

The Components of Credibility
    Trustworthiness   Competence   Dynamism
    The Components in Combination

Factors Contributing to Credibility
    Initial Credibility   Derived Credibility

The Importance of Credibility in Persuasion
    Practical Uses
    The Receiver's Need to Have Confidence in the Persuader

PERSUADING THROUGH LOGIC

The Importance of Logic in Business Persuasion

Factors in Strengthening the Logic of the Message
    Use the Need-Plan Pattern
    Offer Sufficient Proof to Support Your Claims
    Use a Two-Sided Rather than a One-Sided Approach Where Appropriate
    Use Sound Reasoning   Use Logic-Oriented Language
    Make Your Conclusions and Recommendations Explicit

A Closing Word on Logic

Being clear—the focus of the past five chapters—is a prized virtue in business communication. Often, however, just being clear is not enough. You must be persuasive as well. Postponement of a deadline; obtaining new equipment in your department; a change in your vacation schedule; adoption of a new procedure; abandonment of an old one; selling a product; placating a customer—achieving any of these desired ends, and many more, will require persuasion. So you write a memo, letter, proposal, or request, or you make an oral presentation, hoping in each case to win the approval, authorization, or goodwill you seek. Throughout your career, much of the satisfaction you derive from your work will depend on your success in persuading others.

What brings persuasion about? Irrefutable logic? An elegant style? Some magic formula? Advice through the centuries has contained a great deal of wisdom—but also much hokum. Fortunately, since around World War II, research in communication has yielded many insights, some confirming ancient wisdom, some disconfirming it, and some introducing concepts essentially new. It will be the objective of this chapter to present the best of both old and new that can aid in expanding your ability to persuade.

WHAT WE MEAN BY PERSUASION

Persuasive communication aims at influencing the beliefs, attitudes, or specific actions of others. For our purposes this definition does not include deceit or coercion. It is true these may be used by the fly-by-night salesperson, the fast-buck artist, or even by some established businessmen or women. But such tactics have no legitimate role in the business organization (nor anywhere else for that matter). For on the job, maintaining the confidence of others (most of whom will remain our associates for long periods of time) is essential. To the degree that we weaken this confidence we also weaken our capacity to persuade. Whatever the short-term gain may be, it seldom is worth the loss of confidence by others that results.

With these thoughts in mind, let us examine the reader or listener to discover what may cause him or her to be persuaded.

THE THREE FACTORS OF PERSUASION: AN OVERVIEW

Many theories of persuasion have appeared through the years. The approach in this text will rest on the proposition that persuasion results from the operation of three basic factors: the needs of the persuadee (person being persuaded), the credibility of the persuader, and the logic of the message (Figure 9.1). The first, in the structure of this theory, is the primary factor and *must* be present, in combination with at least one of the other two. Usually, all three are present.

This approach, consistent with concepts enduring since Aristotle (fourth century B.C.) to the present day, offers a framework within which the whole range of persuasive theories and techniques may be meaningfully organized.

1. The primary, most basic persuasive factor consists of the *other person's needs as a person*. Identifying this as the most basic factor rests squarely on the assumption that human behavior is not logic-oriented but *need*-oriented; that we influence other people not primarily because our arguments are logical, but because they meet (or are perceived as meeting) one or more needs of the other person. This assumption does not mean that logic is unimportant; only that its importance is secondary.[1]

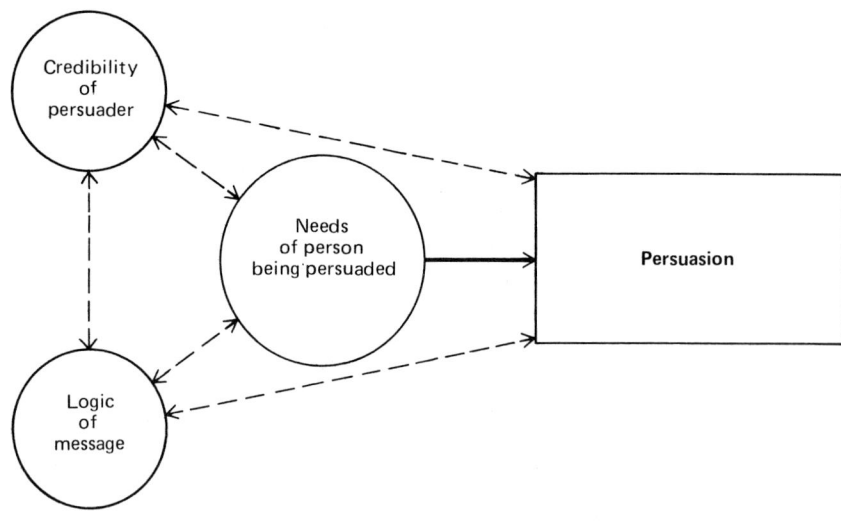

FIGURE 9.1
Three-Factor Model of Persuasion

This position is consistent, of course, with the implications of the Maslow Hierarchy discussed in Chapter 3.

2. A secondary factor is the *persuader's credibility*. Defined briefly, credibility refers to the confidence in the persuader felt by others as a result of what they perceive to be his or her trustworthiness and competence. If they feel he or she is honest and *knows* the subject, they are more inclined to be persuaded than otherwise. Sometimes, they may rely wholly on credibility alone, as would be true in accepting without question the advice of someone highly regarded; for instance, one's family doctor or minister. But frequently the reader or listener wants to "see for him- or herself," so turns to the other secondary factor: logic.

3. The other secondary factor, the *logic of the message,* refers to the use of sound data to support, through sound reasoning, one's inferences or conclusions. Implicit in this definition is the notion that the person being persuaded understands the reasoning and accepts the conclusions because they "make sense" to him or her. In other words, satisfied that the argument is sound, one adopts it as part of one's own belief system.

Following this quick overview of these three factors, let us examine each one more closely.

ADAPTING TO THE RECEIVER'S NEEDS

To adapt to anyone's needs, we first must discover what they are. Providing insight into the receiver's needs, therefore, will be the objective of this section of the chapter.

First we shall review the Maslow Hierarchy, introduced in Chapter 3, then show how its utility is increased through use of another concept, the Consistency Principle. Finally, we shall point out the common denominator in all decision-making: the need to make a "good decision."

The Maslow Hierarchy in Persuasion

Before reading further, it would be well to review the discussion of the Maslow Hierarchy of Human Needs in Chapter 3. Five levels of needs (listed in order from highest to lowest) were described: self-actualization or achievement; esteem or status; love or affiliation; safety or security; and physiological or survival.

Also from Chapter 3, you may recall our classification of people into two broad categories: achievement seekers and status or security seekers. From this, it would appear that for some, the dominant need on the job will be for achievement; for others, the need for status or security. However, esteem remains a potent (though secondary) need for the achievement seekers; while the need for affiliation with selected others is an important secondary need for all—not as an end in itself, but as a means of providing the kind of working relationship essential for satisfying their dominant needs.

The Consistency Principle

For understanding the persuadee's needs, the Maslow Hierarchy is a powerful tool. But its power is increased when we couple it with another contribution of modern psychology: the Consistency Principle.

Since the early 1940s, several forms of consistency theory have gained prominence, generating considerable research among psychologists and communication scholars.[2] The form attracting probably the greatest attention has been the theory of *cognitive dissonance,* first propounded in 1957. Cognitive dissonance will be referred to later as we explain and show applications of the consistency principle.

The Basic Premises of the Consistency Principle   The central notion of the consistency principle is based on three premises:

1. Humankind prefers a state of psychological equilibrium (consistency, harmony, balance, or freedom from anxiety).
2. Loss of the sense of equilibrium creates a feeling of tension, or drive.
3. The result of the tension or drive is an attempt to restore the state of equilibrium.

Premise 1 seems self-evident, requiring little comment. All of us, we may assume, prefer to be "in balance," free of anxiety. But premises 2 and 3 require elaboration.

Premise 2: Loss of Equilibrium. What may cause loss of one's sense of psychological equilibrium? The answer is that one's equilibrium is disturbed when one is confronted with a situation involving *cognitions* (information or beliefs) that conflict with cognitions one already holds.

For instance, if you have considered Joe Jones to be a loyal, dependable friend, but someone tells you that Joe is running you down behind your back, you doubtless will suffer some loss of equilibrium, or cognitive dissonance (literally, disharmony between the established cognition and the new). Such disturbing information would be bound to be upsetting.

Here are other examples that would probably create cognitive dissonance in most people:

Established Belief	*New, Conflicting Belief*
You consider yourself well thought of by most people.	You are told that many of your associates consider you tactless.
You are confident of getting a job following graduation.	The news reports tell of increasing unemployment.
You feel you are doing very well on the job.	Your boss tells you that you must improve drastically to be considered for promotion.

Note, however, that for significant dissonance to result, the new information must conflict with beliefs that are relevant to one's dominant needs. In the examples above, believing that you are well thought of by most people would be relevant to your need for affiliation. The beliefs that you are doing well on the job, or that you will get a job following graduation, would be relevant to your need for security; also, very likely, your need for esteem, and perhaps achievement.

On the other hand, if the conflicting information presents no threat, little if any dissonance will result. You are unlikely, for example, to experience much anxiety if told that Ottawa instead of Montreal is the capital of Canada; or that Saturn, not Pluto, is more distant from Earth.

In other words, the greater the threat seems, the greater the dissonance or anxiety; the less it seems, the less the dissonance.

Premise 3: Restoring Equilibrium. The person experiencing dissonance may resort to any of several ways of reducing the dissonance in order to restore equilibrium. How one goes about doing this has important implications for our possible success in attempting to persuade that person.

1. Reject the conflicting belief. If the new information conflicts with an important belief that is well established, rejecting the new information is a strong likelihood. When this occurs, the odds for persuasion are greatly reduced.

The tendency to reject conflicting ideas has been described by Jesse Nirenberg, an industrial psychologist, in this manner:

> As people move through life they build up a wardrobe of ideas and points of view. These ideas are comfortable. They fit well. They suit the taste of the individual and he feels at ease with them. Like an old shoe, they have become shaped to his contours.
>
> He's reluctant to discard any of these ideas for something new. When he tries on new ideas they feel awkward. They're not cut quite right for him. He misses the security of the old ideas, and sometimes scarcely recognizes himself when holding the new ones. . . .
>
> The truth is that he isn't likely to be swayed merely by logic to give up any of his ideas for new ones.[3]

Rejecting the new as a means of maintaining equilibrium is a natural recourse—which sheds further light on the resistance, referred to in Chapter 3, of the older manager to accepting new ideas.

To the extent that the new seems "far out," rejecting it is all the more probable. Thus, a person will more likely reject a drastic proposal (unless the need seems overwhelming for accepting it) than he or she will a more modest proposal that "seems reasonable." Any idea that appears too extreme falls into one's "latitude of rejection," and will appear to one even more extreme than it is. Thus, in attempting to persuade another, we must be cautious in going "too far." The more extreme the other person sees a request or proposal, the easier he or she can justify rejecting it outright. For instance, in applying for a job, to request a salary $3000 higher than offered may result in the prospective employer's responding, in effect, "Forget it. I can hire someone else." However, he or she may be willing to consider a request for $500 to $1000 more.

2. Devalue the conflicting information. For whatever reasons, the person confronted with the conflicting information may find it impossible or inconvenient to reject it outright. But one may attempt to devalue it. For instance, to return to the examples above, if told one is tactless, one may rationalize, "So what? I believe in being frank. People respect you more. Besides, it's very seldom that anyone thinks I'm tactless."

Or if one hears that the job market looks unpromising, one may respond, "That may be true in general, but not in my case. I've got connections. . . ." And so on. To the extent that one can devalue the conflicting information, one can also reduce any anxiety caused by it.

Coping with such rationalization usually means producing evidence so strong that it cannot be easily brushed aside. In addition, using one or more of the techniques suggested below for employing the consistency principle to our advantage will help in coping with the persuadee's rationalization.

3. Abandon the old, accept the new. Although this is not the most probable means of dissonance reduction, it does occur from time to time. Some of the reasons include: the old belief no longer seems sound; it has become increasingly difficult to maintain; it may no longer be relevant to one's needs anyway; more and more people are accepting the new belief; the new belief seems increasingly sound. People do not abandon old ideas and beliefs readily (and probably should not, for sake of their personal stability); however, when the scales are sufficiently tipped, people do change. Over a lifetime they may change a great deal.

Persuasion is by no means impossible!

Using the Consistency Principle in Persuasion We have seen how the drive for consistency can block persuasion. Let us see how it can also aid. Suggestions for using the consistency principle in persuasion include the following:

1. Link the conflicting information to a more relevant need (or needs) of the persuadee. This suggestion, of course, rests on our premise that human behavior is basically need-oriented.

To illustrate, suppose you work in a department where, except as secretaries and clerks, women have never been employed. An opening exists, and you have a well-qualified friend, Ms. Evans, whom you would like to see get the job. But your supervisor, Mr. Danville, feels that this is a job for men only, and women need not apply.

However, another of Danville's beliefs is that a high rate of production in his department is important. Now, if production has lately been declining to the point that his reputation as a top producer and his end-of-year bonus are threatened, keeping production up has now become highly important to his need both for esteem and security. The idea of hiring Ms. Evans might now prove very attractive.

This would depend, of course, on your ability to convince Danville that Evans could indeed contribute significantly to improving production (without creating other problems in the process). If you succeeded, you would have positively linked the conflicting cognition (hiring a woman) with a more pressing need (improving production), and your odds for success would be fairly good.

2. Utilize the conformity effect. "Conformity effect" is a convenient term for the everyday occurrence of a person's behavior being influenced by the behavior of others. Conformity represents a kind of consistency, since in the process of conforming, one changes one's views so they will be more consistent with the views of others. Thus, one reduces the possibility of threat to one's needs for affiliation or security that might result if one is regarded by others as the "oddball" in the group.

The drive for conformity has been demonstrated experimentally many times. One of the best known examples is the line-judging experiment. "Naïve" persons (i.e., persons not aware of the true nature of the experiment) were asked to judge the relative lengths of a series of lines which clearly were not equal in length, yet were reported to be by the other persons in the experiment (who were actually confederates of the experimenter). The result was that the naïve persons concurred with the majority over 30 percent of the time that the lines were equal in length, even though they could plainly see that such was not the case.[4]

From your own everyday experience, you have witnessed the conformity effect many times—clothing and hair styles being two notable examples.

To return to the question of Danville's hiring Evans, it is easy to see, first, how the conformity effect could complicate his decision. For if not only in his department, but throughout the organization, no women professionals have ever been hired, then clearly his hiring her would be an act of nonconformity.

Of course, it is possible that the conformity effect might not apply here. Others in the organization might care little, one way or the other. Or Danville might be a strong-willed person who, once he has made up his mind, cares little about what others think. But such factors would have to be great enough to outweigh the tendency to conform. Lacking such overriding factors, Ms. Evans's chances would probably remain slim.

Suppose Danville *is* inclined to conform to the traditional practice of not hiring women? How could you use the conformity effect to conform to what *you* desire? It would depend, of course, on the situation. Perhaps you could show that some people he respects in the organization feel that hiring women would be desirable. Or you might show that in similar jobs elsewhere hiring women has worked out well. Simply being aware of the conformity pressures he may face should help you decide on a more intelligent approach.

Few people like to be out "in left field." To the extent you can show them that they are not all alone—or that unless they change they *will* be all alone—you are utilizing the conformity effect persuasively.

One caution: the conformity effect should be used with sound judgment. A person persuaded because of conformity pressures alone can make some very bad decisions. A good decision should be based on reasons more compelling than simply that "everyone else is doing it this way." Bad decisions tend eventually to harm the persuader as much as the persuaded; thus neither conformity tactics, nor any other tactics, should ever be used to influence reaching a questionable decision. (What constitutes a "good decision" will be discussed later in this chapter).

3. Create a sense of anxiety, then offer a means of resolving it. This is a third way of using the consistency principle to advantage in persuasion. Because of the strong drive to reduce feelings of anxiety within oneself, a potentially powerful persuasive technique is to create anxiety which the persuadee will tend to resolve in our favor. This technique is often used on indifferent students by professors with such admonitions as "If you don't meet X requirement [getting your work in, attending class more regularly, or whatever] you will fail the course." More often than not the technique works!

In persuasive messages on the job, the most common application of this technique is found in use of the need-plan pattern. Convincing the supervisor that a need exists stirs up dissonance; offering a plan for remedying the need provides a means of eliminating the dissonance—or at least reducing it.

Examples such as the following will illustrate:

Need (Dissonance Arousing)	*Plan* (Dissonance Reducing)
Morale in the department is low.	A gripe session would help clear the air.
Customer complaints show dissatisfaction with X product.	Modifying Z design feature would end the dissatisfaction.
Vendor Y is unable to meet our demands.	Securing an additional vendor would assure our supply.

Of course, it's quite possible the boss already is painfully aware of the need, so the dissonance already exists. In this case, it is simply a matter of stating the need, and analyzing and reinforcing it if necessary. The persuasion results if you can sell your proposal as the best means of remedying the need (thus reducing the dissonance). If the person you are trying to persuade is not aware of the need, so feels no dissonance over it, then of course you must convince him or her of both the need (in order to create dissonance) and your plan (in order to reduce dissonance).

4. Concentrate on key features. A particularly effective technique for using the consistency principle is to concentrate on two or three *key* features of your proposal—a technique long utilized by successful salespeople. If one is "sold" on these key features, one will tend to sell oneself on other features as well, as one seeks to bring all one's perceptions concerning the idea into one consistent whole.

Thus, in attempting to sell your boss, Mr. Danville, on hiring Ms. Evans, you could concentrate on her efficiency, or dependability, or experience, or whatever key selling points Danville would be most impressed by. As he becomes sold on these key features, other positive features will tend to appear more positive, and any negative features less negative. An everyday illustration of this principle is found in the saying, "Love is blind." To the young man in love, his girl friend's virtues seem heightened and her deficiencies unimportant as he creates an idealized image, unmarred by disturbing inconsistencies. (And presumably she responds in kind—at least until they're married and the honeymoon ends!)

5. Involve the other person in actively advocating what he or she has been neutral on or even opposed to. This advice is based on a principle (known as "counter-attitudinal advocacy"—advocating something counter, or contrary, to what one believes) that says, in effect, that what one advocates one begins to believe in—even if previously one was opposed to it. Numerous examples illustrate this concept. High school debaters have been found to end up believing more strongly whichever side they have been debating on. A person asked to lead a fund-raising campaign becomes increasingly persuaded of the merits of the drive. When put in a position in which one must support some point of view or course of action, one begins to be persuaded by the reasons for supporting it. Not to be persuaded would mean that one's actions and beliefs were not consistent with each other. The need for consistency results in self-persuasion.[5]

A Few Words in Summary on the Consistency Principle In its various forms, the Consistency Principle is a potent factor in human behavior, deriving its effect from its linkage to such needs as those in the Maslow Hierarchy.

The relevance of the principle to persuading others is twofold: (a) it can act as a major barrier to successful persuasion; (b) it can also, used effectively, provide leverage in successful persuasion. Its importance to persuasion should not be underrated.

The Common Denominator: A "Good Decision"

Regardless of your persuadee's particular needs, one common denominator applies in all cases: the need to make a "good decision." Making a good decision is dissonance-reducing; making a bad one, dissonance-arousing.

What is a good decision? A "good decision" can be defined both objectively and subjectively. Objectively, a good decision is one that will benefit the organization, while a bad decision is one that will harm it. Therefore, in making a proposal, you must show how the company will benefit (e.g., by increased production, greater profits, lower costs, ability to compete more effectively, increased efficiency, increased worker satisfaction, improved company image, and so forth). If it is a request from which you, rather than the company primarily will benefit, at least you must avoid any impression that the company may be harmed.

Subjectively, from the point of view of the decision-maker, a good decision is one that seems sound in terms of his or her own need pattern—achievement, security, or whatever. Not only that, if the decision is one he or she must justify to others, such as a supervisor or associates, it must appear logically sound—or one must be able to make it appear sound—to them as well. "Good" decisions help satisfy psychological needs; "bad" decisions tend to threaten them.

Let us illustrate. Suppose you have an idea for a new computer application. To put this idea into effect you will need to sell your supervisor on the idea. If much money is involved, or other departments affected, he or she will need to sell others as well, for the more money required or the wider the area affected, the farther up the organization the idea must go for ultimate approval.

If the approvers (whoever in the organization must be persuaded) are primarily achievement-oriented, they must be convinced of the need for this computer application, must understand specifically what computer you are proposing and what it will do, and must see what the payoff will be in terms of their goals for the organization—increased production, improved ability to compete on the market, or whatever.

On the other hand, let us suppose that the approvers are more security minded. They, too, will be interested in these questions, but probably will be more hesitant, more cautious in being convinced of the need and benefits. If not familiar with computer jargon, they probably will be more reticent in raising questions to clarify what they are not sure of. They may need extra reassurance that the benefits will indeed exceed the cost; likewise, that adopting the system will not bring more problems than it solves. It will probably be helpful to cite other organizations or people they have confidence in who have already adopted the system and been happy with it.

If status is their primary concern, they may buy the idea simply because it is "the thing to be doing." I know of one instance in which an executive, some time ago, approved purchase of a computer, which then gathered dust for two years before finally someone ordered an investigation on what use to make of the equipment!

Whatever the case, all the approvers will view the proposal through the filter of their dominant needs. But in each case also, both esteem and affiliation (belongingness) needs will lie latent just under the surface. No administrator wants to earn a reputation for making bad decisions that may damage his or her esteem, in the eyes either of others or him- or herself. Nor will one be anxious to make decisions that might strain one's working relationships with the associates one values.

Finally, your supervisor's security needs could conceivably be threatened. Enough bad decisions—or even one bad enough—could end chances for promotion; or lead to demotion; or in extreme cases, even to dismissal.

To sum up, in satisfying the objective needs of the company, the manager seeks to serve his or her own needs as well. Therefore, a crucial ingredient in successful persuasion is to give a person every legitimate reason to feel that if he or she approves, his or her own needs as well as those of the organization, will be met.

PERSUADING THROUGH CREDIBILITY

At the outset of this chapter we specified three factors embracing the whole of persuasion: the receiver's needs, the persuader's credibility, and the logic of the message. We specified also that of these three factors, the first must always be present, along with at least one of the others, and that usually all three will be present. It is time to elaborate more fully on this.

Interrelationship of the Three Persuasive Factors

To help explain interrelationship of the three factors, it will be convenient to classify persuasive situations in a table such as Figure 9.2.

From Figure 9.2 a number of observations may be made:

1. Even in persuading oneself on a course of action, at least some degree of need must be felt, and if the situation is critical, a high degree may be present. For example, to turn on the air conditioner, one must feel some need to be more comfortable. To quit one's job and return to college for advanced study, one must feel a high degree of need.

2. The more far-reaching and costly the object of persuasion, the higher degree of need is required. A proposed new office layout costing thousands of dollars would require substantial proof of need.

3. In situations of medium scope, if the persuader's credibility is high enough, he or she may succeed without having to present a logical case. An example would be a highly regarded engineer recommending a design change in a product component, but without going into detail as to why. However, the recommendation must not seem *il*logical, and he or she should have reasons on hand if they are called for.

4. In situations of medium scope, even though the persuader's credibility may be low (initially), if the logic is sufficiently compelling, the persuasion may be successful. An example might be a young graduate, just new in the department, who offers a well-reasoned case for a change in product design.

5. The wider the scope and the higher the cost, the greater the necessity for a high degree of both credibility and logic, in addition to strong need. An example might be a multimillion-dollar proposal from a vice president that a new product line be developed and a new plant erected for producing it.

To sum up: Keep in mind the approver's need for reassurance (to reduce any anxiety) that a decision he or she makes will be a good

FIGURE 9.2
Relationship between Level of Approval Required and Persuasive Factors Required

Level of Approval Required	Scope of Effect	Typical Examples	Persuasive Factors Required
Personal	One's own operations	Whether to write Mr. A today or tomorrow Whether to quit the job or seek a transfer	Low degree of need and logic (though a high degree may be present)
Supervisor: tacit (supervisor informed; may object if he or she wishes)	Within the department	Deferring an assignment until next week Responding to a customer in a certain way	Medium degree of need, credibility, and/or logic
Supervisor: routine	Within the department	Request for supplies Request for time off	Medium degree of need, credibility, and/or logic
Supervisor: special	Within the department	Proposal for a new procedure Proposal for a revised layout	Medium degree of need, credibility, and logic
Higher management: special	More than one department	Proposal for reorganization of departments Proposal for a new warranty procedure	High degree of need, credibility, and logic

decision. The greater the scope of operations the decision affects or the greater the risk involved, the greater his or her need for reassurance becomes. It is the role of credibility and logic to provide this assurance.

What We Mean By Credibility

Earlier we defined credibility as "the confidence placed in the persuader by the reader or listener as a result of what is perceived to be the persuader's trustworthiness and competence." From this definition we shall see that credibility is by no means a fixed, unchanging quality, but one which varies from one situation to the next.

Variables of Credibility

Since credibility is not a fixed, unchanging quality, it will be useful to identify the principal factors which influence it.

The Receiver One variable derives from the fact that credibility does not consist of any objective set of traits the persuader possesses, but rather of the traits he or she is seen by the reader or listener as possessing. Just as "beauty is in the eye of the beholder," so credibility is in the mind of the receiver. Obviously, then, one's credibility varies from one receiver to another. As a persuader, for instance, you may impress some people favorably (as a close companion or boy friend), others neutrally (as a professor or casual acquaintance), and still others unfavorably. As expressed by Joseph Thompson, "source credibility ["source" referring here to the persuader] is the result of an interaction between two or more individuals."[6]

Subject Matter One's credibility varies also in terms of subject matter. This is because a vital component of credibility is the persuader's competence, and few people are experts or specialists in more than a few areas. Thus, your history professor may possess high credibility in history, but not in chemistry. A doctor's credibility is usually limited to medicine; often, in fact, to only a single branch of medicine.

Time Finally, one's credibility varies from one time to the next. In broad terms, we could represent one's credibility over a lifetime as in Figure 9.3.

This graph suggests, of course, an average to which naturally there are many exceptions.

In narrow terms, one's credibility may vary even from moment to moment. For example, during an oral presentation, your credibility may be mildly positive in terms of your personal appearance before you start speaking, drop a bit after some hesitant opening remarks, rise sharply with a perceptive analysis of a problem, then fall very low as you offer some questionable evidence in support of a far-out claim. In the question period you may succeed in improving it somewhat.

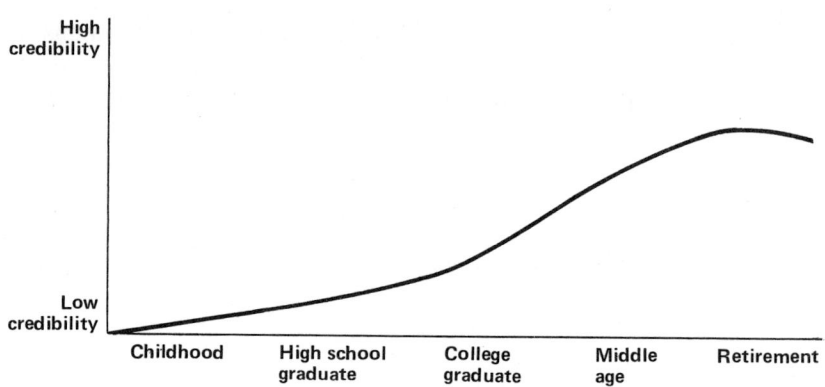

FIGURE 9.3 Typical Relationship between Credibility and Age

The Components of Credibility

We have identified the two main components of credibility already: trustworthiness and competence. It is time now to become more specific.

Trustworthiness Trustworthiness includes such qualities (again as perceived by others) as fair-mindedness, honesty, sincerity, warmth, dependability, integrity, openness, and cheerfulness.

Competence Competence includes such attributes as intelligence, education, training, experience, and expertness.

To illustrate these two components, if we are inclined to take people's advice or point of view seriously because we feel that (a) "they really know what they're talking about, and (b) *believe* in it," then the competence and trustworthiness aspects of their credibility are effectively at work.

Dynamism This is a third component we have not mentioned yet. Dynamism connotes such qualities as being aggressive vs. being meek, being emphatic vs. being hesitant, being frank vs. being reserved, being forceful vs. not being forceful, being bold vs. being timid, being active vs. being passive, and being energetic vs. being listless. Dynamism is generally regarded not so much as an independent component by itself as an "intensifier" of the other two.[7] This point is consistent with findings by James McCroskey from studies he conducted in which he found that the dynamism of a communicator affected the receiver's perceptions of the other two credibility components as well. "A dynamic source was observed consistently to be more competent, and usually more trustworthy, than a passive source."[8]

To test this notion, think of two professors who could be described as follows:

Professor A: meek, hesitant, reserved, forceless, timid, passive, listless, honest, sincere, well educated, intelligent

Professor B: aggressive, emphatic, frank, forceful, bold, active, energetic, honest, sincere, well educated, intelligent

Now ask yourself: Which of these two likely would have the greater persuasive impact on his or her students? Note that each, as described, is equally trustworthy (honest and sincere) and equally competent (well educated and intelligent). Yet the chances are that because of his or her dynamism, Professor B would *appear* more trustworthy and competent, eliciting from others greater feelings of confidence.

Political parties are well aware of the critical role played by dynamism. Between two aspiring candidates equally trustworthy and competent, the party will more likely place on the ticket the more dynamic of the two, because they know he or she will more likely bring in the votes.

Quite by chance, since writing the above, I overheard a conversation between two men. Said one man: "How was the meeting last night?" "Great," was the reply. "The speaker's a great guy; really dynamic. What he says is only about half as important as how he says it." This brief exchange is related here not to suggest that *what* one says is unimportant, for it is not unimportant. But the man's reply does indicate the kind of effect created by dynamism on the *impact* of what one says.

The Components in Combination So which component of credibility is most important? The best answer is: all three. Thompson advises a "*balance* between the various factors that determine trustworthiness, competence, and dynamism."[9] A person perceived as high on competence but low on trustworthiness will tend to be *less* persuasive, rather than more, for such a person will appear dangerous. In fact, if one appears ruthless and unscrupulous, the more competent one seems, the less trust others will want to place in one. Likewise, a person seen as high in trustworthiness but low in competence will also be less persuasive, for he or she will appear as a well-meaning bungler in whom we would not be inclined to place much confidence. And a person high in dynamism but low in both competence and trustworthiness will be seen as a blustering scoundrel or scatterbrain. Finally, as we have already observed, trustworthiness and competence alone, lacking the dynamism, are relatively ineffectual. Thus, strong credibility requires a blend of all three.

Factors Contributing to Credibility

What factors contribute to one's being perceived as possessing high credibility? In answering this question, it will be convenient to discuss credibility in two categories: *initial* and *derived*. *Initial credibility* refers to the persuader's image in the mind of the receiver *before* the receiver is exposed to the message. *Derived credibility* refers to the receiver's image of the persuader as the receiver reads or listens to the message.[10]

Initial Credibility Factors contributing to initial credibility include the following:

1. Being already known personally in a favorable light. Example: a salesperson on good personal terms with his or her client as opposed to a new salesperson who has never met the client.

2. Being regarded as an expert on the subject at hand. Example: a cost analyst about to offer advice on the financial feasibility of a project as opposed to a design engineer on the same subject.

3. Having a reputation for honesty and fair dealing. Example: an employee of unquestioned integrity as opposed to another employee commonly thought to be a slick operator.

4. Possessing status or rank in the organization. Example: a department head as opposed to an assistant professor, or a general superintendent as opposed to a first-line supervisor. (Sometimes, to add credibility, reports written by someone at a lower level are countersigned by the boss, or accompanied by a cover letter written by the boss. Similarly, a "low status" speaker is given higher initial credibility by being introduced by a high credibility person.)

5. Holding values similar to those of the receiver. Example: being identical to (or similar to) the receiver in terms of age, race, religion, education, income, politics, hobbies, and so on; the reason is that we feel more comfortable with those who seem like us than we do with those who seem different.[11]

Naturally, the stronger these factors, or the greater the number the persuader is perceived as possessing, the greater his or her initial credibility. If, for example, you possessed all of them to a high degree, you would virtually have your audience persuaded before you opened your mouth—provided your objective was relevant to their needs.

Derived Credibility Once the audience starts listening (or the reader starts reading), what they hear or read influences their perceptions still further. As stated above, this is where derived credibility takes over. Factors affecting derived credibility include:

1. Showing an understanding of company or customer needs. Example: an advertising agency salesperson showing insight into the needs of a struggling young company as opposed to a competing salesperson who thinks only in terms of large, successful companies; or a complaint manager responding sympathetically to an aggrieved customer as opposed to a complaint manager unable to put him- or herself in the shoes of the customer.

2. Appearing well informed with up-to-date information. Example: a sales engineer familiar with the latest federal safety regulations as opposed to one who has not kept up. (Even when the information does not advance one's argument, appearing well informed still tends to advance one's credibility. The response seems to be, "Even though I don't agree on this point, this guy does seem to know his business." However, if seeming well informed is to enhance one's credibility, the information must be fresh and new. If it appears only as "the same old stuff," it leaves

the receiver unimpressed.[12] Appearing well informed is particularly important in responding to questions following an oral presentation. Too many "I don't knows" can reduce one's credibility in terms of competence, while bluffing can reduce it in terms of trustworthiness as well.

3. Being clearly organized. Example: a proposal clearly organized and easy to follow as opposed to one badly organized and confusing to follow. (As explained above in Chapter 4, "Structure," poor organization has a strong negative effect on credibility; good organization a mild positive effect.)

4. Appearing fair-minded; "seeing both sides." Example: a salesperson who is generous concerning the competitors as opposed to one who runs down the competitors while conceding no disadvantages on his or her own side. (As will be shown below, very seldom is a person persuaded because X has all the advantages while Y has none, for rarely is this the case. Rather, one is persuaded as one sees that X has more advantages, in terms of one's needs, and fewer disadvantages than does Y. The persuader who fails to grasp this principle will seem less competent and honest, thus tending to lose in credibility.)

5. Expressing oneself effectively. Example: a letter from someone who is a competent writer as opposed to a letter from someone who appears illiterate, or a talk by a speaker who is fluent as opposed to a talk by a speaker who is hesitant (providing the fluency is not so smooth that it seems insincere).

6. Not putting the receiver on the defensive. Example: a letter which handles a touchy issue with tact and diplomacy as opposed to one which criticizes the receiver and puts him or her down. (As explained in Chapter 2 in discussing communication falloff, putting the other person on the defensive only stimulates an angry, emotional response—hardly conducive to successful persuasion.)

Again, the stronger these factors, or the more of them appear in the message, the greater the persuader's derived credibility. And as between the two categories of credibility—initial or derived—the derived is the more important, for it confirms or disconfirms the initial reaction. Thus, a strong message tends to enhance low initial credibility, while a weak message tends to erode high initial credibility. This principle offers hope to the newcomer not yet well known, while discouraging the long-termer from resting too complacently on his or her laurels.

The Importance of Credibility in Persuasion

It is doubtful whether people in general appreciate the great importance of strong credibility as a persuasive factor—even though the sad experience of President Nixon and others has demonstrated the devastating effect when credibility is lost. Its importance is better understood if we examine

(a) its practical uses, and (b) the receiver's need to have confidence in the persuader.

Practical Uses The practical usefulness of credibility has been demonstrated repeatedly in experimental studies. In one such experiment, three separate audiences of college students were exposed to a tape-recorded talk favoring leniency toward juvenile delinquents. To each group the source was identified differently: first, as a juvenile court judge, next as an anonymous member of the studio audience, and finally as an ex-delinquent out on bail after arrest on dope-peddling charges. The results were that the talk by the "judge" was received favorably by 73 percent of the listeners, while that by the "ex-delinquent" by only 29 percent.[13]

Specifically, here are some of the practical uses of high credibility:

1. Using high credibility as a "bank account." According to this concept, when a highly credible source comments approvingly on a topic not as highly approved by the receiver, the topic tends to gain in evaluation. Thus, if you are well regarded by your receivers and speak out in favor of an unpopular position, you will tend to influence them in favor of that position. However, just as drawing on a bank account reduces the balance, so drawing on your credibility likewise reduces the "balance." Therefore, you would need a high credibility "account" to draw on. In a persuasive presentation, for example, you could build up your credibility in the first half by a perceptive analysis of the problem at hand, thus establishing "credit." You would then be in a stronger position to propose a radical solution with its resultant drain on credibility.

This drain, incidentally, is explained by a variation of the Consistency Principle. In attempting to reconcile the inconsistency posed by high credibility coupled with an unpopular attitude, the receiver tends to bring the two more in line with each other by rating the attitude somewhat more favorably and the source somewhat less favorably.[14] This phenomenon is frequently seen in public affairs when a popular governor or senator risks some of his or her credibility "capital" to promote a view unpopular with some of the voters.

2. Using high credibility in supporting an extreme position. The more extreme a position a persuader takes, the more in need he or she is of high credibility. The reason is that the more extreme the position, the more resistant the persuadee is to accepting it, and he or she will find it easier to reject it if it can be rationalized that "Jones doesn't know what he's talking about anyway." But if Jones is a respected authority on the subject, rejecting Jones's views becomes much more difficult. Nevertheless, the more extreme the position, the more essential becomes not only high credibility *but also* a strong logical case. (However, even these will not avail if the persuader cannot show how the "extreme" proposal would meet the persuadee's needs better than would any other.)

3. Using high credibility in making threats or creating fear. Sometimes it is necessary for the boss to "crack down." ("You do it this way, or else!"), or get tough with his or her supervisor ("Either I get another employee, or else!"). Threats or scares are variant forms of "extreme positions," which naturally the receiver will resist or reject if possible. And the persuadee can do so more easily if the persuader (or would-be persuader) has low credibility; in other words, is someone the receiver feels need not be taken seriously. Anyone who decides to take a hard line had better have high credibility to go along with it—or be able to stick with it and thereby improve credibility.

4. Using credibility in place of logic. As stated above, if the persuadee's decision is of any consequence, normally he or she wants—in addition to having confidence in the persuader—to "see for him- or herself" (that is, look at the logic of the case). But sometimes the logic is too sophisticated for the persuadee, so he or she is virtually forced to rely on credibility alone.

This need to rely so heavily on credibility should not be surprising when we recall from Chapter 3 that the higher managers rise, the more areas there are in their span of control that are outside the particular technical area in which they began their career. Thus, often they will be compelled to rely on subordinates or staff assistants more expert on the subject at hand than they are. If a manager's background is in finance, for instance, he or she must probably rely on the expertise of the electronics engineer concerning the merits of a given item of electronic equipment. True, he or she will want to understand essentially the reasons for or against, but basically, this manager must depend on the expertise and integrity of the electronics specialist in arriving at a judgment. Credibility thus plays the critical role.

The Receiver's Need to Have Confidence in the Persuader We have already referred to the persuadee's need for assurance that if he or she says "yes," the decision will actually be sound. And we pointed out that the role of credibility (along with logic) is to provide that assurance.

Deeper insight in this role is provided by a study conducted for *Steel* magazine some years ago by Dr. F. Robert Shoaf, an industrial psychologist. Shoaf's study, involving depth interviews with 137 high-level executives and purchasing directors in the metal-working industry representing 70 plants in 18 cities, was concerned with learning about the "emotional factors underlying industrial purchases."

A key finding of this study was that the supplier's credibility was far and away the most important consideration in deciding to whom to award contracts:

> At the very top of the list . . . mentioned two and a half times more often than . . . price, stands "Personal Relations"; a good working relationship with suppliers as people. A very

close second is dependability, which to these metal-working buyers, seems to mean honesty, integrity, sincerity. This, too, is more than twice as important as price. . . . [Above] all, they want to feel that they are dealing with . . . ethical and honest houses, whose product quality they can take for granted, and whose personal service, personal attitude, and personal integrity give guarantee of value and of buyer satisfaction.[15]

Thus, both because of its practical effectiveness and the receiver's deep need to feel trust in the persuader, credibility is an invaluable asset in persuasion. Without it, not even one's logic may avail, for if the persuadee has no confidence in the persuader as a person, he or she may have no confidence in the persuader's facts either.

PERSUADING THROUGH LOGIC

As defined at the beginning of this chapter, logic refers to the use of sound data to support, through sound reasoning, one's inferences or conclusions. Its role in persuasion is to enable receivers to see for themselves—thus feel more assured—that agreeing with the persuader would make good sense.

The Importance of Logic in Business Persuasion

The importance of logic in business persuasion is pointed up by John Fielden, writing as Dean of the College of Business Administration, Boston University:

> There are limits to persuasion as reading audiences become better educated and more sophisticated; this is especially true in the case of the well-educated business executive. As the years go by, it will be ever more true that the successful business communications will be those which show the greatest respect for factual evidence marshaled to support points, and avoid distortion or a resort to persuasive gimmicks. . . . The kind of decision today's executive is being forced to make must be based as much as possible on sound, objective information.[16]

The importance of logic is further underscored when we recall that the greater the scope and cost of the persuasive objective, the more imperative the role of strong credibility and sound logic. If the credibility of the persuader is not initially strong, then the need for sound logic becomes all the greater. The persuadee will indeed want to make certain for him- or herself that the case is sound.

Factors in Strengthening the Logic of the Message

Suggestions for strengthening the logic of the message include the following:

Use the Need-Plan Pattern In Chapter 4, "Structure," we described the need-plan (or problem-solution) pattern (which you should review at this point before reading further, pp. 78–79) as the basic pattern in persuasion when approval is sought for a proposed course of action. This is because any proposal consists essentially of a proposed solution to some problem (or, expressed differently, of a proposed plan to remedy some need). If management is not convinced that the need exists, or that the proposed plan would satisfy the need advantageously, they are unlikely to approve.

In addition to the logic of using the need-plan pattern, there is also the psychological gain (discussed earlier in this chapter) from confronting the persuadee with a problem that is dissonance-arousing, then offering a solution that is dissonance-reducing. This means that the persuadee must be brought to realize that a real problem actually does exist, so he or she will become concerned that appropriate action be taken. For example, suppose your department is housed in cramped quarters. If you first can persuade your boss that this situation is no longer tolerable (reduced efficiency, morale, and so on), you will increase the likelihood that he or she will *want* to do something about it. Your supervisor will then be more "ready" to hear your solution.

Considering how simple the concept of the need-plan pattern is, it is amazing how often it is badly used. Following is a list of the common deficiencies in its use:

1. Explanation of a proposal (for example, to purchase a new gadget on the market), but no proof of need and no proof of benefits.

2. Satisfactory explanation of need (say for improved employee motivation), but little explanation of proposal or proof of benefits.

3. Satisfactory explanation of need and proposal, but no proof of benefits (for example, no proof that the new layout would be any improvement over what we have now, or over any other layout).

4. Satisfactory explanation of need, proposal, and benefits, but no matching of proposal against need to show that this proposal would remedy this need (no analysis to show that a proposed plan of employee motivation would have any effect in reducing the number of customer complaints).

5. Failure to include any criteria as a basis for evaluating the proposal (no mention of cost restrictions, feasibility, or any other criteria the proposal must meet, for example).

6. Satisfactory choice and explanation of criteria, but no evaluation of proposal on the basis of the criteria (for example, no evaluation of the proposal against cost, feasibility, and so on).

To the extent that any of these deficiencies are present, the persuader's probability of success is reduced.

Offer Sufficient Proof to Support Your Claims In Chapter 4, "Structure," we showed that messages consist of two elements: general and specific, each needed to complement the other. In a persuasive message, the structure consists of claims or assertions ("The space is too crowded"; "The employees are unhappy"; "Output is down," and so on). But unless these claims are clearly self-evident, they need explanation and supporting data so the receivers can see clearly for themselves and agree on the validity of the claims. The explanation and data may consist of verbal description; graphic aids such as diagrams or statistical graphs; responses from questionnaires; illustrative examples; reference to research (in this case, on the optimum amount of work space per person for maximum output), and so on.

As indicated above, if one's claims or conclusions are likely to sound farfetched or improbable (in other words, "extreme"), adequate support becomes especially important. Even a single claim that remains unconvincing to a skeptical reader may damage the credibility of the entire message.

Use a Two-Sided Rather than a One-Sided Approach Where Appropriate In plain language, this advice means to tell your persuadee, along with the advantages, what the limitations, costs, or disadvantages are.

On the face of it, this might appear like a foolhardy approach to take. But we need to remember, as already stated, that seldom is a person persuaded because X has all the advantages while Y has none. One is persuaded rather because the advantages of X outweigh the advantages of Y (provided, of course, that the advantages are relevant to one's needs).

In fact, research has shown that, in general, the two-sided approach is more effective than the one-sided approach for (a) increasing the amount of persuasion initially (when the message is first received), and (b) *keeping* the receiver persuaded over a period of time. This is true even when the "arguments against" are only included with the "arguments for" without being refuted. It is even more true, of course, when the "arguments against" are also refuted, either partially or completely.

Some interesting research on this concept was reported in *Psychology Today,* October 1974, based on an article in the *Journal of Marketing Research* in May 1974:

> . . . Settle and Golden [the researchers] developed a series of experimental ads and then asked a group of 120 business students to evaluate them. Half of the ads for each product (a pen, a watch, a blender, a camera and a clock radio) claimed the product was superior to the leading brand on five main

features. The others claimed superiority on the three features that Settle and Golden felt a potential consumer would be most interested in, but admitted that the best seller was better on two less important features. While the students' expectations of how well the products would perform dropped a bit when the two features were disclaimed, their increased confidence in the advertiser's claims made up for it.

"At the least," the researchers conclude, "it would be better for the advertiser to disclaim at least one feature of minor importance than to exclude it . . . entirely." So long as the advertiser knows which features his customers regard as important, he should be less reluctant to include varied claims.[17]

Why does the two-sided message prove generally more persuasive? At least four reasons may be offered.

1. Receivers, while reading or listening to the message, are less likely to be preoccupied with devising their *own* "arguments against," (thus diverting their attention from the message). As a result, they pay more undivided attention to the *persuader's* line of reasoning.

2. As indicated earlier in this chapter, persuadees tend to perceive the persuader as more knowledgeable and fair-minded, therefore more credible.

3. Receivers are better prepared ("inoculated" is the term often used) to withstand "arguments against" that others may suggest later or they may think of themselves.

4. Receivers have fewer false expectations which otherwise could leave them disillusioned if later they find them to be unfulfilled.

However, the two-sided approach is not automatically to be preferred. There are variables affecting its applicability.

One variable is the importance of the issue at hand: the less important the issue, the less useful a two-sided approach; the more important the issue, the more useful it is to show both sides. Example: your boss is not likely to be much concerned with hearing both sides if you propose including an additional person on a committee you are head of. But if your committee proposes establishing a series of training sessions involving 40 hours off the job for each employee, the supervisor is quite likely to want to look at the proposal critically from all sides.

A second variable is the credibility of the persuader: the lower the credibility, the more important the two-sided approach; the higher the credibility, the less important. Keep in mind that the function of both credibility and logic is to increase the persuadee's confidence in being persuaded. Consequently, the less confidence one has in the persuader, the more concerned one will be for understanding thoroughly all the costs as well as the gains of whatever is being proposed.

Still a third variable is the persuadee's attitude toward the proposal: the more skeptical he or she is, the more concerned he or she will be to hear both sides. The persuadee will want to be *sure* before committing him- or herself. On the other hand, the less skeptical one is, the less important it is for one to hear both sides. In fact, one probably has already thought of both sides, to a degree at least, and concluded for oneself that the pros appear to outweigh the cons.

Finally, if the persuadee has less than a high school education, or—probably more to the point—is less mentally alert or capable, he or she will be less interested in hearing both sides. Apparently, hearing the cons along with the pros is simply an added mental burden he or she would rather not be bothered with.

In short, the two-sided approach has generally more to recommend it than not. Only if there are specific reasons against it, should you use the one-sided approach instead.[18]

Use Sound Reasoning As in the case of unsupported claims, even one or two instances in which the reasoning appears fallacious may weaken the credibility of the whole message. Among the more important rules in using sound reasoning are the following:

1. Avoid basing arguments on questionable assumptions. "Questionable" here means questionable in the mind of the receiver. Such statements as "No one in management really understands the worker's feelings," or "The successful supervisor is one who closely supervises the workers" are examples of broad assumptions which many readers or listeners would reject. No matter how logical one's arguments based on these assumptions, if the receiver does not accept the basic assumption, he or she will not accept the conclusions either. The persuader would first have to win acceptance of the assumption before basing any argument on it.

2. Avoid unsound or hasty generalizations. Generalizations should be based on a sufficient number of *representative* examples. Statements such as "We tried that once and it didn't work" or "Everybody I've talked to favors a four-day week, so I think it's safe to assume that most people throughout the plant favor it" are not logically convincing. Such conclusions would need to be based on polls or surveys conducted scientifically to be sure that the evidence from the limited sample could be safely generalized to the whole group or situation.

3. Avoid unsound analogies (comparisons). The logic of an analogy is that if two situations are similar in enough significant respects, what is true of one situation will be true of the other. "The success of X policy in the watch industry is proof enough that it would be successful if adopted in our plant" is poor reasoning if the differences between the two situations are so great that what applies in one would not necessarily apply in the other.

4. Avoid unsound causal reasoning. One common fallacy in causal reasoning is the fallacy of single causation—blaming or crediting a single factor as the cause of a complex effect. The argument, "If only the workers would cooperate, we'd have no more trouble" probably overlooks other causes that may be present.

Another common fallacy in causal reasoning is the *"post hoc, ergo propter hoc"* fallacy—"After this, therefore because of this." Example: "Since we started hiring women, production has gone down." (The presence of women on the work force may be purely coincidental with the declining production.)

Use Logic-Oriented Language Research has shown that receivers are more likely to be aware of the logic when "logic-oriented language" is used.[19] Particularly effective are words that show cause-effect relationships, such as "thus," "therefore," and "consequently," or phrases such as "as a result," "so it is possible to conclude," and others. Note: such terminology is not to be used as a substitute for logic; only to point up the logic already there.

Make Your Conclusions and Recommendations Explicit Research has also shown that being explicit in stating conclusions and recommendations is over twice as effective in persuading others as when they are not made explicit.[20] Using the format suggested in Chapter 11 will assure that one's conclusions and recommendations *are* made explicit.

A Closing Word on Logic

Before allowing themselves to be persuaded, people want to be sure their decisions are sound. This is true in general, and especially so in an organization, where the need for a "good decision" is intensified. As we have seen, the credibility of the persuader is one important factor in providing assurance; the logic of the message is another. Thus, a message whose reasoning is comprehensible and sound tends to play a significant role in securing approval from the person one is hoping to persuade.

SUMMARY

1. To be persuaded, people must feel that one or more of their needs would best be met if they accept the persuasion. For reassurance that this would indeed be the case, they then look to the credibility of the persuader, the logic of the message, or both. The greater the risk involved, the more reassurance they require.

2. One's behavior is constantly influenced by one's desire to believe or act in ways consistent with one's needs. This desire for consistency may result in one either (a) resisting persuasion or (b) yielding to persuasion, according to which response one feels will best serve one's needs.

3. Regardless of which personal needs are most dominant, the common denominator in being persuaded is the persuadee's desire to make a "good decision"—good both for him- or herself and the organization.

4. The persuader's credibility consists of the image in the mind of his or her receivers of his or her competence and trustworthiness. How these two qualities are perceived is influenced by the strength of a third quality: dynamism. Credibility may be usefully classified as *initial* (the persuader's reputation before the message is received) and *derived* (the persuader's image as affected by the message). Credibility is especially critical in persuasion when the persuader takes an unpopular or extreme position, or the logic is too complex for the receiver to comprehend readily.

5. Logic is the process of arriving at sound conclusions based on sound evidence through the use of sound reasoning. To be persuasive, it must be understandable to the receiver. Ways of strengthening the logic of the message include (a) using the Need-Plan pattern, (b) offering sufficient proof to support one's claims, (c) using, where appropriate, a two-sided rather than one-sided approach, (d) using sound reasoning, (e) using logic-oriented language, and (f) making one's conclusions and recommendations explicit.

SUGGESTED APPLICATIONS

1. You have just been notified that, for budgetary reasons, the administration at your school has decided to discontinue the program you are majoring in, effective at the end of the current academic year. Since this could have serious consequences for your own future, you are greatly disturbed. Write a letter of 400–500 words to the dean or president, trying to persuade him or her to reconsider the decision. Use as many of the principles of this chapter as you feel would apply in being as persuasive as possible. In a separate memo to your teacher, explain in approximately 200–250 words what persuasive strategies you used and why.

2. Think of the most persuasive person you know and write a description of about 500 words of this person, analyzing the characteristics that account for his or her persuasiveness. Make use of principles discussed in this chapter. If you feel there are other characteristics not mentioned in the chapter, include these also. In writing your paper, use appropriate methods of development of ideas discussed in Chapter 5, "Effective Paragraphing" (pp. 98–111), to support your points.

3. Using the Criteria-Application Pattern explained in Chapter 4 (p. 79), evaluate the following "open letter" in terms of whether you feel it is highly persuasive, mildly persuasive, or not persuasive at all. Base your criteria on the principles from this chapter, and show specifically how

well the editorial satisfies each criterion. In your concluding paragraph, sum up your general evaluation. Your paper should run 400-500 words.

AN OPEN LETTER TO CONSUMERS ABOUT AEROSOLS[21]

From Samuel C. Johnson,
Chairman, Johnson Wax, Racine, Wis.

Dear Customer:

For 89 years my family and our company have endeavored to develop new, modern, efficient quality products.

Our company still is a family venture; I am the fourth-generation member to head it. We have four children who, I hope, will want to carry on the tradition.

Aerosols Today

About 25 years ago, modern technology brought to the American homemaker a familiar symbol of the age of ease and convenience. This was the aerosol can.

As you are no doubt aware, a lot of confusion, misunderstanding and anxiety has developed over the last few months about aerosols. Since we have been closely involved in their development over the past couple of decades and because we know a great deal about aerosols, I want to try to clear up some of the misapprehensions you may have about them.

Fluorocarbons and Ozone

The most important problem right now is that some aerosol cans release a certain kind of propellant gas that some scientists feel may be damaging the upper atmosphere ozone layer around the earth.

Although this was a totally unforeseen concern, scientific investigation is constantly providing a vital public service by calling to our attention things about our environment that may present serious problems.

The particular aerosol propellant under question is a fluorocarbon. It has several trade names, (e.g., Freon, Genetron, Ucon, Isotron). Some scientists feel that the possible impairment of the ozone layer in the upper atmosphere would permit greater penetration of the sun's ultra-violet rays with unforeseen effects on our health. Obviously this is a very serious concern; our own company scientists confirm that as a scientific hypothesis it may be possible, but conclusive evidence is not available one way or another, at this time.

We concur that the pressing need is for reliable scientific investigation; this is being carried on by the Inter-Agency

Task Force on the Inadvertent Modification of the Stratosphere which has concluded that there may be a legitimate cause for concern. In addition, the National Academy of Sciences has stratospheric investigations underway which are expected to be completed early next year. Additional investigations are being sponsored by aerosol manufacturers and suppliers.

Not All Aerosols Contain Fluorocarbons

In the meantime, it is important to note that not all aerosol products sold in this country contain fluorocarbon propellants. As a matter of fact, approximately half of all aerosols use other kinds of propellants, including hydrocarbons and carbon dioxide.

About 15 years ago, Johnson Wax invented what is known as the "water-base" aerosol system that permitted the use of propellants other than fluorocarbons in many household products.

As a result, we have been reducing our use of fluorocarbon propellants over a long period for a variety of different reasons, including the fact that our unique water-base formulations using other propellants are less expensive.

During the past three years, fluorocarbons have made up less than five per cent of the total propellants we use. And because we share the concern of our customers and others and since we are technically equipped to do so in our products, we have made a policy decision.

What Johnson Wax Is Doing

Effective today, our company has removed all fluorocarbon propellants from our production lines in the U.S., and we are aggressively reformulating our product ingredients worldwide to achieve the same goal.

We at Johnson Wax are taking this action in the interest of our customers and the public in general during a period of uncertainty and scientific inquiry. We are taking this newspaper advertisement and other available means to tell our customers so that they may use our aerosol products with greater confidence.

In addition, we plan to inform the consumer by having information available within the next 30 days in stores where our products are sold and by changing as soon as possible the labels of our containers to carry the following statement:

Use With Confidence

Contains no Freon® or other
Fluorocarbons claimed to harm the
ozone layer

Millions of Americans have learned that in order to have the advantages of aerosol cans, they have to exercise common sense, because the aerosol—like the automobile, or even a simple stepladder—can be dangerous if improperly used.

For example, the aerosol can does contain propellant gases under pressure. It could explode if carelessly placed down on a hot kitchen stove. Fortunately, these dangers are so well known that it almost never happens.

What We Believe

We believe that aerosols are good and useful, or we wouldn't manufacture them. As a result, we will manufacture only those aerosols in the U.S. that *do not* contain fluorocarbons. They include:

Pledge furniture polishes
Raid insecticides
J/Wax automotive products
Jubilee kitchen wax
Favor furniture polish
Glade air fresheners
Edge protective shave
Crew bathroom cleaner
OFF! insect repellents
Big Wally foam cleaner
Klean 'n Shine
   multi-surface cleaner
Glory rug cleaner
Shout pre-spotter

Our customers who have welcomed the utility of these products in the convenient aerosol form will continue to be able to depend upon them.

In closing, I want to assure you that we at Johnson Wax will do our best in the tradition of our family to ensure the effectiveness and safety of our products with the best materials available to us.

Sincerely,

SAMUEL C. JOHNSON

4. Select a persuasive message of your choice and follow the directions for item 3 above. Examples could include another editorial from a magazine or newspaper, a letter to the editor of your daily newspaper, or an advertisement.

NOTES

[1] For a brief, pertinent discussion of the fallacy of the Rational Man Concept, see Erwin P. Bettinghaus, *Persuasive Communication* (New York: Holt, Rinehart, and Winston, 1968), pp. 26-27.

[2] Two books offering excellent discussions of consistency theory are Roger Brown, *Social Psychology* (New York: The Free Press, 1965), Ch. 11, "The Principle of Consistency in Attitude Change," and Arthur R. Cohen, *Attitude Change and Social Influence* (New York: Basic Books, Inc., 1964), Ch. 5, "Cognitive Models of Attitude Changes."

[3] Jesse S. Nirenberg, *Getting Through to People* (Englewood Cliffs, N.J.: Prentice-Hall, Inc., 1963), p. 114.

[4] Solomon Asch, "Effects of Group Pressure Upon the Modification and Distortion of Judgment," in Harold Guetzkow (ed.), *Groups, Leadership, and Men* (Pittsburgh, Pa.: Carnegie Press, 1951).

[5] For a much more complete discussion of counter-attitudinal advocacy, see Gerald R. Miller and Michael Burgoon, *New Techniques of Persuasion* (New York: Harper & Row Publishers, 1973).

[6] Joseph W. Thompson, *Selling: A Behavioral Science Approach* (New York: McGraw-Hill Book Company, 1966), p. 171.

[7] For a prime source on credibility, see David K. Berlo, James B. Lemert, and Robert J. Mertz, "Dimensions for Evaluating the Acceptability of Message Sources," *The Public Opinion Quarterly,* Vol. 33 (Winter, 1969-70), pp. 563-576.

[8] James C. McCroskey, *An Introduction to Rhetorical Communication* (Englewood Cliffs, N.J.: Prentice-Hall, Inc., 1968), pp. 60-61.

[9] Thompson, p. 173.

[10] For a more extensive discussion of initial and derived credibility, see McCroskey, Ch. 4, "Ethos: A Dominant Factor in Persuasive Communication," pp. 58-74. (McCroskey uses the Greek term, *"ethos,"* in place of the more current term, "credibility.")

[11] For a more complete development of this point, see F. G. Evans, "Selling as a Dyadic Relationship—A New Approach," *American Behavioral Scientist* (May, 1963), p. 76.

[12] See James C. McCroskey, *Studies of the Effects of Evidence in Persuasive Communication* (East Lansing, Michigan: Michigan State University, 1967), p. 45.

[13] H. C. Kelman and C. I. Hovland, "'Reinstatement' of the Communicator in Delayed Measurement of Opinion Change," *Journal of Abnormal and Social Psychology,* Vol. 48 (1953), pp. 327-335.

[14] A more complete discussion of the "bank account" concept is found in McCroskey, *An Introduction to Rhetorical Communication,* pp. 44-49.

[15] Quoted in Hector Lazo, "Emotional Aspects of Industrial Buying," in *Dynamic Marketing for a Changing World,* Robert S. Hancock (ed.), Proceedings of the 43rd National Conference of the American Marketing Association, American Marketing Association, Chicago, 1960, pp. 258-265.

[16] John Fielden, "For Better Business Writing," *Harvard Business Review,* Vol. 43 (January, 1965), p. 169.

[17] "To Sell Your Product, Admit It's Not Perfect," *Psychology Today,* October, 1974, pp. 35-36.

[18] For a detailed account of the original studies on two-sidedness, see Carl I. Hovland, Arthur A. Lumsdaine, and Fred S. Sheffield, "The Effects of Presenting 'One-Sided' vs. 'Both Sides' in Changing Opinions on a Controversial Subject," in *Experiments in Persuasion,* ed., Ralph L. Rasnow and Edward J. Robinson (New York: Academic Press, 1967), pp. 201-225. For less detailed discussions, see Raymond S. Ross, *Speech Communication,* 2nd ed. (Englewood Cliffs, N.J.: Prentice-Hall, Inc., 1970), pp. 164-167; also McCroskey, *An Introduction to Rhetorical Communication,* pp. 156-197; and Bettinghaus, pp. 154-157.
[19] Bettinghaus, p. 159.
[20] Carl I. Hovland and Wallace Mandell, "An Experimental Comparison of Conclusion Drawing by the Communicator and by the Audience," *The Journal of Abnormal and Social Psychology,* Vol. 47 (July, 1952), pp. 581-588.
[21] Reprinted with permission of Johnson Wax.

FOUR SPECIFIC APPLICATIONS

10 WRITING EFFECTIVE LETTERS AND MEMOS

IMPORTANCE OF BUSINESS LETTER WRITING

CONCEPT VS. APPLICATION

CREATING A POSITIVE IMAGE

Be Prompt in Responding

Give Attention to Appearance

Convey a Positive Tone
    Begin on a Positive Note
    Accentuate the Positive; De-emphasize the Negative
    Use Words with Positive Connotation

Offer Postdecision Reassurance

Use a You-Attitude

Give Attention to Your Reader's Sense of Self-Esteem
    Personalize the Message
    Avoid Putting the Reader on the Defensive
    Sell; Don't Tell   Be Courteous
    De-emphasize What the Reader Already Knows

Write in a Natural, Informal Style

Maintain a High Quality of Writing
    Review of General Principles
    The Opening and Closing Paragraphs

PARTS OF A LETTER

Standard Parts
    Heading   Inside Address   Salutation
    Body   Complimentary Close   Signature

Supplementary Parts
    Attention Line   Subject Line   Initials   Enclosures
    Copy Designation   Postscript   Second-Page Headings

ADDRESSING THE ENVELOPE

FORMATS AND MECHANICS

Semiblock

Modified Semiblock

Full Block

Simplified

Specialized

APPLICATIONS FOR EMPLOYMENT
The Letter of Application
    Opening Paragraph   Middle Paragraph   Closing Paragraph
    Style   Parts of the Letter

The Personal Résumé
    Mailing the Letter of Application and Résumé
    Further Correspondence   A Few Parting Words

MEMOS
Function

Form

Content and Style
    Informality   Relevance   Completeness   Tact

Of all the writing you do from now until retirement, writing memos and letters is almost certain to be the most common.

IMPORTANCE OF BUSINESS LETTER WRITING

Assume that you will retire in 35 years, with an average of 48 work weeks per year, five days a week. That comes to 8400 work days. Now assume further that over the years you will write on the average one letter per day. That means 8400 letters composed, mailed, and typed; 8400 read. The number of hours involved is impossible to tally; dollar costs are impossible to project ($3.79 for an *average* business letter in 1975)—not to mention the successes and failures created by these letters. A good share of your career will literally ride on a postage stamp—and a good share of the nation's business as well.

Why the continued torrent of letters in this age of direct dialing? Despite the advantages of communicating by telephone (immediate response, two-way exchange, vocal cues, and informal atmosphere), communicating in writing offers advantages the telephone cannot match:

1. In letters you can formulate your message with greater care—choose just the right word; avoid the ill-chosen phrase.

2. Letters provide a record that can be referred to later for information that is lengthy or complex. You might call a prospective employer about a possible job, but you would also send a letter of application with a personal résumé.

3. Letters provide documentation for the record. You may agree on the telephone to follow procedures x, y, and z; you would then follow up with a letter confirming the agreement.

4. Letters are a faster way to reach large numbers of people, as in a sales letter to 50,000 prospects.

5. Letters are less expensive for reaching people in distant locations, especially in foreign countries.

Letter writing seems destined to remain with us. With the cost increasing each year (writer's time, typist's time, stationery, postage, and such overhead costs as facilities and space), the value attached to letter-writing ability is bound also to increase.

CONCEPT VS. APPLICATION

An advertisement received recently featured an "executive portfolio" containing models of letters for "every occasion." Just open the portfolio to the right page, and presto!—there's the recipe, just like in a cookbook. By such means, the busy executive should have no trouble writing letters of inquiry, replies to letters of inquiry, letters of complaint, replies to letters of complaint, letters of congratulation, letters of sympathy, announcements, sales letters, collection letters, letters of recommendation—and so on and on. He or she may not know *why* (two tablespoons of seasoning here, one tablespoon there), but at least he or she would know *what*.

In this text, we shall confine ourselves to general guidelines, with two exceptions. One will be the letter of application. The other will be the letter of transmittal for a formal report or proposal (to be covered in Chapter 11). For other special types, the general guidelines presented here provide a foundation.

The general guidelines are discussed under three headings: creating a positive image, the parts of a letter, and standard formats. Following this treatment of letters, the chapter includes a brief section on memos (which may be thought of as letters to others within an organization instead of to people outside).

CREATING A POSITIVE IMAGE

The characteristic that most distinguishes letters from memos, reports, and proposals is *tone*. The reason is that letters generally are addressed to people outside the organization whom we see less regularly. Since there is less opportunity for maintaining a working relationship with these people through face-to-face association on a day-to-day basis, the letters we send must help do the job for us.

However, there is no assurance that letters will indeed promote a favorable relationship. They may or may not. Consider, for example, letters you have received. Ask yourself if you haven't formed (subconsciously, perhaps) impressions such as these:

> This guy sounds like a stuffed shirt.
> I wonder if this character ever got beyond the eighth grade.
> Here's a woman who really sounds human.
> This fellow turns me off fast.
> Whoever wrote this must be a walking dictionary.
> I wish all letters were as well written as this one.

Even if you already know the writer, his or her letter still creates an impression, adding to or detracting from the image you already hold. By the same token, every letter we write conveys an image (not only of us, but of the company we represent). In fact, to anyone receiving a business letter, that letter to a large degree *is* the writer or the company—cold and machinelike, or warm and human. This is why letters are so critically important in affecting the nature of relationships between an organization and the people outside.

Imagine you have purchased a stereo. After 91 days a speaker goes dead. You call the dealer. He says, "Sorry. Ninety-day warranty. Write the manufacturer." So you do; a week later you receive this reply:

> Dear Sir:
>
> In reply to your letter of June 19th concerning your purchase of our Quadriphone Stereo, Model XL911125A in which you claim that one of the speakers "went dead," as you put it, we regret to advise that since this product, as your letter of complaint admitted, is now out of warranty, there is nothing we can do about it.
>
> Certainly, however, you can find a reputable dealer in your own area who can effect the needed repairs at, we're confident, a reasonable cost.
>
> Trusting that you will remain one of our loyal customers, we remain,
>
>   Very truly yours,
>   ANGELMUSIC MFG. CO.
>
> Josiah R. Prudent,
> Manager, Claims

A response such as this would, of course, be extremely unlikely. But it does make a point. If you *were* to receive such a letter, there's no doubt about it: You would form an image—almost certainly negative—of Mr.

Prudent and his whole so-and-so company. The good name that their advertising department spends thousands each year to promote is destroyed as far as you are concerned.

Using the language of persuasion (Chapter 9), you can readily note that *image* relates closely to credibility, since the image conveyed by the letter strongly affects the credibility of the writer. Is he sincere? Fair-minded? Does he show concern for the reader? Does he appear intelligent? Experienced? Does he sound confident and positive? Always bear in mind that the only important image a letter creates is the image in the mind of the reader.

Sometimes credibility is so important that a letter may carry the signature of someone higher up, even though he or she may not personally have written the letter (beyond perhaps editing it a bit). The higher the status, remember, the higher the initial credibility (other things being equal).

The question now becomes, how can *you* write letters that will create in your reader a positive image of you and your organization? Suggestions to be offered include these:

Be prompt in responding
Give attention to appearance
Convey a positive tone
Offer postdecision reassurance
Use a you-attitude
Give attention to your reader's sense of self-esteem
Write in an informal, natural style
Maintain a high quality of writing

Be Prompt in Responding

It is safe to say that no one who wants something enjoys being put off. Think of instances when you have been in a store or restaurant and someone who came in after you was waited on first.

The same principle applies to letters; the only difference is that it's the letter that's late instead of the person. But the annoyance can be just as great. If you write a letter of application for a job—then hear nothing for a month, you're annoyed, puzzled, frustrated. The same would be true if it were a request for a favor, an inquiry for information, or an order. If the letter from Josiah Prudent, for example, had arrived six weeks later (instead of only one week), your reaction would be even more negative.

The owner of a flourishing mail-order business selling tropical fish food advertises and follows diligently the practice of getting an order in the mail *the same day it arrives* (unless on a weekend). This practice has paid off. Other businesses follow similar practices, and if they cannot respond immediately they drop a short note (or prepared form) explaining why, and when the information or order may be expected.

If—as happens occasionally—you do find you have neglected to respond promptly, an approach such as this may help:

> Sorry I haven't replied sooner. Frankly, I've been swamped (out of town, or whatever the reason).

Or:

> I'm dismayed to discover that two months have passed since your letter to me of July 20.

However, the need for such "outs" should be infrequent. Unless you are completely sincere, they may seem thin. Used very often, they will seem thin anyway.

Give Attention to Appearance

If you had an appointment for a job interview, you would probably want to look your best because you realize that first impressions are important. They may not be accurate, nor fair, nor lasting; but if they are negative, they are a handicap at the outset.

If you send a letter of application—or any other kind of letter—that letter, in effect, is *you*. Since you're not there in person, the reader must form his or her impression of you indirectly, through the letter. If the impression is unflattering, it is not that the reader wants it to be. You have given him or her little choice; again, you've created needlessly a handicap to overcome.

Suppose you were to receive the following reply from the dean of a school of business administration you are thinking of attending. How would your impression of the response affect your decision about whether to apply? Doubtless you would wonder about the calibre of the institution (especially the dean) and what kind of value they place on prospective students to send such a letter:

> Miss
> Dear/Johnson:
>   Thank s for your ~~letter of~~ inquiry of March 13 concerning our program in
> business administration at Paradise State University. ~~We appreciate~~ We're
>   always happy to answer such letters.
>   You'll be ~~un~~interested ti know that . . .
>   Sincerely yours,
>   Ramus Jones
>   Dean, School of Business Adm nistration

Convey a Positive Tone

The reader's initial impressions based on promptness and appearance are soon followed by his or her impressions of the general tone of the letter; the more positive the tone, the more favorable the impression.

Conveying a positive tone depends on *feeling* positive—that is, possessing an attitude that is genuinely felt and believed in. Such an attitude is important for at least two reasons. One is the effect on the reader. In the words of Bob Levoy, a business and professional consultant, "Psychologists have proved that the manner in which we perceive another person does have a definite effect on how we behave toward that person *and also how that person responds to us* [italics mine]."[1] A letter with a positive tone is more likely to evoke a positive response than one with a tone that is negative.

The other reason for possessing a positive attitude is its effect on oneself. Just as one's attitude affects others, so it affects oneself as well. If I tell myself "I can't," my chance of succeeding is less than if I tell myself "I can." If I am convinced at the start that I will probably fail, my behavior will be such that probably I will.

Several factors contribute to conveying a tone that is positive:

Begin on a Positive Note Letters may be classified in two broad categories: "good news" and "bad news" (or a combination of both). "Good news" says "Yes . . ." "We're offering you the contract . . ." "You'll receive a refund." "Bad news" says, "Sorry, but no."

If the letter offers good news, there is no problem: just start with the good news. You might say, "You'll be happy to learn that our board has reviewed your proposal carefully and approved it," then follow with the relevant details.

However, if the letter bears bad news, the approach must be different. The following steps suggest how:

1. Begin with a positive note anyway. This might consist of telling the reader what you *can* do, or commending him or her on his objectives, or showing understanding for his or her problem.

2. Explain the rationale on which your "no" will be based.

3. Say "no" as tactfully and positively as possible.

4. Close on a positive note, such as offering helpful suggestions, thanking him or her for the interest, wishing him or her luck, or whatever seems most appropriate.

A "bad news" letter illustrating the above approach is shown in this response from a local environmental club to a request that it contribute to a national fund-raising campaign:

> Dear Mr. Slocum:
>
> Your letter of February 14 asking for a contribution generated considerable interest at our last business meeting. Our club is deeply interested in your objectives of improving the nation's environment. We feel encouraged that groups like yours are developing such ambitious goals and are taking positive steps to achieve them.

Unfortunately, our organization is not in a position to respond as we would like. About a year ago we adopted the policy of focusing our resources on environmental problems in our immediate community. In fact, we have just depleted our treasury in completing a project for beautifying a notorious eyesore in the downtown area. Therefore, regretfully, our response must be that we cannot contribute the hundred dollars (or even some lesser amount) that your group has requested.

Best wishes, anyway, on your fund-raising campaign. Perhaps at a later time we can participate in some other phase of your program.

Sincerely yours,

Ophelia Tullius
President

Accentuate the Positive; De-emphasize the Negative This advice can take a variety of forms. It may mean stressing the advantages and downplaying the disadvantages. It may mean emphasizing what you (or your company) *can* do rather than dwelling on what you cannot do. Or it may mean focusing on the pleasant and overlooking the unpleasant. At heart, it means learning to think of a glass of water as being half full instead of half empty, or the sky as being partly sunny instead of partly cloudy.

Observe the contrast in tone in the following examples:

Negative	*Positive*
The price tag of $10.95 is pretty high, we admit, but we also feel that the convenience of our battery-powered "Mosquito-Scat" is worth it.	The convenience you'll enjoy of being free of pesky mosquitos is well worth the $10.95 for our handy, proven, battery-powered "Mosquito-Scat."
I've never had any experience selling, but I feel sure I could do it if you'd give me a chance.	My two and a half years as a paper carrier has given me a lot of confidence in dealing with people.
It's too bad that this is the first payment this year you've sent in on time, but we do appreciate it and hope you'll keep it up.	We appreciate receiving your June payment right on time. Your continued promptness will re-establish your credit with us and benefit us both.

Use Words with a Positive Connotation The connotation (emotional meaning) of words can strongly influence how they will be interpreted.

You would never see an ad, "Ladies' Snotrags for Sale," but you might find: "Ladies' Dainty Linen Handkerchiefs for Sale." In either case, of course, the item is the same, but the emotional reaction of potential customers would be sure to range from intense disgust to pleasant desire.

In business letters, be cautious of using such terms as "failed," "mistake," "neglect," "complaint," "cheap," "dissatisfied," or "loss." In the examples below, note how the choice of words can change the tone from negative to positive.

Negative	*Positive*
For *cheap* bargains galore . . .	For *inexpensive* bargains galore . . . (*or:* Bargains galore for the *thrifty* shopper . . .)
We're sorry we *failed* to answer promptly.	We're sorry we were *unable* to answer more promptly.
We feel your *complaint* about your new power mower is unwarranted.	We *regret* you've experienced difficulty with your new power mower.

Offer Postdecision Reassurance

Psychologists have discovered that people often undergo a period of anxiety *after* making a decision of any consequence ("Did I do the right thing?" and so on). Realizing this, we can help others in such situations dispel their anxieties more easily. One way of doing this is by writing a letter. The payoff will probably be an increase in goodwill or (in the case of a purchase) additional business perhaps from the customer or his or her friends. Comments such as these can be helpfully reassuring:

To a recent purchaser:

> We know you'll be happy with your new Safeguard Burglar Alarm System. Like the hundreds of satisfied customers in whose homes we've installed Safeguard, you can now rest peacefully at night, secure in the knowledge that Safeguard never goes to sleep. Or you can leave for a weekend—or an extended vacation—blissfully certain that your property will be safeguarded day and night.

To a new employee:

> Welcome as our newest client services representative at Missouri Market Research, Inc. We know you'll enjoy working with our staff, both the oldtimers and the newcomers, like yourself. We know, too, that you'll find the work challenging, with ample opportunity for advancement. As questions arise, I want you to feel free to come in to talk with me. Best wishes for a long and satisfying career with us.

Use a You-Attitude

Of all the principles stressed in recent years about business letter writing, probably none has been stressed more than the *you-attitude*. What this means basically is being able to see a situation and to write about it understandingly from the *other* person's point of view, keeping foremost in mind such questions as: What is his or her problem? Reason for writing? Emotional feelings about the subject at hand? Information or action desired? Technical expertise?

The you-attitude does *not* necessarily mean agreeing. One can see another's point of view and still disagree. But it does mean being able to visualize the other person's position, then adapting accordingly. It means learning to think of a letter, not as something you stuff in an envelope, but as a means of stirring up a response in the mind of the recipient—another person with needs and concerns just as real and important to him or her as yours are to you.

Note that we are talking about an attitude—something far more deep-rooted than just choosing the "right word." It implies a concern that is real; not a phony gimmick like an automatic smile that one flashes on and off.

Notice the contrast in these examples:

Type of Letter	*"I" or "We" Attitude*	*"You" Attitude*
Application	I would like to apply for this position because I need the money.	My experience in meeting the public while selling shoes would prove valuable for this position.
Request for a Favor	I am writing a term paper on pest control and wonder whether you could send me some literature I could use.	Your reputation as an expert on pest control has led me to ask for a favor. Do you have any literature on this subject that would be helpful for a term paper I am writing?
Refusal of a Request	We cannot send you any literature on pest control since we receive so few requests of this kind that it would not pay us	In response to your request for some literature on pest control, we're sorry we must disappoint you. We receive

Type of Letter	"I" or "We" Attitude	"You" Attitude
	to keep any on hand.	so few requests of this kind that we have no spare literature on hand. However, two sources that could help you are: [names and addresses given here].
Receipt of an Order	We are happy to receive your order.	Your order for _____ should reach you by Monday.
Collection	We have been extremely lenient up to this point.	If you wish to maintain your credit with us, it will be necessary that you send your payment at once.
Congratulations	I would like to congratulate you on your new position.	Congratulations on your new position.

As you reflect on these examples, please note again: It is not the wording itself that creates the attitude, but the empathy underlying the wording.

Figure 10.1 is an example of a letter with a you-attitude that is unmistakable. "You" (or a variation) appears eleven times. More importantly, the letter is adapted to two interests of the reader: pride in the community, and being able to receive credit on his or her income tax return for contributions to the foundation.

Furthermore, when the writer does use "we" or "our," in almost every instance these include the reader as well. There is a profound psychological difference between "we" meaning "our business," "our firm," or "our organization" and "we" meaning "you and I."

Finally, there is the handwritten note in the upper righthand corner, which goes far to personalize a letter whose typed salutation is merely "Dear Fellow Citizen." The tone of this note conveys likewise a you-attitude.

Letters addressed to a particular individual ("Dear Howard" or "Dear Miss Stevens") may also be personalized further by using the recipient's

FIGURE 10.1 Letter Illustrating You-Attitude. (Written by Norman J. Wing. Used with permission of author.)

June 6, 1975

Dear Fellow Citizen:

Have you or your family noticed the exceptionally attractive face of Spring this year? Landscaped and planted areas have made their mark in many parts of our community. These have symbolized that there are people like you who desire to make Flint an attractive city--a city that has pride in itself and confidence in its future.

For the past two years the Flint Environmental Action Team (FEAT), with the help of others like yourself, has been expending a great deal of effort to improve the appearance of our city. Now we would like to share with you a recent development we think you'll be interested in.

For some time, the board of directors of FEAT have realized the need to provide this community with a public trust for environmental improvement so that contributions you make would be tax deductible. You will be happy to learn that we have completed forming the FEAT Foundation and have been granted by the Internal Revenue Service the tax-deductible status of a public-supported trust. This allows the Foundation to keep and use tax dollars that might otherwise leave the community.

Please note the enclosed card describing the goals of the FEAT Foundation. With your tax deductible contributions, you are taking part in personally helping us attain goals that will create a more beautiful city . . . . one that we can all be proud of!

Won't you help Flint move forward with FEAT?

Sincerely,

Norman J. Wing, President

BOARD OF DIRECTORS

Norman J. Wing, President • Linda J. Tapp, Vice-President • Mrs. Bruce M. MacArthur, Secretary • Linda S. Roeser, Treasurer • Homer E. Dowdy
Frederick A. Ellis • Mrs. Stephen A. Evanoff • Richard J. Figura • Paul V. Gadola, Jr. • Jack Hamady • Katherine S. Huber • Alton A. Miller
Gordon Suber • James E. Tomblinson • Mrs. Pat Wallace • Barb Spaulding Westcott • Dr. Robin Widgery • Gerald Wyatt • John C. Yurk

NINE TWENTY-FIVE SOUTH AVON • FLINT, MICHIGAN 48503

name within the body of the letter; for example, "We believe, Miss Stevens, that you will agree . . ." or "Howard, this is an opportunity you'll want to consider seriously." This technique—if it sounds natural, is sincere, and is not overdone—is another useful means of expressing a you-attitude. It is a technique often used (and sometimes misused) in business letter writing.

A caution must be added. Simply using "you" does not guarantee a "you-attitude." "You misrepresented the facts again" states the case from the *writer's* point of view and is likely to put the reader on the defensive. "I'm afraid I did not understand your offer" puts the point tactfully with consideration for the reader, even though it begins with "I." The essential feature of the "you-attitude" is not the use necessarily of "you," but the attitude underlying the language.

Give Attention to Your Reader's Sense of Self-Esteem

An extension of the you-attitude is giving attention to the reader's sense of self-esteem. A veteran of successful business letter writing has observed, "The first and most basic fact to realize is that every individual, regardless of his station in life, has a certain amount of personal pride, dignity, ego, or 'face.'"[2]

Among the techniques for dealing positively with the reader's esteem needs are the following:

Personalize the Message Personalizing a letter by using the recipient's name has already been mentioned in connection with the FEAT letter. In addition, the letter may be personalized by references pertaining to him or her personally (as distinct from the main topic of the letter). For example, you might add (even as a postscript if the letter is quite informal), "By the way, I really appreciate your suggestion on the best restaurants to try on my trip to Denver—especially The Old Prospector's Inn. It was fabulous!" This conveys the feeling that he or she is important *as a person*, quite apart from any role in the business at hand.

Avoid Putting the Reader on the Defensive When one feels threatened (by being criticized or deflated), one tends to become defensive, and when one becomes defensive one's concern is no longer with the message itself, but with protecting one's ego. One becomes angry, one makes alibis, one thinks of comebacks and cut-downs; in short, one reacts emotionally rather than logically. If a letter seems "threatening" to the reader, the intended meaning may become distorted or fail to get through at all. Communication in an atmosphere of trust is far easier than in one of distrust.

This point becomes more vivid if you imagine yourself as the recipient of such messages as these:

Defensive-Arousing	*Not Defensive-Arousing*
We are surprised that you failed to read the directions more clearly.	If you will read the directions carefully, you will note that . . .
Because you neglected to include the instructions . . .	Because we were unable to locate the instructions . . .
You claim that you sent out the order March 17.	We have not yet received your order of March 17.

> You should have known better
> than to fail to bring in
> the motorbike for a checkup.

> For best service (as the
> instruction manual explains
> on p. 7) the motorbike
> should be brought in for
> a checkup after 30 days.

Sell; Don't Tell   Another practice that irritates a reader's sense of self-esteem is giving directions without explaining the rationale. Suppose you've purchased a car. Six months later you receive a letter from the manufacturer that says, in effect, "Take your car to your dealership for an adjustment in the steering mechanism as soon as possible." Period. No word of explanation why. Besides some feelings of alarm and puzzlement, you would doubtless feel distinctly irritated. In the words of John Harwood:

> Customers like to be sold. It's one thing to tell someone bluntly that his car is out of warranty . . . or that he should return to his selling dealer for a minor adjustment . . . but it's an entirely different thing to explain . . . WHY.[3]

If we simply "tell what," it's like issuing a personal command: "You do this because I said to"—that implies a relationship that says, "I'm in a position to order you around." But if we tell *why,* we're saying in effect, "Here's the reason, and it has nothing to do with my trying to tell you what to do. As a rational person, you can see for yourself."

Be Courteous   Three assumptions underlie the advice to be courteous: people like to be treated courteously; in writing letters you prefer being thought of as courteous; and even if you don't, you would be more effective (other things being equal) if you did.

In face-to-face communication, courtesy is often exhibited less by what we say than by how we say it: tone of voice, facial expression, and all those nonverbal cues that suggest how we feel about others. But in writing—although such nonverbal factors as promptness and appearance are important—the expression of courtesy depends more on verbal than on nonverbal cues.

Yet—as is true of the you-attitude—the words themselves are not the essence of courtesy, but only symbols of the inner attitude. Those whose courtesy is only word-deep run the same risk of being thought phony as do those who say, "Be sincere—whether you mean it or not!" The depth of feeling basic to a true sense of courtesy was well expressed by Walter Weir, a leading copywriter in the advertising business, when he said:

> I believe one best prepares himself for communicating by . . . genuinely loving all the countless other human beings with whom he inhabits the earth. I do not believe one can be a cynic and communicate effectively.[4]

You may have supposed that in the "cold, hard world of business" there is no room for courtesy. Yet, even in business, people still have human needs. Meeting these needs helps promote a favorable working relationship. As stressed already, unless there is a good relationship between communicators, their attempts to communicate with each other become vastly more difficult.

To illustrate the use of courtesy in letter writing, here are excerpts from actual business letters. Note that most of them are from the opening or closing portion of the letter, where a positive impression is especially important:

> Your welcome letter was in my mail when I returned to the office this week.
>
> I just can't tell you how glad I was to hear from you.
>
> We appreciate the opportunity of correcting the misunderstanding.
>
> I'm sorry if I've caused you needless inconvenience.
>
> Best wishes for the Holiday Season.
>
> Best personal regards.
>
> Good luck!

Each of the last three examples, incidentally, was the final paragraph of the letter.

De-emphasize What the Reader Already Knows Often, by way of identifying the subject at hand or supplying a link in our chin of reasoning, it is necessary to mention information the reader is aware of. But to express this as if he or she were not aware can be insulting ("You're too dumb to remember, so I'm reminding you").

For instance, there is a distinct difference psychologically between saying:

> We had a telephone conversation this morning. In this conversation I mentioned that . . .

And:

> In our telephone conversation this morning, I mentioned that . . .

The grammatical means by which the change is made is simple: the information already known is subordinated. This is, it is expressed—in this case—as a prepositional phrase rather than as a sentence (or independent clause). It could be subordinated also by being expressed as a dependent clause: "When we were on the telephone this morning, I mentioned that . . ."

Similar expressions used for subordinating information that the reader already knows include:

> As you probably recall . . .
>
> If you will recall . . .
>
> As you already know . . .

This advice, however, has exceptions. If "what the reader already knows" is a point you do wish to stress, then it *should* be expressed as a sentence or independent clause, as in this example:

> In your letter of July 16 you assured us that our order would be shipped by July 23. Now you tell us you can not possibly ship it before the 26th. We're confused.

The question becomes, then, one of deciding how much to emphasize what the reader is already aware of. As a rule, maintaining a cordial relationship is important enough to de-emphasize the already known.

Write in a Natural, Informal Style

This advice, in the final quarter of the twentieth century, may seem unneeded. It would be, except for at least two reasons. One is that some people who express themselves naturally enough in conversation seem to feel that in writing they must suddenly become formal (and unnatural). Thus, the same person who might say over the telephone, "I'm looking forward to meeting you," may write in a letter, "I would deem it a pleasure to make your acquaintance."

The other reason is that throughout the first half of this century many business people wrote in a style wholly stilted and unnatural. This would not concern us here except that some of you entering business may encounter older colleagues who still write in such a style, having acquired it early in their own careers from the practice then still quite common. Unless otherwise advised, you may unintentionally carry on a tradition that is more out of date than high button shoes and kerosene lamps.

How this style got started, incidentally, reveals clearly why it is now old-fashioned. According to J. H. Menning and C. W. Wilkinson, well-known authorities on business correspondence, this style

> . . . goes back to the times when businessmen first began to have social status enough to write to kings, princes, and others at court. Feeling inferior, they developed a slavish, stilted, and elaborately polite style to flatter the nobility. They "begged to advise" the nobleman that his "kind favor of recent date" was "at hand" and "wished to state" that "this matter" would "receive our prompt attention" and "begged to remain your humble and obedient servant." . . . Unfortunately, too many

[businessmen] sheepishly follow somebody else, learn all they know about letter writing from the letters they receive, and thus continue an outmoded, inappropriate, and unnatural style.[5]

While the formal style has long since been replaced, we must point out that the informal style is not the only one acceptably in use. J. Harold Janis, as well as others, has identified four current styles in good standing:

1. Official—used in legal correspondence; characterized by such expressions as "heretofore," "aforementioned," and "pursuant to."

2. Formal—used in letters of introduction and recommendation and other correspondence of an impersonal nature.

3. Informal—used in most correspondence; stresses the "human relations function" more strongly.

4. Familiar—used in correspondence of concern primarily to themselves between people who know each other well.[6]

Of the four, the informal is by far the most common. It is the style found in nearly all the examples in this chapter. The familiar, while sometimes used in letters, is more commonly found in personal memos.

Maintain a High Quality of Writing

In Chapter 9, on persuasion, considerable emphasis was placed on the importance of the communicator's credibility. One of the factors contributing to credibility is "expressing oneself effectively." In other words, in conveying a positive image in letter writing, one critical factor is whether the letter seems well written.

Review of General Principles   Since all of Part 2, "Being Clear" (except for Chapter 8 on graphic aids), focuses directly on writing well, simply refreshing your memory on the ingredients of good writing should suffice for our purposes here.

Briefly, we can say that—in addition to all we have offered above on the tone of the letter—a letter is well written if it observes the following principles. (The number in parentheses after each statement is the number of the chapter in which the principle is developed.)

1. There is an effective balance between the general and specific. (4)

2. An appropriate choice is made between the direct and indirect approach (for good or neutral news, direct; for bad news, indirect). (4)

3. Ideas are developed clearly and sufficiently for the understanding and belief of the reader. (5 and 9)

4. There is a clear, logical sequence of and relationship between ideas, both within and between paragraphs. (5 and 6)

5. Paragraphs are appropriate in length (usually shorter in letters than in most other writing). (5)

6. Each paragraph deals with a single main topic. (5)
7. Complete sentences are used (though exceptions are allowable in sales letters, where attention-getting devices may outweigh grammatical correctness). (6)
8. Ideas are given the amount of emphasis they warrant in terms of the purpose of the letter. No confusion is created about the *main* points to be made. (5 and 6)
9. Sentence length is most effective for the kind of ideas being expressed. (6)
10. The writing is not wordy. (6)
11. Correct grammar and punctuation are observed. (7)
12. Words and phrases are used correctly. (7)

The Opening and Closing Paragraphs   In addition to the general principles just restated, two trouble spots unique to letter writing call for special attention: the opening paragraph and the closing paragraph, which contribute heavily to the image conveyed by the letter.

Guidelines to observe in writing the opening paragraph include the following:

1. Tie in (where relevant) to previous correspondence ("In reply to your letter of June 30 . . ."; "Thanks for your inquiry concerning . . .").
2. Use a you-attitude if possible.
3. Begin with a positive tone.
4. Avoid stilted language ("In reply to yours of the 3rd, we herewith wish to state . . .").
5. Keep it brief (usually one to three sentences).

Guidelines for composing the final paragraph are quite similar:

1. End on a positive note (even when the content of the letter has been "bad news").
2. Be specific in what action (if any) is desired; do not leave the reader hanging in midair.
3. Avoid outworn or insincere phrases ("Trusting you are well, I respectfully remain, Yours truly, Jacob Garder).
4. Keep it brief (sometimes a single short sentence).

Occasionally—if there is just no more to say because the main part of the body has said it so well—a separate, closing paragraph may be omitted completely.

To illustrate the importance of good writing, suppose in this course you receive a final grade with which you're unhappy. Not only are you unhappy; your parents are too. Therefore (having convinced yourself that you're the victim of an injustice), you decide to write the teacher, who happens to run into the dean a few minutes later and shows her your letter. How impressed do you think the dean would be that your grade was too low? (Note that it's the quality of writing we're interested in here. Since you're on your best behavior, the tone is quite acceptable.)

> Dear Proffesor Bell;
> The other day I got my grades and I must say I was verry dissapointed with the grade I received in Eng. 105, it was a D. My parents are disapointed too. And upset, just like me.
> I was always did good in h.s. english and must say I looked forwerd to taking coll. eng. and enjoyed it to since, may I say quiet honestly I always enjoyed your lectures and themes; and the class in general. It was a good class that I see where it was required even if some didn't like it to much some of the time; and some most of the time. But I did. So since I enjoyed it and almost always got my assignments in on time and you gave me several C's and a B I don't see why I should end up with a D when some others that didn't like it so much got C's and one girl (I won't mention her name) got a B and she didn't work as hard as I did.
> So hoping you'll reconsider your grade, I remain
>
> Respectfully yours,
>
> Timothy Campbell III
>
> P.S. My parents both read this letter and agree, they think eng. is important to. Anyone.

We can imagine the dean's response: "I don't see either why you gave him a D. I'd have flunked him."

PARTS OF A LETTER

Business letters generally include six parts that are standard. In addition, various supplementary parts may be used.

Standard Parts

The parts that are standard include, in this order: (1) heading, (2) inside address, (3) salutation, (4) body, (5) complimentary close, and (6) signature. The content, function, and punctuation of these parts will be discussed here. Their location in the letter will be illustrated below under "Formats and Mechanics."

Heading The heading consists of the sender's address (including ZIP code), followed by the date. On personal business stationery (a plain sheet of good quality typing paper), both the address and date will be typed. Since company stationery has its own letterhead (name of company, address, and usually telephone number), only the date need be added.

A typical heading for a letter on personal business stationery would look like this. (Note that instead of abbreviating, all words are spelled out.)

>2954 Helber Street
>Scottsdale, Arizona 85257
>September 30, 1975

Typical headings on company letterhead will be illustrated later in examples illustrating various formats.

Inside Address Because the envelope is usually discarded and the letter often filed, the address on the envelope is repeated inside, *exactly* as typed on the envelope. Included are the addressee's name with appropriate title, position (if any), street address, city, state, and zip code. If the letter is to a company whose letterhead uses abbreviations, use the same abbreviations; otherwise, spell out the word. The one standard exception is the new two-letter abbreviation for each state recently developed by the Post Office for use with the zip code.

Various examples of inside addresses are shown here. (Note that a title of some kind is included in each one.)

Mr. David A. Cotnoir 1125 East 8th Street Milwaukee, WI 53211	(the title here is "Mr")
Ms. Clara T. Harris, Director Personnel Department Amrose Paper Products, Inc. 1416 Tobin Drive Amherst, MA 01002	(but not "Director Ms. Clara T. Harris"; the business title or position should *follow* the name)
Miss Vicki Lott, Sales Department Briteway Lamp Company 5208 Crestline Rd. Westport, CT 06880	
Christopher Lowe, M.D. 2222 Eisenhower Drive Lexington, KY 40206	(but not Dr. Christopher Lowe, M.D., since the second title means the same as the first)

(Note: "Ms." is used if it is not known whether the woman is single or married, or if it is known that she prefers "Ms.")

Salutation The salutation sets the tone for the letter. Salutations may be broadly classified as formal or informal, with the writer choosing the salutation most appropriate in terms of degree of formality, importance of the occasion, how well he or she knows the receiver, and the kind of relationship between them. Typical examples are these:

Formal:

>My dear Mr. Shane:
>Dear Senator:
>Dear Mr. Chairperson:
>The Honorable Ellen Sanders:

Formal and Impersonal:

>Gentlemen: Dear Sir:
>Ladies: Sir:

Informal:

>Dear Miss Sanders:
>Dear Ms. Gibson:

Informal and Personal:

>Dear Jaki:
>Dear Ralph:

Note that the punctuation following the salutation is normally a colon (never a semicolon). In purely personal correspondence a comma is used, while in business correspondence between close friends a comma is permissible. In Europe and South America, a comma instead of a colon is used in business as well as in personal correspondence.

Body The body is the message of the letter. Since the entire preceding section, "Creating a Positive Image," concerned the body, nothing further will be added here.

Complimentary Close The complimentary close should match the salutation in tone, so may range from formal to informal. Only the first word is capitalized, while the last word is followed by a comma.

More Formal:

>Respectfully submitted,
>Very truly yours,
>Very sincerely yours,

Less Formal:

>Yours truly,
>Sincerely yours,
>Sincerely,
>Cordially,

Signature The signature also should match the tone of the rest of the letter. If the correspondents do not know each other, or the writer is clearly speaking for the company, the signature will tend to be more formal. If the opposite is the case, it will tend to be more informal.

More Formal:

Very truly yours,
CAPITAL DESIGN COMPANY

Daniel J. Dickey

Daniel J. Dickey
Director of Marketing

Yours truly,

Daniel J. Dickey

Daniel J. Dickey
Director of Marketing
Capital Design Company

Less Formal:

Sincerely yours,

Brian D. Fogle

Brian D. Fogle
Director of Public Relations

Cordially,

Brian

Brian D. Fogle

Cordially,

Brian

Brian D. Fogle
Director of Public Relations

Note that for legibility the sender's name is always typed (four spaces below the line above), with the signature *above* the line.

As a rule, the signature should match the salutation in formality. That is, if the recipient is addressed as "Dear Miss Pavlik," sign, "Michael D. Shaughnessy"; or if "Dear Ruth Ann," sign "Mike." However, there may be exceptions, usually because of differences in age or status. Thus, a professor might be addressed, "Dear Professor Mariotti," with the signature, "Tonjia." He, in turn, might reply, "Dear Tonjia" and sign "John Mariotti."

Supplementary Parts

In addition to the standard parts described above, any of the following supplementary parts may also be used:

Attention Line If you are writing primarily to a company rather than to an individual, and wish to indicate what person or position in the company the letter is intended for, use an attention line. For instance, in a letter complaining about a product you (or your company) have purchased, the attention line might look like this:

> Angelmusic, Inc.
> 825 Morewood Street
> Winston-Salem, North Carolina 27102
>
> Attention: Director of Customer Relations
>
> Gentlemen:

Or you could express it either of the following ways:

> Attention: Mr. Josiah R. Prudent
> Gentlemen:

or:

> Attention: Mr. Josiah R. Prudent
>
> Dear Sir:

The use of either "Gentlemen" (more commonly used) or "Dear Sir" implies that you are addressing the company as an organization rather than Mr. Prudent as a person. To put it differently, you have nothing against Mr. Prudent personally; it's the company you are directing your complaint to, regardless of who happens to be in charge of complaints (or purchasing, shipping, receiving, personnel, sales, or whatever).

The attention line appears two spaces below the inside address, and may be either centered or begun at the left-hand margin, as shown above. If an attention line is included in the letter, the typist will include a comparable attention line on the envelope.

Subject Line Use of a subject line is a convenience for the reader, since it identifies immediately what the letter is about. Besides, it helps the writer get off to a faster start. An additional reason for a subject line is that some companies now make a practice, upon receiving a letter, of making an extra copy—one to be filed by name of sender, the other by subject. A subject line, intelligently formulated, is an obvious aid.

The subject line may appear (a) above the salutation (but below the attention line), (b) on the same line as the salutation, or (c) below the salutation—whichever looks best (or company procedure dictates). For emphasis, it is often in solid capitals or underlined. The word "Subject" may be used but is not necessary, since the fact that it is a subject line is obvious anyway. Two examples of subject lines are shown here:

> King Cole Novelties, Inc.
> 1916 Hopkins Road
> Iowa City, Iowa 52290
>
> Attention: Purchasing Director
>
> Gentlemen: PRICE REVISIONS, 1976 CATALOG

Ms. Shaheen Shaw, Sales Representative
Beauty Eye Products
900 South Mississippi Avenue
San Antonio, Texas 78284

Subject: Regional Sales Meeting, September 12

Dear Ms. Shaw:

Initials The typist is usually identified by initials located at the bottom, two spaces below the typed name, and at the left margin. Traditionally, the sender's initials have also been included (to the left of the typist's), but since this needlessly repeats information already given (in the typed names), the practice is becoming less common. Variations of how the initials may appear include:

    sl   RPW/sl   RPW:sl   rpw/sl   rpw/s   /s   s.

Whether a colon or slash mark is used is optional; the trend is away from using either. If the person writing the letter types it him- or herself, including his or her initials as typist is also optional.

Sometimes, as mentioned earlier, a letter signed by one person is actually written by an assistant or subordinate. When this occurs, the initials should indicate this. For instance "EK:Kjs" might mean that the letter was written by King for the signature of Edward Kennedy, and typed by Jayne Smith.

Enclosures If enclosures are included, a notation just below the initials is a reminder to the sender not to overlook including them. The notation also informs the recipient that they were to have been included (and, of course, probably are). The enclosure notation may look like this:

    Encl.: 3

    Enclosures: Sales Brochure, KRM Copier
                  Test Report on KRM Copier

When only the number of enclosures is shown, presumably the titles were indicated in the body of the letter.

Copy Designation If others than the addressee are to receive a copy of the letter, their names are shown in a list (often called a *distribution list*), preceded by the abbreviation: "CC:" or "cc:", or the words "Copy to:". The information of who else besides the addressee are receiving the letter is both a courtesy and convenience to sender and receivers alike. On the extra copies (either carbon, or run off on a copying machine), the sender's signature consists often of only his or her initials. In addition, the sender may add a brief note in longhand, either to personalize the copy a bit, or to add information relevant only to that recipient.

If the list needs less than a line or two, the names are usually typed horizontally across the page; but if it is longer, they are more often arranged in a vertical column. In either case, the order is usually alphabetical.

Postscript A postscript is presumably an afterthought. Thus, the more formal the letter, the less acceptable a postscript, for it suggests careless planning. In an informal letter, however, a postscript may be quite acceptable. And in sales letters, postscripts are often used deliberately as attention devices. In any event, the postscript seldom exceeds two or three sentences.

Second-Page Headings Since letterhead stationery is used for the first page only, and plain paper after that, it is customary to include the recipient's name, date, and page number on succeeding pages; for example:

    Mrs. Karen Andreski, April 23, 1977   p. 2

This detail is one that the typist should take care of with no special instructions. However, it should be stressed that the writer cannot take for granted that the secretary will necessarily handle all such details properly. Some secretaries have more limited commercial training than do others; some have less natural aptitude; some are less attentive to detail; some are less dedicated to their work. In their commercial courses they are exposed to various forms, some inefficient and outmoded. It is the responsibility of the writer to decide which forms are to be used, as well as whether the spelling, punctuation, and so on are correct. The popular notion that "the secretary will take care of everything" simply is not sound, and it is irresponsible for the writer to try to hide behind this fallacy.

ADDRESSING THE ENVELOPE

If you type your own letter, you will of course type the address on the envelope as well. To take advantage of the new rapid-sorting equipment of the United States Postal Service, follow these directions (Figure 10.2):

1. Place the address in a block form (having a uniform left margin) at least one inch from the left and ⅝ inch from the bottom.
2. Type the address in all capitals, single spaced; omit punctuation.
3. Type the attention line, if one is used, above the second line from the bottom.
4. Type city, state, and ZIP code on the last line. Use the new two-letter abbreviation for the state, followed by two spaces, then the ZIP code.[7]

FIGURE 10.2
Envelope
Addressed to
Recipient in the
United States

```
J. Parrott Enterprises
P.O. Box 419
Atlanta, GA 30333




                    NATIONAL ALPHA-OMEGA CORP
                    ATTN MRS MARIANNE DALIEGE
                    104 WOODHAVEN DRIVE
                    BOCA RATON FL   33432
```

A list of the two-letter abbreviations for states is shown here:

Alabama	AL	Montana	MT
Alaska	AK	Nebraska	NE
Arizona	AZ	Nevada	NV
Arkansas	AR	New Hampshire	NH
California	CA	New Jersey	NJ
Colorado	CO	New Mexico	NM
Connecticut	CT	New York	NY
Delaware	DE	North Carolina	NC
District of Columbia	DC	North Dakota	ND
Florida	FL	Ohio	OH
Georgia	GA	Oklahoma	OK
Guam	GU	Oregon	OR
Hawaii	HI	Pennsylvania	PA
Idaho	ID	Puerto Rico	PR
Illinois	IL	Rhode Island	RI
Indiana	IN	South Carolina	SC
Iowa	IA	South Dakota	SD
Kansas	KS	Tennessee	TN
Kentucky	KY	Texas	TX
Louisiana	LA	Utah	UT
Maine	ME	Vermont	VT
Maryland	MD	Virginia	VA
Massachusetts	MA	Virgin Islands	VI
Michigan	MI	Washington	WA
Minnesota	MN	West Virginia	WV
Mississippi	MS	Wisconsin	WI
Missouri	MO	Wyoming	WY

When addressing a letter to a foreign country, copy the address exactly as given, since practice abroad differs from that in the United States. Note that in the address in Figure 10.3, the name of the city is on the line *above* the street address; also that the zip code precedes the name of the city rather than following it (although in larger cities in Germany another number may follow the name specifying a particular region within the city—e.g., 634 Berlin 20). Note further that the name of the country is typed in capitals (or underlined): WEST GERMANY or West Germany.

The lines of the address should be approximately equal length. If the addressee's position or the company's name is too long, the name may be continued on the next line, indented two spaces; thus:

>Mr. Gerald Lustenberger
>Publicity and Community
> Relations Coordinator
>Kalamazoo County Community
> Mental Health Services
>1700 West Aurelius Road
>Kalamazoo, MI 49007

Our discussion of standard and supplementary parts is intended to provide only a general awareness, not a rigid rule book. Practices vary from company to company, department to department, secretary to secretary—as well as from one year to the next and one generation to the next. The above description, "Parts of a Letter," is not one to be slavishly followed, but rather intelligently adapted.

FORMATS AND MECHANICS

To ensure familiarity with current practice, five basic formats will be described and illustrated: semiblock, modified semiblock, full block, simplified, and specialized.

FIGURE 10.3
Envelope
Addressed to a
Foreign Country

```
Elanor Lumianski
732 Archer Street
Syracuse, NY   13120
U.S.A.
                        Mr. Udo Abel
                        Assistant Manager
                        Hotel Kaiserwilhelm
                        407 Marbach/Neckar
                        18 Elizabethkirchstrasse
                        WEST GERMANY
```

Regardless of format, rules governing spacing are fairly uniform:

Doublespacing between letterhead and date.

Four to eight spaces between date and inside address.

Doublespacing between all other parts.

Single spacing within all parts.

Margins varying between one and two inches, depending on length of letter, and greater margin at the bottom than at the top.

Semiblock   Probably the most common format of the past generation has been the *semiblock*. It has two distinguishing features: the date, complimentary close, and signature are either centered or located on the right; the paragraphs are indented (usually five spaces). The advantages of the semiblock are that it looks more traditional and appears well balanced on the page. Note the points mentioned above that Figure 10.4 illustrates.

1. Date, complimentary close, and signature on the right; paragraphs indented.
2. Effective use of margins for attractive layout on page.
3. Double spacing between parts; single spacing within.
4. Reference in opening sentence to occasion for writing.
5. Polite closing paragraph.
6. Consistently informal, though businesslike tone throughout.

Modified Semiblock   The *modified semiblock* is identical to the semiblock except that the paragraphs are not indented. It maintains the balance of the semiblock format, yet avoids the inconvenience of indenting paragraphs. Figure 10.5 illustrates not only the modified semiblock format, but also the following supplementary parts of a letter:

1. Attention line
2. Subject line
3. Initials of sender and typist
4. Copy designation (distribution list)

This letter also illustrates effective use of listing (the numbered list of five conclusions that the letter summarizes).

Full Block   Increasingly common is the *full block* format, which differs from semiblock in two ways: *all* lines begin at the left: the paragraphs are not indented. The advantages are that since all lines begin with the left margin, it is slightly less bothersome to type, and it appears more up to date. A disadvantage is that the layout of the page appears a bit lopsided.

FIGURE 10.4
Semiblock Format.
(Written by Ms.
Kareen Hagopian.
Used with permission
of author.)

THE CHICAGO CHAPTER

SOCIETY FOR TECHNICAL COMMUNICATION
1639 WEST FARGO AVENUE
CHICAGO IL 60626

TELEPHONE:
(312) 761-7132

February 20, 1975

Mr. Frank E. McElroy
National Safety Council
425 North Michigan Avenue
Chicago, Illinois 60611

Dear Frank:

    It is a privilege to have you as a member of the panel of judges for the 1975 International Technical Publications Competition.

    This competition, sponsored by the Society for Technical Communication (STC) is designed to provide annual recognition for outstanding achievements in our field. The documents to be evaluated are winning entries from regional competitions held throughout the past year in the United States and Canada. Entries from Africa and Israel may also be considered. Approximately 300 documents in 11 categories will be judged, and awards will be presented to the winners May 14 to 17 at the Disneyland Hotel in Anaheim, California.

    Enclosed is a list of the 1975 International Judges. Like you, each has been selected on the basis of his or her known expertise and contribution to the field of communication. Like you, each has achieved a respected position in a respected profession.

    The judging (being held in the Chicago area this year for the first time) will take place on Saturday, March 8, at Bell Laboratories in Naperville, Illinois. It will start at 9:15 a.m. and continue through the day. You will, of course, be the guest of STC for lunch. Instructions for getting to Bell Labs are enclosed.

    If you have not yet sent us a brief biography and picture, please do so as soon as possible. Ronald Schelkopf of Industrial Communications is STC's national information director and will be handling press releases and publicity.

    Please feel free to call me either at work (690-2007) or at home (773-1930) if you have any questions regarding the above. Meanwhile, I'll be looking forward to seeing you on March 8.

    Sincerely,

Kareen Hagopian
Kareen K. Hagopian
Chairman, Judging
1975 STC International
Publications Competition

cc: R. F. Ellis
    D. Saxner
    R. M. Schelkopf
    M. A. DeMarco

FIGURE 10.5 Modified Semiblock Format. (Written by Mr. Merrill Reinig. Used with permission of author.)

CHEVROLET MOTOR DIVISION

General Motors Corporation

Saginaw Manufacturing Plant
2328 East Genesee Avenue
Saginaw, Michigan 48605

February 1, 1971

Cutler-Hammer, Inc.,
Industrial Systems Division
4265 N. 30th Street
Milwaukee, Wisconsin 53216

Attention: Mr. C. J. Weiss

Subject: CHEVROLET DISC BRAKE COMPUTER PROJECT MEETING January 28, 1971

Dear Sir:

The following is a summary of our discussions and what I understand to be the conclusions of our meetings in Milwaukee on January 27th through January 29th, 1971.

1. The first P.D.P. 15/30 (Machine "A") will be shipped to Saginaw on April 23, 1971 on a moving van, straight through to this location. The I.O. panels for this project will be shipped with the machine.

2. A "Pert" type chart explaining the Cutler-Hammer plan to meet the schedule, as presented to myself and Mr. Wade of Cutler-Hammer on January 22, 1971 by Mr. B. C. Rae, will be completed and delivered to Chevrolet by February 12, 1971.

3. Mr. Leonard Kaczorowski from Chevrolet will be involved in the total system concept, and a written schedule including a list of areas of how this will be accomplished, will be sent to Chevrolet. Mr. Kaczorowski will submit a report of this progress bi-weekly to Chevrolet.

4. Mr. B. Wiseman will remain in Saginaw as the computer project field installation supervisor until completion of the project.

5. A written description of each program will be submitted for review and approval before program coding is started. This will be all that is required at this location for approval of programs. Program flow charts and program listing will not be required until the computer system is installed.

6. Chevrolet will approve the written descriptions within two days of receipt and will assist in every possible manner to expedite the installation and completion.

FIGURE 10.5 Modified Semiblock Format (continued)

        Cutler-Hammer, Inc.   Page 2

In addition to the above items, please submit a progress report on the Pert chart every two weeks to assist in monitoring the progress of the project.

                                                        Very truly yours,

                                                        M. C. Reinig
                                                        Project Engineer

MR:ds

cc: Mr. R. Hopps
     Mr. E. O. Vahala
     Mr. E. Nead
     Mr. B. O. Rae
     Mr. R. Wade
     Mr. R. Winter
     Mr. L. Kaczorowski
     File

FIGURE 10.6 Full Block Format. (Written by Mr. James N. Holly. Used with permission of author.)

LUNDY ELECTRONICS & SYSTEMS, INC.
LUNDY TECHNICAL CENTER

3901 N.E. 12TH AVENUE   POMPANO BEACH, FLORIDA 33064   305-943-1500

November 4, 1974

Prof. Roger Wilcox
Department of Communications and
Organizational Behavior
General Motors Institute
Flint, Michigan 48502

Dear Prof. Wilcox:

Thank you very much for the planning and course materials you sent me. I also appreciated the opportunity to talk with you on the phone about my request.

During that conversation you mentioned an interest in the types of courses being offered and the texts being used at Florida Atlantic University, so I have enclosed a fall book list and a descriptive list of the courses offered.

Again, thank you.

Yours very sincerely,

LUNDY TECHNICAL CENTER

James N. Holly
Publications Manager

JNH:q
Enclosure

FIGURE 10.7
Simplified Format.
(Written by Albert J. Rapuano. Used with the permission of both Mr. Rapuano and Mr. Kyros.)

COLONY SQUARE HOTEL • PEACHTREE & 14TH STREET, ATLANTA 30361 • (404) 892-6000

OFFICE OF THE GENERAL MANAGER

June 2, 1975

Mr. Nicholas P. Kyros
Vice President/Director of Marketing
Sheraton - O'Hare Motor Hotel
6810 North Mannheim Road
Rosemont, Illinois 60018

Nick...I did not want you to spend your very first day without having any mail to open or read, so I decided to send you this brief note of best wishes and good luck in your new job.

You know the job you have to do, and I am sure in your tenure at the Pick Congress you realized the right and wrong ways of going after business. There is no doubt in my mind and in the minds of others that you'll do a great job. You'll go far for a punk Greek kid.

Seriously though, I want you to call me whenever you have any questions or whenever you feel that I could be helpful. Just continue to maintain an aggressive and sophisticated sales attitude and you will not have any problems at all.

Again, Nick, Good Luck...

Albert J. Rapuano

FAIRMONT HOTEL AND TOWER, SAN FRANCISCO • FAIRMONT HOTEL, NEW ORLEANS
FAIRMONT HOTEL, DALLAS • FAIRMONT COLONY SQUARE HOTEL, ATLANTA
For information or reservations at any Fairmont Hotel, call Toll Free 800-527-4727 (in Texas, call 800-492-6622)

Figure 10.6 illustrates the full block format. Special features additionally illustrated by this letter include:

1. The use of "courtesy" language for a favor received.
2. The name of the company in solid capitals just above the name of the writer.
3. The initials of the writer and typist.
4. The notation "Enclosure" (which was already identified in the body).

FIGURE 10.8
Specialized Format.
(Written by Mr. Marvin N. Schoenhals. Used with permission of author.)

August 19, 1975

A Free Gift To Area Residents:

Now that The Owosso Savings Bank has opened two offices near you, we'd like to get to know you. Before I tell you about our very special offer, I'd like to tell you a little about our Bank. Even though we're Flint's newest bank, we're 84 years old. We were founded in 1891 and have over $115,000,000 in total assets. That's large enough to serve you - but still small enough to know you.

We always try to do more for you than most banks. We pay the highest rate on savings the law allows. We've had our **FREE PERSONAL CHECKING** since 1958, and it's just what it says - free checking. There's no minimum balance to maintain, no monthly service charge, no per check charge, no clubs to join. The only thing you have to pay is the normal cost of having your checks imprinted. We offer the full range of banking services. In short, if you have a banking need, we can meet it.

SPECIAL $5.00 INTRODUCTORY OFFER

As a special offer to introduce ourselves, we'd like to give you a $5.00 savings account. **FOR THE FIRST 500 PEOPLE WHO BRING IN THIS LETTER AND OPEN A FREE PERSONAL CHECKING ACCOUNT WITH A $50.00 INITIAL DEPOSIT - WE'LL OPEN A SAVINGS ACCOUNT AND DEPOSIT $5.00 IN IT FOR YOU.** Why not stop in to one of our offices today, get your $5.00 savings account and more importantly, get to know us.

Sincerely,

Marvin Schoenhals

Marvin N. Schoenhals
Vice President - Retail Banking

P.S. Our new Carman Plaza Office will be open early in September.

Clio Plaza Office   Beecher Road Office   Carman Plaza Office
G 4377 Clio Road   4508 Beecher Road   G 3302 Corunna Road
Phone 785-4774   Phone 733-2230   Phone 234-6644

Simplified

The *simplified* format, advocated by the National Office Management Association (NOMA), is like the full block in that all lines begin at the left margin. However, the salutation and complimentary close are omitted, although the recipient's name is often included in the first line or two.

Thus far, the simplified format has not been widely accepted; to many it seems too radical a departure from accustomed practice. Whether it saves more time for the writer is doubtful, since he or she may spend more time devising an appropriate way of including the recipient's name in the first part of the body than would be spent simply writing, "Dear Ray."

FIGURE 10.9
Specialized Format.
(Written by Mr. Gene
Gish. Used with
permission of author.)

GENE GISH
510 MERCHANDISE MART PLAZA
CHICAGO, ILLINOIS 60654

January 23, 1976

TO WHOM IT MAY CONCERN:

Mr. Charles Glanville was employed with Field Enterprises Educational Corporation during the period from January, 1967, to October, 1975. His responsibilities were to employ, train, and supervise a sales staff in the Upper Peninsula of Michigan. In addition, his duties involved servicing and selling to the public and parochial schools, colleges, and universities in the area.

Mr. Glanville carried out fully his responsibilities to our specifications and beyond our requirements. He was also a compatible executive to work with, and had the ability to develop high performance from his subordinates.

I would recommend Charles in any field of management or supervision involving sales.

We would re-employ him were the opportunity to arise.

Sincerely,

Gene Gish

GG/ah

In the example (Figure 10.7), the result is a cross between a letter and a friendly, informal memo. Note that the use of the recipient's name in the first sentence of the body in this particular example sounds very natural, while the closing sentence, "Again, Good Luck," makes a standard complimentary close unnecessary. At first reading, the reference "a punk Greek kid" may seem like an ethnic slur, but in the context of this letter it simply reflects a relationship warm enough to warrant such ribbing. The absence of the writer's or typist's initials further personalizes the tone of the letter.

Specialized

In addition to the four standard formats just described, many specialized formats are used in business. In these, no rules are standard, the only limitation being the writer's ingenuity in devising a layout (and content) that best suits the particular purpose of the letter (for example, to sell a product, introduce a person, or collect an overdue payment).

Figures 10.8–11 illustrate various specialized formats. Study them critically to discover how well each seems adapted to the particular purpose

**FIGURE 10.10
Specialized Format**

Internal Revenue Service   **Department of the Treasury**

Date: July 8, 1974

Person to Contact: Mr. Morris
Contact Telephone Number:
(202) 964-4441
Your Letter Dated:
4-19-74

Dr. Ethel M. Wilcox
Department of Speech Communication
University of Toledo
Toledo, OH 43606

Dear Dr. Wilcox:

We want to reply as quickly as possible to your request for records under the Freedom of Information Act. However, we regret that there will be a delay for the reason we have checked:

☐ We have asked that the records be sent to us from another location.
☐ We need more time to collect all of the records you requested.
☐ We must determine which records will be most responsive to your request.
☐ We are unable to locate the records you requested and need more time to make a thorough search.
☒ We must first examine the records to make sure the information may be disclosed.
☐ We have asked another agency for help in answering your request.
☐

If you have any questions, please contact the person whose name and telephone number are shown above.

Thank you for your patience and cooperation.

Sincerely yours,

C. S. Gibb

Chief, Disclosure Staff

Washington, D.C. 20224   Form M-6111 (3-74)

FIGURE 10.11
Specialized Format.
(Used with permission of Rolling Stone Magazine.)

1255 Portland Place
Boulder, Colorado 80302

It's difficult,
to ask for money and say just enough to get it without offending.

So, I'll be brief and to the point:

>The amount due on your
>ROLLING STONE subscription
>is still outstanding.

Won't you please send us your payment today? We can then stamp PAID on your account and we'll both feel better for it.

Sincerely,

David Obey
for ROLLING STONE

P.S. If you've already mailed in your payment, then please disregard this letter.

for which it was intended. What changes, if any, in format would you suggest?

APPLICATIONS FOR EMPLOYMENT

The purpose of a letter of application and résumé are not directly to land a job, but to create a positive impression and to secure an interview. The interview may lead to a job, but seldom if ever will a letter or résumé—no matter how well written—directly secure a job.

However, a letter or résumé that is badly composed can easily eliminate a candidate from a chance for an interview. A colleague who served on the school board in a small town told of 36 applications submitted for the position of principal. Of these 36, two out of three were so miserably written that only the remaining 12 candidates were considered further.

The letter of application and the personal résumé should be considered as two parts of a whole; the letter provides the general; the résumé, the specific. A mistake to avoid is sending the letter without the résumé, or the résumé without the letter. Neither by itself is complete.

The Letter of Application

Considered a bit differently, the letter of application provides a bridge between the résumé and the position being applied for. Thus, you might use the same résumé in applying for 15–20 job possibilities, but alter the letter appropriately in adapting to each situation. How this is done will be seen later as we examine the role of each section of the letter. But first, a word about whether the application (and résumé) are solicited or unsolicited.

A solicited application is in response to an invitation to apply. The most common example is the response to a classified ad, such as Figure 10.12.

Another kind of solicited application—less common, but more advantageous when it happens—is the personal invitation. Suppose your major is forestry, and you've been employed by the park board. Near the end of your second summer your supervisor says, "Jack, how would you like to apply for a regular job when you graduate? Send us a letter of application and your résumé along in February or March." This doesn't mean that the job is automatically yours. But it does mean that your supervisor thinks enough of your work—and you—to want you included among those to be considered.

In either case—whether the solicited application is by advertisement or in person—you know there's a definite job out there waiting for someone.

The unsolicited application, by contrast, is the one you send in "cold." You are prepared, let's say, to be a medical lab technician, but neither personal contacts nor classified ads turn up any leads. Sources you may then consult include the yellow pages for a list of hospitals and clinics, state or city employment agencies, professional journals, or university placement services. Having compiled a list of possible prospects, you send a letter to each, hoping for at least a few replies.

Basically, the two types of letters are identical except for the first paragraph.

Opening Paragraph If the application is solicited through a classified ad, the most natural way to begin is by referring to the ad. (Incidentally, prospective employers appreciate this kind of opening because it indicates to them which ads are being read.) Thus, you might begin a letter in response to one of the *Times* ads this way:

> This is in response to your ad in *The New York Times,* October 22, for a Spanish-English speaking accountant. I would like to be considered for the position.

Or, if you are applying for a job with the park board as a result of your supervisor's suggestion, you could begin:

FIGURE 10.12 Classified Ad. (*The New York Times,* October 22, 1975, p. 84L. Used with permission of The New York Times.)

Acctcy (2 needed) New Jersey. Promotable type. Background in account analysis, general ledger & statement prep. Salary $13-15M Deg. nec. Special consideration to Female & Minority Candidates. Call crijudi kdiek yui-ioio dyfkdk lsiwpk kdiski kdkk Madison Ave/43 St agency, fee paid by Co.

ACCOUNTANCY/Mid NJ Chem'l corp seeks acctg degreed indiv to work on Controllers Staff. Indiv should have MBA finance or econ. 6 Mos-1 yrs ind'l corp exp prefd. Salary $13-$15,000. F/Pd. Call heydi iekdh, kdjisifyk, kdlk Assoc. kdj Mad Av/40th St. Agency Suite kdkk.

ACCOUNTANCY/INVENTORY-Major midtown corp seeks inventory clerk with min 1 yr exp. Exclnt bnfts. Sal to $160. For more info contact at our agency today. Lsi kdhdisk, luy-iuek. kdkd Assoc. 160 B'way.

Acctcy: Spanish-English speaking Accnt. with min 2 years general accounting exp. Degree prefd, but not nec. Starting sal $12,000+. Mr. Hgdohkd kdj-oiuy. nihisgt Fin'l Services, we E. kd, agency. Fee Pd.

Acctcy, to $18M. Large metal commodities trading firm, prefer similar exp but will consider public/ind'l exp. EDP knowl. High visibility. Mr. Hkdkdk uio-poop. lhdgdgk Fin'l Services kj E. er, agency.

ACCOUNTANT STAFF
Mdtn SS co seeks coll grad w/2-3 yrs exp public exp. Steamship exp. very desirable Excel. fringe bnfts. Send resume & sal desired kdjkjki xcbidi.

Accounting Trainees $8M
NO EXPERIENCE NECESS. Should have basic college acctg (6 credits). FREE TUITION for Nite Students
FEE PAID Call: ieie dkdkd hgiisi Agency we John St. qwoixji

ACCOUNTING $10-11K FEE PAID
Major service org. seeks degreed indiv w 1 yr acctn/finance bkgrnd to work in budget area. Excellant bnfts & working conditions. Call hgf rinkdh at uyi-etei, nhgb Recruiting Systems, rew 5th Ave/ent. 45th St. (Agency).

ACCTG CLERKS $166-175
Some exp or college credits. Excel oppty to develop into Full Acctnt
FEE PAID Call: hghg opwqrm benernd Agency qw John St. ufti-oput

Acctg Clerk, $160-for midtown service firm. Min 1 yr exp. Coll credits prefd but not nec. Good training prog plus tuition. Mr. Hiidiciks at opo-utre. Wryghg Agency, we E 44/Mad. Fee Pd.

> For the past two summers I was employed by the park board under the supervision of Mr. Ruth, Director of Maintenance. Near the end of last summer, Mr. Ruth suggested that I apply for a regular position when I graduate in May.

Each of these openings consists of a straightforward reference to your source of information.

If the application is not solicited, the opening paragraph requires a different strategy. Since there's no "invitation" to refer to, you must secure the reader's attention by other means. Certainly, an unimaginative opening like the following is unlikely to excite much interest:

> I am submitting my résumé for your inspection in case you happen to have a job.

On the other hand, an opening like the following risks coming on so strong that it turns the prospective employer off at once:

> If, by chance, you are looking for someone to inject fresh blood into your firm and bring you the benefits of an up-to-the-minute business education, look no further. I'm your man. [Or, "I'm your woman."]

The approach must fall somewhere in between: neither too dull, nor too brash or gimmicky—yet original and positive enough to elicit favorable reaction. Here are two possible approaches:

> Your firm has often been mentioned at City College for its outstanding success with the Spanish-speaking community. As a major in accounting, with a Spanish-speaking background myself, I feel sure I could fill a position in your firm very effectively.
>
> Dr. Marilyn Harris [assumed here to be well known to the reader] has suggested that with my major in journalism, my editorship of the college paper, and my generally outgoing temperament, I would do well should you have an opening in your Community Relations Department.

To sum up: The opening paragraph should be brief, refer to the lead if solicited, be neither too dull nor too way-out if unsolicited, and identify the nature of your qualifications and the kind of job you are seeking.

Middle Paragraph The function of the middle paragraph or paragraphs, whether the application is solicited or not, is to highlight those portions of your résumé that represent your strongest qualifications relevant to the position. In so doing, it elaborates on qualifications already mentioned in the opening paragraph—yet not in such detail that the reader feels little need to refer to the résumé. On the contrary, having read your letter, he or she should feel impelled to study your résumé to satisfy him-or herself on the factual evidence in support of the general claims in your letter.

Closing Paragraph The principal aim of the closing paragraph is to secure an interview. The paragraph can be as simple as these:

> I shall be happy to come to St. Louis for an interview at your convenience.
>
> From Wednesday, May 12, through Saturday, the 15th, I shall be in Minneapolis attending the ASI Conference [this assumes your reader knows what ASI means; otherwise, use the full name] at the Hotel Leamington. During this time I would welcome the opportunity for an appointment with you if at all possible.
>
> Won't you please suggest a time when I can come to your office so we can discuss further how I can best contribute to your organization?

If your school address and home address are different, you can specify, "After April 29 I may be reached at _____; telephone _____." Of course, if this information is in the résumé, there is no need to repeat it here.

Style Everything that has been stressed above on creating a positive image in a letter applies with double force to the letter of application.

Remember: until you have your interview, your letter is *you*. Thus, for a brief refresher, it may help to review these key points:

1. Give meticulous attention to appearance. Cheap-looking paper (16–20-pound bond is recommended), uneven margins, unsightly erasures, or unclean type are almost certain to eliminate you at the outset from being considered. For your signature, use blue, blue-black, or black ink.

2. Convey a positive tone. Being apologetic, sounding uncertain, or failing to stress your key strengths are unlikely to create the image of a prospective employee who would have much to offer.

3. Use a you-attitude. Your prospective employer is more interested in what you can do for the company than in what the company can do for you. (For this reason, discussion of salary and other benefits should be deferred to the interview—and late in the interview at that.)

4. Give attention to your reader's sense of self-esteem. Use enough "I's" to sound human, yet not so many as to sound conceited. In highlighting your strengths, avoid giving the impression that you have all the answers. Be courteous, but avoid sounding subservient. What the recipient already knows, de-emphasize; for instance, don't write, "Your company is now in a strong growth trend" (which he or she doubtless knows better than you). Subordinate the point instead; for example, "Because your company is now in a strong growth trend . . ."). Do *not* use a form letter of application; each letter should be an original typed copy adapted to this one recipient alone.

5. Write in a natural, informal style. Avoid the extremes of being either too formal or too chummy.

6. Maintain a high quality of writing. An opening sentence, "I have been adviced to write you . . ." can elicit a negative response right away. *Proofread carefully*. Then have someone with a keen eye for good writing proofread it as well. And be absolutely certain of the recipient's name and position (if addressing a person). A letter intended for Dr. Lorraine Bagwell, Dean of Academic Affairs, may never be read if the inside address begins "Dr. Loren Bugwell, Chairman of Academic Affairs." She may or may not be vain, but she *is* interested in candidates who take pains to be correct. If directories or other sources fail to yield the correct information, call the person's secretary, who will be quite willing to provide the correct spelling and title.

Parts of the Letter   Include all six of the standard parts described above. A letter beginning simply "Dear Sir" (with no heading or inside address) is unlikely to receive much attention. Yet I've seen more than one such letter, written by applicants presumably serious in their quest for a job.

If you do not know the name of the recipient, address it, for instance:

Director, Personnel Department
ABC Company
492 North Michigan Avenue
Denver, CO 80210

Dear Sir:

The only supplementary part ordinarily used is "Enclosure" (for the résumé). If someone else types the letter, the identifying initials should, of course, be shown. If the letter goes past one page, a second-page heading should be included; normally, a letter of application ought not exceed a single page.

Figure 10.13 is an example of a letter of application.

The Personal Résumé

The personal résumé, often called a "vita" (pronounced "veeta"), is a compilation of all the data concerning an applicant that would likely be of interest to a prospective employer. Since each résumé is a verbal portrait of the person it describes, no two résumés will be quite alike, either in substance or style. However, résumés generally include information concerning most or all of the following categories:

1. Name, address, telephone number (including area code). If the applicant's address and telephone number will be different following graduation, these should be given, too.

2. Date on which the résumé was written (to indicate how up to date it is).

3. Application photo (cannot be legally required, but may be desirable if it's an attractive shot); may be printed on résumé, or—less desirable—attached with a paper clip.

4. Career objective.

5. Education (beginning with the most recent)—degree(s), college(s), major and minor, grade point average, dates of attendance.

6. Job experience (beginning with the most recent)—kind of job, name of company, location, dates of employment.

7. Awards and achievements—school or community.

8. Personal data—age, height, weight, health, marital status, number of children (if any), military status, hobbies.

9. References—three to five, including usually one or more professors in one's major field and one or more employers, together with title, position, address, and telephone number (including area code).

These categories are usually arranged in roughly the order shown above. Variations may include placing personal data near the beginning along with name and address, or awards and achievements in the education category. In general, a younger person with little job experience will list education ahead of jobs, while an older person will list job experience

FIGURE 10.13
Sample Letter of
Application

519 River Drive, Apt. B-2
Columbus, OH 43402
January 25, 1977

Mr. Mark Iott, Operations Manager
Great Lakes Marketing Associates, Inc.
4334 Central Avenue
Toledo, OH 43615

Dear Mr. Iott:

A family friend, Ms. Loreen Berry, of Toledo Survey Services, Inc., has told me that you are looking for a client service representative to join your firm around April 1. I feel sure I could do an excellent job in meeting your needs.

As you can see from the attached résumé, I shall graduate from Ohio State in March with a major in marketing and minors in psychology and sociology. With strong interests in these fields, along with considerable experience in working successfully with people, I feel I could represent Great Lakes effectively in serving present clients and in selling your services to new clients. The references listed on the résumé will gladly testify to my qualifications for this kind of work.

I would welcome an opportunity for us to discuss further in person how my ambitions and interests could contribute to Great Lake's already solid reputation in market research. Please write or call as to when I may make an appointment. I shall be happy to drive to Toledo any time for a meeting at your convenience.

                                        Sincerely yours,

                                        Lyman A. Atwater

                                        Lyman A. Atwater

Enclosure: Personal Résumé

ahead of education. In any case, the categories should be arranged in the order most advantageous to the applicant.

As with the letter of application, appearance is of utmost importance. It will pay to experiment as much as necessary to achieve the most attractive layout in terms of spacing, indenting, centering, headings, and columns. The résumé should be typed, error free (clear type, preferably with a carbon ribbon for a cleaner, sharper image) on $8\frac{1}{2} \times 11$ good quality paper. Copies (have 20–30 run off) should be of high quality—Xerox or comparable process. For an especially attractive résumé, you may wish to have it printed, though, of course, the expense will be greater. If there are two or more pages, they should be numbered (upper right corner) and stapled carefully (upper left corner) with all sheets perfectly aligned. (Do not leave sharp staple ends protruding for the reader to snag a finger on.)

Figure 10.14 illustrates most of the points discussed above. However, this example should not be considered a model, since each person's résumé should reflect his or her own individuality, and each letter of application should be adapted to the particular situation.

Mailing the Letter of Application and Résumé Yours may be but one of literally dozens of applications. If so, how can you be sure that yours will stand out? You can't, of course; but such tactics as these may help:

1. Mailing your letter and résumé in a 9×12 envelope.
2. Sending your application special delivery.
3. If not special delivery, getting your application in as early as possible—if convenient, even delivering it personally.

There is no need to include a reply envelope. Few firms expect one, preferring to use their own stationery anyway.

Further Correspondence Don't feel that your correspondence is over when you mail your application. If you receive a request for an interview, reply promptly to confirm that you will be there (unless, of course, your reply would not arrive until after the appointment).

Following the interview, write immediately again, if for no other reason than to say thanks for their interest and time. Perhaps at the same time you can offer additional information about yourself that your résumé did not contain nor the interview bring out. If you were given a company brochure to take home (as is often the case), you can comment favorably, though briefly, on it.

If, following your letter of application you have not heard after a couple of weeks, do not hesitate to write (or call), inquiring whether it actually has arrived. Such a letter should be brief—and tactful.

Finally, if you are offered the job, reply again promptly, expressing your appreciation, confirming your acceptance, and attending to any other relevant details. If you are not offered the job, write anyway thanking them for their consideration.

FIGURE 10.14 Personal Résumé

Personal Résumé

LYMAN A. ATWATER
January 21, 1977

Application Photo

Personal

Birthdate:	November 28, 1955	Birthplace:	Twinsburg, Ohio
Height:	5'9"	Weight:	150
Marital Status:	Single	Military Status:	I-H
College Address:	519 River Dr., Apt. B-2 Columbus, OH 43202	Home Address:	2735 Fairmount Avenue Cleveland, OH 44112
Telephone:	(614) 269-4364	Telephone:	(216) 523-4702

Career Objective

Sales position with a market research firm providing experience in handling accounts with a wide variety of client firms. Would like eventually to advance to managerial responsibilities; perhaps eventually own my own market research company.

Education

A.B. (March, 1977) in business administration; major in marketing (GPA: 3.4); minors in psychology and sociology (GPA: 3.2).

Courses leading to an understanding of marketing in today's world.

Marketing	Marketing Theory	Retailing
Managerial Marketing	Channels of Distribution	Consumer Behavior
Marketing Research	Advertising	

Courses related to marketing:

    Business Administration:
      Principles of Management
      Administrative Behavior
      Managerial Finance

    Sociology:
      Problems in Quantitative Analysis
      Problems in Qualitative Analysis
      Demographic Analysis
      Population Studies

    Psychology:
      Motivation
      Learning and Thinking
      Social Psychology
      Organizational Psychology
      Human Performance
      Research Methodology

FIGURE 10.14 (continued)

<u>Extra-Curricular Activities</u>

Alpha Kappa Psi (Professional business fraternity): Treasurer, two semesters.

Interests include: tennis, water skiing, travel, music.

<u>Work Experience During College</u>

(Proportion of college expense earned: 75 percent)

September, 1974-present:	Ohio State University Catering Service
September, 1976-present:	Student Manager (in charge of approximately 50 waiters; includes supervising banquets, scheduling, hiring, and discharging personnel)
September, 1975-March, 1976:	Banquet Supervisor
September, 1974-March, 1975:	Waiter
Summers, 1973-1976:	Salesman, Tom Elliott Shoe Store, Cleveland

<u>References</u>

Dr. Stanley R. Auston,
Professor of Marketing
College of Administrative Science
Ohio State University
Columbus, OH 43210
Telephone: (614) 422-0043

Mr. Thomas Elliott, Jr., Owner
Tom Elliott Shoe Store
108 Erie Avenue
Cleveland, OH 44114
Telephone: (216) 942-7100

Mrs. Marian Stronheim
Supervising Manager
Ohio State University Catering Service
Columbus, OH 43210
Telephone: (614) 422-2340

Credentials may be obtained from:

                Placement Service
                Ohio State University
                Columbus, OH 43210

A Few Parting Words A personnel director recently listed some "errors of commission and omission" he has noted in applications. These are worth sharing:[8]

1. Don't apply for positions for which you are not qualified academically or by experience.

2. Don't get carried away and send voluminous heavy enclosures (e.g., a research paper)—unless you're willing for them to be thrown away.

3. Keep your résumé up to date so it includes your latest employment, marital status, and so forth.

4. Be sure your list of work experience is complete and accurate. Do not leave unexplained gaps.

5. If the company requires you to complete an application form, be sure it jibes with your résumé. Do not enter "Refer to résumé" when the résumé does not contain the information requested.

One final word: There is no assurance that your application—no matter how well written—will lead to an interview. But the more interviews you have, the greater the odds that sooner or later you will find what you want.

MEMOS

Function

Memos are a form of internal communication. Their function is to provide others, in writing, with information useful to the ongoing operations of an organization. Common examples of memos include announcements, reminders, inquiries, and clarification.

Memos move in all directions: from supervisor to subordinate, subordinate to supervisor, equal to equal—at any and all levels of the organization. However, it should be added that they move downward more readily than upward; also, that if the information in a memo moves either up or down more than one level, it may be modified in the process, with some resultant falloff in original meaning.

Form

In addition to the message itself, the essential elements of a memo are: subject heading, receiver's name or distribution list, date, and sender's name.

Usually the memo has blanks at the top (each company has its own form) to be filled in for specifying the subject, receiver(s), and date. Also included may be a blank for the sender's name. Including the sender's name at the top is especially important if the memo runs more than one page, so the reader can see at once who the sender is. If the memo is all on one page, placing the sender's name at the end is quite satisfactory. The memo need not necessarily be signed, but if it is, this indicates (presumably) that the sender has read it after it was typed.

A typical memo heading (not filled in) looks like this:

    SUBJECT: DATE:
    TO: FROM:

Content and Style

Several characteristics of memos having to do with content and style deserve emphasis. These include informality, relevance, completeness, and tact.

Informality Memos range in tone from extremely informal to fairly formal. For instance, a memo to a colleague (who is not in at the moment), in the form of a note left on his desk, might look like Figure 10.15 (with the reply included).

On the other hand, the wider the readership and the more important the subject, the more formal the memo will be. For example, a memo from the president officially announcing a long-rumored merger of two major divisions within the organization will be very carefully worded and fairly formal.

In general, however, memos tend toward informality. More often than not, the writer is writing under pressure, on subjects of routine concern, to persons he or she sees frequently. So memo writing as a rule is less concerned with formalities than with "getting the job done." Thus, the "Dear ____" and "Sincerely yours" found in letters are dispensed with.

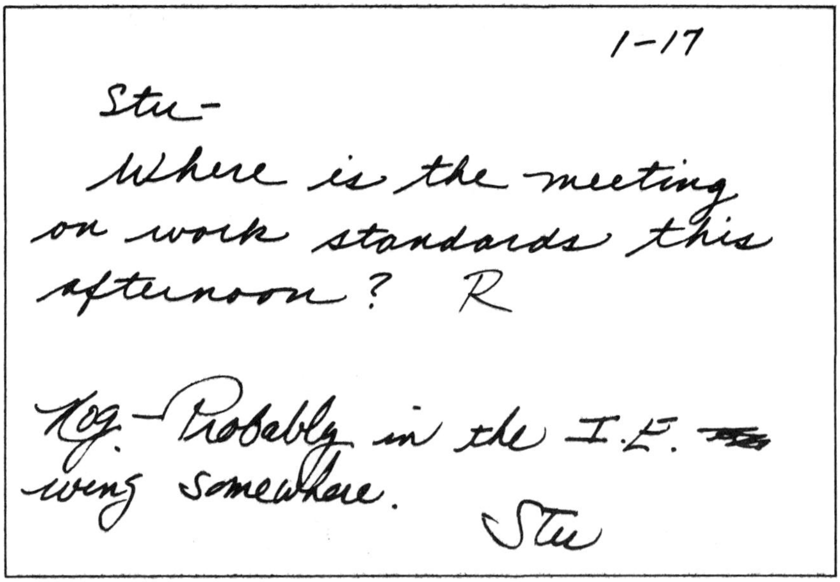

FIGURE 10.15
Informal Memo

1-17

Stu—
Where is the meeting on work standards this afternoon? R

Rog.— Probably in the I.E. wing somewhere.
Stu

The tone is typically more casual and personal than in a report or proposal (see Chapter 11, "Writing Effective Reports and Proposals").

Relevance   What is relevant in a memo is determined by the subject heading, which should therefore be precise:

> *Too broad:*   Manpower
> *Sufficiently precise:*   Manpower Needs in Dept. 12-A, 1977

Because the primary concern in a memo is with getting the job done, the memo should contain only what is relevant to the subject heading. The following passage recording the writer's moods—even though the subject might be "Indoctrination Procedure for New Employees"—would be irrelevant:

> Monday was a day I'll long remember . . . my first day on my new job! Eagerly I arrived at 7:30, only to discover that in my haste I'd left my new office keys at home, so back through the traffic I drove, hoping against hope I'd not be late my first day.

Entertaining as this might be in a letter "back home," it has little relevance to the subject at hand.

Relevance implies, too, that even though a passage may be task-oriented, if it is not related to the subject at hand, it belongs instead in another memo. Thus, the two subjects of (a) a revised shipping procedure and (b) a retirement party would demand two different memos.

Completeness   Information in a memo should be sufficiently complete for the needs of the reader.

One all-too-common omission is the date. Suppose two memos, either or both undated, are issued by the personnel department concerning sick leave procedures. The employee files these in a folder, then six months later has occasion to refer to the subject. Which memo is later (and therefore more up to date)? All kinds of inconvenience could conceivably result from the simple omission of the date. *Memos always should be dated.* (If the memo concerns a telephone call received, the exact time should be recorded as well.)

Other common omissions result from failure to answer questions of the who? what? when? where? why? how? variety. For example:

> There will be a meeting Monday, May 9, of the Metric Committee in the green conference room.

When on Monday??? Or take this example:

> Please complete the attached form and return it to your foreman as soon as possible. The new safety glasses will be available July 15. The charge, payable to the cashier in the Payroll Office, will be $3.50.

If the "attached form" must first be stamped "Paid" by the cashier before being returned to the foreman, the misunderstanding caused by this procedure not being made clear can cause lost time and considerable irritation.

An extra minute's worth of time reviewing the memo *from the reader's point of view* can easily save a great deal of inconvenience and annoyance.

Tact Even though memos are primarily task-oriented, they ought not be tactless. If the reader feels put on the defensive, his or her emotions quickly interfere with any rational, positive response. Reflect, for example, on your own probable reaction to such assertions as these:

> I am getting very tired of the lousy cooperation I'm getting around this place.
>
> The situation is getting worse, and somebody besides me is to blame.

Such outbursts may help the writer air his or her feelings, but are unlikely to solve the problem.

Figure 10.16 illustrates the characteristics discussed above.

FIGURE 10.16
Sample Memo. (Dan Evans, Jr. Used with permission of author.)

GENERAL MOTORS INSTITUTE

```
SUBJECT:  Copy Center                    DATE:  February 28, 1974

TO:   All Institute Personnel


Effective March 4, 1974, the Copy Center will open in its new
location, Room 1-706D A.B.

HOURS:   7:30 a.m. to 4:45 p.m.  Monday thru Thursday
         7:30 a.m. to 4:30 p.m.  Friday


Each job requested from the Copy Center must be accompanied
by a "Copy Center Request" form GMI-243, available in supply
Friday, March 1.

All Copy Center work will be printed with black ink on a good
quality white bond paper on one side only. Work to be
```

printed on two sides should be requested on a Printing Order; it will then be run on a tandem press that prints both sides at the same time. Collating can be done simultaneously to a maximum of 100 sets of not more than 50 sheets per set. Larger orders must be requested on a Printing Order. Maximum number of copies of any one original will be 300 sheets.

HELPFUL HINTS TO THE SECRETARY:

1. Type on a standard white bond paper.

2. A clean typewriter and a good ribbon will produce sharper copy.

3. Signatures will reproduce best if signed with a black pen.

4. Make corrections by using white correction fluid or correction tape.

Most requests can be handled on a "While you wait" basis; collating and stapling will, of course, take longer. Please arrange your work to allow us as much time as possible on longer collating and stapling jobs.

SECURITY:

There will be no students in the Copy Center. When tests or other confidential material is printed, all scrap and masters will be shredded. If tests are to be delivered they will be wrapped before delivery.

TRANSPARENCIES—GMI Personnel:

A transparency maker will be available in the Copy Center for Faculty and Staff use.

TRANSPARENCIES—Student:

Students make a great many transparencies for use in class presentations so arrangements have been made for them to use the transparency maker located in Audio Visual, Room 2-337 A.B.

Dan Evans, Jr.

SUMMARY

1. A prime consideration in letter writing, as opposed to other forms of writing, is that of creating a positive image. Factors which contribute to a positive image include: (a) being prompt, (b) giving attention to appearance, (c) conveying a positive tone, (d) using a you-attitude, (e) giving attention to the reader's sense of self-esteem, (f) writing in a natural, informal style, and (g) maintaining a high quality of writing.

2. A business letter conventionally consists of six standard parts: heading, inside address, salutation, body, complimentary close, and signature. In addition, there are at least seven supplementary parts that may be used depending on the situation.

3. The three most common formats for business letters are the semiblock, modified semiblock, and full block. A fourth, the simplified format, has failed thus far to gain general acceptance. In addition, various formats are in use to meet specialized needs.

4. The letter of application and personal résumé are designed to go hand in hand, the first being more general; the second, more specific. The objective of the two together is to secure an interview that could result in a job.

5. Memos constitute an important form of internal communication and have the function of providing information useful to ongoing operations within the organization. Characteristics of memos include (a) use of a memo heading, (b) a generally informal style, (c) relevance of content to the subject heading, (d) sufficient completeness of information, and (e) tact.

SUGGESTED APPLICATIONS

1. You have received a final grade of D in a course in which you had expected to receive a B. You are very upset, as are your parents. Upon your return to campus you try to make an appointment, but discover that the professor is on leave as guest lecturer for the semester at another school several hundred miles distant. Write a letter to resolve the discrepancy, hopefully to your satisfaction.

2. You are a field service representative for an auto manufacturer with about two dozen dealerships in your area. Recently, one of your oldest and most successful dealers has decided to build a brand new dealership. He sends you a copy of the blueprints drawn up by a local architect, and immediately you note that the plans are badly conceived. The showroom is too long and narrow, the owner's office is too big and the salespeople's offices too small, there is no adequate waiting room for customers, and the exterior design is a generation behind the times. In fact, you are certain that he has paid no attention to a brochure you sent about a year

ago containing guidelines for any dealer planning to rebuild or remodel. Write a letter (less than a page) in which you seek to remedy the situation before it is too late.

3. Write a reply to the following letter, just received, which your boss has turned over to you to handle:

> 513 S. Bassett St.
> Pewaukee, Wis. 53072
> Feb. 16, 1977
>
> Melody House, Inc.
> 800 Kiowa Lane
> Iowa City, Iowa 52740
>
> Dear Sir;
>   I saw your add a few weeks ago in a magazine for a Secret System that you said I could learn how to play a guitar in only one week. Well, my son had a guitar he never used anymore and it was just setting in the closet gathering dust so I decided I might as well order your Secret System.
>   Well, your system must be pretty secret alright because I don't think its any good. I have studied the chords in all those photographs and charts and diagrams and they don't make head nor tail to me. You claim I could learn a song a day and after 3 weeks I've learned only part of one song.
>   So I think your advertising is totaly misleading and should be looked into by the postal athorities. I demand a full refund of the full 5.98 plus .50 postage I paid plus, for that matter, the thirteen cents for the two letters I sent—thats a total of 6.72. If I don't get it all back I am going to write the magazine for carrying false advertising.
>
> Very truly yours
>
> Amos Scott
>
> P. S. I am returning your Secret System under seperate—after I get my refund

4. A professional society you belong to holds monthly dinner meetings at which the main feature is usually a speaker from this particular profession. Recently you have learned from a friend that a nationally known figure in your field will be lecturing at a university about 60 miles away the same afternoon as the date for your dinner meeting two months from now. If you could somehow persuade this person to attend your meeting as the main speaker that evening, it would be the highlight of the year. Write a letter to persuade the person to accept your invitation. (Note: Your treasury will permit an honorarium of $50.)

5. Write a letter to King Cole Novelties, 2980 Canhan Avenue, Seattle, WA 98164, ordering favors for an annual banquet that an organization you belong to is holding in six weeks. The favors you have in mind are miniature gavels with the organization name and "Annual Banquet, 19__" imprinted on the head. You're not certain of the price, but another organization you know of ordered similar gavels a year ago for $1.45 each.

6. Select an advertisement from the "Help Wanted" section of the classified ads in a newspaper and write a letter of application. Draw up a personal résumé (supplying fictitious—though realistic—data as needed) to accompany the letter.

7. Assume that you are a supervisor and have become aware of a widespread practice of employees using copiers for their own personal business. Income tax forms, church programs, kids' library paper, and who knows what are being duplicated by the score. And all of it is costing a pretty penny, not to mention time being squandered in this piracy. So, feeling that this practice has gotten way out of hand, you decide to write a memo to put an end to it. (Adapted from Marvin H. Swift, "Clear Writing Means Clear Thinking Means . . ." *Harvard Business Review,* January-February, 1973, pp. 59–62.)

8. You are head of a department of salaried employees in which your people are expected to put in a full eight-hour day. Lately, you have been noticing increased laxity in observing the rules. Some workers are straggling in 10–30 minutes late; some arrive on time but then head for the cafeteria for breakfast. Others are taking longer lunch hours than allowed, while still others are leaving 20 minutes to half an hour early once or twice a week. At the same time, you notice that work output for the department is down from a year ago. You decide to write a memo in an effort to get the department to "shape up."

9. You have been a member of an engineering design department for about five years and have progressed very satisfactorily. About a year and a half ago a young man not long out of college, Ed Jones, joined your department. Ed is outgoing, friendly, a real "go-getter," and it is obvious that your boss, Mr. Smithereens, is quite impressed with him. In fact, you've seen Smithereens having lunch with Ed frequently in the cafeteria and have heard him comment more than once on the "bright future" he feels Ed has. However, you do not trust Ed. At least twice you have known him to include others' ideas in his conversations or formal reports as if they were his own, without giving credit to the source. Furthermore, you have heard by the grapevine that in his first job following graduation he was asked to leave, and that the glowing letter of recommendation from his former employer was really a means of getting rid of him. Now you are asked by Smithereens to write an evaluation of Ed that can be used in considering him for a promotion with increased responsibilities.

NOTES

[1] Bob Levoy, "The Power of Expectation," *Meetings and Conventions*, September, 1975, pp. 34 and 178.

[2] John H. Harwood, *The Responsive Business Letter,* Pontiac Motor Division, General Motors Corporation, Pontiac, Michigan, 1970, p. 9.

[3] *Ibid.*, p. 14.

[4] Walter Weir, *On the Writing of Advertising* (New York: McGraw-Hill Book Company, 1969).

[5] J. H. Menning and C. W. Wilkinson, *Communicating through Letters and Reports*, 5th ed. (Homewood, Ill.: Richard D. Irwin, Inc., 1972), p. 37.

[6] J. Harold Janis, "A Rationale for the Use of Common Business-Letter Expressions," *Journal of Business Communication,* October, 1966, pp. 3–11.

[7] From "Secretarial Addressing for Automation," United States Postal Service, August, 1974.

[8] James Northway. Used with permission of author.

11 WRITING EFFECTIVE REPORTS AND PROPOSALS

REPORTS AND PROPOSALS IN THE BUSINESS WORLD
Reports
    Function Served in Business by Reports   Characteristics
Proposals
    Function   Characteristics
Reports and Proposals: A Passing Comment

REAL WORLD VS. VERBAL WORLD
Factual Statements
    Nature of Factual Statements
    Suggested Guidelines for Making Factual Statements
Inferences
    Nature of Inferences
    Suggested Guidelines for Making Sound Inferences
Value Judgments
    Nature of Value Judgments
    Suggested Guidelines for Offering Value Judgments
The Objectivity-Subjectivity Continuum
Suggested Guidelines in Choosing Language
The Verbal World and the Real World: A Closing Word

A CLASSIFICATION OF REPORTS AND PROPOSALS

THE COMPONENTS OF A FORMAL REPORT OR PROPOSAL
Cover
Title Page
    Elements   The Title
Memo or Letter of Transmittal
Abstract
    Function   Types   Writing the Abstract
Table of Contents
    Function   Elements

Introduction
        Function   Elements   Organization   Style

Findings, Conclusions, and Recommendations
        What They Are and How They Differ
        Where They Are Located   Guidelines on Format

Discussion
        Content of the Discussion
        Style of Writing in the Discussion

Appendix

Footnotes
        Function   Frequency of Use in Business Writing
        Placement   Form

Bibliography

Distribution List

SAMPLE REPORTS AND PROPOSALS

Sample AVO

Sample Memorandum Report

Sample Memorandum Proposal

Sample Request

Sample Letter Report

Sample Formal Proposal

More than you may now realize, success in your career will depend on your proficiency in writing effective reports and proposals. At the conclusion of a report writing course in a plant several years ago, a senior executive nearing retirement declared, "I wish that this course had been made available to me at least 25 years ago. I am sure it would have had a marked beneficial influence upon my career."

    Depending on your job, you may write fewer reports and proposals than you do memos and letters. But chances are the ones you do write will be more demanding and require special skills beyond those needed in memos and letters. Thus, this chapter.

    The purpose of this chapter will be to (a) help you understand better what reports and proposals are used for in business, (b) offer some guidelines for effective reporting and proposing, and (c) explain the components and formats typically found in formal reports and proposals. By way of illustration, some sample reports and proposals will be included.

REPORTS AND PROPOSALS IN THE BUSINESS WORLD

Although reports and proposals are similar in appearance, they serve basically different functions. Understanding the difference is essential to using them effectively.

Reports

As mentioned in Chapter 1, the function of reports in general is to inform us of situations or events we are not in a position to observe directly for ourselves. Thus, we flip on the radio or glance through the newspaper and note that the Red Sox have lost again to the Tigers, the temperature in Chicago is 71°, IBM stock is up one-eighth, and the President is in California for a few days.

Such information differs in source from the knowledge, for instance, that we have a nasty headache, it's raining outside, and the bore down the hall has just walked into our room. Such knowledge we gain directly through perception by our own senses. But since it is literally impossible to be all places at all times, a vast amount of the information we "know" reaches us only indirectly through reports from others—or, often, reports of reports, reports of reports of reports, and so on.

Function Served in Business by Reports In business and industrial organizations, reports serve several purposes:

1. To provide management with information needed—either immediately or at some future time—for sound decision-making, or in informing others of decisions already made. Just as none of us can be all places at all times, so no one in management can either. Yet managers *must* keep informed on what is happening if they are to make intelligent decisions on company policy and operations—and intelligent decision-making, we must remember, is a critical responsibility of management. But the *only* way management can keep abreast of the bulk of information they need is indirectly through reports—short or long, informal or formal, oral or written. In simplest terms, reports serve as management's eyes and ears. In addition, managers report downward: policy decisions or operational procedures; while any of us may report horizontally to convey information to colleagues in our own or other departments.

2. To provide information "for the record": such as test reports of lab studies, minutes of meetings, or trip reports to suppliers. (Not only reports, but letters, proposals, and sometimes memos may also be filed for future reference.)

3. To serve as evidence in court cases. Sometimes this use is by the company. But often it is by others taking legal action *against* the company. Through what are known in law as "rules of discovery," reports may now be obtained from company files by government agencies (as, for

instance, the Federal Trade Commission or the Environmental Protection Agency), or by attorneys in product liability suits against the company.

Suppose, for example, you are a designer in a company that manufactures plastic toys, and your company is sued by the parents of a child who has lost the sight of an eye because one of your toys splintered in his face. The attorneys for the parents could obtain a court order requiring your company to supply them with any documents (drawings, memos, reports, and so on) having any bearing whatsoever on the design or manufacture of that product. The lawyers' objective, of course, would be to find evidence that your company was in some way negligent.

Failure to produce all such documents could subject your company to serious penalties, so it would be risky to destroy or try to hide them. One might suppose that if damaging passages of the reports could be deleted or altered, this would be advantageous to the company in the lawsuit. But such trickery could easily be exploited by the attorneys for the plaintiff to their own advantage. And if the reports had been inaccurate, incomplete, or distorted to begin with, they would have been worse than useless in the original production of the toy. So the importance of responsible, accurate reports from the start becomes evident.

Characteristics   An appreciation of the function served by reports on the job shows why the following characteristics are important:

1. *Accuracy*. Reporting the situation or event as it actually is or was.
2. *Objectivity*. Reporting the facts of the situation or event rather than one's biases or feelings about the facts.
3. *Completeness*. Reporting *all* the facts that are relevant.
4. *Selectivity*. Reporting *only* the facts that are relevant.
5. *Impartiality*. Reporting all or both sides. (This differs from objectivity, since one can be objective in reporting only one side.)
6. *Interpretation*. Providing background meaning where necessary for the reader's comprehension, or drawing legitimate conclusions to show what it "all adds up to."
7. *Clarity*. Explaining the situation or event in terms clear to the reader.

Proposals

Function   The purpose of a proposal is to persuade. More specifically, it seeks to secure authorization for some course of action (a new program, product line, purchase of new facilities, expansion of facilities, or whatever) that the proposer feels would benefit the company. Put differently, the writer is proposing a solution to a company problem. This implies, of course, informing the reader of the nature of the problem or need, and of the solution being proposed. Thus, proposals utilize the techniques of reporting, but in addition employ techniques of persuasion as well to achieve their objective. (A review of Chapter 9, "Persuading Your Reader or Listener," would be relevant here.)

A variation of a proposal is a request. The approach in either is basically the same, but whereas in a proposal the benefits are expected to accrue primarily to the company and only secondarily to the proposer, in a request the benefits are primarily for the proposer him- or herself. Common examples of requests are those asking for time off, permission to attend a conference, or for equipment needed in performing one's job.

Characteristics   Because proposals must inform as well as persuade, they require all the qualities of effective reports. However, the characteristics that distinguish proposals from reports are the following:

1. Showing the reason for the proposal by identifying and analyzing the problem or need the proposal is intended to remedy.
2. Explaining exactly what is being proposed.
3. Explaining how the proposal would remedy the problem or need.
4. Showing the benefits to the company, leaving no doubt that they would outweigh whatever the costs might be.

Reports and Proposals: A Passing Comment

Drawing a hard and fast line between reports and proposals is not easy. Expressed in broad terms, reports inform; proposals persuade. Yet, any report must at least persuade the reader that the information is accurate, while some reports go so far as to include recommendations which have the effect of persuading, yet are offered in the spirit of "This is what I would do if I were you, but it's your problem, not mine." Thus, as part of a report, you might recommend to your boss: "If you really want to get this new policy across, I would recommend that you first give everyone a copy, than follow up with a meeting."

Likewise, while any proposal aims at securing approval for some course of action, perhaps 80–90 percent of any proposal is informative: what the need is, what the alternatives are, the advantages and disadvantages. But the information is selected and arranged to support the ultimate objective: approval from the boss.

REAL WORLD VS. VERBAL WORLD

To gain further insight into the nature of reports and proposals, it will repay us to explore what is often known as the Verbal World, and its relationship to the Real World. The reason is that while reports and proposals form an important part of the Verbal World, their usefulness in business depends on how accurately they correspond with the Real World.

The Real World–Verbal World concept can be depicted by the model in Figure 11.1.

As indicated in this model, the Real World is the world of facts: objects, situations, events, and so on. For instance, this page is a fact; so is the

WRITING EFFECTIVE REPORTS AND PROPOSALS

FIGURE 11.1 Model of Real World Compared with Verbal World

	Objectivity ———————————————————————— Subjectivity			
Real World	Verbal World (Messages)			
	Factual Statements (Based on Observation)	*Inferences* (Conclusions Based on Reasoning)	*Value Judgments*	
Facts (Objects, Situations, Events, etc.)			Professional (Based on Facts, Reasoning, and Criteria)	Personal (Based on Bias)

chair you are sitting on (or bed you are lying on), the clothes you are wearing, the temperature surrounding you, or any sounds you can hear (or can't hear, for that matter). All matter, all motion, all sensations, all things that exist are part of the Real World.

The Verbal World (the world of words) comes into being the moment we start talking or writing about the Real World. Clearly, the two worlds are not the same. For instance, the word "apple" is obviously not the same as the object itself. A catalogue description of the courses you are enrolled in is not the same as the courses themselves—as you well know! "For sale, '72 Chevy, low mileage, clean" is not the same as the car itself. Indeed, the Verbal World may bear little resemblance to the Real World it represents. And, of course, the less the resemblance, the less useful it is.

From Figure 11.1 you will note that the Verbal World consists of three kinds of content: factual statements, inferences, and value judgments. For writing effective reports or proposals, it is important to understand each of these along with the guidelines suggested below for formulating them.

Factual Statements

The part of the Verbal World closest to the Real World consists of factual statements.

Nature of Factual Statements Factual statements tell "what is" and are based on direct observation. "This page is white" is a factual statement. "The room is warm" is another. However, it must be understood—as illustrated especially by the second example—that strictly speaking we never report facts as such, but only our own perceptions of the facts. Thus, five people may witness an accident and offer five different versions of what happened. Their reports are not of the accident itself (the "real world"), but rather of their perceptions of the accident—what each of them saw or heard.

The extent to which one's report of a situation or event matches the Real World depends on a number of conditions:

1. Having sufficient time and opportunity to observe the situation directly; a fleeting glance may not be enough.
2. Possessing a sound sense of vision, hearing, and so on (aided, perhaps, by such devices as gauges, thermometers, speedometers, and stethoscopes).
3. Freedom from internal or external distractions (a state of nervousness; a sudden loud noise).
4. Ability to understand the significance of what one observes (realizing, for instance, that "P-2" on a survey questionnaire form is a code meaning "Packaging Group No. 2).
5. Ability to observe objectively, free from personal biases, prejudices, desires, or anxieties.
6. Ability to use language accurately.

To the degree that any of these conditions is lacking, the accuracy of one's factual statements (that is, the report) describing the Real World will be lessened.

Suggested Guidelines for Making Factual Statements Special guidelines to keep in mind in making factual statements include these:

1. Report the facts objectively as observed and measured. Reporting objectively means reporting on the *object* itself (hence, "objectively") rather than on one's feelings about the object. To illustrate:

Objective Factual Statements	Subjective Factual Statements
The temperature is 93 degrees and the humidity 97 percent.	The room is unbearably stuffy.
Five students out of 35 received a passing grade on the exam.	The results of the exam were disastrous.

2. Report *all* the relevant facts, regardless of whether they (a) fit preconceived notions or biases or (b) appear positive or negative. If, for instance, you were attempting to persuade your boss to purchase X brand of office equipment instead of Y, you would not be providing him or her with a complete picture of the Real World if you failed to include that X brand has a much higher maintenance cost than Y brand. Nor would you be giving your supervisor an accurate impression if you told him or her that all employees in the department were happy with their vacation schedules when two of them have complained to you how unhappy they are. You might be a good "yes" person, but not an accurate reporter, and in the long run your credibility would suffer.

3. Put the facts into perspective. Reporting that a given metal has a 3.4 percent sulphur content is of little value unless the reader understands that a range of 2.7 to 3.8 percent is acceptable. Otherwise, the fact by itself may do little more than prompt the question, "Is this good or bad?"

Inferences

The second kind of content in the Verbal World consists of inferences.

Nature of Inferences. Inferences are conclusions drawn through reasoning from facts or from other inferences. Whereas factual statements are based on observation and can be made only *after* the observation, inferences are based on reasoning and can be made *any* time, before or after. In reports and proposals, inferences are the conclusions the data "adds up to." (In common usage, conclusions often include value judgments as well as inferences. For example, someone may "conclude" that Jackson is a "fine fellow." However, we shall use "conclusion" to refer only to inferences. When an evaluation is offered, we shall use the term "value judgment.")

The narrow distinction between inferences and factual statements is illustrated by a story told about Cordell Hull, Secretary of State under Franklin Roosevelt. Hull was traveling by train back to Washington with a friend, when the latter, looking out the window, noticed a flock of sheep grazing on the hillside. Seeking to impress Hull with his power of observation, the friend remarked, "I see that these sheep have been recently shorn." Hull studied a moment, then replied, "On *this* side, anyway!"

The difference between factual statements and inferences is further clarified by examples such as the following:

Factual Statement	*Inference*
The inspection sample shows a scrap rate of 2.6 percent.	Scrap for the whole run will probably not exceed 3 percent. (Generalizing from a limited number of instances.)
The cost of steel has risen.	The cost of automobiles will rise. (Reasoning from cause to effect.)
Grievances in Dept. X are high.	Evidently the supervisor can't get along with the employees. (Reasoning from effect to cause.)
The sign on the door says, "Dir. of Quality Control."	Office of the Director of Quality Control. (Reasoning from the sign.)
Computer programming has cut production costs at Plant X.	Computer programming would probably cut costs at our plant. (Reasoning from analogy.)

Note that in these examples factual statements are more nearly *certainties,* while inferences are only *probabilities.* In other words, there is greater certainty that factual statements will correspond to the Real

World than that inferences will. However, the sounder one's observation and reasoning, the stronger the probability that one's inferences will also correspond with the Real World.

Suggested Guidelines for Making Sound Inferences Since inferences are the product of observation and reasoning, suggested guidelines for making sound inferences include the following:

1. Observe the conditions just discussed for making accurate observations.

2. Observe the relevant suggestions from Chapter 9, "Persuading Your Reader or Listener," for strengthening the logic of the message:

    a. Offer sufficient proof to support your claims. A conclusion (or inference), for example, that "the fire probably would not have occurred if a different type of wiring had been used" is of little value without factual evidence to support it. Likewise, such a prediction as, "Unless flame retardants are added, catastrophic results are likely to occur," is useless without careful data to support it.

    b. Avoid unsound or hasty generalizations. An inference that a new type of food mix would "go over big because our family is just crazy about it" is unreliable because it generalizes from too small a sample ("our family") to the whole buying public.

    c. Avoid unsound analogies or comparisons. Just because a new bonus plan at Company M has reduced labor unrest there does not necessarily prove that a similar bonus plan at Company N would have comparable results. Conditions at the two companies may be far too dissimilar.

    d. Avoid unsound causal reasoning. If production has declined since Supervisor O'Hare took over, it does not mean necessarily that O'Hare is to blame. It might be the quality of production stock instead, or some other factor.

    e. Make your conclusions explicit. Facts do *not* necessarily speak for themselves. Simply giving data to your supervisor that you can no longer keep up with your workload since he increased it last month may not make the point that you need an assistant unless you make this point explicit. He may conclude that you're not quite up to it, and give the job to someone else instead.

3. Finally, offer conclusions only when it is within your professional competence to do so. This is a difficult guideline to adhere to, for we live in a society that seems to expect us to have a ready opinion on almost any subject that comes up—politics, the economy, the environment, race relations, international relations, how to raise children, how to treat criminals, and so on without end. It takes a brave person to say simply, "I don't have an opinion."

    Yet, in accurate, responsible report and proposal writing, this is exactly the attitude the writer should take, *unless the subject is within his or her area of professional expertise.* Specialists usually understand this; an obstetrician will be unlikely to offer opinions on one's hearing problems, or a hearing specialist on having babies—even though each of these specialists is an M.D. It is only the nonspecialist who is quick to rush in with opinions on all subjects from A to Z—a temptation we should guard against scrupulously. It is quite legitimate—indeed desirable—to *raise questions* when one is not sure, but not to offer opinions unless one is qualified by training or experience to do so.

Value Judgments

The part of the Verbal World farthest removed from the Real World consists of value judgments.

Nature of Value Judgments A value judgment is—rather obviously—a statement that evaluates. Something is good or bad, desirable or undesirable. In other words, a judgment places a *value* or rating on something, either by itself ("Rimmerstein is a good supervisor") or in comparison with something else ("Rimmerstein is a better supervisor than Ingleschmidt").

One kind of value judgment often found in reports and proposals is a recommendation. For instance, "We should hire a second secretary" implies that doing so would be desirable. (However, "A second secretary is needed" is not a value judgment; only a conclusion, or inference. Such a statement does not say that one *should* be hired; there may not be enough money, or there may be no space to house one.)

From the Real World–Verbal World Model, you may note that value judgments fall in two categories: professional and personal. Professional judgments are based on observation or reasoning, along with generally accepted criteria (standards), or criteria convincingly developed from one's expertise. Such judgments are the kind one would expect from a doctor, lawyer, plumber, electrician, accountant, scientist, and so forth—as long as the judgment concerns a subject in his or her field. Basically objective, these judgments reflect the best thinking of the person, regardless of personal preference.

Personal judgments, on the other hand, spring primarily from the person's bias, with only such observation and reasoning being employed as help support that bias. An interesting feature of personal value judgments is that they tend to reveal more about the person judging than about the thing being judged. The employee who grumbles, "The company is out to gyp you every chance they can," (an implied judgment) reveals more about him- or herself than he or she does about the company.

Suggested Guidelines for Offering Value Judgments Three guidelines to keep in mind in offering value judgments are these:

1. Avoid making value judgments not supported by sufficient evidence and sound reasoning. Thus, a recommendation that space in the parking lot should be reallocated should be based on such factors as (a) an investigation of the number of cars in various categories (workers, supervisors, visitors) now occupying the parking spaces, and (b) conclusions as to the actual needs of the drivers and passengers of these cars.

2. Avoid making value judgments that are beyond your immediate scope of professional competence. You would not expect your math professor to offer medical advice; nor your neighbor, the plumber, to offer legal advice. So should you avoid offering opinions in areas outside your own field of expertise—for instance, on the economic outlook if you are not an economist, or on computer technology if this is not your field.

3. Avoid offering value judgments prompted by personal bias or preference instead of sound evidence and reasoning. Offering value judgments based on either incompetence or prejudice is irresponsible, partially because the consequences can be so adverse. A remark that "Hiring women and minorities only spells bad news" can do irreparable harm to the many candidates who do possess the needed qualifications. Or a declaration by Mr. Big Brass that "As long as I'm boss we'll have none of this participative management nonsense around here" can result in loss of motivation, even active rebellion harmful to the company.

A special temptation, sometimes difficult to avoid, is the biased judgment born of sheer frustration. An executive illustrated this point with a sentence in a letter from one of his field service representatives: "This design is asinine. No engineer in his right mind would ever design anything like this!" Evidently the field service representative had been trying in vain to call attention to some fault in a product, and finally in desperation had written the above. He succeeded in getting through all right, but it was unfortunate he had to resort to such extreme rhetoric. Such an utterance, if it ever should appear in a product liability suit against the company, could be acutely embarrassing—both to the company and to him.

The Objectivity-Subjectivity Continuum

In the Real World–Verbal World Model (Fig. 11.1), you will note across the top a dotted line stretched between the words "Objectivity" at the left end to "Subjectivity" at the right. This to remind us that only in the Real World (the world of objects) do we find complete objectivity.

When we make factual statements, we become at least slightly subjective as to what we observe, what we fail to observe, how we interpret what we observe, and the language we use in describing what we observe.

Inferences are subject to all the subjective factors just listed, plus any resulting from any weaknesses in our reasoning (hasty generalization, faulty analogy, and so on).

Finally, value judgments are vulnerable to all the subjective factors involved in making factual statements and inferences, plus those based on whatever criteria or standards we rely on in arriving at our judgments. Thus, a designer will tend to evaluate a product in terms of appearance, an accountant in terms of return on investment, a production supervisor in terms of ease of manufacturing, a salesperson in terms of sales appeal, and so on. No matter what criteria are used, they inject an additional degree of subjectivity.

The greater the objectivity—that is, congruence with the Real World—the better. Such congruence is an ideal that seldom if ever can be achieved. But as long as we recognize the importance of objectivity in writing reports and proposals, and make an honest effort to achieve it, we will probably not stray far afield. It is only when our observations are careless, our reasoning fallacious, or our biases intrusive that our reports or proposals are likely to become unduly subjective.

Suggested Guidelines in Choosing Language

The problem of writing reports and proposals so the Verbal World they present bears close resemblance to the Real World they represent is often made more difficult by a poor choice of language. Some guidelines concerning choice of language are given here:

1. Avoid "either-or" classifications—unless, of course, they actually apply. It is true that some Real World questions can be accurately answered yes or no. "Are you under 20 years of age?" is an example. "Are you a female?" is another.

But much of the Real World cannot be meaningfully divided into "either-or" categories. Some time ago my wife and I purchased a portable TV set. A week or so later we received a card from the store manager with ten questions, each to be answered by placing an "x" in a "yes" column or a "no" column. "Was the salesman courteous?" "Did he answer your questions well?" and so on. After reviewing the questions, I wrote at the bottom, "Most of these questions cannot be meaningfully answered "yes" or "no"! The salesman was courteous, yes; but we have known others more courteous, some less so. He answered our questions satisfactorily; some salesmen have done better, some poorer.

This store manager had fallen into the trap of thinking of the Real World as dichotomous; divided into two parts (yes or no, good or bad, success or failure, black or white, and so on). We are equally guilty when we make such statements as "I am a failure," "I like my new boss," "Schafer is a liar," all of which are misleading representations of the Real World they describe. "I've failed two tests this past week" may be accurate, but it does not mean I *always* fail at everything I do—or even often. Certainly I don't like everything about my new supervisor; some things about him I like better than others, and some days I like him better than I do on other days. And Schafer certainly doesn't *always* tell lies. In fact, from this statement we cannot be sure whether he told one "little" lie once or tells "big" lies repeatedly.

Put differently, part of the Real World is like a light switch; it can be described as "either-or." But much of it is like a thermometer; it can be accurately described only on a scale of some sort. The idea of degrees is illustrated fairly well by the following item from a survey given to a group of college students:

> How challenging to your intellectual ability do you find the curriculum at this school?
>
> | | |
> |---|---|
> | Very challenging | 27% |
> | Moderately challenging | 36% |
> | Fairly challenging | 18% |
> | Not particularly challenging | 9% |
> | Not at all challenging | 2% |
>
> [The percentages represent the number of responses to each category.]

2. Quantify where possible; steer away from relative terms. Such terms as "excessive," "a lot of," or "frequently" fail to present a precise image of the Real World. "The cost was excessive" could mean that it was 5 percent over the limit or 50 percent. "A lot of scrap" could mean there were 5 parts in a hundred that had to be scrapped, or 35 parts.

3. Use specific, concrete language for describing the facts. "Defective" is often too general a term; it could mean that one key on a typewriter is not functioning, or that none of them are. "Failed" is another word that is far too general; so is "accident." One late afternoon my wife had an "accident"; one of several chicken pies she was baking slithered off on the floor and was ruined. Twenty minutes later our son in college called to report another accident: his VW had been rammed from the rear; no one was hurt, but there was several hundred dollars' worth of damage. Such a word as "accident" is an "umbrella term"; it can cover anything from a spot of mayonnaise on one's suit to a 20-car pile-up on the freeway. To depict the Real World clearly, specific, concrete language does a much better job than general, umbrellalike terms.

4. Avoid being ambiguous. An ambiguous expression can be interpreted in two or more ways. In a handout I once used in a training program I used the heading, "Importance of Writing to an Engineer." One sharp-eyed joker in the audience raised his hand and asked, "Who in hell wants to write an engineer?" In another instance, a test report contained this sentence, "This vehicle is acceptable for wind steer at speeds of 60 to 100 m.p.h." This appears to imply that the driver had better reach 60 m.p.h. in a hurry, because apparently the vehicle was unsafe at less than 60!

5. Be straightforward, clear, and concise. As one of my colleagues likes to express it, "Make it CLEAR, SIMPLE, and EASY TO UNDERSTAND." An example of how *not* to write is illustrated in this 1970

Associated Press report of a government edict from Prague, Czechoslovakia:

> Because Christmas Eve falls on a Thursday, the day has been designated a Saturday for work purposes. Factories will close all day, with stores open a half day only. Friday, December 25, has been designated a Sunday, with both factories and stores open all day. Monday, December 28, will be a Wednesday for work purposes. Wednesday, December 30, will be a business Friday. Saturday, January 2, will be a Sunday, and Sunday, January 3, will be a Monday.

If you can discover the Real World hidden in this verbal maze, you're probably ready for promotion.

The Verbal World and the Real World: A Closing Word

The Verbal World we live by is important. Businesses have failed or suffered serious losses, and careers have been ruined or locked at a standstill because people have created a Verbal World of their own—or depended on a Verbal World created by others—that simply failed to correspond to reality.

In business communication, therefore, understanding just how important the Verbal World is and doing everything possible to make sure it conforms to the Real World is of the utmost concern.

A CLASSIFICATION OF REPORTS AND PROPOSALS

Reports and proposals have been classified in various ways. Sometimes they are classified by function, such as sales reports, test reports, or feasibility reports; sometimes by intended readership, as internal (within the company) or external (outside the company). Often they are classified by frequency: daily, weekly, monthly, annual; sometimes as progress reports or final reports. Or they may be classified as short or long, informal or formal. In public life, especially, reports may be identified by the writer, or the head of the committee producing the report, as the Warren Report (on the John F. Kennedy assassination) or the Rockefeller Report (on activities of the CIA).

All of these classifications are valid and useful. However, in this chapter we shall classify reports and proposals according to *form,* specifying the factors influencing which form is appropriate to the situation. In this respect, the form of the report or proposal—that is, how we "dress it up"—can be compared to how we ourselves dress up for the occasion. For everyday work at the office, our dress is usually quite ordinary. If we are expecting visitors, we may dress up a bit more. For very special occasions, such as a crucial conference with a vice president or a luncheon with an important client, we probably will dress in our best.

With this analogy in mind, we may classify reports and proposals according to two factors:

1. How routine or special they are in terms of scope and importance of subject and number and status of intended readers.

2. Whether they are intended for internal or external readership (within or outside the organization).

The influence on form of these factors is summarized graphically in Figure 11.2.

Some explanatory comments on the classification in Figure 11.2 may prove helpful:

1. A memorandum report or proposal is one using a memo heading. It looks like a memo (though it may be longer), but it serves the purpose of a report or proposal. Whereas a memo typically serves as a reminder or an announcement incidental to everyday operations of the business, a memorandum report—just as does a longer, more formal report—provides information necessary for the reader in present or future decision-making. And a memorandum proposal—just as a longer, more formal proposal—seeks authorization for some course of action desired by the writer. (Incidentally, the terms "memorandum proposal" and "letter proposal"—although entirely logical in our classification—do not seem to be commonly used in business. Commonly used instead are the terms "memorandum report" and "letter report"—often, unfortunately, whether their function is to report or propose.)

2. The direct approach, which provides the reader at the outset with the gist of the report or proposal, is the approach commonly preferred in business, for it is enormously time-saving for the reader. The indirect approach, which builds up to the essential message, is most useful when the subject is new or controversial, and the writer wishes to "educate" the reader or to avoid triggering a negative reaction before the reader has proceeded far enough to understand the rationale behind the proposal. (See Chapter 4, "Structure," for a more detailed discussion of the direct vs. indirect approach.)

3. In the main category, "Special Reports and Proposals," the prefatory sections contain the gist of the whole message. Consequently, these sections should be expressed in terms readily understandable to *any* intended reader, whatever his or her background. The discussion and appendix, on the other hand, may be more technical. (For further elaboration, see again, Chapter 4, the section, "The Direct vs. Indirect Approach.") Incidentally, note that in our classification the introduction is considered prefatory. This is because of the general orientation it provides the reader.

4. There are degrees of how "special" a special report or proposal may be. If it is very special, such as an important report or proposal addressed

FIGURE 11.2 Classification of Reports and Proposals

Routine Reports and Proposals		Special Reports and Proposals	
Internal			
Name: Memorandum Report; Memorandum Proposal (usually under 4–5 pages)		Name: Formal Report; Formal Proposal (usually over 4–5 pages)	
Components:		Components:	
Direct Approach	*Indirect Approach*	*Direct Approach*	*Indirect Approach*
Memo heading	Memo heading	*Prefatory Sections:*	*Prefatory Sections:*
Introduction (with or without a heading)	Introduction (with or without a heading)	Cover	Cover
Conclusions	Discussion	Title page	Title page
Recommendations (if any)	Conclusions	Memo of transmittal	Memo of transmittal
Discussion	Recommendations	Abstract	Abstract
Distribution list	Distribution list	Table of contents	Table of contents
		Introduction	Introduction
		Findings (if listed)	*Discussion:*
		Conclusions	Detailed development and support
		Recommendations (if any)	Conclusions
		Discussion—detailed development and support	Recommendations
		Supplemental Sections:	*Supplemental Sections:*
		Appendix (if needed)	(Same sections, when needed, as listed in column at left)
		Footnotes (if needed)	
		Bibliography (if needed)	
		Distribution list	
External			
Name: Letter Report; Letter Proposal (usually under 4–5 pages)		Name: Formal Letter Report; Formal Letter Proposal (usually over 4–5 pages)	
Components: Same as above, except uses a business letter format (heading, inside address, complimentary close, etc.), instead of a memo heading.		Components: Same as above, except for a letter of transmittal serving as a separate cover letter (instead of a memo of transmittal) which is usually bound into the report or proposal.	

to an executive committee, it may contain all or nearly all the components, planned and typed or printed with great care to create a highly positive impression. Similarly, a report to corporation shareholders may be printed on glossy paper with colorful photos and attractive artwork. Such reports or proposals are "all dressed up" to suit the occasion (though we must caution that appearance by itself is never an adequate substitute for solid content). The use of the term formal in this context, by the way, need not—indeed, should not—mean that the style is stilted and sterile; only that additional use is made of prefatory and supplementary components to adapt to a wider, more diversified, and perhaps higher status audience.

On the other hand, a more ordinary report intended only for one's supervisor or immediate department will probably make less use of the full range of components. It probably will not have a cover; the abstract may be part of the memo of transmittal or introduction; and it may have no need for any of the supplemental components at all.

In short, there is no standard format that applies to all situations or all companies. The most that our classification can do is to provide broad guidelines to be intelligently adapted to each situation.

THE COMPONENTS OF A FORMAL REPORT OR PROPOSAL

As we have already seen, any report or proposal is made up of a number of component parts. How many of these may be used depends, as we have seen, on how "special" the report or proposal is. The full range of components includes all of these.

Cover

A cover, when used, dresses up the report or proposal and adds to the degree of formality. More practically, it protects the document (which implies enough use over time to warrant protection). Because the cover (when used) is the first part the reader sees, it should be neat and attractive. Sometimes a standard cover is provided by the company; other times—as in a report for the public—a special cover is designed, containing perhaps a color photo of the company's latest product or some eye-appealing design.

Principal elements of the cover are the title and author's name (which might be an agency or committee, rather than only an individual). Sometimes the date is included, and perhaps a report number specified by the company, such as "Research Publication, ABR-1833."

In some instances, a clear plastic cover may be used. In this case, the title page, revealed through the cover, for all practical purposes *is* the cover.

Title Page

Elements The title page contains at least four elements, usually in this order: (a) title, (b) to whom submitted, (c) by whom written, and (d) date. In addition, the title of the receiver and sender and their affiliations are often shown.

As with the cover, special attention should be paid to creating a favorable initial impression. It is certain that the title page will create an impression of some sort. If it is messy or contains misspelled words, creating a negative impression, this constitutes an unnecessary handicap at the outset that the rest of the paper must make up for.

Figure 11.3 illustrates an acceptable title page. The essential elements are included—centered, well-grouped, and attractively spaced. Note that the most important element, the title, is in all caps.

The Title Wording of the title warrants special attention. In business writing, the function of the title is to *inform*—to suggest accurately yet briefly what the selection contains so readers can readily determine its relevance to their interests. This contrasts with the function of titles in popular writing whose aim is to attract attention and "sell." Thus, the title *Jaws,* very successful commercially, would be utterly useless in business writing.

A good title for a report or proposal should satisfy at least two criteria:

1. It should be a "good fit" in that it reflects what the document contains—no more and no less. "Selecting Apprentices" is too general; such a title could embrace a wide range of subjects. "The Revised Apprentice Selection Procedure at IBX" would be more exact. Conversely, "The Absenteeism Problem in Dept. 14" is not inclusive enough if the gist of the report (or proposal) consists of *solutions* to the problem. In this case, "Proposed Solutions to the Absenteeism Problem in Dept. 14" would be better.

2. It should be concise. Sydney Harris, the columnist, tells of a thesis written by a steel mill worker for a master's degree in psychology. The original title was "Why the Foreman Hates the Boss," but this got changed to "Emotional Coefficient Correlatives in Interpersonal Relationships Between Management and Supervisory Echelons." In Harris's words, the original was "frank, direct, clear, and forceful," while the revision was "timid, muddy, pretentious, and evasive."[1]

For trimming the verbiage while retaining the sense here are two suggestions:

    a. Omit unnecessary terms. Thus, "A Survey of Present Methods for the Reduction of Advertising Costs" can be trimmed to "Present Methods for Reducing Advertising Costs"—or, perhaps, simply "Reducing Advertising Costs."

    b. Divide the title into two parts, consisting of title and subtitle. For example, the title shown earlier could be rephrased as:

FIGURE 11.3 Title Page

```
              ABSENTEE CONTROL CENTER:
           A PROGRAM TO CONTROL ABSENTEEISM




                      Prepared for
                  Prof. Roger P. Wilcox
                 General Motors Institute




                           By
                     Karl L. Bossung
              Saginaw Malleable Iron Division




                    January 20, 1977
```

ABSENTEE PROBLEM IN DEPT. 14:
PROPOSED SOLUTIONS

This two-part arrangement has the advantage that the key words come first—something sure to be appreciated by the busy reader searching through a list of titles in an index or file cabinet for the particular information he or she is after.

Memo or Letter of Transmittal

The memo or letter of transmittal is a cover memo or letter. It says in writing what you might say in person if you were to walk into your supervisor's office and say "Here's that report you requested."

The only difference between a memo of transmittal and a letter of transmittal is that the format differs according to the recipient. If the report or proposal is addressed to someone within the organization, a memo format is used; if to someone outside, a letter format. If it's addressed to someone in another division of the same corporation, you might use either, but the better you know the other person, the more likely you would use the memo format. (For the difference in format between the two, you may wish to review Chapter 10, "Writing Effective Memos and Letters.")

Regardless of format, the content of the transmittal remains the same. Most typically, the elements include:

Recipient's name, the date, and the subject
Reason or occasion for submitting the report or proposal
Title or topic of report or proposal
Purpose and scope of report or proposal
Acknowledgments, if in order, to any who gave special assistance
The hope that the report or proposal is acceptable
Willingness to discuss it further if desired
Signature

In addition, the writer may mention additional problems, not developed in the report or proposal, that he or she feels might warrant further investigation.

The tone of the memo or letter, while businesslike, is relatively more personal and informal than the tone of the report or proposal itself.

If the memo or letter is intended to be read only by the person requesting it, it may be submitted separately or clipped to the cover so it need not be included in the distribution to other readers. Otherwise, it is usually bound in the report immediately following the title page.

Figure 11.4 illustrates a typical memo of transmittal, and Figure 11.5 a typical letter of transmittal.

Abstract

An *abstract* is a condensation of the report or proposal in miniature; "synopsis" is another name given it.

FIGURE 11.4 Memo of Transmittal (Written by Roger Poisson. Used with permission of the author.)

SUBJECT: Slide Bar Assembly   DATE: July 15, 1973

TO: Shirl D. Wray

This report is a summary of the results that I have found during the investigation you requested concerning the problem of the malfunctioning of some of the 10-Slide Tuner slide bar assemblies.

The nature of the problem and the reason some of the slide bar assemblies are failing is explained in this report. The findings are definite, and concrete conclusions have been drawn. Recommendations are listed that will eliminate the cause of the slide bar assembly malfunction.

I would like to acknowledge Messrs. Heinz Heise, of the Metal Lab, Chet Zarger, of the Product Assurance Dept., and Cliff Jones, of the Receiving Inspection Dept. for the help and special assistance they have given me during this project investigation.

If you have further questions, I shall be happy to discuss them with you.

                                              Roger Poisson

FIGURE 11.5 Letter of Transmittal

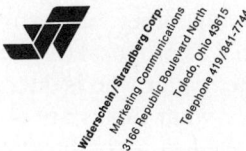

October 27, 1976

Mr. Milo Howard
Director of Marketing
Zamovar Products Corporation
Columbus, Ohio 43210

Dear Mr. Howard:

Enclosed you will find our report of consumer reactions to your proposed new product, "Dent-O-Mint" toothpaste with the capless tube.

We conducted our consumer panel discussion on October 19, in Marion, Ohio. The response, as you can see, was generally favorable, although there were some reservations concerning the parcticality of the capless feature.

We've enjoyed serving you in this project, and if you have further questions we'll be happy to discuss them with you.

Sincerely,

Lawrence F. Berry, III
Vice President
Marketing Research

LFB:sdh

Function Usually an abstract is only 100–200 words in length, and its function is to enable the busy reader to gain a quick overview without having to read the entire report or proposal. As more than one survey has revealed, nearly all managers read the abstract, compared with fewer than half who read the entire paper. For this reason, the abstract should be written in language that *any* intended reader can understand, at least in a general way, whether his or her background is sales, accounting, electrical engineering, or whatever. Although one of the first components of a formal report or proposal to be read, it is one of the last to be written, for its contents are drawn (or "abstracted") from the complete work. The shorter the report or proposal, the less need there is for an abstract.

Types Abstracts are generally classified as being of two types: *descriptive* (or topical) and *summary*. The *descriptive abstract* is like a table of contents written in paragraph form. It names the topics, but gives little or no information about them. Its value is mainly for the reader who wishes merely to get a preview of the coverage; if then he or she is interested sufficiently, he or she will read further. Descriptive abstracts are fairly common at the beginning of articles in professional journals, such as *The Management Review* or *Machine Design*.

The *summary abstract,* on the other hand, summarizes the main information contained in the report or proposal (or the article, if published in a journal). It is intended for the reader who is interested in the actual gist of the report rather than merely what topics are covered.

A third type sometimes used is a combination of the first two. It is useful in a formal report or proposal on a controversial topic, when giving the reader the recommendations at the outset might easily arouse a negative reaction before he or she has read far enough to react knowledgeably. The writer summarizes the problem being discussed, but states only that solutions will be offered and recommendations made. The reader must then continue reading to discover what these solutions and recommendations are.

Writing the Abstract   In writing an abstract, keep in mind the following guidelines:

1. Present in general terms and nontechnical style the main and subtopics (if a descriptive abstract) or the gist of the report or proposal (if a summary abstract). Avoid specific, detailed analysis, illustrative examples, and so on.

2. Make no attempt, unless necessary, to use the exact wording of the report or proposal, but *do* maintain the organization and relative emphasis given to the ideas.

3. Use an impersonal approach. Focus on the ideas of the report or proposal rather than on your own personal role in the investigation.

4. Give careful attention to the quality of writing. Remember the abstract is the section of your report or proposal that will be read by more people than will any other. It should represent your "best face."

Examples of several kinds of abstracts are shown in Figures 11.6, 11.7, 11.8, and 11.9.

FIGURE 11.6
Descriptive Abstract

Abstract

This report is on the 1976 Bond Drive held at Colonial Industries in April. The reason for the drive and the sequence of steps are explained. Also, the final results are given and the general strategy evaluated.

FIGURE 11.7 Summary Abstract. This abstract gives the reader an informative synopsis in 163 words of the substance of an article containing over 3500 words, plus two pages of graphs, photos, and diagrams and their explanatory comments. It illustrates excellently the characteristics of a well-written summary abstract, the "report in miniature." (Wayne A. Daniel and Joseph T. Wentworth, "A Study of the Physical Mechanism of Exhaust Hydrocarbon Emission," *General Motors Engineering Journal,* Vol. 10, no. 1, 1st Quarter, 1963, pp. 14–20.)

A Study of the Physical Mechanism of Exhaust Hydrocarbon Emission

Much research is being done by the automotive industry to obtain more information on automotive engine exhaust hydrocarbons—their formation, their expulsion, and their reactions in various environments. Typical of the research investigations is one recently completed by the General Motors Research Laboratories. This investigation, which represents one phase of a continuing program by General Motors, confirmed the hypotheses that wall quenching (the failure of flames to touch the walls of the combustion chamber) is the main reason for unburned hydrocarbons and that a significant portion of the quenched hydrocarbons is not exhausted from the engine's cylinder. Further studies showed that hydrocarbon concentration of the exhausted gases varies with time during the exhaust stroke of the piston. Additional information also was presented on the hydrocarbon concentration gradients along the exhaust pipe and hydrocarbon reaction in the exhaust pipe. These findings have provided a basis for enumerating several factors which determine the amount of hydrocarbons reaching the atmosphere from an automotive engine's exhaust system.

FIGURE 11.8 Summary Abstract for Proposal Using a *Direct* Approach. Note that the recommended solution is specified in the abstract; thus, the reader knows without reading further what is being proposed.

Abstract

When Calcutech, Inc., was established in 1973, the number of employees was under 200. With room for over 400 vehicles, the parking area was more than adequate. However, the expansion of facilities in 1975 resulted in increasing the work force to over 300. At the same time, since part of the parking area was used for expansion, the number of available spaces was reduced to fewer than 300. The present parking shortage will be seriously worsened when the projected additional expansion in 1977 is completed. Although on-street parking is now being used, this is unsatisfactory, and will be out of the question when the new city regulation goes into effect July 1.

This proposal considers two solutions: (a) acquisition of adjacent property and (b) construction of a parking ramp. On the basis of a careful comparison, construction of a ramp is strongly recommended.

FIGURE 11.9 Combination Abstract for Proposal Using an *Indirect* Approach. Because management has previously opposed it, the idea of a ramp is not specified until the argument for it is stated in the proposal itself.

Abstract

When Calcutech, Inc., was established in 1973, ...
....
....
....
....
the question when the new city regulation goes into effect July 1.

This proposal considers possible solutions and offers recommendations for what is considered to be the most feasible solution with the greatest long-range benefits.

Table of Contents

Function Like the abstract, the table of contents provides the reader with a quick overview of the report or proposal—in fact, an even quicker overview, since it is arranged in topical outline form. In addition, it offers a guide, by means of page numbers, to where sections of interest may be found.

Elements The table of contents includes the following elements:

1. The title, TABLE OF CONTENTS (usually in caps).

2. Headings indicating the following prefatory sections that are used: memo or letter of transmittal (unless it will be detached and not included for general distribution), abstract, and introduction. (Note that even though the table of contents is itself a prefatory section, it is not listed.)

3. All first- and second-order headings from the introduction and discussion; also, third-order headings, unless including these would make the table of contents too long. All headings shown in the table of contents *must* appear in the report or proposal, but—as just noted—third-order headings may be omitted if desired. The word "discussion," incidentally, is often not used as a heading; the first major heading of the discussion is used instead. Use of numbers and letters with headings is optional, but since they tend to clutter the appearance, they are often omitted when the report or proposal is relatively brief and informal.

4. The heading "Appendix," along with each item or class of items included in the appendix.

Not included in the table of contents are references to graphic aids (Fig. 1, Table 3, and so on), since these are not headings. If more than five or six illustrations are used, it is often desirable to list them separately under a title such as "List of Illustrations" or "List of Tables." This list may appear on the lower half of the page containing the table of contents. Or, if this arrangement would appear crowded, the list of illustrations may appear on the next page instead.

5. Page numbers. Page numbers are shown in a vertical column on the right. Prefatory sections are numbered with small roman numerals (i, ii, etc.), beginning with the title page (although the numeral is not actually shown on the title page itself, nor is the title page listed in the table of contents). Beginning with the introduction, the page numbering starts anew, this time with Arabic numerals, and continues on through the appendix if there is one. Only the beginning page number for any given section is shown in the table of contents. Thus, if the heading were "Functions of Department," the page number shown might be "6," rather than "6–8."

In the report itself, a consistent plan of numbering should be followed. The first page number of a section is often centered at the bottom. For pages within a section, the number is often placed in the upper right

FIGURE 11.10 Table of Contents

TABLE OF CONTENTS

	Page
Memo of Transmittal	ii
Abstract	iii
INTRODUCTION	1
CONCLUSIONS AND RECOMMENDATIONS	3
DESCRIPTION OF PRESENT SITUATION	4
Patient Load	4
Facilities	5
PROPOSED IMPROVEMENTS	8
Additional Staff	9
Additional Facilities	11
EVALUATION OF PROPOSED IMPROVEMENTS	15
Benefits	15
Cost Estimate	16
CONCLUSION	17
APPENDICES	18
Appendix A. Patient Load During 1976	19
Appendix B. Breakdown of Treatment by Categories	20

LIST OF ILLUSTRATIONS

Figure 1. Layout of Present Facilities	6
Figure 2. Proposed New Layout of Facilities	13
Figure 3. The E-Z-Bak Dental Chair	14
Figure 4. The E-Z-Access Dental Cabinet	14
Figure 5. Table of Projected Costs	16

corner, a good half inch from either side. Some companies require this form: "Page 6 of 14." The most important point to remember is that—except for the title page and table of contents, all pages in a report or proposal should be numbered.

Like the abstract, the table of contents is one of the last components to be written. It cannot be completed until the page numbers are known. Further, it serves as a useful check on how adequate and consistent the use of headings has been.

Also, like the cover and title page, an attractive layout is important, for the table of contents is one of the components contributing to the reader's initial impression.

A sample table of contents is shown in Figure 11.10.

Introduction

Function The function of the introduction is indicated by the literal meaning of the word "introduce": "to lead into." An introduction thus leads the reader into the body of the report itself (although it is quite true that having read the introduction, a reader may decide he doesn't wish to be lead any further).

The question arises sometimes as to how the introduction differs from the abstract. Stated briefly, the abstract, as explained earlier, is a synopsis of the entire report expressed in general terms, while the introduction contains only the preliminary information helpful in preparing the reader to get into the detail of the report or proposal itself. If the report were a lake, one might say that the abstract provides simply an overview of the lake, while the introduction prepares one for swimming it.

Elements Although authorities differ, it would seem that the introduction to a formal report or proposal should contain elements accomplishing at least the following four steps:

1. Identify the subject. Usually this means identifying the general subject area, then specifying what particular phase or phases of the subject area the report or proposal will be concerned with. In other words, the introduction will make clear the scope and limitations of the report or proposal: what it will cover and what it will not cover.

2. Explain why the report or proposal is being written. This typically means referring, in general terms, to whatever problem has given rise to the investigation, including how serious or far-reaching the problem is. Thus, the reader can see how the report or proposal "makes sense" in light of this problem, and can determine how relevant the problem is to his or her own interests.

3. State the purpose of the report. This should be stated in a single sentence: ". . . to report and evaluate the sales success of our new

Sof-Tint Ceiling Tile, Design RX-3"; ". . . to review the pros and cons of adding to our warehouse facilities" (if the writer wishes to use a direct approach; or if he wishes to use an indirect approach); ". . . to propose ways for alleviating our storage problems." However, even though the purpose should be stated explicitly in a sentence, this sentence may well serve as the topic sentence of a paragraph in which the purpose is elaborated upon.

4. State the plan of development. This can usually be accomplished in a single sentence, such as, "The report will explain the steps involved in the selection procedure, the test administration, and the employment interview." Regardless of whatever else the introduction may contain, the plan of development is invariably the final step.

In addition to the four steps listed above, any of the three additional kinds of information described below may be included, depending on the situation:

1. Background information. If the intended reader or readers are not familiar with the problem situation or the topic in general, background information should be included—but only as much as the reader is likely to need.

2. Definition of key terms. Key terms should be defined in the introduction if they (a) are likely to be unfamiliar to the reader, (b) will be used in a special sense, even if familiar, and—most important—(c) will be used throughout the report or proposal. If they are terms that will be used only once or twice, or only in a limited portion of the report or proposal, they should be defined in the discussion when first used rather than in the introduction. Or, if the report or proposal contains a fair-sized list of terms needing definition, they should be defined in a glossary in the appendix.

3. Methodology. If the report or proposal is based on research, the method of research employed should be explained—whether a lab test, telephone survey, use of questionnaires, controlled experiment, or whatever. If explaining the methodology becomes too complicated, it can be identified in general terms in the introduction, then explained in detail in a special section in the appendix. Explaining the methodology is important to (a) give credibility to the study (and the writer), and (b) permit any who desire to repeat the study for their own purposes.

Organization A useful concept is to think of the introduction as being organized in the form of an inverted pyramid—i.e., progressing from "the broad to the specific."[2]

Both of the introductions in Figures 11.11 and 11.12 illustrate the inverted pyramid pattern.

FIGURE 11.11
Sample Introduction

APPRENTICE SELECTION PROCEDURE: RECOMMENDED IMPROVEMENT

<u>Introduction</u>

Over the years, Heritage Tool Co. has done an effective job selecting people for their apprenticeship program. The success of these selection practices is attested to by the fact that, until recently, only a small proportion of those entering the program have left because of inability to handle the related training courses or because of unsatisfactory work performance.

During the past two years, however, an increasing number of apprentices have had difficulty in performing well both in the courses and on the job. As a result, more of them have been dropping out prior to completion of their program.

One related question has been the minimum selection requirements established in 1964 by the Bureau of Apprenticeship and Training of the United States Apprentice Plan. Heritage has found these requirements adequate in the past, but the recent difficulties raise doubts about whether these requirements continue to be adequate.

The purpose of this report is to analyze the problem and offer recommendations for correcting it. Included are a description of the problem, an examination of the selection requirements as they currently apply to our needs, an examination of present training procedures, and recommendations for correcting the problem.

FIGURE 11.12 Sample Introduction (Lynn V. Rigby and Verner E. Gibbs, "Measurement of Reader Satisfaction by Questionnaire," *Proceedings: The 19th International Technical Communications Conference,* Society for Technical Communication, Inc., Washington, D.C., 1972, p. 173.)

MEASUREMENT OF READER SATISFACTION BY QUESTIONNAIRE

Introduction

Every guide to better writing says "know your audience," but few guides say much about "what to know" or "how to find out." After years of experience, we each feel that we <u>do</u> know our audience, but are our opinions really valid? Are they, or would they be, supported by research? And if we wanted to test our assumptions about our readers or their acceptance of our publications, how could we go about it?

For many years, Sandia Laboratories has been publishing a continuing series of instructions covering the operation, calibration, and maintenance of electronic systems designed to test products built by subcontractors. We have developed and delivered hundreds of test systems, which are found from coast to coast and are used by persons with widely varying interests, experience, and training. We wanted to <u>design</u> our instructions to "optimally" satisfy the needs and preferences of this varied audience; what did we need to know?

In talking among ourselves (as designers and technical writers), it became clear that despite years of working with our readers, we really couldn't describe them in design terms. We were very glib with practiced expressions (such as "a competent electronics technician"), but we disagreed widely on what such expressions had to do with the legibility, readability, usability, and accessibility of our instructions.

To resolve this disagreement, we conducted a survey of our readers. The results of the survey are reported below. Emphasized are four main conclusions which emerged: (1) Publications should be designed to meet reader needs and expectations, (2) Effective design must be based upon systematic measurements of reader needs and preferences, as determined by their abilities, habits, and concept of their role, (3) Questionnaires may be the only practical way to obtain valid data on a specific audience.

Style The introduction is quite likely to be read by readers of varied backgrounds seeking further overview of the report. Consequently, the style of the introduction, like that of the abstract, should be nontechnical. Furthermore, it should be well written, so the reader's attitude toward the writer and report or proposal will be definitely favorable.

Note that in Figure 11.12 the final three sentences, which serve as a preview, also summarize the results, just as one might find in an abstract. By way of comparison, the abstract of this article (an abstract more nearly descriptive than summary) is included here:

> If you haven't measured reader response to your publications, you may be missing the target. We used a multiple questionnaire survey to measure reader satisfaction with a continuing series of instructions for using electronic test equipment. The return data gave us an objective basis for substantial improvements. For those who haven't considered this approach, we include here a brief guide to audience definition and questionnaire design.

Findings, Conclusions, and Recommendations

What They Are and How They Differ In terms of the Real World–Verbal World Model described earlier in this chapter, *findings* correspond to factual statements, *conclusions* to inferences, and *recommendations* to value judgments. For example:

Finding: There is a 15-minute overlap between the schedules of the first- and second-shift supervisors. [Statement based on direct observation.]

Conclusion: One cause of the inadequate communication between the first-shift supervisors and the second-shift supervisors is lack of time. [An inference reached through reasoning.]

Recommendation: The overlap between shifts should be increased from 15 minutes to 30 minutes for the supervisors of those shifts. [Implies a value judgment that this would be desirable.]

Note that the conclusion in the example depends on the finding, and the recommendation on the conclusion. This kind of relationship should exist among all recommendations, conclusions, and findings. Note, too, that while findings and conclusions refer to what *is,* recommendations refer to what (in the writer's opinion) *should be.* In fact, the term "should" is typically found in recommendations that are properly worded.

As indicated earlier, anyone under proper conditions can report findings; only those who are qualified by training or experience should offer conclusions or recommendations.

Where They Are Located In practice, findings are usually found only in the discussion and appendix, although occasionally a summary of the main findings is included in a special section just preceding the conclusions and recommendations. When the direct approach is used, the conclusions and recommendations generally are located immediately following the introduction. When the indirect approach is used, they are located at the end of the discussion.

Guidelines on Format Guidelines on format include these:

1. Use a separate heading for each category included: one for Findings, one for Conclusions, and one for Recommendations—in that order. Grouping them all under one heading, "Conclusions and Recommendations," leads to reader confusion as to which are conclusions and which are recommendations.

If there are subcategories, each containing several items under a given category, use subheadings to show this. For example, if your report consisted of an evaluation of three brands of paint, you could list the conclusions concerning each brand under a separate subheading.

2. Arrange the items in each category in a vertical list and number each item separately. If they are expressed in paragraph form, the reader can easily finish reading the paragraph and not be sure whether, for instance,

there are three conclusions or four. If listed and numbered, they can scarcely be misread.

3. Observe the rules of parallelism in formulating each list. (Consult the index, if necessary, for references on parallelism in earlier chapters.)

4. Be sure each item is in the proper category. It confuses the reader and reflects on the credibility of the writer if, for instance, a recommendation appears in the list of conclusions.

5. State each item concisely. Any extended elaboration belongs in the discussion. Remember, at this point the reader wants a *quick* overview. Placing after each item the page numbers (in parentheses) where the elaboration may be found in the discussion is an aid to the reader who wishes to read further.

6. Use a single page (or more, if necessary) for showing the findings (if included at this point), the conclusions, and recommendations. This helps the reader in seeing the logical relationship among them.

Samples of typical findings, conclusions, and recommendations are shown in Figures 11.13 and 11.14.

FIGURE 11.13
Conclusions and Recommendation from a Proposal on "Reducing Development Time for New Products"

<u>Conclusions</u>

1. Development times can be greatly reduced using this program. (Pages 6 and 7)

2. The reduced development times would lead to significant savings for the corporation. (Page 8)

3. The difficulty in replacing development engineers would be reduced, although not eliminated. (Page 9)

<u>Recommendation</u>

It is recommended that the general vibrations program be purchased from Amco Corporation and put into immediate use. (Page 10)

FIGURE 11.14
Findings, Conclusions, and Recommendations from a Proposal on "Eliminating Warpage in Company Parking Tags"

<u>Findings</u>

1. The current parking tag is a laminate consisting of two layers: one clear, the other pigmented. (Page 3)

2. Both layers of the tag are vinyl acetate-vinyl chloride copolymer. (Page 4)

3. The two layers act like a "bimetal strip," thus causing the warpage. (Page 4)

<u>Conclusions</u>

1. There is an immediate need to eliminate the warpage problem of the IBX parking tag. (Pages 6 and 7)

2. The tag can be feasibly made by a number of suppliers. (Pages 8 and 9)

<u>Recommendations</u>

1. The tag should be made from a single layer vinyl acetate-vinyl copolymer strip. (Page 10)

2. The Purchasing Department should request bids from appropriate suppliers. (Page 11)

Discussion

If you use the direct approach in your formal report or proposal, all the sections described thus far are prefatory. If you use the indirect approach, all the sections except the conclusions and recommendations are prefatory; they, of course, will come at the end of the discussion.

Whichever approach is used, the prefatory sections, as noted earlier, serve to provide the reader with a quick overview. The longer the report or proposal, the more indispensable the overview becomes, for it can convey in minutes (or less) what otherwise might require a half hour or more to read. This is why the prefatory sections are the part of the report most generally read.

You might ask, then, since this is true, why bother with the discussion at all? The answer is that for those readers who *are* interested, it is in the discussion that they will find the data explaining or supporting the conclusions and recommendations. It is only through the discussion that they can "see for themselves."

Content of the Discussion   Depending on which of these are appropriate to the situation, the discussion may include any or all of the following topics:

Description (more detailed than in the introduction) of the general situation.

Explanation, in as much detail as needed, of any problem or problems the report is concerned with.

Analysis of the cause or causes of the problems.

Statement and clarification of the criteria (standards) the solution to the problem should meet.

Explanation—clear and complete—of each solution investigated.

Evaluation of each solution in terms of how well it would solve the problem within the limits of the criteria.

Style of Writing in the Discussion   Whether a report or proposal, the style of writing should be straightforward and informative. More specifically, it should utilize effectively the principles presented in Part 2, "Being Clear," on structure, paragraphing, sentences, grammar, punctuation, and word usage, or graphic aids. Indeed, frequently graphic aids (figures and tables of various kinds) are used in the discussion section of reports and proposals.

Also used freely are main headings and subheadings. Use of headings and subheadings is not because people in business are simple-minded readers who must have everything pointed out to them, but because they are invariably under pressure, and headings help them locate more rapidly whatever they may be looking for. This makes sense when you realize that—unlike short stories and novels—reports and proposals are not necessarily read through from beginning to end. They are more like textbooks, in which often the user looks for and reads only those portions that pertain to his or her own particular interests.

In addition, use of headings practically forces the writer to organize his or her plan of presentation clearly, while at the same time providing the reader with a "tour guide" to the plan.

Samples of discussions will be found in the specimen reports and proposals later in this chapter.

Appendix

The appendix is the first of several supplemental sections that are included, if needed, in a formal report or proposal. Three other such sections, or items, are footnotes, bibliography, and distribution list.

Materials that may be placed in the appendix include:

A glossary of special terms.

Tables of test data (in fact, some test reports may contain as many as 30–40 pages of test data in the appendix, with only four or five pages of discussion preceding).

Samples of forms (such as might be used in a personnel department for hiring employees, or for processing benefits).

A copy of a questionnaire used in a survey.

A tabulation of responses to the questions on the questionnaire.

A detailed description of a special research methodology (included for the benefit of anyone who might wish to check the validity of the research or replicate it).

A question that often arises concerning the appendix is this: How does one decide what belongs in the appendix and what in the discussion? A safe guide to follow is that if most readers would need to refer to the material to understand the development of ideas in the discussion, place it there. If not, place it in the appendix.

A possible exception to locating relevant figures and tables in the text occurs when there are so many of them that they "bury" the text. If the reader must leaf through several pages of figures for every page of text, he or she would prefer solid text with the figures in the appendix. But this seldom happens. In any event, the convenience of the reader is the primary guideline to follow.

Footnotes

Function The kind of footnote of main concern here is the kind used for crediting sources of direct quotations or distinctive ideas borrowed from other writers. Such footnotes serve at least three purposes: (1) they give due credit to the author from whom you have quoted or borrowed; (2) they permit readers, if they wish, to consult the source themselves; and (3)—perhaps most important—they strengthen your own credibility by showing you to be honest, fair-minded, and informed on what others have written.

On the other hand, if you *overuse* footnotes—so you appear to depend too heavily on others for your ideas, with but little contribution of your own—you risk damaging your credibility, for you may appear to have little of your own to offer. The solution, of course, is not to omit the footnotes, but to think through your material so thoroughly that basically your message *is* your own.

(Another kind of footnote is the kind providing incidental commentary on a point in the text, or perhaps defining a term. However, such footnotes are not as likely to be used in business writing as in, for example, a textbook, for they tend to slow the reader—who, let us remember, is typically in a hurry and impatient to keep moving. Incidental comments, when included, are more likely to be enclosed in parentheses within the text, or omitted altogether.)

Frequency of Use in Business Writing Since reports and proposals in business (unlike many college term papers) are ordinarily based on the writer's own investigation, there usually is little need to credit other sources. This is especially true of production reports, test reports, field reports, and the like. Research reports are the principal exception.

Placement Traditionally, footnotes crediting sources are placed at the bottom of the page that contains the material being credited—a location convenient to the reader. However, when so many footnotes are used that the reader is unlikely to refer to them constantly anyway, an alternative arrangement may be used. This is to group them in a list, headed "Notes," directly following the appendix (or the discussion if there is no appendix). Before deciding which arrangement to use, it would be wise to determine which arrangement is preferred in your organization. Many companies have their own stylebooks containing rules on footnotes. When this is the case, the company stylebook should be used.

Form If as many as three or four sources have been cited, these should be shown in a bibliography or list of references at the end of the report or proposal. When this is the case, the footnotes need be no more elaborate than necessary to identify which source is being referred to; for example:

[1]Argyris, p. 71.

If more than one source by the same author is included in the bibliography, they should be distinguished by adding the title:

[1]Argyris, *Personality and Organization,* pp. 122–123.
[2]Argyris, *Integrating the Individual and the Organization,* p. 98–100.

On the other hand, if there is no list of references (since so few have been used), the first footnote used for crediting a source must give all the information that would be contained in a full bibliographic reference—plus the specific page numbers where the quotation or distinctive idea may be found. Later footnotes referring to the same source need be no more complete than those shown above. Although several footnoting systems are in use (and none accepted as *the* standard), the one shown below is widely used. Note that in the form shown below the data concerning publication is important enough to be included, yet incidental enough to be shown parenthetically.

1. For a book with one author:

    [1]Chris Argyris, *Personality and Organization* (New York: Harper and Brothers, 1957), pp. 122–123.

2. For a book with two authors:

    [2]Robert L. Kahn and Charles F. Cannell, *The Dynamics of Interviewing* (New York: John Wiley and Sons, Inc., 1957), p. 178.

3. For a book with no author given:

    [3]*A Guide for Authors* (Boston: Houghton Mifflin Company, 1974), pp. 28–29.

4. For a selection in a book consisting of a collection of articles:

    [4]Robert F. Bales, "How People Interact in Conferences," in *Communication and Culture,* ed., Alfred G. Smith (New York: Holt, Rinehart and Winston, 1966), pp. 97–100.

5. For an unpublished work:

    [5]Gary M. Richetto, "Communication Training for Organizational Change Agents" (paper given at annual convention of the Western Speech Communication Association, 1973), pp. 7–9.

6. For an article in a periodical:

    [6]Robert L. Kahn, Barbara A. Gutek, Eugenia Barton, and Daniel Katz, "Americans Love Their Bureaucrats," *Psychology Today,* June, 1975, p. 69.

7. For an article in an encyclopedia:

    [7]"Plastics," *Encyclopedia Americana* (1973), Vol. 22, p. 222.

8. For a newspaper article:

    [8]"Museums Merchandise More Shows and Wares to Broaden Patronage," *Wall Street Journal,* August 14, 1975, p. 1, col. 1.

9. For a pamphlet (use same form as for a book):

   ⁹G. E. Densmore, "Public Speaking for Business Men," *Fifth Annual Conference on Speech Communication in Business and Industry* (Ann Arbor, Michigan: Department of Speech, University of Michigan, 1956), pp. 5–10.

10. For an interview:

    ¹⁰Interview with Dr. Arnold E. Schneider, Dean Emeritus, College of Business, Western Michigan University, April 18, 1975.

11. For referring to a source previously footnoted:

    ¹¹Richetto, p. 11.
    ¹²"Museums Merchandise More Shows and Wares to Broaden Patronage," p. 1.
    ¹³Densmore, p. 7.
    ¹⁴Richetto, pp. 3–4.

Bibliography

A bibliography is a list of sources concerning a particular subject (in this case, the subject of the report or proposal). Sometimes the list contains all the sources consulted, whether referred to or quoted from in the discussion. Other times, the list contains only those sources that have actually been used (and, of course, footnoted); in this case, the term "References" or "List of References") is the more appropriate heading. If the references are fewer than four or five, a separate list may be omitted entirely, since the footnotes provide the same information anyway.

When the writer does compile a separate list, it is typically located at the end. However, this practice is not standard. Some writers locate it before the appendix; others within the appendix. This is another point on which you should check concerning the preferred practice in your organization.

Items in a bibliography are listed alphabetically according to the last name of the author (or the first word of the title if the author's name is not given). However, if a list of references (as opposed to a full bibliography) is shown, the items may be arranged by number in the same order in which they were first referred to in the discussion. When this is done, one may dispense with the footnotes, replacing them with nothing more than a number in parentheses in the text corresponding to the number of the appropriate item in the reference list. To illustrate, in the following sentence, "Richetto identifies eight steps in the organization development

FIGURE 11.15
Sample Bibliography

<u>Bibliography</u>

Argyris, Chris, <u>Personality and Organization</u>. New York: Harper and Brothers, 1957.

Bales, Robert F., "How People Interact in Conferences," in <u>Communication and Culture</u>, ed. Alfred G. Smith. New York: Holt, Rinehart and Winston, 1966.

Densmore, G. E., "Public Speaking for Business Men," <u>Fifth Annual Conference on Speech Communication in Business and Industry</u>. Ann Arbor, Michigan: Department of Speech, University of Michigan, 1956.

<u>Guide for Authors, A</u>. Boston: Houghton Mifflin Company, 1974.

Kahn, Robert L. and Charles F. Cannell, <u>The Dynamics of Interviewing</u>. New York: John Wiley and Sons, Inc., 1957.

Kahn, Robert L., Barbara A. Gutek, Eugenia Barton, and Daniel Katz, "Americans Love Their Bureaucrats," <u>Psychology Today</u>, June, 1975, pp. 66-71.

"Museums Merchandise More Shows and Wares to Broaden Patronage." <u>Wall Street Journal</u>, August 14, 1975.

"Plastics." <u>Encylopedia Britannica</u>, 1973.

Richetto, Gary M., "Communication Training for Organizational Change Agents." Paper given at Western Speech Communication Association, 1973.

Schneider, Arnold E., Dean Emeritus, College of Business, Western Michigan University. Interview, April 18, 1975.

process (6)," the "6" refers to item number six in a list of references at the end.

When the bibliography is fairly long, the sources may be grouped under such subheadings as "Books," "Periodicals," "Government Bulletins," or whatever subheadings seem appropriate.

Although bibliographic items contain basically the same information as do footnotes, in form they differ in at least four ways:

1. The author's last name, when available, comes first (to facilitate alphabetical arrangement). If more than one author is given, only the first author's name is written with the last name first.

2. In a footnote, the first line is indented about three spaces; in a bibliography, all lines *except* the first in each item are indented about three spaces.

3. The parentheses used in footnotes are omitted in the bibliography.

4. Page numbers are not usually shown in a bibliography; when they are shown, they will be the page numbers of the entire reference.

If a bibliography were to be compiled from the footnotes shown above, it would look like Figure 11.15.

Although you may have little occasion to use footnotes or to list references in business writing, when you do—do it right! You may never know what inconvenience you cause some unknown reader by an inaccurate or incomplete footnote, or what negative impressions you may create of both your organization and yourself by a sloppily drawn-up list of references. Recording the information accurately and correctly is tedious. By the same token, it is one indication of whether you have the capacity for attention to detail that characterizes the alert mind.

Finally, as a practical step, I cannot emphasize too strongly the importance, when consulting other sources, of copying accurately *all* the information (title, source, page numbers, date, and all the rest) you will need for possible footnotes or bibliography later on. Few tasks are as dismal as retracing one's steps trying to find the lost source of some valuable information.

Distribution List

Although the distribution list (which specifies who are to receive copies) is the last section to be considered here, its location in the report or proposal varies.

Depending on its length and importance—as well as what is customary practice in the company—it may appear on the cover (though rarely), on the title page, or on a separate page at the end.

In memorandum reports and proposals (depending on the same factors as above), it may be included in the memo heading or at the end. In a letter report or proposal it appears at the end, as in an ordinary letter.

SPECIFIC APPLICATIONS

SAMPLE REPORTS AND PROPOSALS

In the following pages are five typical examples of business reports and proposals, ranging from "routine" to "special." These examples illustrate many of the principles and techniques discussed earlier in the chapter.

Sample AVO

An AVO (Avoid Verbal Order) is a type of memorandum report frequently used in industry. Since "verbal" as used here stands for "oral," "AVO" really means "Put It in Writing." It is especially useful as a form of communication between supervisors of different shifts. Thus, it is important that it be very clear, as there may be no opportunity for the receiving supervisor to "get with" the sending supervisor to clear up misunderstandings.

In Figure 11.16 the foreman of the second (or afternoon) shift is leaving a note for the foreman of the first (or next morning) shift informing him that a particular drill has had to be repaired, but should be ready for use first thing the following morning. Note that the purpose of the report is simply to inform—accurately, objectively, completely, concisely.

Sample Memorandum Report

Figure 11.17 illustrates well most or all of the characteristics of effective writing discussed earlier in this chapter: accuracy, objectivity, completeness, selectivity, impartiality, interpretation, and clarity.

Effective organization is also demonstrated. The heading and introduction at the beginning adequately orient the reader to what is to follow. Locating the conclusions and recommendations ahead of the discussion

FIGURE 11.16
Sample AVO. (Written by James H. Myers. Used with permission of author.)

Avoid Verbal Orders

Electro-Motive Division
General Motors Corporation

Number/

Date 8/12/73 Sunday 10:15 a.m.

To: T. Garstka

RE: Baker Drill, E.M. #1932, Department 2120.

The above machine has had the drilling fixture removed and sent to the Tool Room for repairs, as the fixture would not index. The Tool Room disassembled the fixture and found it to have a bad shaft. They made a new shaft and have now reassembled the fixture.

Per R. Fuchs, of Machine Repair, this fixture should be reinstalled on the drill, so that the machine will be ready to run by 7:00 a.m. Monday 8/13.

Signed J. Myers

CC: 1-B. Massow
    1-File

EMD 338D

FIGURE 11.17 Sample Memorandum Report. (Written by S. L. Alexander. Used with permission of author.)

Inter-Organization

Detroit Diesel Allison Division of General Motors Corporation
13400 West Outer Drive ▌ Detroit, Michigan 48228

To: Mr. J. E. LaBelle   **Address:** K-15

From: S. L. Alexander   **Date:** January 3, 1972

Subject: Progress Report on Performance of Oil Separators

Introduction

This report concerns the performance of three General Motors Manufacturing Development gravity oil separators (see attached) on washers in Department 502, 132, and 521. The oil separators were observed during the period from October 15 through December 4, 1971.

Conclusions

Department 502 - DE 32406

1. The solution life has been extended from two weeks to seven weeks.

2. Only 400 pounds of cleaner was required for supplemental additions during the seven weeks. Before the oil separator was operating, the average daily addition of cleaner was 200 pounds. The total amount of cleaner saved during the period was 10,300 pounds; approximately 10,000 pounds of cleaner valued at $1,500 was saved during the seven-week period.

3. The oil separator removes 98 percent of the oil that goes into the washer, thereby eliminating the problem of parts leaving the washer with an oily film.

4. The oil separator is capable of keeping the oil content at less than 0.20%.

Department 132 - DE 28853

1. This separator is capable of operation at near maximum efficiency but did not because of crowded location in the department and difficulty in servicing it.

Department 521 - DE 29212

1. The oil separator in Department 521 can be installed on another washer because the sources of oil that caused contamination in the washer have been eliminated.

FORM DA-3 (Rev. 4-74)

Mr. J. E. LaBelle
Page Two
January 3, 1972

Recommendations

1. Explore the possibilities of using the oil being removed by the separators in some other operation within the plant.

2. Set up a checklist whereby Maintenance can inspect the oil separators daily.

3. Future installations of oil separators should be wired electrically so they can be operated when the washer is not being operated.

4. Spare and replacement parts should be specifically held for the separators so when there is a need for repair work it can be performed without a long delay.

Discussion

Department 502

During the seven weeks in which the solution was used without being changed, approximately twenty-five drums (1,250 gallons) of oil were removed. Also during the period approximately 1,275 gallons of oil were added to the washer. From those figures it was calculated that 98 percent of the oil added was removed.

Samples were taken from the washer during the first week of the new charge and other samples were taken on November 11 and November 29, 1971. The percent of oil content on those days was as follows:

October 21, 1971	0.04%
November 11, 1971	0.09%
November 29, 1971	0.18%

Personnel, supervisors, inspectors, and operators have noticed a marked improvement in cleanliness of the blocks. Since the separator is capable of removing most of the oil from the washer and large quantities of cleaner are not required, the problem of blocks leaving the washer with an oily film and cleaner deposits have been eliminated.

Department 132

Since November 15, 1971, fourteen drums (700 gallons) of oil were removed from the washer. The oil separator is capable of removing far more oil than was collected during the period noted, providing that the supervisors in Department 132 take an interest in the successful operation of the separator. On numerous occasions, oil was observed overflowing from the collecting drums onto the floor where in turn a sump pump would return the oil back to the washer. At other times the intake would be almost completely

Mr. J. E. LaBelle
Page Three
January 3, 1972

clogged with debris and only a small flow of solution would be passing through the pump. This could be prevented if the skimmer intake is checked at least twice per shift to remove debris that sometimes collect at the intake. Also, supervision should not allow the water level to fall below the skimmer intake and should notify Maintenance of any malfunction of the pump and/or motor.

Department 521

When this separator was installed, a cutting oil operation prior to the washer accounted for most of the oil contamination. The cutting oil has been eliminated and replaced with coolant. Another source of contamination was excessive hydraulic oil loss on the washer. The oil leak was repaired during the first week of November. The separator would be more beneficial if it was installed on another washer within the plant.

                                                S. L. Alexander, Chemist
                                                Metallurgical Processing

cc: M. D. Opachak
     H. A. Roth
     W. F. Rushman
     File

makes it easy for the reader to get the main ideas before proceeding (if he or she wishes) to the more detailed explanation in the discussion. (A graphic aid in the form of a diagram, referred to in the introduction, is omitted in this copy.)

Finally, clear readability is achieved through the use of main and subheadings, listing, direct, simple paragraphs and sentences, and the choice of easy-to-understand language.

Incidentally, this was the writer's first technical report on the job. It was written following exposure to concepts presented in a report writing program he had taken in his plant a short time before.

Sample Memorandum Proposal

Figure 11.18 is an actual proposal for the purchase of a new item of equipment. Note that the writer, Mr. Pardoe, uses a persuasive approach that includes (a) explaining the need and giving evidence that it is urgent, (b) proposing a particular solution and showing its advantages, and (c) closing with a positive "action step."

In the present example, there was evidently no need for the writer to be more specific concerning what brand of contact printer should be purchased, or what its specifications should be. In many proposals the case would be strengthened if this information were included, along with (a) reasons why the particular brand specified would be preferable to other competing brands and (b) information on cost and, possibly, how long it would take to pay for itself.

FIGURE 11.18
Sample Memorandum Proposal. (Written by Albert O. Pardoe. Used with permission of author.)

		Classification	UNCLASSIFIED
		Contract No.	
DIVISION	RAYTHEON SERVICE COMPANY		
Operation		Distribution	aa
Department	RSC PUBLICATIONS		
To	R. D. Eames	File No.	
From	A. O. Pardoe	Memo No.	AOP-245
Subject	CAPITAL EQUIPMENT – CONTACT PRINTER	Date	12 May 1971

    Our ability to provide precision printed circuit negatives and positives for EDL is in jeopardy. Our basic problem is an old and beyond-repair contact printing frame (see attached photo) that has seen better days. The vacuum printing frame (printer) was purchased in 1954 (17 years ago) and has been in constant use ever since. Its age is never more evident than when we attempt to meet precision requirements.

    If we are to continue to provide a critical circuit capability for our customers at EDL, the need to purchase a new contact printer is urgent. The Wayland Satellite, where the printer will be located, serves many major programs such as AEGIS, OHD, MSR, SEASPARROW, and TARTAR-D.

    During the past 15 years, we have been providing precision circuits of high quality to EDL. However, especially during recent months, as our equipment deteriorated – so too, our ability to perform. As a matter of fact, since our most recent equipment failure, a good deal of EDL circuit work has been subcontracted. We want that work. We have the precision camera; we have the technical competence; all we need is a good contact printer.

    I urge your approval of this new equipment so that we may once again perform in a manner that is beneficial to EDL and RSC.

                                         A. O. Pardoe, Manager
                                         Graphic Arts & Satellites

AOP: rmn

dc: S. Bull, Jr.
    D. Gagne

    How strong a factual case would be needed would depend on the degree of perceived need, the magnitude of the purchase, and the credibility of the writer. In this case it appears likely that Mr. Pardoe enjoyed high credibility with Mr. Eames.

    The word "Unclassified," by the way, in the upper right corner, simply means "not confidential."

Sample Request

    Securing additional personnel in a business organization is usually difficult. If we assume that funds are available, the principal requirement for such a request is a strong demonstration of need. In Figure 11.19

FIGURE 11.19
Sample Request.
(Written by R. A. Girling, G. D. MacPhail, and L. S. Youngling as a General Motors Institute letter-writing class project. Used with permission of authors.)

GENERAL MOTORS OVERSEAS OPERATIONS

Date: June 16, 1972

To: Mr. John C. Smith,
    Manager Detroit Staff

Subject: Request for Additional Personnel

From: G. L. McYoungir

As you know, the role of the Detroit Office has grown considerably during the past few years. The resultant increase in departmental activities has reached a point whereby our mailroom staff cannot adequately provide the support service required by the Detroit Office.

Some of the more notable factors that have affected our mailroom are:

1. The merger of the GMODC and GMOO Service Departments.
2. The increase in Detroit Staff personnel from 105 to 225 during the past ten years (mailroom personnel has remained constant at 2).
3. The increase in technical assistance to overseas plants (distribution of reports, prints, video tapes, etc.).

In June of 1970 a complete time and motion study of the mailroom activity resulted in increased efficiency and the acquisition of new equipment. However, it was pointed out at that time that the present number of personnel was barely adequate. The merger of the service departments in January of this year nearly doubled the volume of mail and completely inundated the mailroom. Because of the "head count freeze," additional personnel were out of the question.

In an effort to maintain the mailroom operation, it has been necessary to resort to such inefficient and costly means as:

1. Increased overtime for mailroom personnel.
2. Use of higher level personnel from other departments on an overtime basis.
3. Reduction in mail service (resulting in secretarial help making trips back and forth to the mailroom).
4. Use of temporary outside help.

The addition of one third level clerk would eliminate the above and also put the mailroom back into a position of providing the basic support service required by the Detroit Staff.

Therefore, we have attached for your consideration Personnel Request Form 617, requesting a third level clerk for the mailroom.

[signature]

G. L. McYoungir

nearly the entire memo consists of analyzing the situation to show that an additional mail clerk is needed. If the recipient, Mr. Smith, were skeptical of the need or uninformed of the situation, he might require more factual evidence (how much increased overtime, how much use of temporary outside help, and so on) before being convinced. However, in this instance he probably would find the need argument sufficiently convincing.

Sample Letter Report

The letter report in Figure 11.20 is from a member of a Chicago-based firm who is on leave overseas to assist a local branch in setting up a new system. Note that although a letter format is used, the content employs a typical report format. Whereas most business letters carry a fairly personal tone, the only elements of this letter that are personal are the "Dear Lynn," "best regards," "Sincerely," and the informal signature, "Tom."

This particular example happens to be addressed to a member of the writer's home office, but it does not differ essentially from a letter report from one company to another.

Sample Formal Proposal

Figure 11.21 illustrates most of the essential components of a formal proposal: title page, abstract, table of contents, introduction, conclusions and recommendation, and discussion. In addition a copy of the map is included showing the proposed new facility. (Omitted in the version here are several photographs that show the crowded parking conditions.)

FIGURE 11.20
Sample Letter Report.
(Adapted from a letter written by T. R. Brackett. Used with permission of author.)

INTERCONTINENTAL ENTERPRISES, INC.
Rua Formosa 417
P.O.B. 9307
Sao Paulo, Brazil

November 10, 1975

Mr. Lynn Glidden, Director
Department of Administrative Services
Intercontinental Enterprises, Inc.
12750 Lane Highway
Chicago, Illinois

Dear Lynn:

In this letter I'll give you a general summary of my activities at IEB for the week of November 5 and report on the status of the Critical Path Planning System now being prepared for Project 767.

<u>Objectives</u>

1. Train local personnel in Critical Path Planning techniques for control of Project 767.
2. Analyze the total project and assist management in determining the most effective project control system to be used.
3. Set up Project 767 with the selected control system.

<u>Accomplishments</u>

1. Two individuals have been selected for intensive training in C.P.P. and are now progressing in the following areas:
   a. Written material for home study.
   b. Practical in-plant application of techniques.
2. Analysis of the total project is under way and will require at least another two weeks for completion.

<u>Conclusions</u>

I am very optimistic that this project will succeed for the following reasons:
1. Local management is very enthusiastic about the C.P.P. method and is anxious to have it succeed.
2. The individuals selected for training are competent and have the desire to learn.

3. I am receiving excellent cooperation from everyone involved in the project.

I'll report again in another week to keep you up to date. Meanwhile, best regards.

Sincerely,

Tom

T. R. Brackett

TR/bb

FIGURE 11.21 Sample Formal Proposal. (Written by James E. Brendtke. Used with permission of author.)

PROPOSED ADDITIONAL PARKING FACILITIES

General Motors Deutschland

Wiesbaden, Germany

Submitted to Mr. John M. Lawrence

Regional Manager

Prepared by James E. Brendtke   March 24, 1971

TABLE OF CONTENTS

Abstract	iii
Introduction	1
Conclusions	2
Recommendation	2
Proposal to Lease Additional Parking Facilities	3
Appendix	5

ABSTRACT

When GM Deutschland was established in 1967, taking over the premises leased by GM Limited for Frigidaire GMBH, the product lines were expanded. In line with this expansion, personnel, sales volume and inventories increased, but the physical facilities remained unchanged.

The parking in the open compound area, in conjunction with street parking, although crowded, was tolerable. Recently, the parking situation became very critical due to changes and requirements of City regulations. There is but one solution; namely, parking facilities must be expanded.

There is a suitable piece of land adjacent to the present premises which can be utilized to eliminate this critical situation, leasing of which is proposed and recommended.

INTRODUCTION

The premises presently occupied by General Motors Deutschland at 131 Mainzerstrasse, Wiesbaden, Germany, were leased by General Motors Limited, effective January 2, 1963 from the City of Wiesbaden. The property consisted of a "U" shaped building and open parking area. The building housed an office (46 people) and a small finished product and parts warehouse for Frigidaire products.

In 1967, GM Deutschland was founded, absorbing Frigidaire GMBH and taking over the marketing responsibility for U.S. and Vauxhall vehicles, Parts & Accessories, and Power & Industrial products which had formerly been handled by General Motors Continental. Although sales volume, inventories and other related activities, including personnel (102 people) increased, the physical operating facilities remained unchanged. With the increased volume the open area which is utilized for visitor and employe parking has become very critical.

The following proposal analyzes the need for additional parking facilities and shows how we feel the need can best be met.

CONCLUSIONS

1. There is an immediate need to alleviate the overcrowded parking and service area.

2. Only one piece of land is available adjacent to the present premises which is suitable for current needs and possible future expansion.

RECOMMENDATION

In line with the situation as outlined in the preceding introduction and the ensuing report, it is recommended to lease the parcel of land at 133 Mainzerstrasse starting January 1, 1971, through December 31, 1972, at a total rental of DM 90, 100 ($24,617). Your concurrence and approval is requested.

DISCUSSION

Need

GM Deutschland's biggest current problem is one of inadequate parking facilities inside the company compound. The present area can reasonably hold 30 vehicles. There are, however, more than 70 cars struggling to park in this area on any normal working day. In addition to employe parking, there are civilian and military customers, visiting dealers, the company fleet and large articulated highway trucks effecting deliveries to and from our warehouse loading dock. Please refer to attached exhibits 1 through 4 illustrating the present situation.

This situation results in loss of employe time in moving cars to allow trucks to get in and out, and furthermore it often creates safety hazards.

The critical space shortage has developed from a number of unrelated items. They are:

1. The increase in the number of employes.

2. Recent parking regulations whereby the city no longer allows street parking in front of the plant.
3. A city ordinance which requires that employers furnish adequate parking facilities for their employes' cars.
4. No other readily accessible parking areas available nearby.
5. Increase in truck delivery volume resulting from growing sales volume.

Proposed Solution

In answer to our desperate plea for more parking space, the city has offered a triangular piece of ground adjacent to our present property. A plot plan illustrating the present facilities as well as the available new area is shown on the attached exhibit 5.

As will be noted from this plot plan, this piece of land is the only parcel available for expansion, and fortunately is adjacent to our present facilities. Besides, the terms offered by the city are unusually reasonable.

The location of the parcel of land offered is at 133 Mainzerstrasse. The total land area is 29,920 square feet. The lease term, which would run concurrent with our present lease, would be for a period of two years, from January 1, 1971, to December 31, 1972. The total rental would be DM 90,100 (U.S. $24,617).

There are presently four (4) small one-story buildings on the property. The city has agreed to raze the buildings and prepare the land for parking. GM Deutschland would have an approximate cost of DM 20,000 (U.S. $5,465) to provide a suitable gravel surface.

Projecting into the future, as noted the lease covering the present facilities expires December 31, 1972, at which time either new facilities must be available for occupancy or the lease extended. The proposed new property is the only adjacent property which can be used for building expansion. By securing it now there will be an option for the future in that we can either stay in the present premises, if we so desire, or look for more suitable ones. If we do not lease the additional property now this option may not exist later; thus we would be forced to move.

430   SPECIFIC APPLICATIONS

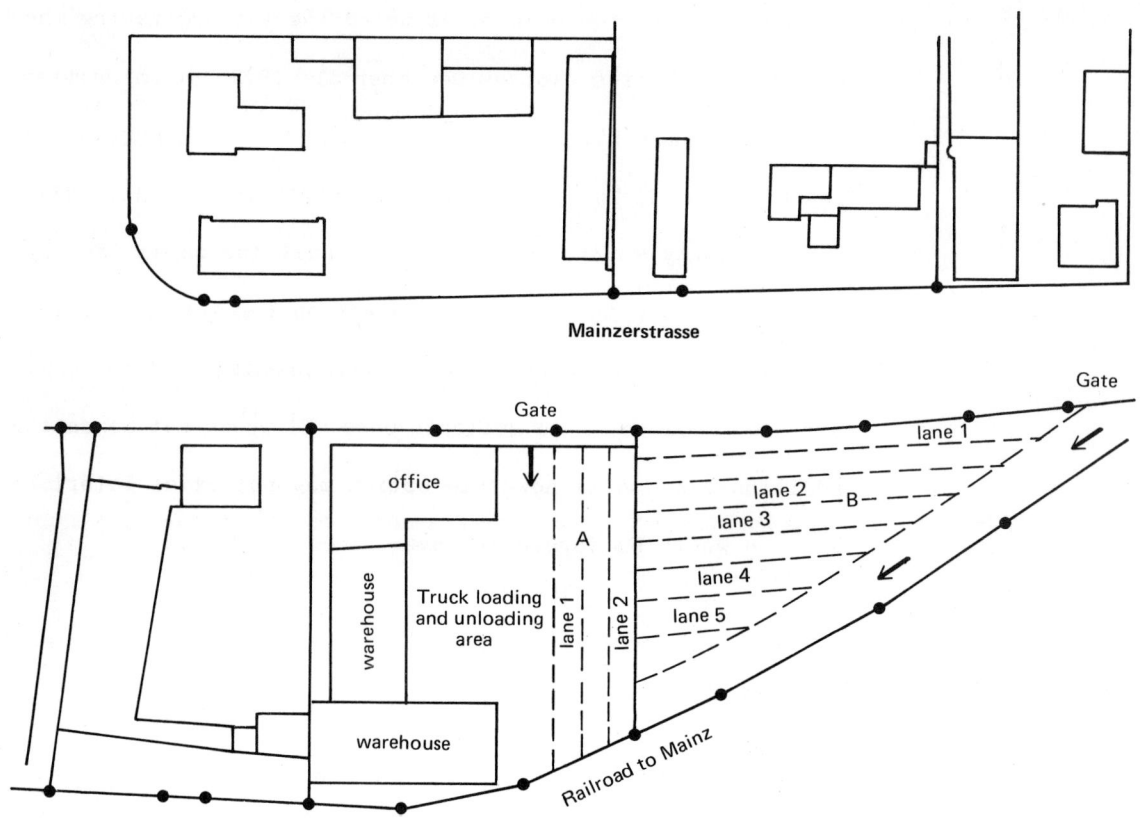

Legend

Present Parking Lot A   Proposed Additional Parking Lot B
                                      lane 1   20 cars
   lane 1   15 cars   lane 2   14 cars
   lane 2   15 cars   lane 3   10 cars
   Totals   30 cars   lane 4   5 cars
                                      lane 5   4 cars
                                      Totals   53 cars

Figure 6. Map of Present and Proposed Parking Areas

SUMMARY

1. Reports provide the eyes and ears for those not in a position to observe directly for themselves; reports inform the reader or listener what is or has been.

2. A proposal seeks authorization for what the proposer thinks should be adopted as the solution to a problem.

3. Reports and proposals are forms of the Verbal World, and their value depends on how closely they correspond with the Real World.

4. Three kinds of statements comprising the Verbal World are (a) factual statements, based on direct observation; (b) inferences, based on reasoning; and (c) value judgments, based on criteria. In reports and proposals these three are represented by factual data, conclusions, and recommendations.

5. The components of a formal report or proposal may include (a) cover, (b) title page, (c) memo or letter of transmittal, (d) abstract, (e) table of contents, (f) introduction, (g) findings, conclusions, and recommendations, (h) discussion, (i) appendix, (j) footnotes, (k) bibliography, and (l) distribution list. The more special, or formal, the document, the more likely it is to use all—or nearly all—these components. The more routine, or informal the document, the less likely it is to use more than the most essential components.

6. If the direct approach is used, the conclusions and recommendations normally follow the introduction; if indirect, they come at the end of the discussion.

SUGGESTED APPLICATIONS

1. The class (or teacher) will select several school-related topics—such as life in the residence hall, parking regulations, cheating on exams—that are likely to be perceived differently by different groups. The class will then be divided into several subgroups of three or four with each subgroup investigating a different source of information or opinion on one of the topics. For instance, one subgroup might interview students, another teachers, another someone in a dean's office, another the campus police—whatever sources seem most relevant. The subgroups should then report their findings (either orally, in writing, or both, as the teacher may direct) in class and compare the differences. What relationship is there between the Verbal World reported and the Real World?

2. Assume that you have been assigned a term paper in another course. Write a memorandum report to the teacher of that course in which you explain your progress to date. Include in your report (a) your general topic and exact title, and (b) a bibliography of eight actual (not fictitious)

sources you would consult. Each source should illustrate a different form as presented in the section in this chapter on how to compose a bibliography. Use appropriate headings, and sign the report.

3. Assume that you are employed by a foundation that gives financial grants to worthy causes. One of your responsibilities is reviewing proposals, and one of the first parts of any proposal you review is the proposal summary, or abstract. Compare the following three summaries and be prepared to defend which you feel is most effective, and why.[3]

A

This proposal to the Trustees of the Blank Foundation requests a grant of $59,000 to underwrite the preparation of a bibliographic monograph of Obscure Disease. Obscure Disease presently afflicts seven million persons from the Southern United States south to Central Argentina.

This monograph will cover the etomological, the parasitological and clinical literature on this subject from 1500 to 1970. It will bring together many widely scattered research findings on this disease, and make them available to the many researchers presently investigating the disease.

The principal investigator will be Dr. Physician of the Microbiology Department at the School of Medicine of Large University. Dr. Physician has been conducting research on Obscure Disease for the past 22 years, and is the preeminent researcher in the field. This research will be conducted under the auspices of Large University School of Medicine, which supports physicians and medical clinics throughout Central and South America.

The following pages outline the problem, objectives, procedures and budget, and give further information concerning participation and institution.

We respectfully invite your serious consideration of this proposal, and trust that the Blank Foundation will find it possible to make a grant in support of this project at this time.

B

The long-range goal of this proposed program is to help students develop into adults who think creatively and independently, learn by observation, work together in inquiring teams, develop judgment and decision making abilities and most importantly, adults who can conceive of more satisfactory alternatives to social problems than passive acceptance or militant violence. In short—this program's aim is to help students to grow into adults who actively practice and participate in democratic citizenship.

The principal investigator will be Dr. Physician of the Microbiology Department at the School of Medicine of Large University.

The following pages outline the problem, objectives, procedures and budget, and give specific information concerning participant and institution.

We respectfully invite your serious consideration of this Proposal, and trust that the Blank Foundation will find it possible to make a grant in support of this project at this time.

C

The long-range goal of this proposed program is to help students develop into adults who think creatively and independently, learn by observation, work together in inquiring teams, develop judgment and decision making abilities and most importantly, adults who can conceive of more satisfactory alternatives to social problems than passive acceptance or militant violence. In short—this program's aim is to help students to grow into adults who actively practice and participate in democratic citizenship.

4. Here is a way to get practice in committee proposals. In any organization, the ability to secure management approval for ideas one would like to see adopted is indispensable. Without it, one's capacity for job satisfaction or personal growth is severely limited.

The following project has proved highly effective in a wide variety of college classes and plant training programs in sharpening insights and providing experience in the persuasive process. Essentially, the project consists of a series of persuasive presentations by committees of three or four students. The purpose of each presentation is to secure approval from an "administrative group" (role-played by other members of the class) of whatever proposal the committee chooses to make. The project is described in detail below:

Objectives

1. To secure a practical understanding of the three factors in persuading others. These are:
    a. Adapting to the needs of the organization and of the management personnel who are to be persuaded.
    b. Enhancing and utilizing one's personal credibility to maximum effect.
    c. Utilizing the need-plan pattern clearly with sound evidence and reasoning.

2. To gain increased proficiency in serving as a member of a group.

3. To gain experience in securing, selecting, and organizing data needed in convincing an audience to accept one's assertions.

4. To gain proficiency in participating in question-and-answer periods.

5. To gain clearer insights into how management tends to react to persuasive attempts.

6. To gain experience in arriving at sound group decisions.

Procedure

1. *Grouping*. The class will be divided, through volunteering, into three- or four-person committees. Each committee will then decide on whatever proposal it wishes to make. In each case, the proposal should be for some specific change in policy or operation at your school (in order to provide a common frame of reference). The presiding officer for the administrative group to which each proposal is addressed will be decided on at this time also. Each committee will be responsible for securing an appropriate member of the administration to visit the class the day of their presentation.

2. *Written Memo*. At the next class meeting each committee will submit to the instructor a memo stating (a) what specific change it intends to propose, (b) what administrative group (as role-played by other members of the class) at your school the proposal is addressed to, and (c) what member of the administration it will invite as a guest observer. The memo should be signed by all members of the committee.

3. *Instructional Reading*. The concepts and techniques discussed in Chapter 9, "Persuading Your Reader or Listener," and in the present chapter should be carefully reviewed for their applicability to this project.

4. *Schedule*. A typed schedule will be distributed by the teacher showing (a) membership of each committee, (b) proposal topic, (c) name of administrative group to be role-played by the class, (d) name of presiding officer of the administrative group, (e) date of presentation, and (f) name of the guest observer. The presentations will be scheduled at the rate of one per class period. Each committee should provide its guest observer with a copy of this schedule.

5. *Preparation*. Each committee will be responsible for preparing a typed formal written proposal observing the guidelines presented in this chapter concerning the cover, letter or memo of transmittal, title page, and so forth. Copies are then to be duplicated by whatever means the teacher specifies

for distribution to the class and teacher at the class meeting preceding the day of their presentation.

6. *Presentation*. On its scheduled day, each committee, sitting in front of the room, will have about 15–20 minutes for answering any questions from the administrative group concerning any phase of the proposal. The presiding officer of the administrative group will be in charge, and should also sit in front of the room.

7. *Decision*. The administrative group, still under the chairmanship of the presiding officer, will be allotted another 15–20 minutes to reach a decision to (a) adopt the proposal, either in whole or in part, (b) reject it, or (c) return it to the committee for "further work." The guest observer may join in the deliberations if he or she wishes (but should be careful not to dominate). Note: It is important that those role-playing the administrative group clearly understand what group they constitute and play their roles convincingly—not as they imagine the actual members of this group would react, but as they themselves would react if they were actually members of this group.

8. *Critique*. Near the end of the class period, the instructor will spend 10–15 minutes offering a critical analysis to the committee in terms of:

    a. The clarity with which their written proposal explained
      1. The problem or need
      2. The criteria against which the proposal was evaluated
      3. The proposal itself
      4. The arguments supporting the proposal
    b. How clearly and convincingly they answered questions during the question period.

The teacher may also comment on the decision reached by the administrative group and how competently it was reached. If time permits, the guest observer may also comment on any of the above points.

9. *Evaluative Paper*. Following the presentations, your instructor may request that you write a paper evaluating the application of any one or more of the persuasive principles or techniques discussed in Chapter 9 relating to (a) the committee's adapting to the needs of the administrative group, (b) the credibility of the committee, or (c) the use of logic in their presentation.

5. This project can easily be converted from a written to an oral proposal by changing directions 6, 8, and 9 above (in addition to reading in advance

Chapter 12, "Presenting Your Ideas Orally"). Items 6, 8, and 9 would thus read:

> 6. *Presentation.* On its scheduled day each committee will have about 20 minutes for making its presentation. The organization should be adapted from the following guide:
>
>> Introduction (identification and importance of problem, relevant background, preview of main topics, and order of speakers)
>> Description and analysis of problem
>> Explanation of criteria
>> Explanation of the specific proposal
>> Arguments showing the benefits of the proposal, including how its advantages would outweigh its disadvantages
>> Conclusion stating explicitly what is being recommended
>
> Visual aids (especially charts and overhead transparencies) should be used freely in the presentation. The time used for the presentation and the responsibilities for its various segments should be shared about equally by the committee members.
>
> 8. *Critique.* Near the end of the class period, the teacher will spend 10–12 minutes offering a critical analysis to the committee in terms of:
>
>> a. The clarity with which they explained
>>> 1. The problem or need
>>> 2. The criteria against which they evaluated the proposal
>>> 3. The proposal itself
>>> 4. The arguments supporting the proposal
>>
>> b. Their speaking delivery (whether forceful, direct, and communicative)
>> c. Their use of visual aids (whether well chosen, legible, reasonably neat, and well utilized)
>
> In addition, the teacher will give each member of the committee a written evaluation of his or her delivery and organization. The instructor may also comment on the decision reached by the administrative group and how competently it was reached, and may invite the guest observer to comment also.
>
> 9. *Suggested Topics.* The topic of your proposal should be whatever your group can do the best job with. You must be able to convince your administrative group that a need for whatever you are proposing actually exists, devise a feasible solution, and support your entire case with adequate, authentic evidence. The following list illustrates the kind of topics suitable for this assignment:

Campus-town relations Advisors in dormitories
Campus parking and traffic Making adjustments for
Protection for coeds late working students
  at night Compulsory attendance
Exam scheduling Improved laundry facilities
Noise in dormitories Improved library hours

10. *Evaluation Form.* The following evaluation form may be used by the teacher for evaluating each committee presentation. After completing the form, the teacher may wish to make copies for distribution to all the members of the committee.

Committee: 1.   Class:
No.   2.   Hour:
           3.   Date:

EVALUATION

Committee Presentation

	Excellent			*Poor*	
1. Organization (need-plan sequence, general vs. specific, continuity, introduction, transitions, summary)	5	4	3	2	1
2. Visual aids (relevant, adequate, legible, well used)	5	4	3	2	1
3. Delivery (communicative, confident, audible, free from distracting mannerisms)	5	4	3	2	1

Administrative Group

1. Leadership (Ch.)	5	4	3	2	1
2. Decision (soundness based on need and plan)	5	4	3	2	1
3. Interpersonal relationship and participation	5	4	3	2	1

Evaluator:

NOTES

[1] Sidney Harris, "Ph.D. Dissertations: A Lesson in Futility," *The Detroit Free Press,* December 5, 1960.

[2] See Robert R. Rathbone and James B. Stone, *A Writer's Guide for Engineers and Scientists* (Englewood Cliffs, N.J.: Prentice-Hall, Inc., 1962), p. 20.

[3] Norton J. Kiritz, "The Proposal Summary," *The Grantsmanship Center News,* October–November, 1974, pp. 8–10.

FIVE: PRESENTING YOUR IDEAS ORALLY

12 THE ORAL PRESENTATION

SPEAKING COMPARED WITH WRITING
Advantages of Writing vs. Speaking
Advantages of Speaking vs. Writing
    Creating a Positive Relationship
    Formulating the Message
    Utilizing Two-Way Communication

OVERCOMING SPEECH FRIGHT
The Problem of Speech Fright
    Symptoms   The Underlying Nature of Speech Fright
    Additional Consequences of Self-consciousness

The Solution to Overcoming Speech Fright
    Replace Negative Attitudes with Positive
    Utilize Audience Reactions   Get Experience
    Additional Payoffs from Overcoming Speech Fright

DELIVERING THE SPEECH
Body Communication
    Posture   Facial Expression
    Eye Directness   Gestures

Vocal Communication
    Audibility   Expressiveness

Manuscript vs. Extemporaneous
    Why Business People Often Read Their Speeches
    The Case Against the Manuscript Speech
    The Case for the Extemporaneous Speech
    The Oral Style Compared with the Written Style
    The Written and Oral Styles Illustrated

USING VISUAL AIDS

Differences between Visual Aids and Graphic Aids
      The Listener-Viewer Situation
      Variety of Visual Aids Available

Advantages and Limitations in the Use of Selected Visual Aids
      Three-Dimensional Objects   The Chalkboard   Charts
      The Overhead Projector   The Opaque Projector
      The 2- by 2-Inch Slide Projector

Precautions in Using Visual Aids

MAKING SURE THE MAIN POINTS STAND OUT

HANDLING QUESTIONS FROM THE AUDIENCE

Preparing for Questions from the Audience
      Develop a Positive Attitude   Plan Your Answers

Deciding When Questions Should Be Raised

Listening to Questions and Replying to Them
      Listening   Replying

The main emphasis of this book thus far has been on written communication. Nearly all of Part 2, "Being Clear," focused on problems in writing. Chapter 11 focused solely on written reports and proposals. Sometimes, however, you will be asked to present reports or proposals orally. It could be a committee presentation to your department, or a department presentation to higher management. It could be a talk in your community to a local service club, a class at the high school, or a board of some civic group you belong to. It could also be a talk before a professional society at a local, regional, or national meeting.

Many people, unfortunately, upon receiving such an assignment, view it with great apprehension. I have known highly capable people in responsible positions who became very uptight over the prospect of facing an audience. To them it was not an opportunity, but an ordeal.

Since facing audiences is a prospect you also will encounter, we shall endeavor in this chapter to provide you with insights and guidelines that will help you face them confidently and constructively.[1]

SPEAKING COMPARED WITH WRITING

Comparing speaking with writing will shed useful light on the particular advantages of each.

Advantages of Writing vs. Speaking

Perhaps the main advantage of writing is that it allows for a more deliberate formulation of the message, an advantage especially important in policy statements or legal documents. The more important the message, the more important it is to put it in writing.

One reason for this advantage is, of course, that the writer has more time for formulation than does the speaker. But this is not the only reason. In the words of Horowitz and Newman, "writing represents a more serious commitment than speaking. Psychologically . . . there is something about putting pen to paper . . . that creates inhibitions. . . . Apparently, the . . . [writer] feels that what is spoken can be taken back, but what is written may stand as a self-recrimination forever."[2] Thus, putting ideas in writing not only allows more careful formulation, it also encourages it.

A second advantage, virtually equal in importance, is that what is written is "permanent"—at least until lost or discarded. Thus, it can be studied at length if need be, and can provide a permanent record. (One could argue that tapes are permanent, too, and can be studied at length if need be. But the practical inconvenience of filing and reviewing tapes eliminates them from serious consideration on this score.)

Additional advantages of writing vs. speaking include these: writing can more easily present extensive factual information (such as tables of data in an appendix); it is usually more convenient and certainly less expensive for reaching large numbers (as by means of a newsletter or shareholder's report); and is less expensive for long distance transmission (a telex or cablegram vs. a transocean telephone call).

Advantages of Speaking vs. Writing

The principal advantages of speaking vs. writing can be summed up in terms of the three factors discussed in Chapter 2 on reducing communication falloff: (a) creating a positive relationship, (b) formulating the message, and (c) utilizing two-way communication.

Creating a Positive Relationship   For promoting a positive relationship between sender and receiver, speaking has a much greater potential than writing. When we write, the manner in which we transmit ideas is very impersonal: sheets of paper covered with symbols. The reader may have little notion what the writer looks like, or vice versa. Even if the words create a positive image, the reader may have little assurance of the kind of person behind those words; even if he or she knows the writer, the written words still lack the personal impact.

When we speak, however, the means by which we transmit our ideas is exceedingly personal: it is you or I, a flesh-and-blood being, standing in person before our audience. Through the tone of our voice, the vitality of our manner, the directness of our delivery we can evoke a sense of trust impossible to arouse through the printed page alone. Any college student who drives 500 miles home on a weekend to see his girlfriend is well aware of the superiority of spoken, face-to-face communication in promoting a positive relationship!

Formulating the Message While it is true that speaking does not permit as *careful* a formulation as writing, it often permits a more *precise* formulation. One reason is presented by Horowitz and Newman, who point out that while speaking is "looser" (more verbose) than writing, it is not *vaguer*. "It is looser because it is less inhibited. . . . But it is also richer, fuller, and more precise—the last because of its elaboration."[3]

Another reason is that oral communication offers more cues to the meaning than does written. In writing, the principal cues are the word symbols themselves, while in speaking there are the word symbols *plus* the manner in which they are uttered. Such cues as vocal inflections, pauses, forcefulness, facial expression, and gestures can combine to bring out subtleties of meaning impossible on the printed page.

Utilizing Two-Way Communication Two-way communication is enormously facilitated when we speak as compared with when we write. The feedback may be nonverbal, in the form of expressions of interest, boredom, comprehension, or confusion on the faces of our audience. Or it may be in the form of questions and comments during the question period.

This feedback, in turn, affects our own behavior as speaker. Observing audience reactions, we can define a term here, or simplify a point there as we suspect that our meaning is not entirely clear. Further, by being alive to audience response, we can become more "turned on," more absorbed with "getting through"—both important in gaining confidence and rapport.

The purpose of this comparative analysis has not been to establish that oral communication is superior to written, or vice versa, for each has its own particular advantages. Indeed, one well-known study concluded that for most effective results, *both* should be used.[4] Thus, it is not uncommon for a written policy statement to be followed by a staff meeting to clarify the implications, or for a telephone call to be followed by a letter of confirmation. Similarly, an oral report or proposal is often accompanied by a written version, or vice versa.

The purpose of our examination of written vs. oral has been rather to emphasize the advantage of presenting ideas orally when the occasion arises. For it is important that when you are faced with an oral assignment, you regard it as it should be regarded: an opportunity, not an ordeal.

OVERCOMING SPEECH FRIGHT

The advantages awaiting you from presenting your ideas orally in a face-to-face setting can be considerable. But they will be more easily realized as you overcome the specter of speech fright that so often proves a nightmare even to very capable persons.

However, you *can* overcome it (if you haven't already)! From experience with thousands of students, both undergraduate and adult, over more than a third of a century, I feel safe in predicting that, whatever your anxieties, you can become confident and communicative in front of an audience.

Let us proceed to analyze the problem, then offer our solution.

The Problem of Speech Fright

The reason for examining the problem first is that understanding a problem is often the first step in correcting it.

Symptoms   When speech fright occurs, the symptoms tend to fall in three categories:

1. A feeling of *nervousness*. The speaker experiences "butterflies" in the stomach, a quickened heartbeat, increased perspiration, nervous cough, and so on.

2. A feeling of *inferiority*. The speaker feels inadequate for the situation or inferior to the audience. He or she is certain they are sitting there passing scornful or amused judgment on him or her. This feeling of inferiority may occur before or after the speech as well.

3. A feeling of *wanting to withdraw*. The speaker looks away from the audience, mumbles in a low tone, seeks security behind the lectern. Privately he or she wishes to "sink through a hole in the floor." Often the desire to escape grips one *before* the speech. One is tempted not to show up, or hopes that "something will happen to call the whole thing off."

Of course, these feelings may appear in various combinations in varying degrees of intensity with different people. If you have experienced any of these feelings, you're normal! In fact, studies have revealed that among beginning speakers, over 90 percent undergo at least some of these symptoms. One study of 420 college students in beginning speech courses showed that only 6 percent claimed that speaking was initially "a pleasurable experience unaccompanied by any fears or doubts."[5]

The Underlying Nature of Speech Fright   Simply indentifying these symptoms of speech fright is not enough. To cope effectively with the problem, we must recognize that essentially speech fright is nothing more or less than a case of self-consciousness in a speaking situation. Of the three basic elements in the situation—the speaker, the message, and the audience—the speaker's mind is on him- or herself instead of where it should be: on his message and audience. This self-consciousness results in a wholly negative set of attitudes toward all of these elements; undue anxiety concerning oneself, apathy toward one's message, and inferiority or indifference toward the audience.

Redefined, we can see that speech fright is by no means limited to standing in front of an audience. The salesperson who paces the street working up enough nerve to knock on a prospect's door is experiencing a form of speech fright, as is the teenager who vacillates before the telephone, unsure whether to call for a date with a girl he's just met.

Additional Consequences of Self-Consciousness The experience of speech fright, distressing as it may be to the speaker, is only one unhappy consequence of negative attitudes, and not the most serious at that. In fact, studies have shown that the speaker is likely to sense much more keenly than the audience his or her own feelings of nervousness: shaking knees that to a speaker can be quite unnerving, may scarcely be noticeable to the audience at all. (As one student expressed it, "My nervousness is inside me, so I'm the one who notices it most.")

At least three further consequences of self-consciousness may result, all sharply reducing speaker effectiveness. These are:

1. Poor speaking delivery. The speaker tends to talk in an impersonal, mechanical manner; lifeless, monotonous, evoking little interaction or rapport with the audience.

2. Audience boredom and loss of attention. As a result in large part of the miserable delivery, members of the audience quickly tend to lose interest. Since the speaker presents no strong stimulus to hold their attention, they begin to glance at their watches, lapse into daydreaming; even, if possible to slip away unnoticed.

3. Loss of speaker credibility. Worse yet, the speaker's credibility diminishes in the eyes of the audience. This is easy to understand when we recall (from Chapter 9) the vital role played by dynamism in the overall credibility of the speaker. The dynamic speaker may not actually *be* more competent or trustworthy than a lackluster counterpart, but—other factors being equal—he or she *seems* so. The speaker who mumbles and drives an audience to boredom will scarcely come across as dynamic. Likely such a speaker will evoke as little confidence as he or she does attention.

The Solution to Overcoming Speech Fright

The cure for speech fright is amazingly simple, in theory, at least, if not always in practice—though actually, it is fairly simple in practice as well. The answer is essentially threefold.

Replace Negative Attitudes with Positive The most critical step is clearly implied by our analysis of the problem. It is to drive out the negative attitudes by replacing them with positive. Doing this involves basically two steps:

1. Get turned on with your message. Choose a subject you have a strong feel for; a feel for its importance both to you and your listeners. If you are

given a subject whose relevance you fail to grasp, look far enough into it to discover its consequences for the well-being of your audience until you *do* feel fired up. A speaker with a message is seldom overcome with speech fright.

I vividly recall a black student in a speech class a few years ago, a shy, quiet girl with a sweet smile and unassuming manner. Then one day in a series on "a personal belief," a white student preceding her was giving his views on the case against forced busing. Suddenly I noticed Mary furiously revising her notes, and when she stepped before the class her eyes flashed with indignation as she launched into an attack on the injustice of segregation as she had known it. She was turned on! Any self-consciousness she may ever have felt was forgotten.

However, an important caution here: becoming turned on with one's message, important though this is, falls short of the mark if we are to become both confident *and* communicative, for one can get so absorbed in the subject that while one does indeed forget oneself (thus shedding one's self-consciousness) one forgets the audience as well! A guest professor at an evening forum I once attended spoke brilliantly for twenty minutes—addressing the flag at one side of the platform! His content and organization were superb; so was his self-confidence. But he exhibited no awareness of his audience. We could all have slipped out and I doubt he would have noticed—or cared much if he had.

In replacing negative attitudes with positive, therefore, a second step is necessary.

2. Get concerned with getting through to your audience. This step is even more critical for achieving communicative effectiveness. It involves reminding yourself that your primary reason for speaking is to create within the minds of the audience an understanding of, a feeling for, a conviction concerning the message you are presenting. This objective *must* be the goal riding uppermost in your mind if you hope to become an effective speaker.

Now, when you replace the negative attitudes of apathy and indifference with the positive attitudes of being turned on toward your message and concerned for getting through to your audience—what happens to your self-consciousness? It dissolves! You simply have no time left to be anxious for yourself.

But this is only part of the cure for speech fright. It is the most crucial part, but to be fully effective, two additional ingredients are required.

Utilize Audience Reactions We mentioned above, as one consequence of negative attitudes, audience boredom and loss of attention. By replacing the negative attitudes with positive, you can expect instead rapt attention and lively reactions from your audience. These reactions you should use. As the authors of a textbook on discussion have expressed it, "We have yet to hear of a good public speaker who does not hunt for those faces in the crowd that say, 'I am with you; keep it up.' When he finds those faces, he keeps looking at them."[6]

The value of audience reaction is described by a beginning speaker in this account of how he gained confidence during a speech:

> About a week ago I gave a talk demonstrating techniques of girl watching. I am basically a quiet, timid person, so I was nervous and not looking forward to giving the speech, and I began to wonder if girl watching was a proper topic with girls in the class. After considerable thought, I decided to use a humorous approach, but felt unsure how the class would react.
>
> I cannot express enough the relief I felt when I started to speak. As soon as I heard laughing, my fears were dispelled. I found the audience, especially the girls, laughing at things I hadn't even thought would be funny. I realized then that my talk was a success. To me, the most important part of the speech was the audience's acknowledging that they liked what I was doing.[7]

Realizing the value of reaction from the audience in establishing a positive relationship with them, the effective speaker not only awaits their reaction, he or she creates it. One can use humor to provoke laughter, as did the speaker on girl watching. One can evoke, by the warmth of one's opening remarks, a corresponding warmth from the audience. Underlying such techniques, one can—and should—think of one's talk not as a presentation *to* the audience but as a conversation *with* them. The speaker does the talking, to be sure, but he or she looks for their nonverbal response as a means of enhancing his or her sense of worthwhileness as a speaker in their midst.

Picking up reassuring feedback from the audience, by the way, is a prime reason for maintaining direct eye contact with your audience instead of looking over their heads, at the floor, or keeping your eyes glued to your notes.

Get Experience As important as positive attitudes and audience reaction are in overcoming speech fright, one is unlikely to achieve full success overnight. Just as acquiring proficiency in any art requires time and practice, so it is true in speaking. Any speech teacher will testify that the anxieties of beginning speech students normally diminish with each succeeding talk. Likewise, a study of 60 nationally prominent successful speakers revealed that in nearly all cases, speech fright disappeared after the beginning of "regular and frequent 'practical' speaking careers."[8]

The key word at this point is "experience." Reading about speech fright is helpful for the insights it offers, but only through experience can those insights be applied. As one with once put it, "The way to become a good speaker is that everytime anyone is fool enough to ask you to speak, you be fool enough to do it!''

Additional Payoffs from Overcoming Speech Fright   From the speaker's standpoint initially, overcoming the bogey of speech fright may seem rewarding enough in itself. But this is, in a sense, a neutral reward; one has simply rid one's self of old fears. The most satisfying rewards are more positive. They consist of the reverse of the unhappy consequences discussed above of dull delivery, audience boredom, and weak credibility. In place of these, as one forgets oneself in a genuine concern for one's message (assuming, of course, that one has a message) and one's audience, one can expect rapt attention and lively reactions. One can also expect one's credibility to be heightened. Rewards such as these can prove profoundly satisfying. To conclude with the words of one student, "When a person can get all of those rambunctious butterflies to fly in an orderly and effective pattern, he can use this nervousness as a catalyst for an effective and exciting talk.''

DELIVERING THE SPEECH

One advantage, just mentioned, of a presentation that is oral as compared with one that is written is the opportunity for the speaker to convey his or her meanings more vividly through effective use of body and voice.

Body Communication

Body communication refers to what listeners see in the speaker's delivery as opposed to what they hear. Four of the most important aspects in body communication are posture, facial expression, eye directness, and gestures.

Posture   A common tendency of inexperienced speakers is to slouch. They stand with their weight mainly on one leg, sometimes shifting back and forth in a slow uneasy teeter. Or, instead of slouching, they stand with their feet wide apart as if straddling a ditch, or with feet close together like a prim schoolgirl. Either way, the effect is one of self-conscious awkwardness. With such a posture, the speaker conveys little sense of feeling at ease or of showing any real desire to communicate with his or her listeners.

A speaker's posture should be alive and erect (yet not rigid like a fence post), with the weight distributed about equally on both feet and leaning forward just a bit instead of away, as if subconsciously wanting to escape.

Facial Expression   The face is the mirror of our emotions. A speaker who is unsure of him- or herself or the message and indifferent or apprehensive concerning the audience will reveal these moods unmistakably on his or her countenance. Such a speaker will be unlikely to arouse much feeling of rapport or interest or confidence in him or her on the part of the audience.

The speaker's face should instead reveal a lively interest in the message and genuine warmth and rapport with the listeners. If you can forget your anxiety by becoming really absorbed with your ideas and audience, your facial expression will reinforce rather than detract from the message.

Eye Directness Inexperienced speakers seem to want to look everywhere except toward the audience: at their notes, at the floor, at the ceiling—even out the window. Yet such indirectness destroys any sense of communicating with the listeners. Moreover, it robs the speaker of the benefits of reading the feedback in his or her listeners' eyes and faces.

A speaker should look the listeners in the eye. One should see them as individuals who, one hopes, will respond with interest, understanding, and belief. In so doing, one should avoid focusing too long on any one person, but include instead the entire audience, as if in a lively conversation with them all.

Gestures One of the most frequently asked questions by beginning speakers is, "What should I do with my hands?" An answer that many have found helpful is to think of speaking as something that involves the whole body, including hands and arms—then let your hands respond accordingly. (This happens in informal conversation, anyway.)

Gestures may be used for various purposes: to *describe* (as the spiral staircase gesture), to *emphasize* (raising the index finger with "Now, just a minute . . ."), to *enumerate* ("There are three good reasons . . ."), or to *point* (pointing to a location on a graph or diagram—usually with a pointer).

One's gesturing will be more effective if the following principles are kept in mind:

1. Gestures should involve the whole body—not just the hands. For example, in pointing to a diagram, turn the whole body instead of pointing with one hand as if the arm were attached loosely at the shoulder.

2. Gestures should be varied. The speaker should avoid relying on a single gesture, such as a right-hand chop repeated over and over. With two hands and the variety of gestures just described, such distracting monotony can be easily avoided.

3. Gestures should be definite and complete. It helps to think of a gesture as consisting of three stages: approach, stroke, and return. Too often a gesture fails to rise above a timid approach. To be effective, it should include an uninhibited motion (above waist level), with the stroke (climax of the motion) coordinated with the stressed syllable of the word it reinforces: "The *sec*ond objection . . ."; ". . . shaped like *this* . . . ." The return follows naturally from the stroke.

4. Gestures should be spontaneous. Gestures that are specifically rehearsed appear stilted, besides contributing to a sense of self-consciousness. The speaker should be so absorbed with the message and the audience that gesturing occurs spontaneously as a natural response to the occasion—just as in an animated conversation.

It is not necessary, of course, to gesture constantly. Between gestures, the hands may be clasped loosely in front (often at waist level) or behind, or simply left to hang freely at the sides. Not recommended is the belligerent-looking hands-on-the-hip stance, or the hands-stuffed-in-the-pockets posture, although one hand slid casually into a pocket may be acceptable in an informal situation, if not left there indefinitely. In fact, the speaker should avoid "freezing" in any position, for the longer he or she remains frozen, the more uncomfortable he or she will feel—and the audience as well.

Body communication is an important aspect of an oral presentation. If ineffective, it can detract from the message. If effective, it can reinforce it—by as much as 20 percent, according to one authority.[9]

Vocal Communication

Vocal communication is even more of a factor than is body communication in getting through to the audience. In fact, a group of college speech teachers, after listening to more than fifty recorded student speeches, concluded that vocal delivery is "almost twice as important in determining the effectiveness of self-introductions, and . . . almost three times as influential . . . in . . . attempts to 'sell' an idea."[10]

Two aspects of vocal communication we shall consider here are audibility and expressiveness.

Audibility "Audibility," which means being heard at all times, is the least that the audience has a right to expect. Otherwise, for them, the message is lost completely.

At least three factors contribute to vocal audibility. One of these is sufficient projection; that is, speaking with enough volume and force to be heard. The second factor is clear articulation: speaking distinctly—especially with unfamiliar terms—to be sure the listener does not confuse, for instance, "acidic" with "acetic" nor "sodium chlorite" with "sodium chloride." The third factor is appropriate rate of speaking; not running one word into the next in a clutter of sounds.

Expressiveness Expressiveness is the opposite of speaking in a monotone. Achieving it involves varying the voice to bring out the numerous shades of meaning: major ideas, incidental idea, similar ideas, contrasting ideas, serious ideas, humorous ideas, ideas in a series, ideas at the end of a sentence, ideas at the end of a whole division of the speech.

The key factor in expressiveness is variety. The variety may be in rate of speaking: hurried or deliberate, pauses of varying frequency and length, extra duration given to key words. The variety may also be in pitch inflections: rising inflections to signify emphasis or cue the listener that the thought is not yet complete; falling inflection to indicate the end of a thought. Or the variety may be in degree of force: greater force for more important ideas, reduced force for less important. In practice, the experienced speaker uses all three kinds of variety simultaneously to give expressiveness to his or her ideas. In such an ordinary sentence as "I am *determined* to complete this project," a speaker can emphasize "determine" by (a) giving a rising pitch inflection to the stressed syllable (the middle syllable, *ter*), (b) giving extra force to the same syllable, and (c) pausing a brief instant at the end of the word to "set it off" and let the impact of the emphasis sink in. Try repeating "I am *determined*" half-a-dozen times to get a sense of how the emphasis is achieved.

Expressed in broader terms, a speaker can utter a sentence such as "So today in this report, I'm going to give you the results of several study contracts which we let," in a flat, unvarying tone that reflects no interest nor animation whatsoever. Or one can say it so one sounds alive, confident, and communicative. It belabors the obvious to point out which manner is more likely to evoke both the understanding and interest of the audience and to elicit a positive attitude toward the speaker.

As a bit of parting advice, expressiveness should not be flawed by such distracting mannerisms as "uh," "and uh," and "you know." Nor should it be marred by slovenly articulation, as in these examples:

gonna	*for*	going to
probly	*for*	probably
firs	*for*	first
gimme	*for*	give me
hunderd	*for*	hundred

Even though the listener will doubtless understand what is meant, such careless speech habits reflect unfavorably on the speaker's general competence—especially as the occasion becomes less casual and more formal.

Manuscript vs. Extemporaneous

Classified by method of preparation, four ways of delivering a speech are available: impromptu, memorized, manuscript, and extemporaneous.

The first two are unsuited for prepared presentations on the job. "*Impromptu*" means "without preparation," or "off the cuff"—so by definition does not apply to a presentation that is prepared (although responses in the question period are impromptu). The *memorized* method is also unsuited; it places too great a strain on the speaker's memory, besides sounding affected and unnatural.

However, the other two methods are commonly used. The *manuscript* method, which means writing the speech in advance and then reading it, seems a favorite in the business world, for the phraseology can be carefully chosen and the style carefully polished. If the occasion is sufficiently formal or the message of critical importance, the manuscript method may be justified. But the precision and polish risk being more than offset by the tendency of the manuscript to be dull and lifeless. Because of the popularity of this method in spite of its disadvantages, it will pay to examine more closely why business people rely on it so heavily.

Why Business People Often Read Their Speeches Among reasons accounting for the common reliance on a manuscript appear to be these:

1. The extreme pressure under which business figures operate, especially those in higher management. Often they simply lack the time for preparing their own talks to meet the speaking demands thrust upon them, so they delegate this task to speechwriters. For the busy executive, the written speech may be born from practical necessity.

2. The desire for security. Speakers are concerned they may miss a point or forget a choice phrase, so they reason that if their speeches are word for word in front of them, they cannot possibly forget.

3. The feeling that a speech is a performance. Speakers become more concerned with impressing their listeners than with communicating with them. So they abandon the vigorous, conversational style of everyday communication for a style that is formal, polished—and dull and unnatural.

4. The example set by other speakers in the business world. Because manuscript speaking is so prevalent for reasons such as those above, newcomers to the business world see this as the norm, which they naturally then proceed to perpetuate.

The Case Against the Manuscript Speech This reliance on the manuscript method, while in some cases warranted, is generally to be deplored. Most speakers (and even speechwriters) find it exceedingly difficult to write a speech that doesn't sound written or to read one that doesn't sound read. The result: an ordeal for both the speaker and audience.

In terms of our analysis of speech fright above, a speaker reading a manuscript is hampered both in getting turned on with the message and becoming genuinely concerned with getting through to the audience. Instead, one is more preoccupied with words than with ideas, and with not losing one's place in the script. Self-assurance, dynamism, rapport with audience, credibility—all these tend to suffer, often badly.

The Case for the Extemporaneous Speech It is necessary first to clear away a common confusion concerning the meaning of "extemporaneous": it does not mean "off the cuff"; as noted earlier, that type of speech is "impromptu." On the contrary, an *extemporaneous speech* is planned—preferably, very carefully planned. One researches the subject as thoroughly as needed, decides on one's purpose, how to introduce the subject and adapt to the audience, what the main and subpoints will be, how to develop each point, and how to conclude. In the process of planning, one organizes one's ideas in outline form—revising as many times as necessary—until eventually one ends up with a speaking outline.

All these steps may—and should be—followed in preparing a manuscript speech as well. But here the similarity ends. Instead of writing the speech, later to be read, the extemporaneous speaker works solely from an outline. Some speakers rehearse the speech aloud a number of times; others simply think through their ideas to themselves to fix in mind the sequence of ideas and their relationship to each other. In either case, the speaker leaves for the actual presentation the exact choice of wording.

The advantages from this approach are substantial:

1. Unlike the impromptu speech, the extemporaneous speech may be carefully planned (although leaving room for occasional impromptu remarks inspired by the immediate occasion).

2. Unlike the manuscript speech, the extemporaneous speech allows the speaker much greater freedom in interacting with the audience through a lively eye contact and animated facial expression.

3. Unlike both the manuscript and memorized speech, the extemporaneous speech fosters an oral style as compared with a written style. Since the oral style is generally regarded as more enjoyable and easier to listen to than the written style (about 10 percent more, according to one study),[11] the oral style merits further examination.

The Oral Style Compared with the Written Style Simply put, the oral style is the style of expression used in talking, while the written style is the style used in writing. Among the characteristics distinguishing the two styles are the following:

1. The oral style is less polished. An excellent analysis concerning polish is offered by Leland Schubert:

> In writing you ought to be more careful with your grammar, sentence structure, and choice of words than you are in speaking. When you're writing, there's no reason not to be careful. Time is usually on your side; grammars and dictionaries and guidebooks are available. Nine out of ten times you can rewrite as much as you need to. . . .
>
> A speaker, on the other hand, is expected only to be sensible, clear, and to the point, because the speaking situation is quite different from the writing situation. The speaker's time is always somewhat limited; he is always obliged to think more rapidly than the writer; and often he has to think on his feet. A

good speaker, of course, knows the rules of grammar and sentence structure, and he's had enough experience to enable him to think and speak reasonably grammatical and well-constructed sentences. But neither he nor his audience expects absolute literary accuracy or a polished literary style. We are willing to overlook a few errors in speaking. We expect less formality.[12]

Schubert adds, "The language of a speaker, with exceptions too rare to mention, should be simple, colloquial, and, above all, human—with many of the normal human weaknesses."[13]

2. The oral style is more personal. A speaker using an oral style is more personal, just as he or she would be in a conversation. The difference between oral and written style in being personal is similar to the difference between the style of a telephone conversation and a letter confirming the telephone conversation.

Being personal means that the speaker is more direct in referring to the audience ("You fellows probably recall the situation a year ago"); uses personal pronouns more freely ("I," "you," "we"); also uses contractions more freely ("I didn't," "we aren't"); employs colloquialisms, even slang ("We had one devil of a time finding the cause"); and uses dialogue in "conversing" with the audience ("Perhaps you wonder why we did it this way," "Let's review these steps before we move on").

3. The oral style is intended for the ear. It is important to remember that whereas the written style is intended for the eye, the oral style is intended for the ear. A listener ought not be handicapped in followlng the meaning simply because he or she is receiving the message through the sense of hearing rather than the sense of vision.

This means that the pacing of ideas must be slower when presented orally. As Carroll C. Arnold says:

> A reader sets his own pace. He can review, reflect, or relax at his convenience. A listener is at the mercy of the speaker's pace. A wise composer of oral communication therefore builds into his composition those moments of review, reflection, and rest which he anticipates his listeners will need. This is one reason that all effective oral composition exhibits more redundancy than good composition for readers. Listeners need at least some redundancy.[14]

Expressing the same point a bit differently, Sidney Wilcox has observed, "Published speeches are too expanded for written technical style, and written papers intended for publication are too compressed for oral presentation."[15]

In other words, a style adapted to the ear instead of the eye means that the language will be simpler to grasp; unusual terms will be used more sparingly, and when they are used will be spoken more clearly and defined more fully; ideas will be paced more slowly; and the development will be less condensed than in writing.

The Written and Oral Styles Illustrated   Below are the opening paragraphs of two talks. The first is a talk delivered from a manuscript. Quite obviously its style is written. The second is a transcription of a tape-recorded talk given extemporaneously (that is, planned, but not read or memorized). Just as obviously, its style is oral.

Comparison of the two examples will readily reveal that the second example illustrates all three characteristics described above: less polished, more personal, and more adapted to reception by ear. You may judge for yourself which style you consider to be more listenable and intelligible.

The written style:

> The materials handling system of the future must be able to respond to automatically generated material management commands. Whether these commands are directly delivered to the handling systems through such things as hard-wired data links or indirectly through human operator links is largely immaterial—the important point is that the response must be accurate and fast enough to satisfy the particular timing requirements of the overall operation.
>
> This means that more and more materials handling systems will be considered as the transportation or storage subsystems in larger integrated manufacturing or distribution systems. Materials handling systems perform this function today whether they be wheelbarrows or synchronized shift-register controlled conveyors, but they are not looked at this way. The difference in viewpoint will become pronounced as computer-based time-critical information control systems become operational, pacing an entire manufacturing line, plant, or distribution system for more efficient performance.
>
> Thus, in a broad sense, control systems mate with materials handling systems at two levels: The first level consists of the physical equipment controls that sense conditions, make decisions, and manipulate material flow by operating directly on the materials handling equipment. The second echelon control comprises an information handling network that acquires status information (either directly or through manual input), makes decisions based on current demands and established operating rules, and delivers instructions to the physical equipment controls.[16]

The oral style:

> Although, fellow Hoosiers, I think I'm more competent today to discuss sump pumps, Hoosier drivers, and snow shovels, my subject is the design evaluation of 60-cycle alternators. We in the Industrial Power Department are presently engaged in designing several power plants, using the basic T-56 engine as the prime mover. Some of these power plants drive electrical alternators; some drive gas compressors. Of these electrical devices, one has to be extremely mobile. In other words it has to be transportable, and primarily transportable by air. The purpose of this mobility requirement is, of course, to allow the user to generate power in many isolated locations by flying his power plant to the site. Those of you familiar with the electrical equipment know that it is built very heavy, very sturdy and as such it could not be transportable by air as part of a complete power plant. The weight is too great. So our problem, then, is to get someone to design for us a 60-cycle alternator which is light weight, compact, and yet rugged. Now this is something that those manufacturers do not do. They make their equipment to last 20, 30, 40, even 50 years. And so, to protect their reputation, they build it "hell for stout." As a matter of fact, one of the alternators which would do the job we want it to do weighs around 13,500 lbs., and that's too much.
>
> So today in this report, I'm going to give you the results of several study contracts which we let. I'll show you how those results tie in with the criteria judging those results, and I will recommend for you one of the manufacturers as the prime contractor for this job.[17]

Sometimes, the manuscript method may be warranted. But the disadvantages in terms of effectiveness are considerable. So before being tempted by what may appear to be the easy "out" of writing your speech and reading it, consider very carefully whether the gain will be worth the cost.

USING VISUAL AIDS

Visual aids in oral presentations are the counterpart of graphic aids in writing (discussed in Chapter 8). In this section we shall compare visual aids with graphic aids, then discuss the advantages and limitations of six of the most commonly used visual aids.

THE ORAL PRESENTATION

Differences between Visual Aids and Graphic Aids

The Listener-Viewer Situation The most basic difference between visual and graphic aids derives from the fact that when we use visual aids, our receiver is not a reader, but a listener. More accurately, he or she is a *listener-viewer,* for the receiver must both listen and view at the same time. Although the implications of this circumstance seem obvious, they are often overlooked.

First, the aid must be *simple*. A listener-viewer, unlike a reader, has limited time for absorbing the content of the aid. Not only is his or her time limited (by the pace of the presentation), he or she must also pay attention to the speaker's verbal explanation simultaneously. Therefore, it is important not to clutter the aid with a mass of detail which the listener-viewer will not have time to absorb anyway. An especially common mistake is to project onto the screen a table or diagram from a written report; almost always it contains too much detail, too small to be read. Material prepared for a written report should invariably be redone for use in an oral presentation so it is simple and legible enough for the listener-viewer.

Second, the aid (as already implied) must be *legible*. This means fully legible to those farthest away, perhaps 20 or 30 feet; sometimes, of course, even farther. If those in the back row can read the visual aid clearly, you need not worry about those sitting closer. Being legible means that the overall size of the diagram or graph is ample, and the lettering of titles and labels sufficiently heavy and intense. Perhaps the most common complaint when visual aids are used is that the contents cannot be comfortably read. When this is true, the "aid" is no longer an aid, but an annoyance. As obvious as this advice may seem, it is amazing how often it is ignored.

Finally, the aid must be explained, to the extent necessary, for the listener-viewer. A common oversight, for instance, on the part of the speaker in presenting a line or bar graph is to proceed directly to interpreting the plot line or bars without first explaining values on the ordinate and abscissa (the vertical and horizontal axes). This leaves the listener-viewer having to discover for him- or herself what the values are—whether dollars or barrels or whatever, and what the units on the time scale are, when instead he or she should be paying attention to the speaker. Another common oversight is for the speaker to neglect titling or labeling the aid. Even if the speaker identifies the components orally, the listener may easily forget, then again be distracted from giving full attention as he or she attempts, perhaps unsuccessfully, to recall the forgotten term.

Variety of Visual Aids Available A second difference between visual and graphic aids is the greater variety of visual aids available to the speaker. The writer is limited to what can be reproduced on a sheet of paper bound in the report. The speaker, on the other hand, can use gestures, body movement, three-dimensional objects, the chalkboard, flip charts, and projections of various kinds. Because of the greater variety available, visual aids tend to add more to the factors of interest and dynamism in speaking than do graphic aids in writing.

Advantages and Limitations in the Use of Selected Visual Aids

Of the various aids available in oral presentations, we shall describe and evaluate briefly six of the most common. Three of these are *direct* aids (that is, require no projection): three-dimensional materials, the chalkboard, and flip charts. The other three are *projectors:* the overhead, opaque, and 2- by 2-inch slide projection.

Three-Dimensional Objects The two most common kinds of three-dimensional visual aids are *samples* and *models*. A sample is the "real thing"—as an actual sample of a hand calculator or a single-lens reflex camera. The main advantage of using a sample is its authenticity; it shows the appearance concretely and realistically. Further, it may show operation as well if it is a sample of something that operates. One disadvantage is that while it does show the external appearance realistically, as in the example of a camera, it reveals little about the internal appearance or operation. Another disadvantage is that the object may be too small (as the design of a class ring) or too large (such as a space satellite) for practical use as a visual aid. If too large, it often would be too expensive as well.

Thus, models (recognizable representations of the real thing) are often preferable to samples. A foot-high model of a human ear, for instance, is more easily seen and more revealing to an audience than an actual human ear. Or a five-foot-high model of a space satellite would be more manageable and less expensive than an actual satellite. However, even using a model may have its limitations: one might not be available, it might still be too expensive, or—if being shown before a large audience—it might, like the sample—be too small for effective viewing.

The Chalkboard One of the most familiar of visual aids is the chalkboard; a classroom or conference room would scarcely be complete without one. Its principal uses are for presenting (a) visual materials simple to sketch—as a diagram of a street intersection or the name of a chemical compound, and (b) ideas built up a little at a time—as an outline of key points, or a series of mathematical calculations.

The chief advantage of the chalkboard is the ease with which it can be used; material may be added, modified, or erased as the needs of the moment require. On the other hand, it is not well adapted to presenting complicated material (such as a table of statistical data or a diagram of a complex mechanism). Furthermore, in using it, the speaker must be careful not to forget the audience; sometimes the speaker becomes so absorbed with boardwork that he or she virtually forgets the audience—even to the extent of ignoring their needs by writing too small or by getting in the way of what is already written.

Charts   As used here, charts refer to sheets of paper, usually 28" × 32", which can be hung by holes or clamped to a crosspiece across the top of a chart stand. Charts commonly are used for presenting diagrams, graphs, or key ideas.

Using charts offers numerous advantages. As compared with the chalkboard, they:

1. Permit greater attention to the audience, since usually they are prepared in advance, and the chart stand can be positioned to allow for good eye contact.

2. Allow a neater appearance, both because they can be prepared ahead of time and because such devices as colored ink markers and guidelines can be used.

3. Offer greater assurance of being available to refer to during the question period, since they run no risk of being erased.

4. Permit repeated use much more readily (although they are bulkier than projections either to store or transport).

As compared with projected visual aids, charts have the advantage of being simpler to manage—no room darkening required, no electric cords or outlets necessary, no projection lamps to burn out, no screen or projectionist required. Besides the chart stand itself, only a pointer is needed (plus a marker if drawing on the chart during presentation is planned).

However, charts have limitations as well. They:

1. Are not suitable for audiences of over sixty people or so; for larger audiences projections are virtually a must.

2. Require usually more preparation time than does either the chalkboard or many projections (which may require only a few seconds on a copying machine).

3. Offer less work space than the chalkboard (though as many charts as desired may be used in a series).

4. Do not adapt to spontaneous development as well as does the chalkboard.

Nevertheless, in spite of these limitations, charts have proved highly useful before smaller audiences.

In preparing charts, it will help to remember a few guidelines: Include only one basic idea to a chart; better to use three charts for three ideas than only one chart. Keep the chart simple; list key phrases, for example, instead of complete sentences. Use titles and labels so listeners are not preoccupied with trying to identify components when they should be following you. Make the chart legible to everyone in the audience. Give attention to appearance: neatness, balance, spacing, and color. The chart should evoke a positive rather than negative reaction.

FIGURE 12.1 Proper Lettering for Chart

FIGURE 12.2 Improper Lettering for Chart

THE ORAL PRESENTATION

The Overhead Projector Developed during World War II as a training aid, the overhead projector has become (next to the chalkboard) perhaps the most widely and easily used visual aid in the conference room or classroom. Its advantages are numerous:

FIGURE 12.3
Overhead Projection Showing Details Fully Legible

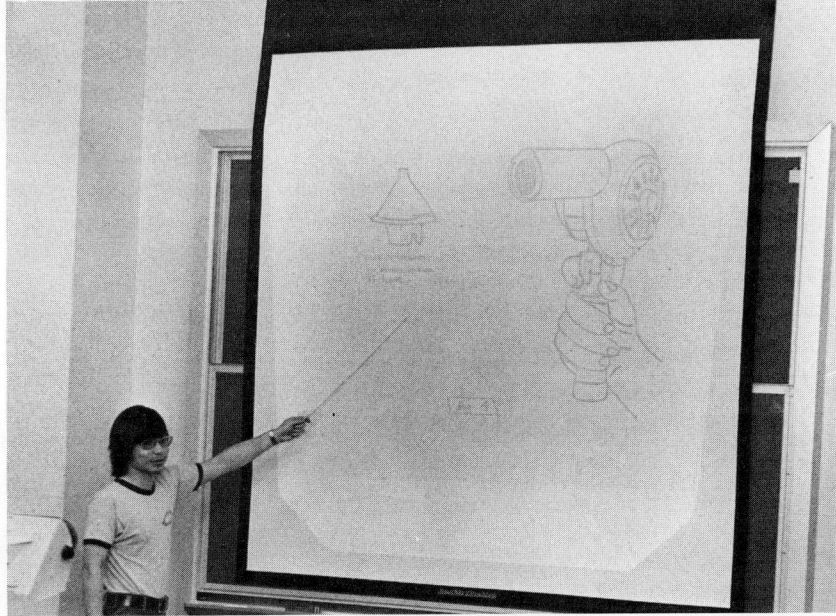

FIGURE 12.4
Overhead Projection with Details Much Less Legible

1. Because of its short focal length, it can be located at the front of the room where the speaker can operate it him- or herself (one advantage) while facing the audience (another advantage).

2. Because the room need be only minimally darkened (usually the front bank of lights turned off), the speaker can see the audience clearly, and they the speaker.

3. With the use of a copying machine, transparencies can be easily and quickly prepared. The master sheet (for example, a diagram drawn on a sheet of typing paper) is run through the copier with a plain sheet of transparency, and in seconds the transparency emerges with the diagram copied on it.

4. Details may be added or information built up at will. The speaker can add detail with a special pencil; overlays (several transparencies hinged so each can be added as desired) can be used; or a portion of the projection (such as the lower half of a list) can be masked until needed, then the mask removed to reveal the rest.

FIGURE 12.5
Speaking Using a Transparency with Several Overlays

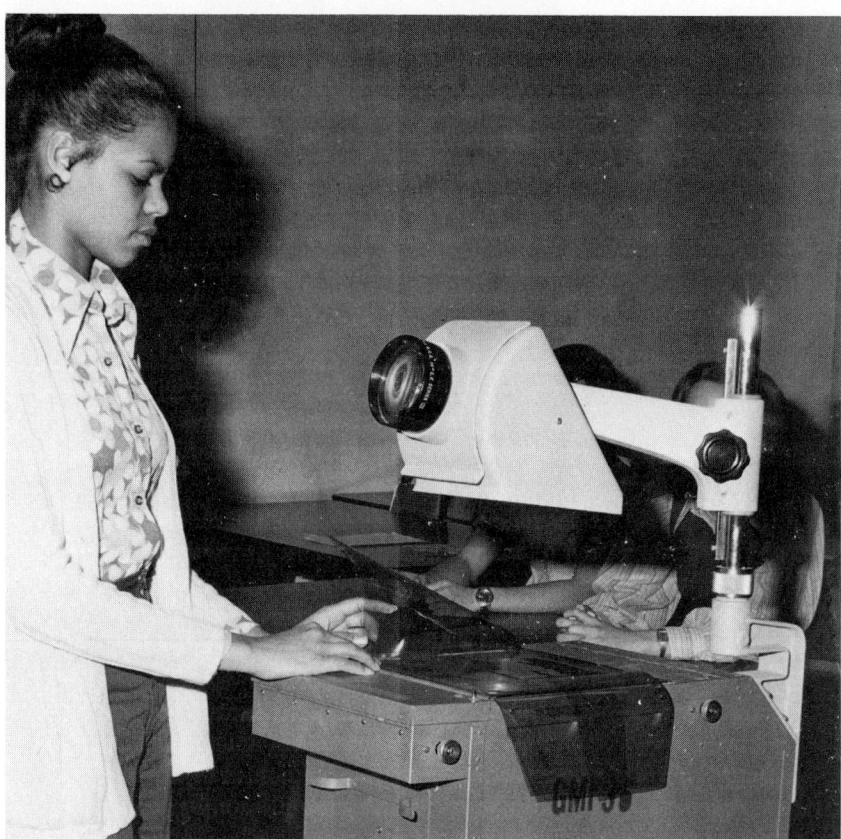

5. Transparencies may be easily stored or transported. Some prefer to have the transparencies mounted in a cardboard frame. Some prefer to punch three holes in the side (as with three-hole paper), place the master underneath each transparency for easy identification, and either place it in a three-ring binder for easy carrying or store it in a file folder until needed again.

In preparing transparencies, we must observe the same guidelines (simplicity, legibility, and so on) as for charts. Typed material is often projected on the overhead, but for distances more than 10 to 20 feet, special type roughly $\frac{1}{8}''-\frac{3}{16}''$ high should be used, or lettering with a felt-tipped pen so the letters are $\frac{3}{16}''-\frac{1}{4}''$ high. With this size, the copy will be visible as far back as 40 to 50 feet—providing a large size screen (usually 84" square) is used. To insure best results, check out projections with different size types or lettering in the room you will speak in.

In referring to specific details on the projected material, you may if you wish point directly to the transparency, using a pencil or other fine pointer. If you do, however, you also run the risk of blocking the screen to part of the audience. Therefore, it generally is preferable to stand to one side of the screen and use a long pointer, referring to the projection instead of the transparency itself.

The Opaque Projector The opaque projector differs from other projectors in that it shows *nontransparent visuals*. Visuals may include any flat opaque material: typescript, photographs (black and white or colored), even such objects as a micrometer or slide rule.

The principal advantage of the opaque projector is that visuals need not be converted into transparencies, thus saving both money and time. But the disadvantages tend to outweigh the advantages. Because the light is reflected off the material instead of passing through it, the room must be quite dark for a satisfactory image, thus reducing visual contact between speaker and audience. Because it is bulky, it tends to block the view of some in the audience. And because the lamp must be brighter (usually 1000 watts) than in other projectors, a more powerful cooling fan must be used, resulting in more noise than in any of the other projectors. Finally, when transparencies are changed, extra light spills out, nearly blinding any viewer who might be looking that way.

If, after considering the disadvantages, you decide to use the opaque projector after all, the main precaution is to insure legibility. As explained earlier, printed graphs and diagrams are almost never suitable for projection. To insure legibility, lettering used in an opaque projector should consist of intense heavy lines $\frac{3}{16}''$ to $\frac{1}{4}''$ high, and the usual guidelines of simplicity should be observed.

Since the heat from the lamp tends to curl paper projections, the paper should be mounted on cardboard. Or, if a series of projections is to be shown, they may be mounted on a long strip of paper (or sheets of paper taped together) and passed through the projector one at a time. This way the projector need not be opened and the strong light spilled out.

The 2- by 2-Inch Slide Projector   This is probably the most familiar projector of all, since it is used in many homes for showing 35-mm slides. Its special advantages include photographic realism and the ability to enlarge any image (limited only by the size of the screen) to a size suitable for any size audience. In addition, of course, slides are small and easy both to store and transport, while with a remote control cord the speaker can usually face the audience. Disadvantages include the expense, but this is not great if you already own your own equipment or have access to equipment. A greater disadvantage, depending on urgency, could be the delay until your film is processed and returned.

Precautions in Using Visual Aids

As their name implies, visual aids are intended to aid. But unless certain precautions are observed, instead of aiding, they may do little more than hinder.

One precaution is to avoid using an aid for the mere sake of using one. The story is told of an oral presentation at the Pentagon in which the speaker was hoping to win a contract for his company. At one point in his talk he stated, "Now this unit comes in three sizes: small [here revealing a chart that said 'small'], medium [flipping to a second chart, 'MEDIUM'], and large [showing now a third chart, 'LARGE']." Gimmickry such as this is not an aid, but an insult to the intelligence of the audience.

A second precaution is to select the aid or combination of aids best suited to the situation. In general, the smaller the audience and the less important the occasion, the more appropriate will be use of a chalkboard or chart stand. As the size of the audience increases and the situation becomes more important, the more likely the overhead or 2- by 2-inch projector will serve better. Often a combination works best: blackboard and chart stand, or two chart stands instead of one, or chart stand and overhead projector.

Special precautions are needed in using projectors. The room must be capable of being darkened readily; the location of electric outlets must be checked out and an extension cord secured if necessary, along with possibly a three-prong adaptor; the equipment must also be checked out to be certain you are familiar with how to turn it on and off, how to insert projections, and how to focus it; a spare lamp should be on hand and you should know how to install it; the projector should be prepositioned and prefocused (though the projector may be set on the floor if desired until needed); the projectionist, if one is used, must be fully briefed on what you want projected and when; and the projections must be in proper sequence.

Another precaution is never to show a visual aid until you are ready to use it. If you have a title chart or slide, you should "lead into" your title before revealing it. Avoid darkening the room or turning a projector on until the moment you begin using it. Similarly, when through, turn it off and the room lights back on.

Finally, make certain your aids, including titles and labels, are easily, comfortably, and fully legible. Legibility to the whole audience is the first, last, and principal prerequisite.

A really effective presentation using visual aids often requires a great deal of planning and hard work—and this must be taken into consideration.

MAKING SURE THE MAIN POINTS STAND OUT

In Chapter 4, "Structure," we emphasized how important it is for the receivers to get the "gist" of the message—what the message adds up to. This is what readers or listeners look for more than anything else in the message. They want to be able to grasp the main points, the central idea, and how they relate to one another to form a unified structure in a way that makes sense.

Assuming, of course, that your message possesses such a structure, you then face the problem of making that structure clear to the receivers. In a written message, you achieve this through the use of such devices as the title or subject heading, a clear introduction and conclusion, main headings and subheadings, and effective topic sentences for the paragraphs. In addition, if the report or proposal is longer and more formal, you will probably include an abstract and table of contents.

In an oral presentation you can use most of these same techniques, though in slightly different form. Instead of a title page you can use a chart or projection showing the title. Instead of a table of contents, you can use a chart or projection showing a preview of main points you will cover. And for headings you can also use charts or projections—or, if the occasion is less formal, write them on the chalkboard as you talk.

Using visual aids for this purpose, incidentally, offers benefits not only to your listener but also to you. First, preparing the visuals forces you to decide precisely what your main and subpoints are to be. In addition, the visuals help you, as well as your audience, to stay on the track. They constitute, in effect, your notes. (Incidentally, if your visual aids are on charts, you can pencil in, legible to you but invisible to your audience, additional reminders of information you wish to remember. But be sure they are sufficiently intelligible so you won't get lost trying to interpret them!)

Whether you use visual aids or not, it is absolutely essential that you make generous use of previews, transitions, and summaries (both internal and final). The listener cannot turn the report back or ahead, as he or she could if the report were written; he or she cannot feasibly take time from listening to check upon points of confusion. Therefore, we must so present the report that a listener is able to stay with us at all times and to develop a sense of direction as he or she listens.

Thus, whether visually or verbally—or both—you must make certain the listener understands clearly your topic or title, your specific purpose, your plan of development, the main headings and subheadings for any section or subsection of your discussion, and your final conclusions. The *structure* of your talk must be unmistakably clear. Remember your listener wants to see ahead where you are going, know where you are at any given point, and understand what conclusions you reach in the end. He or she does not like to feel lost.

HANDLING QUESTIONS FROM THE AUDIENCE

An important advantage of the oral presentation over the written message is the much greater opportunity for two-way communication. Part of this, of course, consists of nonverbal cues: the dynamism and directness of the speaker; the indications of interest, comprehension, confusion, or boredom from the audience. The interaction of such nonverbal behavior determines in large part the nature of the relationship between speaker and audience—whether positive or negative.

But a significant part of the two-way communication is verbal, consisting of questions and comments from the audience, along with the speaker's response. Such verbal exchange can go a long way in clearing away confusion and misunderstanding. It also can strengthen the relationship by allowing the audience to "talk back" instead of being only passive recipients.

Preparing for Questions from the Audience

Handling audience participation constructively benefits from being ready for it. Two kinds of preparation are suggested.

Develop a Positive Attitude Some speakers, unfortunately, seem to resent questions as if they were a reflection on the speaker's competence or integrity. A more objective view is to remember that since falloff is bound to occur, the speaker should expect that there will be some listeners with questions to ask. These questions, then, provide a desirable means of bringing confusion into the open where it can be dealt with effectively. Thus, the speaker should not only expect questions, he or she should encourage them.

From your own experience in the classroom you have learned to sense which teachers dislike and which ones welcome having questions brought up. In your own presentations, you should genuinely try making your listeners feel comfortable in asking questions or offering comments, just as you as a student like to feel comfortable. Any response that makes a listener feel stupid for raising a question is unlikely to improve either his or her understanding of the material or his or her attitude toward you.

Plan Your Answers While it may seem absurd to talk of how to answer questions before they have been asked, several practical suggestions can be offered.

First, "do your homework." Become thoroughly familiar with your subject matter so you will be forearmed. This, of course, has the added benefit of increasing your confidence as you face your audience.

Second, you can anticipate most of the kinds of questions that may arise. Some questions may seek additional information. Other questions may challenge your assertions by disputing your assumptions or supporting data. And still others may ask your opinion on how to interpret a given situation, or whether the situation is "good" or "bad."

In addition, the makeup of your audience offers cues on probable questions to expect. An accountant, for instance, will be concerned about cost, a production supervisor about schedules, a safety engineer with meeting government regulations, a salesperson with customer response, and so on. Knowing this in advance, you can be somewhat prepared. In addition, you can plan your presentation accordingly, thus answering many questions before they need to be raised.

It is well to be fully aware of counterarguments to one's presentation. Giving reasonable answers to questions both reasonable and unreasonable can be a most effective ending to an oral presentation.

Deciding When Questions Should be Raised

It might appear that ideally the listeners should interject with any questions as soon as they pop in their heads. If the presentation is informal enough, to a small enough group, and time is not pressing, this practice has the advantage of clearing up confusion on the spot. But it also involves disadvantages. Expecting questions to be raised at any time could encourage sloppy preparation on your part ("If I'm not clear, they can always break in"). Questions may be raised over trivial points, leaving too little time for more important points. Furthermore, encouraging questions any time may result in questions being asked on points you were about to cover anyway; thus the presentation becomes disjointed through needless interruptions.

Rather than encouraging unregulated questioning, it normally will be preferable to (a) plan the presentation carefully to reduce the need for questions, and (b) ask for questions either following major sections of the talk, or at the end. This way you can better control the time and maintain a clearer sequence of development.

Listening to Questions and Replying to Them

The essence of handling questions from the audience is the actual act of listening and replying.

Listening   As already implied, effective listening depends first on really *wanting* the audience to participate.

Assuming you have such a positive attitude, your main problem then is to make sure you understand each question fully. Understanding may mean asking the questioner, if necessary, to speak up so he or she can be heard. It certainly means listening to the entire question before launching into your reply; also making every effort to understand the question sympathetically from the questioner's point of view, and if in doubt restating it or asking for an elaboration to be sure you are clear what the questioner has in mind. Obviously, you can hardly offer an intelligent response if you are unclear about what the question means or you interpret it wrongly.

Replying   Replying effectively requires a positive attitude also; an attitude free from defensiveness. If you view your response as an opportunity to clarify rather than an annoying obligation, you will create a more positive tone.

In replying to a question, you will find it useful to adapt your response to the purpose of the listener. If the purpose is clarification, offer whatever elaboration—by way of examples, comparison, description, and so on—may seem relevant. If the purpose is to challenge an assertion, do not be afraid to agree if the questioner's position seems sound, or to disagree, if it seems unsound, by pointing out weaknesses in the facts or reasoning.

Finally, in replying to questions, organize your reply for maximum clarity. The following four-step pattern is recommended:

1. Restate the question (as suggested above), paraphrasing it if advisable.
2. State the essence of your answer in a single sentence or two.
3. Elaborate to the extent necessary by giving in a systematic order the points supporting the answer. These can be presented in whatever order seems simplest and most appropriate: time order, space order, topical order (reasons, causes, effects, advantages, disadvantages, and so on).
4. Restate the answer in a single sentence or two.

Such a pattern has the merit of (a) making clear the question you are answering, and (b) expressing your answer at both the general and specific level.

SUMMARY

1. In comparison with speaking, writing has the advantages that it permits more deliberate formulation of the message and is more convenient to file "for the record"; speaking has the potential for promoting stronger

interpersonal relationships, being more precise, and facilitating two-way communication. A combination of both writing and speaking is more effective, when appropriate, than either is alone.

2. Speech fright is best understood as a sense of self-consciousness in a speaking situation. Overcoming it involves (a) speakers' forgetting themselves in their concern for the message and for getting through to the audience, (b) making use of audience feedback, and (c) gaining experience.

3. Visual aids, to be appropriate to the listener-viewer situation, must be simple enough to be easily absorbed, legible to everyone in the audience, and accompanied with sufficient explanation to be clear. The chalkboard and chart stand are usually more appropriate for small audiences and informal situations; while projectors, such as the overhead or 2- by 2-inch, are more appropriate for larger audiences and more formal situations.

4. While it is always important for the main ideas to stand out in a message, a speaker must assume special responsibility in assisting the listener to be certain of the main pattern of development, since—unlike a reader—the listener cannot preview or review the message.

5. Questions and comments from the audience should be regarded positively rather than defensively. To be prepared for audience questions, the speaker should master the material and analyze the audience to anticipate the kinds of questions he or she may expect. In responding to questions, a speaker should first be sure he or she understands the question clearly, then answer it candidly and clearly.

SUGGESTED APPLICATIONS

1. Learning About Yourself as a Speaker

Objectives

1. To increase your understanding of the elements of effective delivery in speaking.

2. To increase your confidence in facing an audience.

3. To help you better understand your own strengths and areas for improvement in speaking.

4. To provide you an opportunity for organizing and developing your ideas clearly in writing.

Procedure

1. *Planning and delivery.* Plan and present a two-minute speech to be videotaped and played back on TV. You may speak on any topic you choose, but keep in mind that you will do better with a topic you can feel "turned on" about and that is narrow enough to develop adequately in two minutes.

In planning your talk, keep in mind the importance of achieving an effective balance between your *main idea* and its *specific development*.

Do *not* write your talk nor try to memorize it verbatim. Simply, *PLAN* it, *THINK* carefully through your ideas, then *TALK* on it. No notes, please.

2. *Written Report.* Following your talk and playback, write a critical analysis (around 300–400 words) of your talk, basing your analysis on data from the feedback sheets you receive from the other students, plus your own feedback sheet as you view the playback. A sample feedback sheet is attached.

Organize your paper as follows: Memo heading addressed to the instructor; introduction identifying your topic and day and date of speaking, giving any relevant background information, and stating the plan of your report (around 50–75 words); discussion, using the major headings and subheadings from the feedback sheet (around 275–350 words); and conclusion summing up the principal implications of your analysis (around 25–50 words).

Please type or use ink. Include adequate headings and subheadings to bring out very clearly the organization of your paper. Proofread carefully before handing in the paper to be sure it says clearly what you want it to say, and is free from misspelling, grammatical error, and so forth.

Speaker _____ Date ____

FEEDBACK ON SPEAKING DELIVERY

Emotional Attitudes	Excellent				Poor
1. "Turned on" concerning message	5	4	3	2	1
2. Genuine interest in "getting through" to the audience	5	4	3	2	1
3. Self-assurance; freedom from self-consciousness	5	4	3	2	1

Body Communication

1. Posture (alive, relaxed but not slouched)	5	4	3	2	1
2. Facial expression (interested, appropriate)	5	4	3	2	1

Body Communication (continued)	Excellent				Poor
3. Eye directness (includes whole audience)	5	4	3	2	1
4. Gestures (varied, appropriate, well-coordinated)	5	4	3	2	1

Vocal Communication

1. Audibility (volume, articulation, rate)	5	4	3	2	1
2. Expressiveness (appropriate rate, use of pauses, duration, pitch inflection, force)	5	4	3	2	1

Freedom from Distracting Mannerisms

1. Physical mannerisms (excessive gesturing, fidgeting, shifting weight, and so on)	5	4	3	2	1
2. Vocal mannerisms ("uh," "and uh," slovenly articulation, and so on)	5	4	3	2	1

Evaluator

2. Demonstration Talk

Objectives

1. To provide further experience speaking before an audience.
2. To sharpen your awareness, both through giving your own speech and through observing others in their speeches, how useful body language can be in communicating ideas.
3. To discover how helpful bodily activity can be in controlling nervous tension while giving a speech.

Procedure   Describe a process or procedure with liberal use of gestures and bodily movement. Use *no* props (this includes the chalkboard) except—if you wish—a chair or table.

Sample topics: directing an orchestra, aiming and firing a pistol, using a tennis racket, basic swimming strokes, kinds of people you have known (students, teachers, salespeople, customers, drivers, or whoever).

Caution: In selecting a topic, choose one well adapted to this particular assignment. For instance, avoid a topic calling for few if any gestures, such as "The Philosophy of Confucius" or "What I Hope to Be Doing Five Years from Now." Similarly, avoid a topic which, while perhaps calling for gestures, is too complicated for the gestures to help out a great deal, such as "How to Operate an Acme-Gridley." Also, avoid a topic too extensive for the time allowed (around four minutes, plus or minus a half minute); better to demonstrate how to saw a board than how to build a birdhouse, or how to use a driver than how to use all six, eight, or ten clubs a golfer might carry. In other words, choose a topic sufficiently limited that you can do well within the allotted time rather than having to rush through, worrying whether you can finish on time.

Suggestion: If you are describing a process or procedure that consists of a series of steps or subtopics, break your description down accordingly, carefully demonstrate each step in slow motion, then demonstrate the steps together—still in slow motion, and finally put them all together in regular motion.

Organization: Start with an introduction that provides some background, including how you happen to be familiar with and interested in this topic, and which ties in with interests your audience have or may have; include also a general preview of how you will explain the subject. Then proceed to the actual demonstration. Finally, conclude with a brief conclusion summing up the main point or points to be remembered.

Another caution: In presenting your speech, avoid becoming so preoccupied with your demonstration that you forget your audience. Remember, your purpose is not primarily to give a demonstration, but to use your demonstration as a means of helping your audience understand your subject as clearly as possible.

Again, no notes please. Plan your talk carefully, think it through thoroughly, but do not write it nor attempt to memorize it word for word.

3. Making Yourself Perfectly Clear

Being able to explain things so others can understand them clearly is obviously a very useful communication skill. The following project is designed to increase both your proficiency and insight into "making yourself perfectly clear." It consists of several activities, and is described below in the order in which these activities will be scheduled.

Objectives

1. To gain increased insight in how to be clearly understood when explaining a situation, procedure, process, and so on, to other people.
2. To gain increased proficiency in organizing and developing your ideas clearly in writing.

Schedule

1. *Written Memo.* Please submit a brief memo to your instructor stating (a) the topic you plan to use and (b) why you selected this topic. For instruction on memo writing, see Chapter 10.

2. *Lab Sessions.* The class will be divided into groups of six each. During the three sessions scheduled for this assignment each group will meet separately, and each half-session a different member will explain to the others in his or her group a situation, procedure, or the like with which he or she is familiar but the others are not. The listeners may take notes, but should not ask questions for at least the first ten minutes; nor should the explainer ask for questions during that time. (This is not to deny the invaluable role of two-way communication in making ideas clear, but only to discourage the explainer from relying on it at the outset to get him or her through.) Techniques the explainer will find especially helpful include:

    a. Relating how he or she happens to be familiar with and interested in this topic.
    b. Showing what value learning about it may have for the listeners.
    c. Explaining how he or she plans to treat the topic (the pattern of organization).
    d. Using previews, transitions, and summaries freely to point up the main ideas and help the listener to stay interested.
    e. Presenting the explanation in terms clear to the others.
    f. Using examples, including personal examples, where relevant.
    g. Using visual aids freely (diagrams, lists of points, and so on) probably on 8½ × 11 paper.
    h. Explaining not only "what" or "how," but "why."
    i. After the first ten minutes, encouraging questions.

3. *Written Report.* Write a report (roughly 350–500 words) on what you have learned about "making yourself perfectly clear." The report should contain:

    a. A brief introduction.
    b. A brief summary of the topic used in the Lab Session.
    c. What ways the explanation was successful and why.
    d. In what ways it was unsuccessful and why.
    e. What changes you would make to improve it were it to be made another time.
    f. A brief evaluation of the "Making Yourself Perfectly Clear" project, along with any suggestions for improvement.

The report should use a memo format, with appropriate topic headings throughout, and should reflect a clear familiarity with principles discussed in Chapter 10.

NOTES

[1] Most of this chapter draws on concepts that are developed much more fully in my earlier text, *Oral Reporting in Business and Industry* (Englewood Cliffs, N.J.: Prentice Hall, Inc., 1967).

[2] Milton W. Horowitz and John B. Newman, "Spoken and Written Expression," *Journal of Abnormal and Social Psychology,* June, 1964, p. 647.

³*Ibid.*

⁴Thomas L. Dahle, "An Objective and Comparative Study of Five Methods of Transmitting Information to Business and Industrial Employees," *Speech Monographs,* Vol. 21 (March, 1954), pp. 21–28.

⁵Howard Gilkinson, "A Questionnaire Study of the Causes of Social Fears Among College Speech Students," *Speech Monographs,* Vol. 10 (1943).

⁶R. Victor Harnack and Thorrel B. Fest, *Group Discussion: Theory and Technique* (New York: Appleton-Century-Crofts, Inc., 1964), p. 443.

⁷From a paper by Gary Tregea. Used with permission of author.

⁸Wade A. Knisely, "An Introduction of the Phenomenon of Stage Fright in Certain Prominent Speakers," unpublished doctoral dissertation, University of Southern California, 1950.

⁹Raymond G. Smith, *Principles of Public Speaking* (New York: The Ronald Press Company, 1958), p. 316. Professor Smith based his judgment on the findings of three experimental studies by other scholars in the field.

¹⁰Paul Heinberg, "Relationships of Content and Delivery to General Effectiveness," *Speech Monographs,* Vol. XXX, No. 2 (June, 1963), p. 107.

¹¹Gordon L. Thomas, "Effect of Oral Style on Intelligibility of Speech," *Speech Monographs,* Vol. 23 (March, 1956), pp. 46–55.

¹²Leland Schubert, *A Guide for Oral Communication* (Englewood Cliffs, N.J.: Prentice-Hall, Inc., 1948), p. 33.

¹³*Ibid.,* p. 36.

¹⁴Carroll C. Arnold, "Reader or Listener? Oral Composition," *Today's Speech,* Feb., 1965, p. 6.

¹⁵Sidney W. Wilcox, *Technical Communication* (Scranton, Penna.: International Textbook Company, 1962), p. 236.

¹⁶Byron K. Ledgerwood, "Control Systems in Material Management," *Proceedings,* Region IV Seminar, International Material Management Society, May, 1969, p. 79.

¹⁷E. P. Neate, "Design Evaluation of 60 Cycle Alternators." Report given in management training program. Used with permission of author.

INDEX

Abbreviations
  of academic degrees, 178
  of dates and places, 178
  familiar, 178
  manuscript, 178-179
  of states, 341
  of titles, 179
Accept-except, 222
Achievement seekers, 42-43
Adapt-adopt, 222
Adverbial phrases, 154
Adverbs, 154
Advice-advise, 222
Affect-effect, 222
Agreement
  pronoun-antecedent, 183-184
  subject-verb, 179-183
All ready-already, 222
All right-alright, 222
All together-altogether, 222
Ambiguity in references, 126-128
Among-between, 222
Amount-number, 222
Analysis, and paragraph development, 99-100
And etc., 223
Apostrophes, 195, 198
Application, letters of, *see* Letters of application
Appositives, 139
Apt-liable-likely, 223

Bad-badly, 223
Balance-remainder, 223
Being that-being as how, 223
Beside-besides, 223
Besides-plus, see *Plus-besides*
Between-among, 224
Biweekly-semiweekly, see *Semiweekly-biweekly*
Brackets, 198
Business correspondence, personal style in, 157-158
Business speaking, characteristics of, 11
Business writing, characteristics of, 10-11

Can-may (could-might), 224
Cannot-can not, 224
Capital-capitol, 224
Capitalization
  for emphasis, 144
  rules for use of, 198-203
Casual-causal, 224
Cause-effect pattern, 79-80
Charts
  flow, 269-270
  organization, 270-271
Chronological pattern, *see* Time pattern
Classification, and paragraph development, 100

Clauses
  adjective, 185
  adverbial, 185
  dependent, 120, 152, 185
  independent, 121, 152, 184-185
  noun, 185
  restrictive, 138-139
Cognitive dissonance, *see* Consistency principle
Coherence
  in paragraphs, 104
  in sentences, 121-134
Colons, 203-204
Combine into one, 224
Commas, 138-139, 204-207
Comma splices, 122-123
Communication
  definition of, 17
  downward, 4, 56-57
  external, 6, 57-58
  horizontal, 6, 56
  importance of
    to employee, 6-7
    on job, 2-6
  internal, 4, 21
  misconceptions in, 12-13
  model of, 20-21
  upward, 4-6, 39
  see also Falloff, communication
Comparison, paragraph development, 101
Comparisons
  of absolutes, 187
  degree of, 186
  illogical, 186
  incomplete, 187
  inequivalent, 186
Complement-compliment, 224
Completeness, in sentences, 120-121
Conciseness
  in sentences, 148-151
  in topic sentences, 97-98
Conclusion, of a message, 82
Conformity effect, *see* Consistency Principle
Conjunctions
  coordinate, 135, 187
  correlative, 188
  subordinate, 188-189

Conjunctive adverbs, 135-136, 154
Consensus of opinion, 225
Consistency Principle
  basic premises, 286-288
  cognitive dissonance, 286
  conformity effect, 289-290
  and persuasion, 288-292
Content-relationship meaning, 27
Continual-continuous, 225
Continuity, in paragraphs, 104-106
Contrast, and paragraph development, 101-102
Council-counsel, 225
Credibility
  "bank account," 300
  components of, 296-297
  definition of, 295
  derived, 298-299
  importance of, 299-302
  initial, 297-298
  interrelationship with logic, 293-295
  in persuasion, 285
  receiver need and, 301-302
  variables of, 295
Criteria-application pattern, 79
Criteria-data, etc., see *Data*, etc.

Dangling modifiers, 125
Dashes
  for emphasis, 143-144
  rules for use of, 208
Data-criteria-memoranda-phenomena, 225
Decision, "a good," 292-293
Decreasing importance, order of, 81
Definition, and paragraph development, 100
Denotative-connotative dimension, 27
Description, and paragraph development, 100-101
Diagrams, 265-269
Differ from-differ with, 225
Direct vs. indirect approach
  case for direct approach, 74-75
  exceptions to using direct approach, 75-77
  in paragraphs, 95
  and patterns of organization, 81
  in sentences, 131-132

Disinterested–uninterested, 225
Disorganized–unorganized, 225
Downward communication, 4, 56–57

Effect–affect, see *Affect–effect*
Effect–cause pattern, 79–80
Ellipses, 209
Emphasis, in sentences, 134–144
  capitalization for, 144
  equal, 134–136
  increased, 139–144
  reduced, 136–139
  repetition for, 142–143
Enthuse, 226
Example, and paragraph development, 102–103
Except–accept, see *Accept–except*
Exclamation points, 209
Explicit–implicit, 226
External communication, 6, 57–58

Factual statement, *see* Real World vs. Verbal World
Falloff, communication
  definition of, 22
  and noise, 28–29
  problems causing, 22–28
  reducing, 29–34
  selectivity in, 27–28
  and trust, 29–31
Farther–further, 226
Fee–honorarium–salary–stipend–wage, 226
Fewer–less, see *Less–fewer*

General and specific ideas
  balance between, 70–73
  general, 68–69
  in paragraphs, 93, 97, 98, 99, 106–108
  specific, 69–70
Generative function of topic sentences, 94–95
Geographical pattern, *see* Space pattern
Good–well, 226
Graphic aids
  checklist for planning, 276–277
  figures
    bar graphs, 256–261
    circle graphs, 261–263
    diagrams, 265–269
    flow charts, 269–270
    line graphs, 248–256
    maps, 272–275
    models, 270–271
    organization charts, 270–271
    photographs, 263–265
  kinds of ideas best presented by, 241
  placement of, 277
  tables
    formal, 242–246
    informal, 246–247
Graphs
  bar, 256–261
  circle, 261–263
  line, 248–256

Hanged–hung, 226
Headings, 87–88
Honorarium–fee, etc., see *Fee*, etc.
Horizontal communication, 6, 56
Hyphens, 209–211

"I," use of, *see* Personal style
If–whether, 226
Imperative sentences, 153
Implicit–explicit, 226
Imply–infer, 227
Increasing importance, order of, 81
Incredible–incredulous, 227
Inferences, *see* Real World vs. Verbal World
Infinitive phrases, 154
In–into, 227
Innovation, new, 228
Inter–intra, 227
Internal communication, 4, 21
Introduction of a message, 82
Irregardless, 227
Italics, *see* Underlining
Its–it's, 227

Jargon, 155–157

Kindly, 227
Kind of–sort of, 227

Lay–lie, 227
Lend–loan, 228

Length of sentences, 140, 144-148
  "ideal," 144-147
  long, 147
  medium, 147
  short, 140, 147
Less-fewer, 228
Letters of application, 349-356, 358, 361
Letter writing
  abbreviations for states, 341
  addressing envelopes, 340-342
  creating positive image in
    appearance, importance of, 321
    closing paragraph, 332
    informal style, 331-332
    opening paragraph, 332
    positive tone, 321-323
    postdecision reassurance, 324
    promptness in responding, 320
    quality of writing, 332-333
    reader's self-esteem, 328-329
    you-attitude, 325-328
  formats
    full block, 343, 347
    modified semiblock, 343, 345
    semiblock, 343, 344
    simplified, 346, 348
    specialized, 347, 349-352
  importance of, 317-318
  parts of letter
    standard, 334-337
    supplementary, 337-340
Liable-likely-apt, see *Apt*, etc.
Logic
  contradictory, 131
  importance of, in persuasion, 302
  and need-plan pattern, 303-304
  rules of sound reasoning, 306-307
  and two-sided approach, 304-306
Loose-lose, 228

Majority-plurality, 228
Management
  power in, 44
  style of, 53-54
Manager(s)
  as communicators, 48-53
  definition of, 40
  job orientation of, 44-48
  as persons of change, 55-56
  psychological motivations of, 40-44
Maps, 272-275
Maslow Hierarchy, 41-42, 285
May-can, see *Can-may*
Memoranda-data, etc., see *Data*, etc.
Memos
  completeness in, importance of, 363-364
  form of, 361-362
  function of, 361
  informality in, 362-363
Misplaced modifiers, 124
Models, 270-271
Moral-morale, 228

Need-plan pattern, 78-79
Needs, receiver's psychological
  adapting to, 285-293
  as basic factor in persuasion, 284
Non-restrictive clauses, 138
Number-amount, see *Amount-number*
Numbers
  combination of words and figures, 191
  figures, when to use, 189-190
  guidelines in using, 192
  words instead of, when to use, 190-191

Oral presentations
  delivering the speech, 448-456
    body communication, 448-450
    extemporaneous speaking, 451-456
    manuscript speaking, 451-456
    oral vs. written style, 453-456
    vocal communication, 450-451
  main points in, making stand out, 465-466
  questions from audience, 466-468
  speaking compared with writing, 441-443
  speech fright, 443-448
    problem of, 444-445
    solutions to, 445-448
  see also Visual aids
Organization
  aids in achieving clear, 82-87

definition, 66
importance of, 66–68
patterns of
  cause–effect, 79–80
  criteria–application, 79
  decreasing importance, order of, 81
  increasing importance, order of, 81–82
  patterns within patterns, 81
  problem–solution (need–plan), 78–79
  rationale for, 77–78
  space (geographical), in, 80
  time (chronological) in, 80
  topical, 80–81
Outlining
  benefits of, 83
  mechanics of, 86–87
  steps in, 83–86

Paragraph development
  amount of, 106–108
  analysis, 99
  classification, 100
  comparison, 101
  contrast, 101–102
  definition, 100
  description, 100–101
  example, 102–103
  guidelines for, 98–111
  reference words in, 105
  statistics, 103
  testimony, 103–104
Paragraphing, functions of, 93
Paragraphs
  coherence in, 104
  concluding, 110
  continuity in, 104–106
  definition of, 93–94
  introductory, 110
  length of, 108–109
  in memos, 110–111
  and topic sentence, 93–94
  transitional, 110
  unity in, 99
Parallelism
  for coherence, 132–134
  for equal emphasis, 135
  for increased emphasis, 140–141

Parentheses
  for reduced emphasis, 138
  uses of, 211–212
Participial phrases, 154
Party–person, 228
Passive voice, 159–161, *see also* Personal style
Periods, 212–213
Personal–personnel, 229
Personal style
  in business correspondence, 157–158
  and choice of pronouns, 162–163
  and passive voice, 159–161
  in reports and proposals, 158–159
  when not to use, 161–162
  when to use, 160–161
Persuasion
  basic factors in, 284–285
  credibility in, 285
  definition of, 283–284
  and logic, 302
  model of, 284
  and receiver's needs, 284
Phenomena–data, etc., see *Data*, etc.
Photographs, 263–265
Phrases, 184
  infinitive, 154
  participial, 154
Plurality–majority, see *Majority–plurality*
Plurals, 192–194
Plus–besides, 229
Possession
  apostrophes used to show, 195
  gerunds, form of, used with, 196
  possessive pronouns, 196
Power, in management, 44
Precede–proceed, 229
Precedence–precedent, 229
Prepositions, 196–197
Principal–principle, 229
Problem–solution (need–plan) pattern, 78–79
Pronouns, and personal style, 162–163
Proposals, *see* Reports and proposals
Proved–proven, 229
Punctuation
  apostrophes, 198
  brackets, 198

Punctuation (continued)
  capitalization, 198–203
  colons, 203
  commas, 204–207
  dashes, 208
  ellipses, 209
  exclamation points, 209
  hyphens, 209–211
  parentheses, 211–212
  periods, 212–213
  question marks, 213
  quotation marks, 214–216
  semicolons, 216–218
  underlining and italics, 218–219

Question marks, 213
Quotation marks, 214–216

Real World vs. Verbal World
  factual statements, 375–376
  inferences, 377–379
  language, guidelines in using, 381–383
  model of, 375
  objectivity-subjectivity continuum, 380–381
  value judgments, 379–380
Reason is because, 229
Reference words, in paragraph development, 105
Refer-refer back, 230
Relationships among ideas
  in paragraphs, 105
  in sentences, 128–129
Remainder-balance, see *Balance-remainder*
Repetition for emphasis, 142–143
Reports and proposals
  characteristics of, 373, 374
  classification of, 383–386
  components of
    abstract, 389, 391–394
    appendix, 406
    bibliography, 409–410
    conclusions, 401–404
    cover, 386
    discussion, 405–406
    distribution list, 411
    findings, 401–404
    footnotes, 406–409
    introduction, 397–401
    recommendations, 401–404
    table of contents, 395–397
    title page, 387–389
    transmittal, memo or letter of, 389, 390, 391
  function served by, 372–374
  personal style in, 158–159
  samples of
    AVO, 412
    formal proposal, 418, 421–430
    letter report, 418, 419–420
    memorandum proposal, 415–416
    memorandum report, 412–415
    request, 416–418
Respectively-respectfully, 230
Restrictive clauses, 138–139
Résumé, personal, 356–361

Salary-fee, etc., see *Fee*, etc.
Security and status seekers, 43–44
Semicolons, 123, 135–136, 216–218
Semiweekly-biweekly, 230
Sentences
  coherent structure in, 121–134
  completeness of, 120–121
  complex, 136, 152, 184
  compound, 152, 185
  compound-complex, 152
  conciseness in, 148–151
  declarative, 153
  definition of, 119–120
  effective, characteristics of, 120
  emphasis in, 134–144
  exclamatory, 153
  imperative, 153
  interrogative, 153
  length of, appropriate, 140, 144–148
  loose, 153
  overloaded, 122
  periodic, 153
  simple, 152, 184
  subordination in, 136
  variety in, 151–154
  word choice in, 154–163
Sequence of ideas, confused, 130–131
Set-sit, 230
Simplicity, in word choice, 155

Sort of–kind of, see *Kind of–sort of*
Space pattern, 80
Specific ideas, *see* General and specific ideas
Spelling, 219–220
Split construction (infinitives), 125–126
Squinting modifiers, 125
Statistics, and paragraph development, 103
Stipend–fee, etc., see *Fee*, etc.
Switching
  point of view, 129–130
  tense, 129–130

Tables, 242–247
Testimony, and paragraph development, 103–104
Their–there–they're, 230
Theory X, 53
Theory Y, 53
Time pattern, 80
Topical pattern, 80–81
Topic sentence
  development of, 98–111
    as element of paragraph, 93–94
    formulation of, 94–98
    generative function of, 94–95
    location of, 95–96
Triteness, 163
Trust, and communication falloff, 29–31
Try to–try and, 230
Two-sided approach, 304–306
Two-way communication, and communication falloff, 32–34

Underlining and italics (underscoring)
  for emphasis, 143
  rules for, 218–219

Uninterested–disinterested, see *Disinterested–uninterested*
Unity in paragraphs, 99
Unorganized–disorganized, see *Disorganized–unorganized*
Up, 231
Upward communication, 4–6, 39

Value judgments, *see* Real World vs. Verbal World
Variety in sentences, 151–154
Verbal World, *see* Real World vs. Verbal World
Verbs, tense of, 220–222
Visual aids
  chalkboard, 458–459
  charts, 459–460, 461
  graphic aids, compared with, 457–458
  opaque projector, 463–464
  overhead projector, 461–463
  precautions in using, 464–465
  three-dimensional objects, 458
  2 × 2 inch slide projector, 464
Vital, 231

Wage–fee, etc., see *Fee*, etc.
Well–good, see *Good–well*
Where–that, 231
Where–when, 231
Whether–if, see *If–whether*
Who–whom (*whoever–whomever*), 231
Who–whose, 232
Word choice
  jargon, 155–157
  personal style, 157–163
  simplicity, 155
  triteness, 163
Wordiness, *see* Conciseness